SIGNIFICANT CASES IN CORRECTIONS

SIGNIFICANT CASES IN
CORRECTIONS

SECOND EDITION

Craig Hemmens
Missouri State University

Barbara Belbot
University of Houston-Downtown

Katherine Bennett
Armstrong Atlantic State University

OXFORD
UNIVERSITY PRESS

Oxford University Press is a department of the University of Oxford. It furthers the University's
objective of excellence in research, scholarship, and education by publishing worldwide.

Oxford   New York
Auckland   Cape Town   Dar es Salaam   Hong Kong   Karachi
Kuala Lumpur   Madrid   Melbourne   Mexico City   Nairobi
New Delhi   Shanghai   Taipei   Toronto

With offices in
Argentina   Austria   Brazil   Chile   Czech Republic   France   Greece
Guatemala   Hungary   Italy   Japan   Poland   Portugal   Singapore
South Korea   Switzerland   Thailand   Turkey   Ukraine   Vietnam

Copyright © 2004, 2013 by Oxford University Press.

For titles covered by Section 112 of the US Higher Education Opportunity
Act, please visit www.oup.com/us/he for the latest information about
pricing and alternate formats.

Published by Oxford University Press.
198 Madison Avenue, New York, NY 10016
www.oup.com

Oxford is a registered trademark of Oxford University Press

Library of Congress Cataloging-in-Publication Data

Hemmens, Craig.
Significant cases in corrections / Craig Hemmens, Missouri State University,
Barbara Belbot, University of Houston-Downtown, Katherine Bennett,
Armstrong Atlantic State University.—Second edition.
pages cm.—(Criminal justice case briefs)
Includes bibliographical references and index.
ISBN 978-0-19-994858-1
1. Correctional law—United States—Cases.
I. Belbot, Barbara.   II. Bennett, Katherine.   III. Title.
KF9728.H46 2013
345.73'077—dc23   2012045383

1 3 5 7 9 8 6 4 2

Printed in the United States of America
on acid-free paper

CONTENTS

ACKNOWLEDGMENTS

Craig Hemmens would like to thank Mary, Emily, and Amber.

Barbara Belbot would like to thank her husband Steve and her mother Ruth Gertrude.

Katherine Bennett would like to thank her son, Joseph Allen Harvey, for his support and encouragement.

The authors would also like to thank the reviewers who helped shape this book:

First edition: L. F. Alarid, University of Missouri–Kansas City; Charles J. Corley, Michigan State University; Carolyn Dennis, Mount Olive College; Christopher Hensley, Morehead State University; Alexander M. Holsinger, University of Missouri–Kansas City; and Patricia Loveless, Penn State Altoona.

Second edition: Michael T. Geary, Albertus Magnus College; Mario L. Hesse, St. Cloud State University; Jessie L. Krienert, Illinois State University; Tom Powell, Paradise Valley Community College.

PREFACE

This book is intended to serve as a supplement to a textbook on corrections law. It may also be used by law school student struggling to understand the law while wading through the myriad (and often contradictory) opinions contained in the typical law school casebook.

While nothing substitutes for reading the original case opinion, the reality is that only those with a passion for the subject and plenty of time can afford to always go first to the source. This book is intended to assist those who are trying to read the original opinion, and to provide more detail than can be contained in a typical textbook.

The book is divided into sections that mirror the typical criminal justice textbook and law-school casebook approach to the subject, so that students and instructors can easily refer to related cases. All the significant United States Supreme Court cases are included, through the 2011–2012 term.

Each case brief follows the same basic format: Facts, Issue, Holding, Rationale, Case Excerpt, and Case Significance. The *Facts* section includes the relevant facts of the case that led to the eventual Supreme Court decision, as well as a brief explanation of the decisions in the lower courts. The *Issue* is the question presented to the Supreme Court for its ruling. The *Holding* is the result, the decision by the Supreme Court. The *Rationale* section contains the explanation of the Supreme Court for its decision. The *Case Excerpt* section provides some of the language from the court's opinion. The *Case Significance* section contains a discussion of why the case matters to criminal justice.

We hope that this book is of use to instructors and students seeking to understand the often arcane world of corrections law. We welcome any comments or suggestions that readers have.

TABLE OF CASES

CASE HOLDINGS

CHAPTER ONE SENTENCING

TOWNSEND v. BURKE, 334 U.S. 736 (1948): The Fourteenth Amendment's due process clause is violated when a defendant is deprived of the assistance of counsel during the sentencing phase of his or her case.

TROP v. DULLES, 356 U.S. 86 (1958): The Constitution's prohibition of cruel and unusual punishment in the Eighth Amendment does not permit Congress to enact legislation that allows a person's United States citizenship to be taken away as punishment for a crime.

NORTH CAROLINA v. PEARCE, 395 U.S. 711 (1969): The Fifth Amendment's double jeopardy clause requires that full credit be given to the time served by a defendant in the event of reconviction for the same offense. The equal protection clause is not violated if a more severe sentence is imposed upon reconviction for the same offense.

WILLIAMS v. ILLINOIS, 399 U.S. 235 (1970): The equal protection clause prohibits requiring indigent offenders to be imprisoned beyond the maximum length of the sentence because they are unable to pay monetary penalties.

UNITED STATES v. GRAYSON, 438 U.S. 41 (1978): A judge is constitutionally permitted to consider a defendant's perjury during his or her trial when determining that defendant's sentence.

ROBERTS v. UNITED STATES, 445 U.S. 552 (1980): The Fifth Amendment's privilege against self-incrimination is not violated when a sentencing judge considers the defendant's refusal to cooperate with the government during the investigation of the crime.

MISTRETTA v. UNITED STATES, 488 U.S. 361 (1989): The US Sentencing Guidelines are constitutional and do not violate the separation of powers doctrine, nor do they delegate excessive power to the US Sentencing Commission, which is responsible for promulgating the guidelines.

HARMELIN v. MICHIGAN, 501 U.S. 957 (1991): The Eighth Amendment does not require proportionality in sentencing unless the sentence is grossly disproportionate to the offense. It also does not prohibit mandatory sentences in cases that do not involve the death penalty.

RENO v. KORAY, 515 U.S. 50 (1995): A defendant in a federal criminal case is not entitled to credit under federal law for time served while awaiting sentencing under restrictive bail release conditions.

KOON v. UNITED STATES, 518 U.S. 81 (1996): When a federal appellate court reviews a decision by a sentencing to depart from the US Sentencing Guidelines, the correct standard is whether the sentencing court abused its discretion.

NEAL v. UNITED STATES, 516 U.S. 284 (1996): A federal sentencing judge is required to follow federal law and the Supreme Court's interpretation of that law when determining the weight of a controlled substance despite the fact that the US Sentencing Commission Guidelines require a different method of calculating weight.

UNITED STATES v. WATTS, 519 U.S. 148 (1997): A jury's acquittal verdict does not prohibit a sentencing judge from considering the conduct underlying the acquitted charge when determining a sentence, as long as the conduct has been proved by a preponderance of the evidence.

UNITED STATES v. BAJAKAJIAN, 524 U.S. 321 (1998): A punitive forfeiture violates the Eighth Amendment's prohibition of excessive fines if it is grossly disproportionate to the seriousness of the crime it is designed to punish.

APPRENDI v. NEW JERSEY, 530 U.S. 466 (2000): The due process clause requires that any fact that increases the penalty for a crime beyond the statutory maximum, other than a prior criminal conviction must be submitted to a jury and proved beyond a reasonable doubt.

SELING v. YOUNG, 531 U.S. 250 (2001): If a statute has been deemed to be civil and not criminal in nature, a person confined under that statute cannot obtain release because "as-applied" to them the statute was punitive and, therefore, violated the double jeopardy and ex post facto clauses.

ALABAMA v. SHELTON, 535 U.S. 654 (2002): The Sixth Amendment prohibits a suspended sentence to be imposed if the defendant had not been afforded counsel at the time he was prosecuted for the offense.

EWING v. CALIFORNIA, 528 U.S. 11 (2003): Ewing's 25 years to life sentence under California's three-strike laws is not grossly disproportionate and therefore does not violate the Eighth Amendment's prohibition on cruel and unusual punishments.

BLAKELY v. WASHINGTON, 542 U.S. 296 (2004): Facts, other than a prior conviction, necessary to increase a sentence beyond the statutory standard range must be proved by a jury beyond a reasonable doubt.

UNITED States v. BOOKER, 543 U.S. 220 (2005): An enhanced sentence under the US Sentencing Guidelines based only on the judge's determination of a fact violates the right to a jury trial under the Sixth Amendment. Only the mandatory provisions of the guidelines are unconstitutional.

KIMBROUGH v. UNITED STATES, 552 U.S. 85 (2007): It is not abuse of discretion for a District Court to conclude when sentencing a particular defendant that the crack/powder disparity yields a sentence "greater than necessary."

GALL v. UNITED STATES, 552 U.S. 38 (2007): Under *Booker v. U.S.* (2005), federal courts have authority to set any reasonable sentence as long as they explain the reasoning. Courts of appeal must review sentences under a deferential abuse-of-discretion standard, taking into account the totality of circumstances, including the extent of the variance from the guideline range, but must give due deference to the District Court's decision that the factors justify the variance.

CUNNINGHAM v. CALIFORNIA, 549 U.S 270 (2007): The California Determinate Sentencing Law violates the Sixth Amendment right to a jury trial because trial judges, and not juries, are permitted to find facts not admitted to by the defendant which can lead to enhanced sentences.

GRAHAM v. FLORIDA, 560 U.S.—(2010): The Eighth Amendment does not allow for a juvenile to be sentenced to life without parole for a crime that is not a homicide.

CHAPTER TWO THE DEATH PENALTY

FURMAN v. GEORGIA, 408 U.S. 238 (1972): A statute that allows judges and juries unbridled discretion when making the decision about whether to impose the death penalty violates the cruel and unusual punishment clause of the Eighth Amendment.

GREGG v. GEORGIA, 428 U.S. 153 (1976): The death penalty for murder is not per se cruel and unusual punishment in violation of the Eighth Amendment. A death penalty statute that focuses a jury's attention on the particular defendant and crime is constitutional.

WOODSON v. NORTH CAROLINA, 428 U.S. 280 (1976): Statutes that authorize the mandatory imposition of the death penalty violate the Fourteenth and Eighth Amendments.

COKER v. GEORGIA, 433 U.S. 584 (1977): The death penalty is grossly disproportionate and excessive for the crime of rape and is considered cruel and unusual punishment.

LOCKETT v. OHIO, 438 U.S. 98 (1978): The Eighth and Fourteenth Amendments require that the sentencing authority not be precluded from considering any aspect of the defendant's character or record and any other evidence the defendant offers as mitigating factors.

GODFREY v. GEORGIA, 446 U.S. 420 (1980): The statutory aggravating factor of "outrageously or wantonly vile, horrible, or inhuman" was not defined so as to provide restraint on the arbitrary and capricious infliction of the death penalty.

PULLEY v. HARRIS, 465 U.S. 37 (1984): The US Constitution does not require a state appeals court before it affirms a death sentence to compare the sentence in the case before it with the penalties imposed in similar cases.

SPAZIANO v. FLORIDA, 468 U.S. 447 (1984): The Eighth Amendment does not require a trial judge to accept a jury's recommendation that a defendant in a capital case be sentenced to life as opposed to death.

LOCKHART v. MCCREE, 476 U.S. 162 (1986): The Sixth Amendment is not violated when a judge removes a prospective juror in a capital case for cause because the juror opposes the death penalty and states that their opposition would make it difficult for them to perform their legal obligations during the sentencing phase.

FORD v. WAINWRIGHT, 477 U.S. 399 (1986): The Eighth Amendment prohibits executing a prisoner who is insane at the time of execution.

TISON v. ARIZONA, 481 U.S. 137 (1987): Major participation in a felony combined with reckless indifference to human life is sufficient to satisfy the Eighth Amendment's requirement that the defendant be culpable of the killing in order to be sentenced to death.

MCCLESKY v. KEMP, 481 U.S. 279 (1987): A statistical study that indicates a risk that racial considerations enter into capital sentencing decisions does not indicate a violation of the Eighth Amendment because it fails to support an inference that the decision makers in a defendant's particular case acted with discriminatory intent.

MAYNARD v. CARTWRIGHT, 486 U.S. 356 (1988): A death penalty statute that allows a death sentence to be imposed based on the aggravating circumstance that murder is "especially heinous, atrocious, or cruel" is unconstitutionally vague.

STANFORD v. KENTUCKY, 492 U.S. 361 (1989): The Eighth Amendment does not prohibit sentencing a juvenile defendant who was over the age of 16 at the time he or she committed a capital crime.

PAYNE v. TENNESSEE, 501 U.S. 808 (1991): The US Constitution does not prohibit a state from permitting the admission of victim impact evidence and allowing the prosecutor to comment about the subject.

HERRERA v. COLLINS, 506 U.S. 390 (1993): Claims of actual innocence based on newly discovered evidence are not sufficient to entitle a defendant to federal habeas corpus relief from a death sentence.

SIMMONS v. SOUTH CAROLINA, 512 U.S. 154 (1994): The due process clause requires that in a capital case when the prosecution argues that the jury should consider future dangerousness when deciding whether to assess death or life, and by law the defendant will never be eligible for parole, the jury must be informed a life sentence means a lifetime of incarceration.

JONES v. UNITED STATES, 527 U.S. 373 (1999): The Constitution does not require that a jury be instructed as to the consequences of a deadlock while deliberating on sentencing in a capital case.

ATKINS v. VIRGINIA, 536 U.S. 304 (2002): Executing mentally retarded convicted capital murderers violates the Eighth Amendment.

RING v. ARIZONA, 536 U.S. 584 (2002): The Sixth Amendment requires that a jury determine all of the facts that must be established before a death sentence can be imposed, including aggravating factors that, if found, allow for the death penalty to be imposed.

ROPER v. SIMMONS, 543 U.S. 551 (2005): The cruel and unusual punishment clause prohibits the execution of offenders who were under the age of 18 when they committed their crime.

ROMPILLA v. BEARD, 545 U.S. 374 (2005): Even in cases where a capital defendant's family members and the defendant himself suggest that no mitigating evidence is available, defendant's counsel "is bound to make reasonable efforts to obtain and review material that counsel knows the prosecution will probably rely on as evidence of aggravation at the sentencing phase of the trial."

BAZE v. REES, 553 U.S. 35 (2008): Kentucky's lethal injection protocol does not violate the cruel and unusual punishment clause of the Eighth Amendment.

KENNEDY v. LOUISIANA, 554 U.S. 407 (2008): The Eighth Amendment prohibits the execution of offenders for the crime of child rape.

CHAPTER THREE ACCESS TO COURTS

EX parte Hull, 312 U.S. 546 (1941): Prison regulations screening petitions for habeas corpus are invalid.

GRIFFIN v. ILLINOIS, 351 U.S. 12 (1956): Indigent prisoners are entitled to adequate and effective appellate review, including a certified copy of trial court proceedings.

BURNS v. OHIO, 60 U.S. 252 (1959): Indigent criminal defendants may not be prohibited from filing a leave to appeal because they are unable to pay a filing fee.

SMITH v. BENNETT, 365 U.S. 708 (1961): Requiring indigent prisoners to pay statutory filing fees before applying for a writ of habeas corpus, or before such appeals will be docketed, violates the equal protection clause of the Fourteenth Amendment.

JOHNSON v. AVERY, 393 U.S. 483 (1969): State regulations that bar inmates from assisting other inmates in preparing writs, absent reasonable alternatives to provide inmate access to the courts, are unconstitutional.

BOUNDS v. SMITH, 430 U.S. 817 (1977): The fundamental constitutional right of access to the courts requires prison authorities to assist inmates in the preparation and filing of meaningful legal papers by providing prisoners with adequate law libraries or adequate assistance from persons trained in the law.

MURRAY v. GIARRATANO, 492 U.S. 1 (1989): States are not required by the US Constitution to provide counsel for indigent capital prisoners in postconviction proceedings.

LEWIS v. CASEY, 518 U.S. 343 (1996): In order to establish a systemic Bounds violation of access to the courts, widespread actual injury must be shown. Prison officials must provide inmates the tools to attack their sentences, directly or collaterally, and to challenge the conditions of their confinement, but an inmate's right of access to courts does not include the right to a law library of legal assistance.

SHAW v. MURPHY, 532 U.S. 223 (2001): Inmates do not possess a special First Amendment right to provide legal assistance to fellow inmates that enhances the protection otherwise available under Turner.

CHAPTER FOUR ACCESS TO THE PRESS, THE OUTSIDE WORLD, AND THE MAIL

PROCUNIER v. MARTINEZ, 416 U.S. 396 (1974): Mail censorship regulations forbidding inmate mail that "unduly complained, magnified grievances, expressed inflammatory political, racial, religious or other views or beliefs," or contained matter deemed "defamatory" or "otherwise inappropriate" violate the First Amendment and the due process clause of the Fourteenth Amendment. Likewise, a ban against law students and paralegals conducting attorney-client interviews with inmates violates inmates' right of access to the courts.

PELL v. PROCUNIER, 417 U.S. 817 (1974): A ban on face-to-face media interviews is not unconstitutional as long as both the media and inmates have access to alternative channels of communication.

JONES v. NORTH CAROLINA PRISONERS' LABOR UNION, Inc., 433 U.S. 119 (1977): Regulations banning inmate solicitation of union membership, union meetings, and bulk mailings do not violate the First and Fourteenth Amendments. Such regulations are "rationally related to the reasonable objectives of prison administration" in that an inmate union may be seen as an adversarial organization at odds with the goals of the prison.

HOUCHINS v. KQED, Inc., 438 U.S. 1 (1978): The media possesses no special constitutional right of access to a prison and its inmates that is different from or greater than that given to the general public.

BLOCK v. RUTHERFORD, 468 U.S. 576 (1984): Inmates do not have a constitutional right to contact visits nor to observe "shakedown" searches of their cells. A blanket prohibition on contact visits and random shakedown searches of cells in the absence of their occupants is a reasonable, nonpunitive response to legitimate security concerns.

TURNER v. SAFLEY, 482 U.S. 78 (1987): A regulation restricting certain correspondence between inmates at difference institutions is reasonably related to legitimate security concerns; a regulation restricting the right of prisoners to marry is unconstitutional and is not reasonably related to legitimate penological objectives.

THORNBURGH v. ABBOTT, 490 U.S. 401 (1989): Federal Bureau of Prison regulations that restrict outside publications if they are deemed by the warden to be "detrimental to the security, good order, or discipline of the institution or if it might facilitate criminal activity" do not violate First Amendment rights and are "reasonably related to legitimate penological interests."

CHAPTER FIVE CONDITIONS OF CONFINEMENT

LEE v. WASHINGTON, 390 U.S. 333 (1968): Mandatory racial segregation in a state prison is unconstitutional.

CRUZ v. BETO, 405 U.S. 319 (1972): Inmates who hold unconventional religious beliefs are entitled to reasonable opportunities to practice their beliefs in as comparable a situation as those who hold more conventional religious beliefs.

BELL v. WOLFISH, 441 U.S. 520 (1979): "Double-bunking," a "publisher-only" rule regarding receipt of books, body-cavity searches, a prohibition against receipt of packages, and a room-search rule do not deprive pretrial detainees of their liberty without due process of law in contravention of the Fifth Amendment or any other constitutional guarantees.

RHODES v. CHAPMAN, 452 U.S. 337 (1981): Double-celling in and of itself is not cruel and unusual punishment prohibited by the Eighth and Fourteenth Amendments.

O'LONE v. ESTATE OF SHABAZZ, 482 U.S. 342 (1987): Prison regulations prohibiting inmates from returning to the building in which religious services are held do not violate freedom of religion rights because such regulations are rationally related to legitimate governmental interests in institutional order and security.

DESHANEY v. WINNEBAGO COUNTY DEPARTMENT OF SOCIAL SERVICES, 489 U.S. 189 (1989): The due process clause of the Fourteenth Amendment does not impose a special duty on the state to provide services to the public for protection against private actors.

WILSON v. SEITER, 501 U.S. 294 (1991): Prisoners claiming that conditions of confinement violate the Eighth Amendment's ban on cruel and unusual punishment must show a culpable state of mind amounting to "deliberate indifference" on the part of prison officials.

RUFO v. INMATES OF SUFFOLK COUNTY JAIL, 502 U.S. 367 (1992): A party seeking modification of an institutional reform consent decree bears the burden of establishing that a significant change in facts or law warrants revision of the decree, and that the proposed modification is suitably tailored to the changed circumstances.

HELLING v. MCKINNEY, 509 U.S. 25 (1993): Prison authorities' deliberate indifference to an inmate's involuntary exposure to environmental tobacco smoke poses an unreasonable risk to future health and constitutes an Eighth Amendment violation.

FARMER v. BRENNAN, 511 U.S. 825 (1994): Prison officials may be found constitutionally liable under the Eighth Amendment for failing to protect inmates if the officials are subjectively aware of the risk of serious harm and disregard that risk, failing to take reasonable measures to decrease it.

JOHNSON v. CALIFORNIA, 543 U.S. 499 (2005): Any type of policy of temporary racial segregation of state prisoners for up to 60 days is subject to a strict scrutiny standard of review for an equal protection challenge to that policy or practice.

CUTTER ET AL. v. WILKINSON, 544 U.S. 709 (2005): The Religious Land Use and Institutionalized Persons Act of 2000 (RLUIPA) is constitutional and means that inmates, even those holding unconventional beliefs, must not be unnecessarily prevented from exercising their religious freedoms. Restrictions on religious exercise of institutionalized persons are subject to a standard of strict scrutiny rather than the more lenient rational basis test.

U.S. v. GEORGIA, 546 U.S. 151 (2006): Title II of the ADA rescinds state sovereign immunity for suits by prisoners with disabilities challenging discrimination by state prisons and is a proper exercise of Congressional power under Section 5 of the Fourteenth Amendment, as applied to the administration of prison systems. Thus, a disabled inmate may sue a state for monetary damages for conduct that violates the ADA.

CHAPTER SIX MEDICAL CARE

ESTELLE v. GAMBLE, 429 U.S. 97 (1976): "Deliberate indifference" by prison personnel to a prisoner's serious illness or injury constitutes cruel and unusual punishment in violation of the Eighth Amendment.

WEST v. ATKINS, 487 U.S. 42 (1988): A physician who is under contract with the state to provide medical services to inmates at a state prison hospital on a part-time basis acts "under color of state law," within the meaning of §1983, when he treats an inmate.

WASHINGTON v. HARPER, 494 U.S. 210 (1990): A mentally ill inmate may be treated with antipsychotic medication against his or her will without a judicial hearing provided that a state first establishes that the inmate is dangerous to himself or others, or is seriously disruptive to the environment and that such treatment is in the inmate's medical interest.

PENNSYLVANIA Department of Corrections v. YESKEY, 524 U.S. 206 (1998): Refusing to allow an inmate to participate in a motivational boot camp, because of the inmate's history of hypertension, violates the Americans with Disabilities Act of 1990 (ADA). The ADA's protections cover prisons and prison inmates as well as any other liberated citizen, and under the ADA, no public entity may discriminate against qualified disabled individuals due to their disability.

MCKUNE v. LILE, 536 U.S. 24 (2002): A prison-based sex offender treatment program that requires offenders to admit to sexual misconduct for which they have not been charged or convicted and provides that if they refuse to participate they lose privileges and may be transferred to a more security facility does not compel offenders to incriminate themselves in violation of the Fifth Amendment.

CHAPTER SEVEN INMATE SEARCHES AND USE OF FORCE

HUDSON v. PALMER, 468 U.S. 517 (1984): The Fourth Amendment prohibition against unreasonable searches does not apply "within the confines of the prison cell." Further, "random and unauthorized" deprivations of property are not violative of the due process clause, so long as postdeprivation remedies are available.

WHITLEY v. ALBERS, 475 U.S. 312 (1986): Use of deadly force during a prison disturbance does not amount to cruel and unusual punishment unless it is characterized by obduracy and wantonness. The question ultimately turns on whether the force is applied in a good-faith effort to maintain or restore discipline or maliciously and sadistically for the purpose of causing harm.

HUDSON v. MCMILLIAN, 303 U.S. 1 (1992): The use of excessive physical force against a prisoner may constitute cruel and unusual punishment even though the inmate does not suffer serious injury. The core judicial inquiry is whether the less than deadly force is applied in a good faith effort to maintain or restore discipline, or maliciously and sadistically to cause harm.

CHAPTER EIGHT DUE PROCESS AND DISCIPLINE, ADMININISTRATIVE SEGREGATION, AND TRANSFER

WOLFF v. MCDONNELL, 418 U.S. 539 (1974): Prioners are entitled to due process under the Fourteenth Amendment in disciplinary proceedings that can result in a loss of good time or assignment to punitive segregation.

BAXTER v. PALMIGIANO, 425 U.S. 308 (1976): Prisoners are not entitled to counsel in prisoner disciplinary hearings, and officials are permitted to give adverse significance to a prisoner's silence during such a hearing.

HUTTO v. FINNEY, 437 U.S. 678 (1978): Courts are permitted to set limits on the amount of time a prisoner can serve in punitive segregation as part of an overall plan to correct constitutional violations.

HEWITT v. HELMS, 459 U.S. 460 (1983): Before a prisoner can be assigned to administrative segregation, he or she must be afforded an informal, nonadversarial evidentiary review of the information supporting administrative confinement. The prisoner is entitled to receive notice of the charges and the opportunity to

submit a statement to the officials who are to make the decision.

HUGHES v. ROWE, 449 U.S. 5 (1980): Unless it is justified by emergency conditions, it violates the due process clause to assign a prisoner to administrative segregation without a hearing. A prisoner can only be assessed his opponent's attorney's fees if the court finds that his or her claim was frivolous, unreasonable, or groundless.

SUPERINTENDENT, Walpole v. HILL, 472 U.S. 445 (1985): Disciplinary findings that lead to a loss of an inmate's good-time must be supported by a modicum of evidence in order to meet due process requirements.

PONTE v. REAL, 471 U.S. 491 (1985): The due process clause does not require prison officials to note their reasons in the administrative record for denying an inmate's witness request at a disciplinary hearing.

MEACHUM v. FANO, 427 U.S. 215 (1976): The due process clause does not afford prisoners the right to a hearing before they are transferred to another facility within the same state, even if the conditions of confinement in the facility to which they are transferred are less favorable than the conditions in the facility to which they are originally assigned.

MONTAYNE v. HAYMES, 427 U.S. 236 (1976): The due process clause does not afford prisoners the right to a hearing before they are transferred to another facility within the same state, even if the transfer for disciplinary reasons.

VITEK v. JONES, 445 U.S. 480 (1980): The due process clause affords prisoners the right to a hearing before they are involuntarily transferred to a mental hospital.

SANDIN v. CONNER, 515 U.S. 472 (1995): Under certain circumstances, states may create liberty interests for prisoners that are protected by the due process clause; however, these interests are generally limited to freedom from restraint that impose atypical and significant hardship on the prisoner in relation to the ordinary incidents of prison life.

JOHNSON v. CALIFORNIA, 543 U.S. 499 (2005): All racial classifications, including the California Department of Corrections (CDC)'s unwritten policy of temporarily racially segregating prisoners, must be subjected to a strict scrutiny standard of review.

WILKINSON v. AUSTIN, 545 U.S. 209 (2005): Inmates have a protected liberty interest in avoiding assignment at the Ohio State Penitentiary (OSP). The procedures set forth in Ohio's New Policy are sufficient to satisfy the Fourteenth Amendment's due process requirements.

CHAPTER NINE LIABILITY AND DAMAGES

PARRATT v. TAYLOR, 451 U.S. 527 (1981): In order to prove a §1983 case, a prisoner must show (1) that the action complained about was committed by a person acting under color of state law; and (2) that the action deprived the prisoner of rights, privileges, or immunities protected by the US Constitution or federal law.

HARLOW v. FITZGERALD, 457 U.S. 800 (1982): Government officials who are performing discretionary functions are not liable for civil damages to the extent that their conduct does not violate a clearly established statutory or constitutional right about which a reasonable person would have known.

SMITH v. WADE, 461 U.S. 30 (1983): Punitive damages may be awarded in a §1983 lawsuit if the defendant's conduct involves callous or reckless indifference to the plaintiff's rights or the safety of others.

CLEAVINGER v. SAXNER, 474 U.S. 193 (1985): Members of prison disciplinary committees are only entitled to qualified immunity, not absolute immunity, when performing their duties as committee members.

DANIELS v. WILLIAMS, 474 U.S. 327 (1986): The due process clause of the Fourteenth Amendment is not triggered by the negligent actions of state officials that cause unintended injury to or loss of life, liberty, or property.

RICHARDSON v. MCKNIGHT, 521 U.S. 399 (1997): Correctional officers employed by a private firm are not entitled to qualified immunity from lawsuits by prisoners charging a §1983 violation.

ALI v. FEDERAL BUREAU OF PRISONS ET AL., 552 U.S. 214 (2008): The text and structure of Section 2680 (c) "any other law enforcement officer" includes all law enforcement officers and is not limited to only officers enforcing customs and excise laws, therefore, the Bureau of Prisons (BOP) is protected by sovereign immunity for prisoners' claims involving lost or damaged property detained by BOP officers.

MINNECI v. POLLARD, 132 S.Ct. 617 (2012): Employees of private prison companies cannot be sued in a *Bivens* type action for violations of inmates' constitutional rights where the conduct is of a type that typically falls within the scope of traditional state tort law.

CHAPTER TEN HABEAS CORPUS AND THE PRISON LITIGATION REFORM ACT

PRICE v. JOHNSTON, 334 U.S. 266 (1948): A Federal Circuit Court of Appeals has the power to issue a writ of habeas corpus commanding that a prisoner be brought before the court for the purpose of arguing his own appeal in a case involving his life or liberty.

ROSE v. LUNDY, 455 U.S. 509 (1982): Title 28 U.S.C. §§2254(b) and (c) provide that a state prisoner's application for a writ of habeas corpus in a federal district court based on alleged federal constitutional violation will not be granted unless the applicant has exhausted the remedies available in state courts. A petition for a writ that contains both exhausted and unexhausted claims must be dismissed until all of the claims have been heard in state court.

MCCLESKEY v. ZANT, 499 U.S. 467 (1991): When a prisoner files a second or subsequent application for a writ of federal habeas corpus, a cause and prejudice standard is to be applied in order to determine if a petitioner has abused the writ through inexcusable neglect in failing to raise a claim in a prior petition.

REED v. FARLEY, 512 U.S. 339 (1994): A state court's failure to observe the Interstate Agreement on Detainers rule that the trial of a transferred prisoner shall be commenced within 120 days of the arrival of the prisoner in the receiving state is not cognizable under 28 U.S.C. §2254 when the defendant registers no objection to the trial date at the time it was set and suffered no prejudice that can be attributed to the delay.

FELKER v. TURPIN, 518 U.S. 651 (1996): Title I of the Antiterrorism and Effective Death Penalty Act which prevents the Supreme Court from reviewing an appellate review panel's denial of leave to file a second habeas petition does not unconstitutionally suspend the habeas writ or restrict the Court's authority to entertain original habeas petitions.

MARTIN v. HADIX, 527 U.S. 343 (1999): The Prison Litigation Reform Act of 1995 limits attorney's fees for postjudgment monitoring services performed after the PLRA's effective date, but it does not limit fees for monitoring performed before that date.

MILLER v. FRENCH, 530 U.S. 327 (2000): The Prison Litigation Reform Act's automatic stay provision is mandatory and precludes courts from exercising their equitable powers to enjoin such a stay. The provision does not violate the constitutional separation of powers doctrine.

BOOTH v. CHURNER, 532 U.S. 731 (2001): The Prison Litigation Reform Act requires prisoners exhaust administrative remedies prior to filing a civil rights lawsuit even when the grievance process does not permit an award of money damages and the inmate seeks only money damages.

ARTUZ v. BENNETT, 531 U.S. 4 (2000): An application for state postconviction relief containing procedurally barred claims is properly filed within the meaning of the Antiterrorism and Effective Death Penalty Act.

DUNCAN v. WALKER, 533 U.S. 167 (2001): A federal habeas corpus petition is not an application for state postconviction or other collateral review within the meaning of 28 U.S.C. §2244(d)(2).

PORTER v. NUSSLE, 534 U.S. 516 (2002): The Prison Litigation Reform Act's exhaustion requirement applies to all prisoner lawsuits about prison life, whether they address general circumstances or particular episodes, and whether they allege excessive force or some other wrong.

BOUMEDIENNE v. BUSH, 553 U.S. 723 (2008): Petitioners have the constitutional privilege of habeas corpus and are not barred from seeking the writ or invoking the suspension clause's protections because they are designated as enemy combatants or because of they are detained at the Guantanamo Bay Naval Base. The Military Commissions Act is an unconstitutional suspension of that right.

BROWN v. PLATA, 131 S.Ct. 1910, 563 U.S.— (2011): The court below did not err in concluding that overcrowding in California prisons was the primary cause of the violations of prisoners' constitutional rights to adequate health care. The evidence supported the conclusion of the three-judge panel that a population limit was necessary to remedy the overcrowding problem. The relief ordered by the three-judge court was narrowly drawn, extended no further than necessary to correct the violation, and was the least intrusive means necessary to correct the violation.

CHAPTER ELEVEN PAROLE

MORRISSEY v. BREWER, 408 U.S. 471 (1972): The due process clause of the Fourteenth Amendment requires that a state afford a parolee due process rights prior to revoking parole. The minimum due process requirements are: "(a) written notice of the claimed violations of parole; (b) disclosure to the parolee of evidence against him; (c) opportunity to be heard in person and to present witnesses and documentary evidence; (d) the right to confront and cross-examine adverse witnesses (unless the hearing officer specifically finds good cause for not allowing confrontation); (e) a 'neutral and detached' hearing body such as a traditional parole board, and (f) a written statement by the fact finders as to the evidence relied on and reasons for revoking parole."

MOODY v. DAGGETT, 429 U.S. 78 (1976): A federal parolee imprisoned for a crime committed while on parole is not constitutionally entitled to a prompt parole revocation hearing after a parole violator warrant is issued and lodged with the institution of his confinement but not served.

GREENHOLTZ v. INMATES OF NEBRASKA PENAL AND CORRECTIONAL COMPLEX, 442 U.S. 1 (1979): The mere possibility of release on parole, unlike parole revocation, does not create an entitlement to due process.

MARTINEZ v. CALIFORNIA, 444 U.S. 277 (1980): The Fourteenth Amendment, which protects deprivation of life by the state without due process of law, does not invalidate a California statute granting absolute immunity to public employees who make parole release determinations. Thus, parole officers are not liable for an injury or death resulting from a parole release decision. The Court did not address whether public officials are absolutely immune from liability in an action brought under the federal Civil Rights Act of 1871.

CONNECTICUT Board of Pardons v. DUMSCHAT, 452 U.S. 458 (1981): The fact that the Connecticut Board of Pardons granted approximately three-fourths of the applications for commutation of life sentences did not create a constitutional "liberty interest" or "entitlement" requiring the board to provide reasons for denying an application for commutation.

JAGO v. VAN CUREN, 454 U.S. 14 (1981): A decision by the Ohio Adult Parole Authority to rescind a parole release order without a hearing does not violate the due process clause of the Fourteenth Amendment. No protected liberty interest is implicated until actual release from prison.

WEAVER v. GRAHAM, 450 U.S. 24 (1981): A Florida statute reducing the amount of "gain time" for good conduct and obedience to prison rules deducted from a convicted prisoner's sentence is unconstitutional as an ex post facto law if applied to prisoners whose crime were committed before the statute's enactment.

BOARD of Pardons v. ALLEN, 482 U.S. 369 (1986): The use of mandatory language ("shall") in a Montana statute created a liberty interest in parole release that is protected by the due process clause of the Fourteenth Amendment.

CALIFORNIA Department of Corrections v. MORALES, 514 U.S. 499 (1995): A 1981 amendment to a California statute that allows a reduction in the frequency of suitability hearings for parole for prisoners convicted of more than one offense involving the taking of a life does not violate the ex post facto clause in regard to prisoners who committed their crimes before 1981.

LYNCE v. MATHIS, 519 U.S. 433 (1997): A Florida statute canceling early release credits to prison inmates after they have been released, resulting in their rearrest and reincarceration, violates the ex post facto clause.

YOUNG v. HARPER, 520 U.S. 143 (1997): A preparole conditional supervision program in Oklahoma was sufficiently like parole to entitle participants to procedural protections, such as due process safeguards set forth in the Fourteenth Amendment.

PENNSYLVANIA Board of Probation and Parole v. SCOTT, 524 U.S. 357 (1998): The federal exclusionary rule, prohibiting the introduction of evidence seized in violation of the Fourth Amendment's protections against unreasonable search and seizure, does not apply to parole revocation hearings.

OHIO Adult Parole Authority v. WOODARD, 523 U.S. 272 (1998): Inmates do not have protected life or liberty interests in clemency proceedings. Voluntary participation in an interview as part of the clemency process does not violate an inmate's Fifth Amendment rights because inmate testimony is not compelled.

GARNER v. JONES, 529 U.S. 244 (2000): Retroactive application of a Georgia law extending intervals between parole considerations does not violate the ex post facto clause.

SAMSON v. CALIFORNIA, 547 U.S. 843 (2006): The condition of release on parole diminishes or eliminates a parolee's reasonable expectation of privacy to the extent that a suspicionless search by a law enforcement officer does not violate the Fourth Amendment.

CHAPTER TWELVE **PROBATION**

EX Parte United States (Killits), 242 U.S. 27 (1916): Courts do not havE THE CONSTITUTIONAL POWER TO DIMINISH OR PREVENT PENALTIES PROVIDED BY LAW.

MEMPA v. RHAY, 389 U.S. 128 (1967): A defendant has a right to counsel when deferred sentencing is being imposed at a probation revocation hearing.

GAGNON v. SCARPELLI, 411 U.S. 778 (1973): The same due process protections mandated in Morrissey v. Brewer apply to probation revocation proceedings. The hearing body should decide on a case-by-case basis whether due process requires that counsel be provided to indigent probationers.

CABELL v. CHAVEZ-SALIDO, 454 U.S. 432 (1982): Statutory citizenship is a constitutional requirement for probation officers and deputy probation officers.

BEARDEN v. GEORGIA, 461 U.S. 660 (1983): Indigent persons on probation can not have probation revoked solely because, through no fault of their own, they fail to pay fines or make restitution.

MINNESOTA v. MURPHY, 465 U.S. 420 (1984): Statements made to a probation officer by a probationer without receiving Miranda warnings are admissible in subsequent criminal proceedings. If the probationer is being questioned by the probation officer while held in police custody, or if the police are questioning the probationer in a "custodial setting," then Miranda protections would apply.

BLACK v. ROMANO, 471 U.S. 606 (1985): Sentencing courts are not required by the due process clause of the Fourteenth Amendment to consider alternatives to imprisonment before revoking probation.

GRIFFIN v. WISCONSIN, 483 U.S. 868 (1987): A Wisconsin law allowing warrantless searches of a probationer's residence by a probation officer and based on "reasonable grounds" is valid and does not violate the probationer's Fourth Amendment rights.

FORRESTER v. WHITE, 484 U.S. 219 (1988): A state court judge does not have absolute immunity from a damages suit under 42 U.S.C. 1983 for his or her decisions to demote and dismiss a court employee.

Judicial functions which fall under administrative, executive, or legislative headings, such as administrative personnel decisions, do not qualify for absolute immunity.

ALDEN v. MAINE, 527 U.S. 706 (1999): Article I of the United States Constitution does not include the power to subject nonconsenting states to private suits for damages in state courts. Accordingly, the State of Maine could not be sued by probation officers for overtime pay and liquidated damages under the Fair Labor Standards Act because the state did not consent to such a suit.

INTRODUCTION

At early common law, and until the middle part of the twentieth century, criminal justice offenders had few rights. The Bill of Rights, with its protections of individual rights against search and seizure, self-incrimination, and the like, applied only to the federal government, not the states. The exclusionary rule and Miranda warnings were unheard of. Once incarcerated, individuals lost almost all of their rights and found themselves at the mercy of correctional personnel. Those under community supervision, be it probation or parole, found their rights and opportunities severely circumscribed. Those convicted of crimes were often treated as "slaves of the state" (*Ruffin v. Commonwealth*, 1871). Most states had "civil death" statutes which stripped convicted individuals of most of their civil rights, such as the right to vote or hold elective office. This loss of rights was justified as a part of the punishment for committing a crime.

Courts took what was referred to as a "hands-off" approach to the rights of prisoners, choosing not to become involved with the affairs of corrections agencies, which were part of the executive branch of government. Courts reasoned that correctional administrators were better equipped to deal with prisoners than judges, and that judicial involvement, through the hearing of inmate complaints, would unnecessarily complicate relations between the executive and judicial branches of government. If prisoners had no rights, then courts need not oversee correctional agencies dealing with prisoners.

Courts also paid scant attention to the rights of probationers and parolees, treating them as essentially equivalent to inmates. Any number of restrictive probation and parole conditions were upheld, with courts often falling back on the rationale that neither probation nor parole was a right, but merely a privilege, something granted by the state which could be modified or revoked at any time.

By the 1940s courts began paying closer attention to the rights of prisoners, as part of a growing trend towards increased protection of individual rights. In 1941 the Supreme Court, in *Ex parte Hull*, held that inmates had a right to unrestricted access to federal courts. This decision signaled the beginning of the end of the hands-off doctrine and the beginning of the era of judicial intervention in corrections. In 1944, in *Coffin v. Reichard*, 143 F.2d 443, a federal district court expanded the scope of habeas corpus to include lawsuits filed by inmates which challenged not their confinement, but the conditions of their confinement.

The civil rights movement of the 1960s and a change in the membership of the Supreme Court resulted in tremendous changes in criminal justice procedure and correctional practices. Under Chief Justice Earl Warren, the Court extended a number of protections to criminal defendants, including the exclusionary rule, Miranda warnings, and the right to counsel at any "critical stage" in the prosecution. The Supreme Court also began to extend protection of individual rights to those convicted of crimes. The Court focused on due process, as the Court in a line of cases required correctional administrators at all levels, from prison to probation and parole, to accord basic procedural rights to criminal justice offenders.

Following the high court's lead, lower federal courts became more receptive to lawsuits brought by prisoners challenging the conditions of their confinement. In *Holt v. Sarver* (1969), a federal district court in Arkansas determined that inmates could challenge as unconstitutional not merely individual practices, but also the totality of the prison's conditions. This form of suit became known as the "conditions of confinement" lawsuit. Federal district courts, formerly absolute in their deference to the wisdom of correctional administrators, became intimately involved in the monitoring and operation of entire prison systems. In 1976 the Supreme Court, in *Estelle v. Gamble*, held that correctional administrators could be held liable for injury to an inmate if the administrators displayed "deliberate indifference" to the situation. While this has proven a fairly difficult standard for inmate plaintiffs to meet, it is nonetheless a far cry from the days of *Ruffin v. Commonwealth*, when inmates where seen as literal "slaves of the state."

Paralleling the increased attention paid by courts to correctional institutions was an increased attention to the rights of those under community supervision. In a series of cases decided during the 1970s the Supreme Court extended a number of due process rights to probationers and parolees, including the right to a revocation hearing, notice of the charges against the individual, and the right to counsel. Recently, as the membership of the Supreme Court has become more conservative, the high court has been less receptive to the complaints of inmates, and has declined to extend further the protections accorded inmates and those

under community supervision. How things will play out in the coming years is anyone's guess. What we can say with assurance, however, is that correctional law remains an area where change can and odes occur with some frequency. That makes study of the subject both interesting and frustrating!

In this book we provide an overview of the development of prisoners' rights as developed by the United States Supreme Court over the past half century. While nothing substitutes for reading the original case opinion, the reality is that only those with a passion for the subject and plenty of time can afford to always go first to the source. This book is intended to assist those who are trying to read the original opinion, and to provide more detail than can be contained in a typical textbook.

The book is divided into sections which mirror the typical criminal justice and casebook approach to the subject, so that students and instructors can easily refer to related cases. All the significant United States Supreme Court cases are included, through the 2011–2012 term. We hope that this book is of use to instructors and students seeking to understand the often arcane world of legal issues in corrections. We welcome any comments or suggestions that readers have.

SENTENCING

INTRODUCTION

For noncapital offenses, in the majority of states the judge who presided at the guilt or innocence trial or accepted a guilty plea is also responsible for making the decision about how to sentence a convicted offender. Sentencing is often a judge's most important and difficult decision. While judges are bound to follow the legislative sentencing scheme in their jurisdiction, they must also weigh concerns about safeguarding citizens, responding to victims, addressing the needs of offenders, and sending messages about what types of behavior will not be tolerated. That task, whether performed by a judge or a jury, is complicated by a criminal justice system where there is no consensus about the ultimate goals of sentencing. The public, elected representatives, and scholars have failed to provide a clear and consistent set of rationales for punishment, and public policy is often muddled.

Public policy has become especially confusing in the last two decades, during which significant changes in sentencing law have been implemented in a patchwork manner across the United States. A fairly common approach to sentencing in every jurisdiction has been replaced as state and federal statutes have been rewritten extensively in some jurisdictions, while far less extensively in others. Rather than rewrite entire sentencing schemes, many states have implemented legislation that if not in direct conflict with laws that remain on the books, works to undermine the purpose of those laws, further muddling what criminal justice policy seeks to accomplish. Indeterminate sentencing laws gave judges discretion to sanction offenders within the parameters set by law. In many jurisdictions, those parameters were broad. On the back end of the criminal justice system, parole boards had broad discretion to release offenders conditionally on parole. The dramatic shift to a more determinate form of sentencing has reduced the discretion available to both judges and parole boards. Mandatory sentencing laws for certain types of offenses further diminish the exercise of discretion. State and federal governments have not adopted change in an orchestrated fashion, making sentencing one of the most difficult criminal justice processes to describe, much less understand.

This chapter reviews the most important US Supreme Court cases about sentencing law to date. Because sentencing has been going through rapid and significant revision, more and more case law has been generated in recent years specifically about the sentencing process and much more can be expected in the future. For many offenders, the sentencing issue is more important than whether they are guilty or innocent, either because they have plead guilty or because the evidence of their guilt is strong enough to support conviction for some type of offense. The Supreme Court acknowledged the importance of the process in *Townsend v. Burke* (1948), when it decided that a defendant's due process rights are violated when he or she is deprived of counsel during the sentencing phase. As recently as 2002, the Court highlighted the importance of the sentencing process when it could result in incarceration. In *Alabama v. Shelton* (2002), the Supreme Court concluded that a suspended sentence, which places a defendant on community supervision, could not be imposed because of a violation of that supervision if the defendant did not have the assistance of an attorney at the time he or she was prosecuted and convicted of the crime.

The Court has struggled mightily with the issue of proportionality and the issue of whether the Eighth Amendment's prohibition against cruel and unusual punishment requires that the severity of a sentence be proportionate to the severity of the crime of conviction. Without addressing proportionality directly, in *Trop v. Dulles* (1958) the Court decided that the Eighth Amendment does not permit a person's citizenship to be taken away as punishment for a crime and noted that the Eighth Amendment draws its meaning from the "evolving standards of decency that mark the progress of a maturing society." In *Harmelin v. Michigan* (1991) the Court addressed the proportionality issue head-on, but significant questions remain. The Court seemed to conclude that that the Constitution does not require proportionality unless a sentence is grossly disproportionate to the offense and mandatory penalties are constitutional as long as the death penalty is not involved. This case sought to clarify previous Supreme Court opinions, but a split decision leaves unresolved whether a disproportionality principle still exists and the extent of its reach. For the first time, the Supreme

Court struck down the amount of a forfeiture as excessive punishment under the Eighth Amendment in *United States v. Bajakajian* (1998).

This chapter also presents cases that addressed other constitutional limitations on the length of a sentence. In *North Carolina v. Pearce* (1969), the Court decided that the double jeopardy clause is violated if a defendant is not given full credit for all the time he or she served prior to a reconviction. Defendants should not lose the time they served because they successfully appealed their conviction and were retried. On the other hand, in that same case, the Court stated that the equal protection clause does not prohibit the imposition of a more severe sentence upon reconviction as long as the new sentence was not a result of vindictiveness. In *Williams v. Illinois* (1970), the Supreme Court Justices interpreted the equal protection clause as prohibiting imposing subjecting offenders to incarceration beyond the maximum term provided by statute solely because they were indigent and unable to pay a fine. In considering how a hate crime statute could increase the penalty of a crime beyond the statutory maximum without violating the Constitution, the Court concluded in *Apprendi v. New Jersey* (2000) that the due process clause mandates that any facts necessary under the statute to support an increase must be submitted to a jury and proved beyond a reasonable doubt.

Because the federal sentencing scheme has undergone the most significant revision of any jurisdiction, this chapter presents a number of important decisions concerning federal law. In *Mistretta v. United States* (1989), the Court upheld the constitutionality of the US sentencing guidelines, ushering in determinate sentencing in the federal criminal justice system. The guidelines remain a fertile area for legal challenge and have spawned many cases. *Koon v. United States* (1996) decided that when a federal appellate court reviews a trial court's sentencing decision that departs from the guidelines, the appeals court should only inquire as to whether the departure was an abuse of discretion. The Court concluded in *United States v. Watts* (1997) that the guidelines do not prohibit a sentencing judge to consider a defendant's conduct, despite the fact that he or she had been acquitted of that offense, in determining a sentence—as long as the conduct was proved by a preponderance of the evidence. The guidelines do not trump federal law when a judge is deciding a sentence in a case that requires him or her to consider the weight of a controlled substance, decided the Court in *Neal v. United States* (1996). This chapter also discusses several other cases that involve federal sentencing statutes, because the trend to federalize criminal law makes it more likely today than ten years ago that an offender will be prosecuted for a federal crime instead of a state offense.

Seling v. Young (2001) introduces a very recent and controversial sentencing law issue involving civilly committing sexual predators after they have served their criminal time. The issue first came before the Court in *Kansas v. Hendricks* (1997) and involved the double jeopardy and ex post facto clauses. The *Seling* case sought to clarify that earlier decision and is an example of how quite often it takes more than one case to explore all of the different aspects of a legal issue.

Just as sentencing statutes are in flux, so are the court opinions that interpret them. The Supreme Court has addressed a number of the most pressing issues, but there is no reason to think that soon there will be consensus about how the laws should be applied. The Eighth Amendment's cruel and unusual punishment clause, the Fourteenth Amendment's due process and equal protection clauses, and the Fifth Amendment's double jeopardy clause remain the primary grounds where battles about sentencing will be fought.

TOWNSEND v. BURKE
334 U.S. 736 (1948)

FACTS
Townsend pleaded guilty to robbery and burglary in a Pennsylvania trial court. He was sentenced to 10 to 20 years in prison. In a writ of habeas corpus filed in federal court, Townsend alleged that when he was brought into court to plead, he was not represented by counsel, offered an assignment of counsel, advised of his right to counsel, or instructed in any detail about the nature of the crimes with which he was charged. He maintained that as a result of lack of counsel, facts about his prior criminal history were misrepresented. Specifically, the judge recited several offenses for which Townsend had been charged but which were either dismissed or for which he was found not guilty. He claimed the misrepresentation caused the court to assess a severe sentence and violated his due process rights.

ISSUE
Is it a violation of a defendant's due process rights to deprive him of counsel during the sentencing phase of his case?

HOLDING
Yes. The Fourteenth Amendment's due process clause was violated because counsel would have been able to take steps to ensure that the sentence was not predicated on misinformation or by a judge misreading the court records.

RATIONALE
The Supreme Court emphasized that the defendant's lack of an attorney during sentencing either allowed the prosecutor to submit misinformation to the court or allowed the court to misread the information presented. "Counsel, had any been present, would have been under a duty to prevent the court from proceeding on such false assumptions." Whether this case was caused by carelessness or design, the results were inconsistent with due process of law. Shortly before this decision, the Court had reaffirmed in *Bute v. Illinois*, 333 U.S. 640 (1948) that due process does not prohibit states from accepting guilty pleas in a noncapital cases from uncounseled defendants. Further, fair and conscientious district attorney's and judges will make honest mistakes. In this case, however, there was reason to think the sentence was not based on fair play.

CASE EXCERPT
"It is not the duration or severity of this sentence that renders it constitutionally invalid; it is the careless or designed pronouncement of sentence on a foundation so extensively and materially false, which the prisoner had no opportunity to correct by the services which counsel would provide, that renders the proceedings lacking in due process."

CASE SIGNIFICANCE
This case was decided before *Gideon v. Wainwright*, 372 U.S. 335 (1963) and its progeny. *Gideon* and the cases that followed established that the Sixth Amendment right to counsel applies to all critical stages of criminal proceedings. There remains, however, no clear cut Supreme Court decision that holds counsel must be present during a sentencing hearing. Federal Rule of Criminal Procedure 32 requires that defendants in federal court must be afforded counsel. Many state rules also require counsel be afforded at sentencing. Defense counsel should be available to present information that will assist the court in making an appropriate sentencing decision. Counsel should be familiar with all the sentencing alternatives and the judge's sentencing

TOWNSEND v. BURKE (cont.)

practices, and must counsel his or her client about the ramifications of different sentencing decisions.

TROP v. DULLES
356 U.S. 86 (1958)

FACTS

Trop, a native-born American and a private in the US Army stationed in Morocco in 1944, escaped from the stockade where he was being held for disciplinary violations. The day after his escape, he voluntarily boarded an army truck while he was walking on a road headed back in the direction of the stockade. He was convicted of desertion and sentenced to three years imprisonment and given a dishonorable discharge. His application for a passport was denied in 1952 on the grounds he had lost his citizenship because of his conviction and dishonorable discharge for wartime desertion pursuant to the Nationality Act of 1940.

ISSUE

Does the Constitution permit Congress to enact legislation that allows a person's United States citizenship to be taken away as a punishment for a crime?

HOLDING

No. Denationalization as punishment for a crime violates the Eighth Amendment's prohibition against cruel and unusual punishment because such a punishment involves the "total destruction of the individual's status in organized society. It is a form of punishment more primitive than torture, for it destroys for the individual the political existence that was centuries in the development."

RATIONALE

The Court noted that the civilized countries in the world were virtually unanimous that denationalization should not be imposed as punishment for a crime. Such a punishment subjects a person to a fate of fear and distress. The person never knows what discrimination they may be subject to, what prohibitions they may face, or when they may be forced to leave their native land. The person is stateless with a constant threat of disastrous consequences that may befall them. Wrote the Court, "the threat makes the punishment obnoxious." The Court acknowledged the exact scope of the phrase "cruel and unusual" can be ambiguous. The

Court noted it had not given specific content to the words of the amendment, but that the words will never be precise and their scope will never be static.

CASE EXCERPT

"The Amendment must draw its meaning from the evolving standards of decency that mark the progress of a maturing society."

CASE SIGNIFICANCE

This case is significant in part because the punishment it addresses is a noncriminal sanction. The loss of citizenship did not occur as a sanction that was assessed after a criminal conviction. It occurred as a civil matter. This case is often remembered for Justice Warren's powerful statement that the meaning of the Eighth Amendment is drawn from "the evolving standards of decency that mark the progress of a maturing society." That statement has marked the stage for many a debate about the scope of the Eighth Amendment. With those words, Justice Warren opened the debate to include evidence about contemporary social standards and beliefs. The exact scope of the Eighth Amendment might be uncertain in any given controversy, but it is clear, says the Court, its scope was not frozen at the time of its enactment. The scope of the amendment evolves as society progresses and matures. The "evolving standards of decency" test has played a pivotal role in many cases involving sentencing, the death penalty, and even conditions of prison confinement. It is one of the Supreme Court's most famous statements and has been the inspiration behind many constitutional arguments.

NORTH CAROLINA v. PEARCE
395 U.S. 711 (1969)

FACTS

Pearce was convicted in North Carolina of assault with intent to rape. The judge sentenced him to prison for 12 to 15 years. Several years later, the Supreme Court of North Carolina reversed his conviction because an involuntary confession had been unconstitutionally allowed into evidence. Pearce was retried and reconvicted. The judge sentenced him to eight years in prison, which, when added to the time he had already spent in prison, was a longer sentence than what was originally imposed. His original sentence, assuming allowances for good time, would have expired in

November 1969. His new sentence with good time would expire in October 1972. Pearce filed a writ of federal habeas corpus. The District Court ruled that the longer sentence was unconstitutional. The Fourth Circuit Court of Appeals agreed. Rice pleaded guilty in an Alabama court to four charges of second-degree burglary. He was sentenced to prison terms that aggregated to 10 years. Two and a half years later, Rice successfully had his conviction overturned because he had not been afforded his right to counsel. He was retried, reconvicted, and sentenced to prison terms aggregating 25 years. He was not credited for the time he served on the original conviction. The federal District Court and Fifth Circuit Court of Appeals agreed with Rice that he was punished by the state for successfully exercising his right of appeal and having his original sentences overturned.

ISSUE
Does the Constitution require, in computing a sentence imposed after conviction upon retrial, that credit be given for the time served under the original sentence? Is there a constitutional bar to imposing a more severe sentence on reconviction?

HOLDING
The Fifth Amendment guarantee against double jeopardy is violated when punishment that has already been served for an offense is not fully credited in imposing a new sentence for the same crime. Imposing a more severe sentence upon retrial does not violate the double jeopardy clause because the power to impose whatever sentence is legally authorized is a corollary of the power to retry a defendant whose conviction has been set aside due to error in a previous proceeding. Imposing a more severe sentence also does not violate the equal protection clause because there is no invidious classification of those who seek a new trial. Nonetheless, due process requires that vindictiveness against a defendant who successfully challenged his original conviction must play no role in the sentence he receives upon reconviction. The reasons for imposing a more severe sentence at retrial must appear in the record and be based on objective information concerning the defendant's conduct after the original sentencing proceeding.

RATIONALE
The Court noted that the prohibition against double jeopardy clearly is violated when punishment that

has already been served is not fully credited when a person is reconvicted. If a person is reconvicted after retrial, the years he or she spent in prison must be returned by subtracting them form the new sentence. Constitutional doctrine is well established and clear, however, that the double jeopardy clause does not impose any restrictions on the length of a sentence imposed upon reconviction. There are no limits on the right to retry a defendant who has his first conviction overturned. At the defendant's behest, the original conviction was "wholly nullified and the slate wiped clean." The Court declined to depart from a principle that has been in practice for 75 years. Neither does imposing a more severe sentence violate the equal protection clause. A person who is retried after his conviction has been set aside may be acquitted or may be convicted and be assessed a shorter sentence, the same sentence, or a longer sentence than what was first imposed. A trial judge is not precluded from imposing a new sentence, more or less severe than the original sentence, "in light of events subsequent to the first trial that may have thrown new light upon the defendant's 'life, health, habits, conduct, and mental and moral propensities.' Such information may come to the judge's attention from evidence adduced at the second trial itself, from a new presentence investigation, from the defendant's prison record, or possibly from other sources." It would, however, violate the due process clause for a judge to impose a more severe sentence as a way of punishing a defendant for having his first conviction overturned because it would have a chilling effect on individuals still in prison exercising their rights to appeal.

CASE EXCERPT
"It simply cannot be said that a State has invidiously 'classified' those who successfully seek new trials, any more than that the State has invidiously 'classified' those prisoners whose convictions are not set aside by denying the members of that group the opportunity to be acquitted."

CASE SIGNIFICANCE
This case clarifies two important issues involving sentencing after a successful appeal, retrial, and reconviction. Time served must be credited to the new sentence. A more severe penalty may be imposed as long as it is clear on the record the judge was not motivated by vindictiveness and had objective information about the defendant's behavior since the first trial that justified

NORTH CAROLINA v. PEARCE *(cont.)*

a more severe sanction. As the result of a series of Supreme Court decisions in the 1960s and 1970s, convicted offenders more frequently exercised their right to appeal and file writs for collateral relief. Retrials and reconvictions became more common. The Supreme Court had a chance to refine its holding in *Pearce in Texas v. McCullough*, 475 U.S. 134 (1986). McCullough was convicted of murder and sentenced by a jury to 20 years in prison. The trial judge granted his motion for a new trial, but he was convicted him a second time. The judge increased his sentence to 50 years in prison. On the record, she explained there was newly discovered evidence during the second trial that McCullough had been out of prison only four months when he committed the murder, and the judge stated she would have sentenced him to more than 20 years if she had set the original sentence. The Texas Court of Criminal Appeals set the sentence aside and remanded the case to the trial court for resentencing in light of *North Carolina v. Pearce*. The US Supreme Court concluded that the sentence should not have been set aside because there were no facts to support a presumption that the judge acted vindictively, and she relied on information that was pertinent and justified an increased sentence. *Pearce* permits a judge to increase a sentence by finding relevant conduct or events that occurred subsequent to the original sentencing. This language, however, was never intended to describe exhaustively all the possible circumstances in which a sentence increase could be justified.

WILLIAMS v. ILLINOIS
399 U.S. 235 (1970)

FACTS

Williams was convicted in an Illinois court of petty theft and assessed the maximum penalty under state law: one-year imprisonment and a $500 fine. He was also taxed five dollars in court costs. As permitted by the statute, the judgment directed that if Williams defaulted on payment of the fine and court costs at the expiration of the one year sentence, he should remain in jail to work off the fine and costs at the rate of five dollars per day. After Williams completed his one-year term, he began serving the imprisonment necessary to satisfy the $505 in fine and costs. On appeal, the Illinois State Supreme Court denied his claim that he

was denied equal protection of the laws when he was incarcerated to satisfy the payment of his fine.

ISSUE

Is it a violation of the Constitution for an indigent convicted offender to be confined beyond the maximum term specified by the statute because he or she failed to satisfy the monetary penalties of the sentence?

HOLDING

Yes. Though a state has considerable latitude in fixing penalties for state crimes, the equal protection clause of the Fourteenth Amendment prohibits subjecting convicted offenders to imprisonment beyond the maximum length of the term provided in the statute solely because they are indigent and are unable to pay monetary penalties.

RATIONALE

Imprisoning convicted offenders for nonpayment of fines dates back to medieval England, and almost all the states and the federal government have laws authorizing incarceration as a result of nonpayment. Most states permit imprisonment beyond the maximum allowed by the statute. In previous decisions the Supreme Court approved of the practice, which has been defended as a coercive device to ensure the offender will pay the fine. In *Griffin v. Illinois*, 351 U.S. 12 (1956), the Court held that failing to provide an indigent defendant with a trial transcript at public expense in order to pursue an appeal violated the equal protection clause. Since that case was decided the Supreme Court has had other occasions to support the basic mandate that justice be applied equally to all and has worked towards weakening the disparate treatment of the poor in the criminal justice process. The Illinois statute in effect exposes only indigent offenders to the risk of imprisonment beyond the statutory maximum. This results in different consequences on two categories of persons, in violation of the Constitution. Nothing in this decision precludes imprisonment if the offender willfully refuses to pay a fine or court costs.

CASE EXCERPT

"The need to be open to reassessment of ancient practices other than those explicitly mandated by the Constitution is illustrated by the present case since the greatly increased use of fines as a criminal sanction has made nonpayment a major cause of incarceration in this country."

CASE SIGNIFICANCE

The year following *Williams v. Illinois*, the Supreme Court decided *Tate v. Short*, 401 U.S. 395 (1971). In Tate, an indigent offender was fined $425 for nine traffic offenses. Under state law only fines could be imposed for these offenses, and if the offender could not pay the fines, he or she could be imprisoned until the fines were satisfied at five dollars per day. The Court ruled that a statute that automatically converts a fine to imprisonment if the offender cannot pay violates the equal protection clause. *Williams* provided the precedent for the *Tate* decision. In 1983, the Court considered whether the equal protection clause prohibits a state from revoking an indigent offender's probation for failure to pay a fine and restitution. Relying again on *Williams*, the Court ruled that in probation revocation proceedings for failure to pay a fine or restitution, the sentencing judge must examine why the probationer failed to pay. According to the majority opinion in *Bearden v. Georgia*, 461 U.S. 660 (1983), probation cannot be revoked solely because a person lacks the resources to pay.

UNITED STATES v. GRAYSON
438 U.S. 41 (1978)

FACTS

Grayson escaped from a federal prison camp, was apprehended two days later by FBI agents, and indicted for prison escape. At his trial, the government presented testimony from the arresting FBI agents to the effect that Grayson denied his true identity when he was apprehended. During his testimony he admitted leaving the camp but stated he did so because another inmate had threatened him, seeking to collect a gambling debt. The government introduced testimony from the alleged assailant who testified there were no threats and no gambling debt. In addition, the government introduced evidence that contradicted Grayson's version of his escape. The jury convicted him, and the District Court judge sentenced him to two years in prison to run consecutive to his unexpired term. The judge commented that one of his reasons for imposing such a penalty was because Grayson's defense was completely fabricated and without any

merit. The Third Circuit Court of Appeals directed that Grayson's sentence be vacated and he be resentenced without consideration of his false testimony. The appeals court was concerned that relying on the defendant's false testimony impinges on his right to testify on his own behalf.

ISSUE

Is it unconstitutional for a judge to consider a defendant's false testimony that the judge observed during the course of trial, when fixing a sentence within the statutory limits?

HOLDING

No. Considering a defendant's false testimony does not constitute punishment for the offense of perjury, and it does not impermissibly chill his right under the Constitution to testify in his own behalf.

RATIONALE

A defendant's truthfulness or lack thereof while testifying is probative of his attitude and his chances for rehabilitation. It is relevant information for a sentencing judge to consider. Judges are not limited to the information compiled in presentence investigation reports.

CASE EXCERPT

"A defendant's right to testify is the right to testify truthfully under oath. If allowing a sentencing judge to consider a defendant's false testimony has a chilling effect on his or her decision to lie under oath, that is permissible. There is no protected right to commit perjury."

CASE SIGNIFICANCE

The *Grayson* decision was the basis for the Supreme Court's more recent decision in *Dunnigan v. United States*, 507 U.S. 87 (1993), which interpreted the US Sentencing Guidelines. In Dunnigan's trial for conspiracy to distribute cocaine, the government's case consisted of five witnesses who testified they took part in or observed Dunnigan's cocaine trafficking. Dunnigan denied possessing or distributing cocaine. She was convicted, and the District Court found she had committed perjury, enhancing her sentence pursuant to the guidelines, which provided for such when a "defendant willfully impeded or obstructed, or attempted to impede or obstruct the administration of justice

UNITED STATES v. GRAYSON *(cont.)*

during the investigation or prosecution of the instant case." The Court of Appeals found the enhancement unconstitutional, concluding that Grayson was based on a sentencing scheme that emphasized rehabilitation and the goal of the Sentencing Guidelines is punishment, not rehabilitation. The high court disagreed, ruling that rehabilitation is not the only justification for increasing a sentence because of perjury. A unanimous Court reiterated all the reasons supporting its previous decision in *Grayson*, which it made clear remains good law under the Sentencing Guidelines.

ROBERTS v. UNITED STATES
445 U.S. 552 (1980)

FACTS
Winfield Roberts was indicted on one count of conspiracy to distribute heroin and four counts of using a telephone conversation to facilitate the distribution. He refused to cooperate with government prosecutors and give them information about his suppliers. The prosecutors warned him that his failure to cooperate would affect the charges brought against him. His first conviction was vacated. On remand, the government asked for two consecutive sentences of 16 to 48 months each and a $5,000 fine. Prosecutors argued that Roberts had a prior criminal history and had refused to name his suppliers. Roberts's defense attorney pointed out that his client had already been incarcerated for two years pending his appeal and his codefendant had been sentenced to probation. Counsel explained that Roberts refused to identify other members of the conspiracy because he was not involved in it. The District Court imposed two consecutive sentences of one to four years and special parole, supporting its penalty in part because Roberts refused to cooperate with the government. Roberts appealed, contending that the judge should not have considered his failure to cooperate because it violated the Fifth Amendment. The Court of Appeals for the District of Columbia affirmed the trial court.

ISSUE
Does it violate the privilege against self-incrimination for a court to consider, as one factor in imposing sentence, a defendant's refusal to cooperate with officials investigating a crime in which the defendant confessed he participated?

HOLDING
No. It does not violate the Fifth Amendment's privilege against self-incrimination for a court to consider a defendant's refusal to cooperate with the government in imposing a sentence—unless there is substantial reason for the government to believe the information would be incriminating and the privilege was invoked in a timely fashion.

RATIONALE
Federal criminal law states specifically there are no limits on the information a judge can consider for purposes of imposing a sentence. This Court has reaffirmed the fundamental principle that a judge may conduct a broad inquiry and is not limited by the information he or she may consider or the source from which it may come (*United States v. Tucker*, 404 U.S. 443 (1972)). There was no misinformation used in this case. It is undisputed that Roberts refused to provide information to the government over a period of three years. It is a citizen's duty to report felonies to the authorities. By declining to cooperate, petitioner rejected an "obligatio[n] of community life" that should be recognized before rehabilitation can begin. This duty is not lessened when the witness to the crime is also involved. Unless his silence is protected by the Fifth Amendment's privilege against self-incrimination, he or she has no less a duty than any other citizen. Roberts's refusal to provide information protects criminals and preserves his ability to resume criminal activities when he is released. Roberts failed to argue to the sentencing judge that his refusal to cooperate was based on the Fifth Amendment. Where the government had no substantial reason to think the information they requested would be incriminating, Roberts could not rely on the privilege unless he invoked it in a timely fashion.

CASE EXCERPT
"Concealment of crime has been condemned throughout our history. The citizen's duty to raise the 'hue and cry' and report felonies to the authorities was an established tenet of Anglo-Saxon law at least as early as the 13th century."

CASE SIGNIFICANCE
Roberts was decided two years after the Supreme Court decided *United States v. Grayson*, 438 U.S. 41 (1978), in which the Court ruled that a judge could consider a defendant's perjury in fixing a sentence.

Both cases examine the type of information judges can use in making sentencing decisions and the scope of their discretion. Under the federal Sentencing Guidelines adopted in 1984, where a defendant agrees to cooperate with the government and provide information about crimes committed by other persons, and in exchange the government agrees the information which incriminates the defendant will not be used against him, the information can not be used in deciding the guideline range that applies to the defendant's sentence, except as provided in the agreement. Also under the guidelines a prosecutor can request that a judge grant a downward departure to a defendant who has provided substantial assistance to the government. The judge decides whether the downward departure will be granted and to what extent.

MISTRETTA v. UNITED STATES
488 U.S. 361 (1989)

FACTS

The Sentencing Reform Act of 1984 abolished indeterminate sentencing and parole in federal criminal cases. Under indeterminate sentencing, Congress defined the maximum and judges used their discretion to impose sentences within the statutory range. The parole board determined the actual duration of incarceration. Congress abandoned indeterminate sentencing as a result of widespread dissatisfaction with the uncertainties and disparities that resulted from the system. In 1984, the federal legislature enacted sweeping reforms in the Sentencing Reform Act (SRA). The SRA created the United States Sentencing Commission, which has authority to promulgate binding sentencing guidelines that establish ranges of determinate sentences for all federal crimes and defendants based on various factors. The Commission is independent within the judicial branch of the federal government. Its seven members are appointed by the president. At least three of the members must be federal judges, selected from a list of six judges recommended by the Judicial Conference. Mistretta pleaded guilty to the distribution of cocaine. He moved to have the Sentencing Guidelines declared unconstitutional on the grounds that the Sentencing Commission was constituted in violation of the separation of powers clause and that Congress had delegated excessive authority to the commission to structure the guidelines. The District Court rejected his arguments. Under the guidelines he was sentenced to 18 months

in prison, followed by three years of supervised release, a $1000 fine, and a special assessment of fifty dollars. Mistretta filed for appeal in the Eighth Circuit, but because of the importance of the issue and pursuant to Court Rules, both parties petitioned for certiorari before the Supreme Court before the appeals court rendered judgment.

ISSUE

Are the US Sentencing Guidelines unconstitutional because Congress delegated excessive legislative power to the sentencing commission? Are the US Sentencing Guidelines unconstitutional because they violate the separation of powers doctrine by placing the commission within the judicial branch, requiring federal judges to serve on the commission and share authority with nonjudges, or by empowering the President to appoint individuals to the Commission and to be able to remove them for cause?

HOLDING

The Sentencing Guidelines are constitutional. Congress did not violate the separation of powers doctrine or delegate excessive power to the commission. The Constitution does not prohibit Congress from delegating to an expert body within the judicial branch the difficult job of creating sentencing guidelines consistent with the direction Congress provided in the SRA. The Constitution also does not prohibit Congress calling on judges with their experience and wisdom to assist in developing sentencing guidelines.

RATIONALE

The nondelegation doctrine is found in the separation of powers doctrine and provides that Congress cannot delegate its legislative power to another branch of the federal government. The nondelegation doctrine, however, does not prevent Congress from obtaining the assistance of one of the other branches. As long as Congress outlines in legislation an "intelligible principle" directing the persons or body authorized to exercise the delegated authority, the delegation is not forbidden by the Constitution. In our increasingly complex society, Congress cannot do its job without the ability to delegate power under broad general directives. As long as Congress clearly delineates the general policy, the agency that is charged with applying it, and the boundaries of the delegated authority, there is no constitutional problem. The delegation of authority to the Sentencing Commission under the SRA is

MISTRETTA v. UNITED STATES *(cont.)*

sufficiently specific and detailed. The task of developing sanctions for hundreds of different offenses committed by a vast array of offenders is the type of matter that is appropriate for a body of experts. Mistretta also claims that the SRA requires the judicial branch to not only exercise their judicial power but legislative power as well, undermining the judiciary's independence and integrity. Mistretta asserts that Congress violates the separation of powers doctrine when it co-opts federal judges into performing the political work of establishing sentencing guidelines and subjecting them to the political whims of the president, and forcing them to share power with nonjudges."

CASE EXCERPT

"Although the unique composition and responsibilities of the Sentencing Commission give rise to serious concerns about a disruption of the appropriate balance of governmental power among the coordinate Branches, we conclude, upon close inspection, that petitioner's fears for the fundamental structural protections of the Constitution prove, at least in this case, to be 'more smoke than fire,' and do not compel us to invalidate Congress' considered scheme for resolving the seemingly intractable dilemma of excessive disparity in criminal sentencing."

CASE SIGNIFICANCE

This decision upheld a significant revamping, the Sentencing Reform Act of 1984, of federal sentencing policy and practice. The SRA revised the old sentencing process in several ways. It adopted a new rationale for imprisonment, rejecting rehabilitation and accepting retribution, deterrence, and incapacitation. It abolished parole in the federal system. It made all sentences determinate. It made the Sentencing Commission's guidelines binding on federal judges. The commission is a unique independent agency within the judicial branch. The *Mistretta* case, decided 8–1, allowed federal sentencing reform to proceed, which, in turn, contributed to sentencing reform throughout the United States.

HARMELIN v. MICHIGAN

501 U.S. 957 (1991)

FACTS

Harmelin was convicted of possessing 672 grams of cocaine and sentenced by a Michigan court to a mandatory term of life in prison without the possibility of parole. He had no prior felony convictions. On appeal, the Michigan Court of Appeals rejected his claim that the punishment was cruel and unusual, thereby violating the Eighth Amendment of the US Constitution. The Michigan Supreme Court denied him leave to appeal.

ISSUE

Is Harmelin's sentence unconstitutionally cruel and unusual because it is significantly disproportionate to the crime he committed? Is his sentence unconstitutionally cruel and unusual because the judge was statutorily required to impose it, without considering the particular circumstances of the crime and the offender?

HOLDING

The Eighth Amendment does not require proportionality in sentencing unless the sentence is grossly disproportionate to the offense. The Eighth Amendment does not require individualized sentencing in noncapital criminal cases. A mandatory sentence that precludes a sentencing judge from considering the particular circumstances of a crime and the offender is constitutional in cases that do not involve the death penalty.

RATIONALE

Mandatory penalties may be cruel, but they are not unusual and have been employed throughout our history. Harmelin's claim that the judge must be required to consider mitigating factors in sentencing finds support in the Court's death penalty jurisprudence where the Court held that it violates the Eighth Amendment to impose a capital sentence without an individualized determination. This Court, however, refuses to extend that doctrine to noncapital cases. The death penalty differs from all other punishments and is irrevocable. Although Harmelin's sentence is unique in that it is the second most severe punishment that can be imposed, life in prison with parole is also unique as the third most severe sentence. There still remains the possibility of a retroactive legislative reduction of the sentence and executive clemency. The framers of the Constitution did not include a prohibition against disproportionate sentences.

CASE EXCERPT

"We think it enough that those who framed and approved the Federal Constitution chose, for whatever reason, not to include within it the guarantee against disproportionate sentences that some State Constitutions contained. It is worth noting, however, that there was good reason for that choice—a reason that reinforces the necessity of overruling *Solem*. While there are relatively clear historical guidelines and accepted practices that enable judges to determine which *modes* of punishment are 'cruel and unusual,' *proportionality* does not lend itself to such analysis."

CASE SIGNIFICANCE

Harmelin is one of a series of cases in which the Supreme Court has struggled with the principle of proportionality in sentencing. The Court first considered the matter in *Weems v. U.S.*, 217 U.S. 349 (1910) and concluded a sentence of twelve years imprisonment at hard labor and the wearing of chains was disproportionate to the crime of falsifying a public and official document and violated the cruel and unusual punishment clause. In the second case, *Rummel v. Estelle*, 445 U.S. 263 (1980), the Court considered the case of a man who was sentenced to life under the Texas recidivist statute. Rummel argued that the life sentence was grossly disproportionate to the three felonies that formed the predicate for his sentence: fraudulently using a credit card to obtain $80 worth of goods, passing a forged check for $28.36, and obtaining $120.75 by false pretenses. Under the recidivist statute the trial judge imposed a life sentence. Concluding that Rummel's punishment was not cruel and unusual, the Supreme Court refused to engage in a proportionality analysis. It noted, "even if we were to assume that the statute employed against Rummel was the most stringent found in the 50 States, that severity hardly would render Rummel's punishment 'grossly disproportionate' to his offense or to the punishment he would have received in the other State." In the third case, *Solem v. Helm*, 463 U.S. 277 (1983), the Court considered whether the Eighth Amendment prohibits a life sentence without possibility of parole for a seventh nonviolent felony. The Solem Court wrote, "the principle that a punishment should be proportionate to the crime is deeply rooted and frequently repeated in common-law jurisprudence. The constitutional principle of proportionality has been recognized explicitly in the Court for almost a century." The Court held that a criminal sentence must be proportionate to the crime for which the defendant is convicted and set forth three criteria for reviewing sentences: (1) the gravity of the offense and the harshness of the punishment; (2) a comparison of sentences imposed in other

criminals in the same jurisdiction; and (3) a comparison of sentences imposed for the same crime in other jurisdictions. The Supreme Court decided that Solem's sentence was disproportionate to his crime. The 5–4 Harmelin decision does not clarify the Court's position on proportionality and the Eighth Amendment. The majority opinion written by Justice Scalia suggests there is no proportionality requirement in the Constitution. Three of the other Justices who made up the majority, however, did not agree with Justice Scalia in the part of the opinion concerning the Eighth Amendment and proportionality. In their concurring opinion, they agreed that strict proportionality is not constitutionally required but suggest that the Constitution forbids grossly disproportionate sentences. In their opinion they emphasized the seriousness of drug trafficking and concluded that Michigan's statute was not grossly disproportionate.

RENO v. KORAY

515 U.S. 50 (1995)

FACTS

Ziya Koray pleaded guilty to laundering monetary instruments. A US magistrate ordered him released on bail, pending sentencing, into the custody of the pretrial services agency. He was confined to a community treatment center operated by the Volunteers of America and was not authorized to leave the facility unless accompanied by a government agent. Several months after his release to the community center, he was sentenced to 41 months in prison. He remained at the center an additional month until he reported to a federal prison camp. Koray requested that the Bureau of Prisons (BOP) credit the approximately 150 days he spent at the Volunteers of America treatment center toward his 41-month sentence. The BOP refused. The District Court refused his petition for habeas corpus, ruling that the 150 days in the community treatment center did not constitute official detention within the meaning of 18 U.S.C. §3585(b). The Third Circuit Court of Appeals reversed. The appeals court agreed that §3585 does not require the BOP to credit defendants whose bail conditions allowed them to be confined outside of a BOP facility. The court disagreed with the bureau that time spent on bail under highly restrictive conditions is not official detention just because the defendant is not under BOP control.

RENO v. KORAY *(cont.)*

ISSUE

Is a federal prisoner entitled to credit against his sentence under 18 U.S.C. §3585(b) for time when he or she was released on bail pursuant to the Bail Reform Act of 1984?

HOLDING

No. A defendant who is released on bail while waiting sentencing is not entitled to any credit for the time he or she served under highly restrictive bail release conditions.

RATIONALE

18 U.S.C. §3585 outlines when a federal sentence of imprisonment begins and when credit should be granted for time spent in official detention before the sentence. The statute specifies that a defendant should be granted credit toward their term in prison for any time spent in official detention prior to the date the sentence began. Section 3585 must be construed in conjunction with the Bail Reform Act of 1984, which authorizes federal courts to place restraints on a defendant's liberty while he is waiting to be sentenced. The act gives a judge two options for dealing with a defendant who is waiting sentencing: (1) release on bail, or (2) order him detained without bail. A defendant who has been released on bail can be made subject to a variety of conditions, including residence in a halfway house. If the judge finds that bail is not appropriate, the defendant is detained and committed to the custody of the attorney general for confinement in a corrections institution. Under the language of the Bail Reform Act, a defendant is detained only when committed to the custody of the attorney general. A defendant who is released on bail with restrictions is not detained. Generally, Congress views the restriction on liberty like those placed on the defendant while he was at the treatment center to be part of a probation sentence or supervised release. It is true that release to a community treatment center while on bail includes restraints on liberty that are not much different than those imposed on a person committed to the custody of the attorney general and assigned to a treatment center. Nonetheless, the distinction is real. A person committed to the attorney general's custody is always subject to the BOP control. They can be reassigned and are subject to BOP disciplinary procedures. A person released on bail is not subject to the bureau's control and not in its custody

CASE EXCERPT

"To determine in each case whether a defendant 'released' on bail was subjected to 'jail type confinement' would require a fact intensive inquiry into the circumstances of confinement, an inquiry based on information in the hands of private entities not available to the Bureau as a matter of right."

CASE SIGNIFICANCE

There had been a series of Courts of Appeal cases addressing the meaning of official detention under 18 U.S.C. §3585. Most courts had determined the defendant was not entitled to credit toward their sentence in similar situations to Koray's. The Third and Ninth Circuits, however, had decided defendants were entitled to credit if the conditions of release were similar to the conditions of incarceration. The Supreme Court accepted this case to resolve the conflict. There was no constitutional issue in this case. It was entirely a matter of statutory construction.

KOON v. UNITED STATES
518 U.S. 81 (1996)

FACTS

Stacey Koon was convicted in federal District Court under 18 U.S.C. §242 for willfully permitting law enforcement officers to use unreasonable force during the arrest of Rodney King, thereby violating King's constitutional rights under color of law. In connection with the same incident, Laurence Powell was also convicted in federal District Court under 18 U.S.C. §242 for willful use of unreasonable force. The applicable US sentencing guideline indicated that they should be sentenced to 70 to 87 months in prison; however, the District Court granted them two downward departures from the range. The first departure was based on Rodney King's misconduct, which the court found significantly provoked the offense. The second departure was based on a combination of factors: (1) Koon and Powell were very susceptible to abuse in prison; (2) they had lost their jobs and would never serve in law enforcement again; (3) they had been subject to successive state and federal prosecutions (both defendants had previously been acquitted on state charges of assault and excessive use of force); and (4) they posed a low risk of recidivism. After the departures, the sentencing range was 30 to 37 months imprisonment. The court sentenced each defendant to 30 months. On appeal, the Ninth Circuit Court of Appeals reviewed each departure and reasons for it de novo, reversing every departure.

ISSUE
Under the US Sentencing Guidelines, should an appellate court reviewing a sentencing court's decision to depart from the guidelines review the departure decision de novo?

HOLDING
When reviewing a sentencing court's decision to depart from the US Sentencing Guidelines, the standard of review for the appeals court is whether the sentencing court abused its discretion.

RATIONALE
The Sentencing Reform Act of 1984 requires a federal district court to impose a sentence within the applicable guideline range in an ordinary case. It does not eliminate all of the court's traditional sentencing discretion. The law permits a departure from the range if the court finds "there exists an aggravati ng or mitigating circumstance of a kind, to a degree, not adequately taken into consideration" by the formula devised by the guidelines. The guidelines apply to a "heartland" of typical cases and do not apply to atypical cases. The guidelines prohibit some factors from being considered for departure and gives guidance on what other factors may or may not be appropriate. If the guidelines do not mention a particular factor, the court must consider the purpose and structure of the guidelines as a whole and decide whether the factor is sufficiently unusual to make the case atypical. Departures based on factors that are not mentioned must be infrequent. Federal law allows appellate review of sentencing decisions; however, appeal courts must grant deference to District Court decisions. Appellate courts do not have wide-ranging authority over their sentencing decisions. In this case, the Ninth Circuit erred in rejecting certain of the downward departures relied on by the sentencing judge. King's misconduct is a valid basis for a downward departure. The guidelines recognize that victim misconduct can be considered in making a departure. The Ninth Circuit also erred when it concluded that certain factors must never be considered for departure. Only the US Sentencing Commission decide which factors are proscribed by law. The District Court did abuse its discretion in relying on the defendants' loss of employment in making a downward departure. It

is expected that public officials who use their authority to violate a citizen's constitutional rights will lose their job and be barred from that type of employment. The Commission considered these consequences in establishing the punishment range for this offense. The District Court also abused its discretion when it considered the defendants' low likelihood of recidivism. The Commission addressed this factor in formulating the sentencing range for the defendants' criminal history category. The sentencing court did not abuse its discretion in relying on Koon and Powell's susceptibility to abuse in prison and the burdens imposed on them by successive prosecutions. When a district court bases departures on both valid and invalid factors, the case must be remanded unless the reviewing court determines that the district court would have imposed the same sentence if it had not relied on the invalid factors. In this case, it is not clear whether the District Court would have imposed the same sentence.

CASE EXCERPT
"A district court's decision to depart from the Guidelines, by contrast, will in most cases be due substantial deference, for it embodies the traditional exercise of discretion by a sentencing court."

CASE SIGNIFICANCE
Before the US Sentencing Guidelines were implemented in 1984, federal sentences were not reviewable on appeal as long as the sentence was within the statutory range. The Sentencing Reform Act allows for limited review, including allowing a defendant to appeal an upward departure and the government to appeal a downward departure. Until the Koon case was decided there was no clear standard for reviewing a sentencing court's departure decisions. The government advocated for de novo review, which would allow an appeals court to make its own fact-findings and decide for itself which departures were warranted under the Guidelines. This Court declined to support the government's position. It upheld the sentencing judge's traditional discretion, or what is left of it under the guidelines. The Court noted that sentencing involves considering unique factors that differ somewhat from case to case, making it unlikely that appeals courts exercising de novo review could establish clear standards for the lower courts. Although the guidelines provide uniformity and predictability to sentencing, the Court wrote, "it has been uniform and constant in the federal judicial tradition for the sentencing judge to consider every convicted

KOON v. UNITED STATES *(cont.)*

person as an individual and every case as a unique study in the human failings that sometimes mitigate, sometimes magnify, the crime and the punishment to ensue. Discretion is reserved within the Sentencing Guidelines, and reflected by the standard of appellate review we adopt."

NEAL v. UNITED STATES
516 U.S. 284 (1996)

FACTS
In 1988, Meirl Neal pleaded guilty in federal court to possession of LSD with intent to distribute and conspiracy to possess LSD with intent to distribute. At the time of the initial sentencing, the method for determining the weight of the illegal substance was based on the whole weight of the blotter paper containing the drug. The total weight exceeded 10 grams, and the District Court found that Neal was subject to a 10-year mandatory minimum sentence as specified in 21 U.S. §841(b)(1). The quantity of the drugs and Neals's prior convictions resulted in a sentencing range of 188 to 235 months imprisonment. The court imposed concurrent sentences of 192 months on each count, followed by five years of supervised release. In 1993, the US Sentencing Commission revised the method for calculating the weight of LSD. Under the amended guidelines, each dose of LSD on a carrier medium must be given the presumed weight of 0.4 milligrams. The revisions were retroactive. Neal filed a motion to modify his sentence, contending that the weight of the LSD attributable to him should now be construed to be only 4.58 grams. The sentencing range would reduce to 70 to 87 months in prison. Most importantly, the 10-year mandatory minimum would no longer bar a reduced sentence because the 4.58 grams under the new guidelines would be far less than the 10 grams which triggered the 10-year mandatory sentence. The District Court ruled that the blotter paper must be weighed in determining whether a defendant crosses the 10-gram threshold, and the 10-year mandatory minimum still applied. The Seventh Circuit Court of Appeals agreed.

ISSUE
Is a federal sentencing judge required to follow 21 U.S.C. §841 when determining the weight of a drug even though the amended US Sentencing Guidelines provide a different method for calculating weight?

HOLDING
21 U.S.C. §841(b)(1) directs a sentencing court to take into account the actual weight of the blotter paper with its absorbed LSD, even though the Sentencing Guidelines require a different method of calculating the weight of an LSD mixture or substance. The revised guidelines are not entitled to deference.

RATIONALE
In 1984, Congress amended the Comprehensive Drug Abuse Prevention and Control Act to calculate penalties by the weight of the pure drug involved. In the Anti-Drug Abuse Act of 1986, Congress went a step further and provided that the total quantity of what is distributed, rather than the amount of the pure drug, should determine the length of a prison sentence. This step addressed the problem of traffickers who were getting lighter sentences because they were supplying diluted or mixed drugs. The 1986 act also provided for mandatory minimum sentences based on the weight of a mixture or substance containing a detectable amount of drugs. Under 21 U.S.C. §841, trafficking in 10 grams or more of a mixture or substance containing LSD mandated at least 10 years in prison. In *Chapman v. United States*, 500 U.S. 453 (1991), the Supreme Court ruled that because LSD cannot be distinguished from the blotter paper or separated form it, §841 requires the actual weight of the blotter paper be weighed. Neal asserts the revised Sentencing Guidelines set up a new method for determining weight that must supersede the old method and established a constructive or presumed weight to the LSD and carrier for each dose. The Court concluded, however, that the Commission's alternative methodology for weighing LSD does not alter its interpretation of 21 U.S.C. §841 in Chapman, stating that "principles of stare decisis require that we adhere to our earlier decision." The mandatory minimum statute and the Sentencing Guidelines both calibrate punishment of drug traffickers based on the quantity of drugs involved. The Commission has noted in the past that mandatory minimums are at odds with the Sentencing Guidelines and the goals they seek to achieve. Nonetheless, the Commission has tried to make the guidelines fit the mandatory minimum scheme established by Congress in 21 U.S.C. §841. Most of the time there is no inconsistency between the guidelines and the statute with respect to calculating the weight of drugs. In 1993, based on a study of the LSD trade, the Commission decided to change the method for weighing LSD for the purposes of promoting proportionate

sentencing. There was concern that the weights of carrier mediums could vary significantly and including their weight could produce disparity in sentencing crimes involving the same amount of actual LSD. The revised guideline stated that the carrier medium should not be included and each dose of LSD should be given a presumed weight of 0.4. The amendment was submitted to Congress, which did not disapprove it within the allotted 180 days, and it took effect. The commentary to the guidelines states that the new method is to be used to determine the base offense level. It never states that the method should replace the actual-weight method approved by the Court in the Chapman case. The Commission also noted that its method does not override the method used for determining weight under mandatory minimum laws.

CASE EXCERPT

"The Commission seems to do no more than acknowledge that, whether or not its method would be preferable for the statute and Guideline alike, it has no authority to override the statute as we have construed it…Entrusted within its sphere to make policy judgments, the Commission may abandon its old methods in favor of what it has deemed a more desirable 'approach' to calculating LSD quantities. We, however, do not have the same latitude to forsake prior interpretations of a statute. True, there may be little in logic to defend the statute's treatment of LSD; it results in significant disparity of punishment meted out to LSD offenders relative to other narcotic traffickers. Even so, Congress not this Court, has the responsibility of revising its statutes."

CASE SIGNIFICANCE

When a drug offender is sentenced under the federal guidelines, his sentence is largely determined by the quantity (weight) and type (classification) of the drugs involved in the case. Determining the quantity of drugs is a very important. In *Chapman v. United States*, the Court interpreted the meaning of the words "mixture or substance" in 21 U.S.C. §841 which provides that the total weight of any "mixture or substance containing a detectable amount" of an illicit drug should help determine the punishment. The Court ruled that in the case of LSD, the statute included the medium on which the LSD is carried. The Court dismissed arguments that the medium is not used to dilute the LSD and, therefore, was not intended to be covered by the statute. The *Chapman* case left a lot of unanswered

questions. The Court addressed LSD without expressly applying its strict interpretation of "mixture or substance" to other drugs. The result was a split among the courts of appeal. Some courts held that the weight of the material that render a drug uningestible should not be calculated for purposes of sentencing. Other courts applied the weight of such a material. The 1993 amendments to the guidelines were intended to clarify the issue by adopting the position that "mixture or substance" does not include materials that must be separated from the illicit drug before it can be used. The amendments went on to specify the presumed weight of marijuana without moisture and LSD without the carrier medium. *Neal v. United States* is significant because it addressed a growing conflict among the appeal courts regarding the balance of authority between the Sentencing Guidelines and the statutory sentencing provisions. *Neal* made it clear that the Sentencing Commission does not have the authority to override or amend a statute. Nonetheless, confusion remains over the interpretation of "mixture or substance" for drugs other than LSD. Neither the *Chapman* nor *Neal* decisions resolved the issue.

UNITED STATES v. WATTS
519 U.S. 148 (1997)

FACTS

A jury convicted Watts of possessing cocaine base with intent to distribute but acquitted him of using a firearm in relation to a drug offense. At sentencing, despite his acquittal on the firearm's charge, the District Court found by a preponderance of the evidence that Watts possessed a gun in connection with a drug crime. The court added two points to his base offense level under the federal Sentencing Guidelines, enhancing his sentence. The Court of Appeals vacated and held a sentencing judge may not rely on facts of which a defendant was acquitted.

ISSUE

Is a judge prohibited from considering conduct for which a defendant has been acquitted when making a sentencing determination on another charge for which the defendant has been found guilty?

HOLDING

A jury's verdict of acquittal does not prohibit a sentencing judge from considering conduct underlying

UNITED STATES v. WATTS *(cont.)*

the acquitted charge, so long as it is proved by a preponderance of the evidence.

RATIONALE

18 U.S.C. §3661 provides that "no limitation shall be placed on the information concerning the background, character, and conduct of a person convicted of an offense which a court of the United States may receive and consider for the purpose of imposing a sentence." In *Williams v. New York*, 337 U.S. 241 (1949), the Court considered the case of a convicted murderer sentenced to death who challenged the court's reliance on information that he had been involved in 30 burglaries for which he had not been convicted, concluding the evidence was relevant at the sentencing stage. The federal Sentencing Guidelines provide that in determining which sentence to impose within the guideline range or whether to depart from the guidelines, a judge may consider any information about a defendant's background, character, and conduct— unless it is otherwise prohibited by law. Commentary to the guidelines allows a judge to rely on the entire scope of a defendant's conduct, regardless of the counts alleged or on which there was a conviction. Sentencing enhancements increase a sentence because of the way the offender committed the crime for which they were convicted. In addition, an acquittal does not prove a defendant's innocence. It only proves the existence of reasonable doubt and is not tantamount to a finding of facts. The guidelines state that facts relevant to a sentencing decision should be proved by a preponderance of evidence. The Court agrees that burden of proof satisfies due process.

CASE EXCERPT

"Neither the broad language of § 3661 nor our holding in *Williams* suggests any basis for the courts to invent a blanket prohibition against considering certain types of evidence at sentencing. Indeed, under the pre-Guidelines sentencing regime, it was well established that a sentencing judge may take into account facts introduced at trial relating to other charges, even ones of which the defendant has been acquitted."

CASE SIGNIFICANCE

This case was significant because it clarified an issue that created a split among the Courts of Appeal. The Court made the very important conclusion that there is no distinction in the sentencing decision-making process between uncharged conduct being considered by the judge and conduct relating to the charge for which a defendant was acquitted.

UNITED STATES v. BAJAKAJIAN
524 U.S. 321 (1998)

FACTS

Customs agents detained Hosep Bajakajian, his wife, and their children while they were waiting in the Los Angeles International Airport for a flight to Cyprus after dogs detected currency in their checked luggage. A search uncovered $230,000. A customs inspector approached Bajakajian and advised him that he was required to report all money in excess of $10,000 in their possession. Bajakajian reported he had $8,000 and his wife had $7,000. Agents discovered $357,144 after a search of the family's carry-on bags, wallets, and purses. Bajakajian was charged with failing to report that he was transporting more than $10,000 outside of the United States and making a false material statement to the US customs agents. Count three of the indictment sought forfeiture of the $357,144. Under federal forfeiture law, if a person is convicted of failing to report he is transporting more than $10,000 outside of the country, a court shall order that person to forfeit to the United States any property involved in the offense or traceable to the offense. Bajakajian pleaded guilty to failure to report, and the government dismissed the false statement charge. The defendant went to trial on the forfeiture issue. The District Court found that the entire $357,144 was subject to forfeiture because it was involved in the offense. The court also found the defendant was transporting the money to pay a valid debt, no other crime was involved, and that he failed to report taking the currency out of the United States because of fear stemming from cultural differences. He had grown up as a cultural minority in Syria and did not trust the government. The District Court concluded that full forfeiture would be too harsh and violate the Eighth Amendment. It ordered $15,000 to be forfeited, three years probation, and a fine of $5,000. The government appealed and sought full forfeiture. The Ninth Circuit Court of Appeals affirmed.

ISSUE

Does full forfeiture of a large sum of money a defendant failed to declare he was transporting outside of the United States in violation of federal law violate the excessive fines clause of the Eighth Amendment?

HOLDING

A punitive forfeiture violates the excessive fines clause of the Eighth Amendment if it is grossly disproportional to the gravity of the crime it is designed to punish.

RATIONALE

The Eighth Amendment provides that "excessive bail shall not be required, nor excessive fines imposed, nor cruel and unusual punishment inflicted." The Court has never applied the excessive fines clause, however, it has explained in a previous decision that the word "fine" means a payment to the government as punishment for a crime. The forfeiture of currency required by federal law in this case constitutes punishment. It is imposed at the end of a criminal proceeding and requires a conviction of failing to report a transfer of currency. The currency in this case is not an instrumentality of the crime. It was a precondition to the reporting requirement only. It is the subject of the crime of failure to report. It did not facilitate the commission of a crime. The constitutional issue is whether the amount of the forfeiture bears some relationship to the gravity of the crime it is meant to punish. Is the fine proportional to the offense? For determining the proportionality issue in a case such as the one before the Court, the standard should be whether the forfeiture is grossly disproportionate. Using this standard, the $367,144 forfeiture is grossly disproportionate to the crime and violates the Constitution.

CASE EXCERPT

"It was only in 1970 that Congress resurrected the English common law of punitive forfeiture to combat organized crime and major drug trafficking. In providing for this mode of punishment, which had long been unused in this country, the Senate Judiciary Committee acknowledged that 'criminal forfeiture represents an innovative attempt to call on our common law heritage to meet an essentially modern problem.' Indeed, it was not until 1992 that Congress provided for the criminal forfeiture of currency at issue here."

CASE SIGNIFICANCE

The Bajakajian case was preceded by another case that held the Eighth Amendment's excessive fines clause applied to drug-related forfeitures of property under federal civil law. In that case, *Austin v. United States*, 509 U.S. 602 (1993), the Court considered the forfeiture under civil law of a mobile home and auto body shop owned by Richard Austin, who had pleaded guilty to several drug law violations. The Justices concluded that whether the forfeiture is labeled civil or criminal does not matter because the Eighth Amendment is not expressly limited to criminal cases. The important issue is whether the forfeiture is punishment. The Court specifically declined to establish a standard for determining whether a forfeiture is constitutionally excessive, deciding that the lower courts should be allowed to consider the question. In Bajakajian, the Supreme Court established the standard they had declined to establish five years earlier. In addition, for the first time the Supreme Court struck down a fine as excessive under the Eighth Amendment.

APPRENDI v. NEW JERSEY
530 U.S. 466 (2000)

FACTS

Charles Apprendi fired several shots into the home of an African American family that had recently moved into a previously all white neighborhood. He was arrested and admitted firing the shots. In a statement to police he said he did not want the family in the neighborhood because of their race. A New Jersey Grand Jury indicted him on 23 counts, alleging shootings on four different dates and various unlawful possession of weapons charges. None of the counts referred to the state's hate crime statute. There were no allegations that Apprendi acted out of racial bias. The New Jersey hate crime statute provides for an extended term of imprisonment if the trial judge finds by a preponderance of the evidence that the offender committed the crime with a purpose to intimidate an individual or group of individuals because of race, color, gender, handicap, religion, sexual orientation, or ethnicity. The extended term authorized for second-degree crimes is between 10 and 20 years. Apprendi pleaded guilty to two counts of second-degree possession of a firearm for an unlawful purpose and one count of a third-degree offense of unlawful possession of an antipersonnel bomb. The other 20 counts were dismissed. Under New Jersey law, a second-degree offense carries a penalty range of five to 10 years. A third degree offense

APPRENDI v. NEW JERSEY (cont.)

has a penalty range of between three and five years. As part of the plea agreement, the state reserved the right to ask the court for an enhanced penalty on one of the second-degree felony counts on the grounds it was committed with a biased purpose. Apprendi reserved the right to challenge the hate crime enhancement The trial judge found by a preponderance of the evidence that the shooting was racially motivated and sentenced Apprendi to a 12-year term on one firearms count and shorter concurrent sentences on the other two counts. The New Jersey High Court rejected Apprendi's challenge to the enhancement statute, ruling that the Constitution's due process clause did not require a jury to make the racially biased finding beyond a reasonable doubt because the hate crime enhancement was a sentencing factor as opposed to an element of the underlying offense.

ISSUE

Does the due process clause of the Fourteenth Amendment require a factual determination that authorizes an increase in a maximum prison sentence be made by proof beyond a reasonable doubt? Does the Sixth Amendment right to trial by jury require a factual determination that authorizes an increase in a maximum prison sentence be made by a jury?

HOLDING

The due process clause of the US Constitution requires that any fact that increases the penalty for a crime beyond the statutory maximum, other than the fact of a prior criminal conviction, must be submitted to a jury and proved beyond a reasonable doubt.

RATIONALE

The Court noted that nothing in our nation's history suggests that judges should not be permitted to exercise their discretion, considering factors related to the offense and the offender's background, when imposing a sentence within the range prescribed by the statute. The New Jersey hate crime law, however, exposes a defendant to a penalty that exceeds the maximum he would have received if he was punished according to the facts reflected in the jury verdict alone. The Fourteenth Amendment's due process clause and the Sixth Amendment right to a jury trial entitle a defendant to a jury determination that he or she is guilty beyond a reasonable doubt of every element of

the crime with which they are charged. A state cannot circumvent these protections by redefining the elements that constitute different crimes by characterizing them as factors that simply impact the severity of punishment. The New Jersey hate crime enhancement statute exposed Apprendi to a greater punishment that what was authorized by the jury's verdict. Just because the New Jersey legislature placed the enhancement provision in the state's sentencing provisions does not mean it is not an essential element of the offense.

CASE EXCERPT

"The New Jersey procedure challenged in this case is an unacceptable departure from the jury tradition that is an indispensable part of our criminal justice system."

CASE SIGNIFICANCE

Apprendi is a significant case. In *Ring v. Arizona*, 122 S. Ct. 2428 (2002), the Court overturned *Walton v. Arizona*, 530 U.S. 466 (1990) and decided that the Sixth Amendment requires a jury—not a judge—to find the existence of an aggravating circumstance for imposing the death penalty. The Court explained that the Apprendi ruling required the Court to overturn Walton because the two decisions were irreconcilable. In the last 15 years many legislatures have enacted statutory sentencing enhancements based on factors that judges have historically considered to justify harsher sentences within the range of sentences already provided for the offense. Many of these newer statutory schemes give discretion to the trial judge to increase the punishment beyond what is provided for the underlying offense and require the judge to determine whether the aggravating factors exist at the sentencing hearing. Since *Apprendi*, there has been a flood of appeals based on the decision. In *United States v. Cotton*, 122 S. Ct. 1781 (2002), the Supreme Court considered whether omitting a fact that enhances the statutory maximum sentence from a federal indictment justifies vacating the enhanced sentence. Cotton was charged with intent to distribute a detectable amount of cocaine and cocaine base. The indictment did not allege any of the threshold levels of drug quantity that could lead to an enhanced punishment. After Cotton was convicted, the judge made a finding of drug quantity and assessed an enhanced penalty. The defendant did not object that the sentences were based on drug quantities not mentioned in the indictment. While the Cotton's appeal was pending, the Supreme Court decided *Apprendi v. New Jersey.* Cotton argued that under *Apprendi* his sentence was invalid because the drug quantity was not alleged in the indictment and not submitted to the jury. The Fourth Circuit Court of Appeals vacated the sentence. In a unanimous opinion, the Supreme Court disagreed and held that a defective indictment does not deprive a court of jurisdiction. The Court also ruled that omitting a fact that enhances the statutory maximum punishment from a federal indictment does not justify vacating an enhanced sentence. Failure to allege those facts did not affect the fairness, integrity, and public reputation of the judicial proceedings. Neither did the government's error affect the defendant's substantive rights since there was overwhelming evidence of the amount of drugs involved. The Supreme Court also addressed the impact the *Apprendi* case has on the US Sentencing Guidelines in *Harris v. United States*, 122 S. Ct. 2406 (2002). Harris sold illegal narcotics from his pawnshop, an unconcealed semiautomatic pistol at his side. He was convicted of violating 18 U.S.C. §924(c)(1)(A), which provides that a person who in relation to a drug trafficking crime uses or carries a firearm "shall, in addition to the punishment for the crime" (1) be sentenced to a prison term of not less than five years; (2) if the firearm was brandished—not less than seven years; (3) if the firearm was discharged—not less than 10 years. The government's indictment did not include a reference to brandishing a weapon or subsection (2), simply alleging the elements of the principal paragraph defining the offense. After Harris was convicted, the trial judge found he had brandished the pistol and sentenced him to seven years in prison. Harris objected on the grounds that brandishing was an element of a second offense for which he was not indicted or convicted. The District Court judge overruled his objections. The Fourth Circuit upheld the sentence. In a 5–4 decision, so did the Supreme Court. The majority concluded that §924 (c)(1)(A) defines a single offense, and that brandishing and discharging a weapon are sentencing factors to be found by the judge, not elements of an offense to be found by a jury. Under the federal Sentencing Guidelines, brandishing and discharging a weapon are factors that affect sentences for many crimes. The incremental increases in minimum penalties are what one would expect in provisions that list factors a judge should consider in

making a sentencing decision. Congress merely dictated the weight to be given to a factor that judges traditionally use in sentencing.

SELING v. YOUNG
531 U.S. 250 (2001)

FACTS

A Washington state statute authorizes civil commitment in a secure facility of sexually violent predators, defined as someone who has been convicted of or charged with a crime of sexual violence and who suffers from a mental abnormality or personality disorder that makes the person likely to engage in predatory acts of sexual violence. The statute provides that when it appears someone who has committed a sexually violent act is about to be released from confinement, the prosecuting attorney can file a petition in which he alleges that the person is a sexually violent predator. The alleged predator is afforded counsel and experts paid by the state if he is indigent, a probable cause hearing, and trial by judge or jury at his option. The state must prove the person is a sexually violent predator beyond a reasonable doubt. If the state succeeds, the person is committed for care, control, and treatment to the custody of the department of social and health services. He has a right to adequate care and treatment and an annual examination of his mental condition. If the exam shows the person is no longer likely to engage in predatory violent sexual acts, he can petition the court for conditional release or discharge. A hearing is conducted at which the state must prove the person is not safe beyond a reasonable doubt. Andre Brigham Young was convicted of six rapes over 30 years. He was to be released from prison in October 1990, and Washington State filed a petition to have him committed as a sexually violent predator. A jury unanimously decided he was a violent sexual predator, and he was confined to the special commitment center. Young appealed, arguing that the Washington statute violated the federal Constitution's double jeopardy clause, the equal protection clause, and the prohibition against ex post facto laws. The State Supreme Court upheld the law, deciding the law was intended to be a civil, not criminal After he lost his case in state court, Young filed a writ of habeas corpus in federal court. The federal District Court granted his writ, but while the case was pending on the

SELING v. YOUNG *(cont.)*

state's appeal, the US Supreme Court decided *Kansas v. Hendricks* (521 U.S. 346 (1997)). The Ninth Circuit Court of Appeals remanded Young's case back to the District Court to reconsider in light of Hendricks. The District Court reconsidered his petition and denied it. Young appealed again and this time the Ninth Circuit reversed the District Court. The important issue, stated the Ninth Circuit, is whether the law as applied to Young is punitive. The Ninth Circuit stated the Hendricks case did not preclude the possibility that the law could be punitive as it was applied. In reaching its decision, the appeals court reviewed Young's claims that conditions of confinement at the center were punitive. The center is located within the state department of corrections and relies on the department for all its essential services, including security. Young contended the conditions he was placed under were not related to a nonpunitive goal and that residents were abused, confined to their rooms, subjected to random searches, and subject to excessive security. Therapy sessions were videotaped and privileges were withheld for refusal to submit to treatment. The center lacked certified sex offender treatment providers. A court appointed resident advocate had reported to the District Court that he had suspected the center was designed to punish and confine persons for life with no hope for release. The Ninth Circuit remanded the case back to the District Court to determine whether the center's conditions caused the law to be punitive as it was applied.

ISSUE

Can a statute deemed civil in nature be deemed punitive as applied to an individual, thereby violating the Constitution's double jeopardy and ex post facto clauses and provide cause to release that individual?

HOLDING

The nature of a confinement scheme cannot be altered based on vagaries in how the authorizing statute is implemented. If the confinement scheme has been found to be civil in nature, an individual confined under such a statute cannot obtain release through an as-applied challenge on double jeopardy and ex post facto grounds.

RATIONALE

The Court proceeded on the basis the Washington law was civil in nature and noted the statute was "strikingly similar" to the commitment scheme the Court upheld in *Kansas v. Hendricks*. Whether an act is civil or criminal in nature is initially a question of statutory construction and what the legislature intended. A court should reject a legislature's manifest intention only where there is the "clearest proof" that the law is so "punitive in either purpose or effect as to negate the State's intention." In *Kansas v. Hendricks*, the Supreme Court concluded there was insufficient evidence that the Kansas law was punitive. Young's claims about the Washington facility for sexual predators are very similar to those the Court reviewed in *Hendricks*. The Court rejected the Ninth Circuit's reasoning that Young should have the opportunity to prove his confinement was actually punitive. The Supreme Court concluded "that an 'as-applied' analysis would prove unworkable" because it would never conclusively resolve whether a particular confinement scheme is punitive, preventing a final determination of the law's validity under the double jeopardy and ex post factor clauses. By its very nature, confinement is not fixed. It extends over time and conditions of confinement can change. How a civil confinement scheme is implemented may vary from time to time and facility to facility. Those variations do not alter the fact that the confinement is civil in nature. The Washington State Supreme Court decided that the statute under which Young is confined is a civil law. The US Supreme Court cannot use an as-applied analysis to avoid the ruling of the state high court. The Court acknowledged that its opinion did not address if conditions of confinement would be relevant for determining the civil or punitive nature of a confinement statute if the state court had not already found the scheme to be civil in nature. Young has remedies. State law requires adequate care and treatment. If the state is not abiding by the terms of the statute, Young can file a lawsuit in state court and claim the state is not fulfilling the law's requirements.

CASE EXCERPT

"An Act, found to be civil, cannot be deemed punitive 'as applied' to a single individual in violation of the Double Jeopardy and *Ex Post Facto* Clauses and provide cause for release."

CASE SIGNIFICANCE

Even though the US Supreme Court upheld the constitutionality of the Kansas violent sexual predator commitment statute, expressly stating it did not violate the double jeopardy and ex post facto clauses, the controversy surrounding such confinement did not end. In *Kansas v. Hendricks*, the Court concluded that the confinement was civil, not punitive. The double jeopardy and ex post facto clauses did not apply because they restrict only punishment. Defining such confinement as "civil," however, did not resolve all the issues. Seling argued that the conditions under which he and others are confined in Washington changed the nature of their confinement. What was labeled "civil" was actually punitive. If confinement is meant as punishment, then the double jeopardy clause applies and he has been subjected to punishment twice for the same offense. If the confinement is meant as punishment, then the Constitution's ex post facto clause was violated because Seling was committed to the violent sexual predator facility pursuant to a law that was passed after he was convicted. The *Kansas v. Hendricks* decision in 1997 did not directly address whether the conditions under which Young was confined could alter the nature of the statute. The *Seling* Court ruled that if the state court has determined the confinement is civil, the US Supreme Court cannot entertain a claim that as it is applied, the confinement is actually for purposes of punishment.

ALABAMA v. SHELTON

535 U.S. 654 (2002)

FACTS

LeReed Shelton represented himself in a criminal trial in an Alabama state court. The trial judge warned him several times about the problems with self-representation but did not offer him the assistance of counsel at state expense. Shelton was convicted of misdemeanor assault and sentenced to 30 days in jail. The court suspended the sentence and placed him on two years of unsupervised probation, assessed a $500 fine, twenty-five dollars in reparations, and $516.69 restitution. The Alabama Supreme Court reversed the sentence on the grounds that the US Supreme Court decision in *Argersinger v. Hamlin*, 407 U.S. 25 (1972) and *Scott v. Illinois*, 440 U.S. 367 (1979) require that counsel be provided in any felony or misdemeanor prosecution that actually leads to imprisonment, even for a short period of time. The Alabama court considered a suspended sentence as a term of imprisonment.

ISSUE

Does the Sixth Amendment prohibit the imposition of a suspended sentence if the defendant has not been afforded counsel in the prosecution of the offense?

HOLDING

The Sixth Amendment mandates that a suspended sentence that may result in the actual deprivation of a person's liberty may not be imposed unless the defendant was afforded counsel in the prosecution of the crime charged.

RATIONALE

The lower courts were divided on the issue presented by this case. Certiorari was granted to resolve the conflict. There are essentially three positions: (1) an indigent defendant may not receive a suspended sentence unless he is offered state-appointed counsel; (2) the Sixth Amendment bars activating a suspended sentence for an indigent defendant who was not afforded counsel but does not prohibit imposing such a sentence as a way of making probation available; and (3) failure to appoint counsel to an indigent defendant does not bar imposing a suspended or probationary sentence for a misdemeanor, even though the defendant might be incarcerated if his probation is revoked. In *Argersinger v. Hamlin*, the Court held that an indigent defendant must be offered counsel in any misdemeanor case that leads to imprisonment. In *Scott v. Illinois*, the Court held the defendant had no right to counsel because the actual sentence imposed was a fine, even though the statute authorized a jail term of up to one year. The actual imprisonment standard has been in force since that time and is still controlling. Applying that standard, the Court concluded the Sixth Amendment does not permit activation of a suspended sentence if the defendant violates the terms of probation. No person may be incarcerated for any offense unless he was afforded an attorney at his trial. The State of Alabama argued that the imposition of a suspended sentence does not require the appointment of counsel because there is no deprivation of liberty. Only if probation is revoked must the state provide counsel. The Court concluded that this approach is insufficient. Providing an attorney after the guilt adjudication stage would not be much help to a defendant. Most jurisdictions already provide a right to counsel that is more expansive than what is mandated by the US Constitution. All but 16 states would have provided counsel to a person in Shelton's circumstances. There

ALABAMA v. SHELTON (cont.)

is little reason to think a rule requiring the appointment of counsel in suspended sentences would have a deleterious impact on the states.

CASE EXCERPT

"A suspended sentence is a prison term imposed for the offense of conviction. Once a prison term is triggered, the defendant is incarcerated not for the probation violation, but for the underlying offense. The uncounseled conviction at that point results in imprisonment, as it ends up in the actual deprivation of a person's liberty. This is precisely what the Sixth Amendment, as interpreted in *Argersinger* and *Scott*, does not allow."

CASE SIGNIFICANCE

This case clarifies the Argersinger-Scott actual imprisonment rule and resolves a conflict among state courts enforcing the constitutional requirements imposed by the rule. The Court relies heavily on the fact most states already provide a right to counsel that is broader than what the Constitution requires.

EWING v. CALIFORNIA

538 U.S. 11 (2003)

FACTS

Gary Ewing, an offender with a history of criminal convictions, was arrested for stealing three golf clubs, each worth $399, from a golf course. At the time he was arrested, he was on parole from a nine-year prison term for convictions in three burglaries and one robbery. Under California's three strikes law, another felony conviction required a sentence of 25 years to life. Ewing was charged with and convicted of one count of felony grand theft for theft of the golf clubs. Ewing requested the judge in his case to exercise discretion permitted under California law and reduce the conviction to a misdemeanor. The judge declined and sentenced Ewing in accordance with the three strikes law. On appeal, Ewing argued the sentence of 25 years to life was grossly disproportionate to the crime and violated the Eighth Amendment prohibition of against cruel and unusual punishments. The court rejected this claim. The California Supreme Court declined to hear the case.

ISSUE

Did Ewing's sentence of 25 years to life, in accordance with California's three strikes law, violate the Eighth Amendment protection against cruel and unusual punishment?

HOLDING

Ewing's 25 years to life sentence under California's three-strike laws is not grossly disproportionate and therefore does not violate the Eighth Amendment's prohibition on cruel and unusual punishments.

RATIONALE

When California enacted the three strikes law, it decided that in order to protect the public safety, the state needed to incapacitate criminals who have already been convicted of at least one serious or violent crime. Nothing in the Eighth Amendment prohibits California from making that choice. Recidivism has been recognized as a legitimate reason for increased punishment and is a serious public safety concern throughout the United States. The state has a legitimate interest in deterring crime. Both incapacitation and deterrence are rationales for recidivism statutes. Criticisms of the three-strike laws should be aimed at the legislature, which has primary responsibility for making the difficult policy choices. The Court is not a "superlegislature" that second-guesses policy choices. Ewing was convicted of felony theft for stealing nearly $1,200 worth of merchandise after having been convicted of at least two violent or serious felonies. Ewing's theft should not be taken lightly. In weighing the gravity of Ewing's offense, it is appropriate to consider also his long history of felony recidivism: "Any other approach would fail to accord proper deference to the policy judgments that find expression in the legislature's choice of sanctions." This Court must full effect to the state's policy choices. Ewing's sentence reflects a rational legislative judgment that offenders who have committed serious or violent felonies and who continue to commit felonies must be incapacitated.

CASE EXCERPT

"Throughout the States, legislatures enacting three strikes laws made a deliberate policy choice that individuals who have repeatedly engaged in serious or violent criminal behavior, and whose conduct has not been deterred by more conventional approaches to punishment, must be isolated from society in order to protect the public safety. Though three strikes laws may be relatively new, our tradition of deferring to state legislatures in making and implementing such important policy decisions is longstanding."

CASE SIGNIFICANCE

This case, along with a case decided the same day and also involving the application of the California three-strike laws, *Lockyer v. Andrade*, 538 U.S. 63 (2003), established that the California three-strike laws do not violate the Eighth Amendment. After examining its previous decisions in *Rummel v. Estelle* (1980*), Solem v. Helm* (1983), and *Harmelin v. Michigan* (1991), the Court ruled that the punishment in both cases was not disproportionate to the crime and that courts must extend due deference to the policy decision makers in the various legislatures. It is now clear that the Court will not engage in deciding proportionality questions related to nondeath penalty sentences.

BLAKELY v. WASHINGTON
542 U.S. 296 (2004)

FACTS

Blakely pleaded guilty to the second-degree kidnapping of his estranged wife. The statutory maximum under Washington State sentencing guidelines was 10 years in prison. The standard sentencing range or presumptive sentence was 49 to 53 months. Under the state's guidelines the judge must impose a sentence within the standard range unless the court finds aggravating or mitigating circumstances by a preponderance of the evidence that justify the exceptional sentence. The judge in Blakely's case conducted a sentencing hearing, found that the defendant had acted with deliberate cruelty, and sentenced him to 90 months incarceration. Blakely argued that the Washington sentencing laws deprived him of his Sixth Amendment right to have a jury determine beyond a reasonable doubt the additional facts necessary to increase his sentence. The state appellate court affirmed his sentence and the state supreme court denied review.

ISSUE

Do facts that are necessary to increase a sentence beyond the presumptive range need to be submitted to a jury and proved beyond a reasonable doubt?

HOLDING

Facts—other than a prior conviction—necessary to increase a sentence beyond the statutory standard range must be proved by a jury beyond a reasonable doubt.

RATIONALE

In this 5–4 decision written by Justice Scalia, the Court turned to the precedent it established in *Apprendi v. New Jersey* (2000). The Court defined the statutory maximum as the "maximum sentence a judge can impose solely based on the facts reflected in the jury verdict or admitted by the defendant." The relevant statutory maximum is not the maximum sentence a judge can impose after he or she finds additional facts. It is the maximum the judge can impose without finding any additional facts. In Blakely's case, the state trial judge had increased the defendant's sentence based on facts that had not been submitted to the jury and proved beyond a reasonable doubt.

CASE EXCERPT

"The Framers would not have thought it too much to demand that, before depriving a man of three more years of his liberty, the State should suffer the modest inconvenience of submitting its accusation to the unanimous suffrage of twelve of his equals and neighbors, rather than a lone employee of the State."

CASE SIGNIFICANCE

After the *Apprendi* decision was rendered by the Supreme Court in 2000, it was clear that sentencing statutes with provisions like Washington State's would be challenged. The *Blakely* decision was highly anticipated. It is most significant for the stage it set for the *Booker v. U.S.* decision rendered by the Court in 2005. Justice Scalia emphasized that reversing the judgment below, is not tantamount to a finding that determinate sentencing is unconstitutional: "This case is not about whether determinate sentencing is constitutional, only about how it can be implemented in a way that respects the Sixth Amendment."

UNITED STATES v. BOOKER
543 U.S. 220 (2005)

FACTS

Booker was convicted of possession with intent to distribute cocaine. Under the US Sentencing Guidelines, based on the defendant's criminal history and the drug quantity, the recommended sentence was 210 to 262 months in prison. The district court judge, however, found by a preponderance of the evidence, that Booker possessed an amount of drugs greater than what the jury found and increased his sentence to 360 months,

UNITED STATES v. BOOKER (cont.)

which amounted to a 30-year sentence instead of a 21-year, 10 month sentence. Booker appealed, arguing that the increased sentence violated his Sixth Amendment right to a jury trial because the judge found facts not admitted by the defendant or found by the jury beyond a reasonable doubt. The Seventh Circuit Court of Appeals held that the sentence violated the Sixth Amendment and ordered the district judge to sentence Booker within the guideline range, based solely on the jury's findings or hold a separate sentencing hearing before a jury.

A federal jury found Fanfan guilty of possessing 500 or more grams of cocaine with the intent to distribute. During sentencing, the judge found Fanfan was the ring leader of a significant drug conspiracy, which combined with his criminal history, resulted in a sentence of 188 to 235 months under the Sentencing Guidelines. A few days before his sentencing hearing, however, the US Supreme Court decided *Blakely v. Washington* (2004), which held that a Washington state judge could not find an aggravating factor that authorized an enhanced sentence that state law would otherwise permit because it violated the Sixth Amendment right to a jury trial. In light of the *Blakely* decision, the federal judge recalculated Fanfan's sentence based only on the jury's findings and imposed a 78-month sentence.

The Supreme Court granted certiorari in both these cases to give guidance to federal courts, many of who were applying the *Blakely v. Washington* decision in federal sentencing hearings.

ISSUES

(1) Does an enhanced sentence under US Sentencing Guidelines based only on the judge's determination of a fact violate the Sixth Amendment? (2) If so, are the Sentencing Guidelines entirely unconstitutional?

HOLDING

An enhanced sentence under the US Sentencing Guidelines based only on the judge's determination of a fact violates the right to a jury trial under the Sixth Amendment. Only the mandatory provisions of the guidelines are unconstitutional.

RATIONALE

In this historic 5–4 decision, the Court wrote a majority opinion in two parts. The first part was written by Justice Stevens. He explained that the Court decided

that the Sentencing Guidelines were unconstitutional because they required the judge to increase a defendant's sentence beyond the maximum guideline range if the judge found facts to justify an increase by a preponderance of the evidence. The Sixth Amendment right to a jury trial was violated because the judge was sentencing an offender based on facts not found by the jury. Both *Apprendi v. New Jersey* (2000) and *Blakely v. Washington* (2004) are precedents for the Court's decision in part one of the *Booker* opinion. In part two, written by Justice Breyer, the Court ruled that to remedy the defect identified in part one it must hold that the federal guidelines are advisory, meaning that judges need only consider the guideline range as one of many factors in making sentencing decisions. The Court chose to expunge the portion of the Sentencing Reform Act of 1984 that made the federal guidelines mandatory.

CASE EXCERPT

"We do not doubt that Congress, when it wrote the Sentencing Act, intended to create a form of mandatory Guidelines system. But, we repeat, given today's constitutional holding, that is not a choice that remains open. Hence we have examined the statute in depth to determine Congress' likely intent in light of today's holding."

CASE SIGNIFICANCE

The mandatory provisions of the federal law had proved to be very controversial. This decision radically changed the law of sentencing in the federal courts. By making the guidelines advisory instead of mandatory, the Court raised many other important legal questions that had to be decided in the years following the *Booker* opinion. How much deference must judges pay to the now advisory guidelines as one of the factors they can consider? How should appellate courts review guideline departures?

KIMBROUGH v. UNITED STATES
552 U.S. 85 (2007)

FACTS

Kimbrough pleaded guilty to distributing 50 or more grams of crack cocaine and several other drug and firearm related crimes. Under the applicable statutes, Kimbrough had to serve a minimum prison term of 15 years. The federal Sentencing Guidelines recommended a range of 228 to 270 months incarceration—19 to 22.5 years. The District Court rejected the sentence, finding that it would be greater than necessary. The court relied, in part, on its view that Kimbrough's case was an example of the "disproportionate and unjust effect that crack cocaine guidelines have in sentencing." The judge was referring to the 100:1 sentencing disparity that originated in the 1986 Anti-Drug Abuse Act. Congress believed that crack was more dangerous than powder cocaine and enacted a statute that imposes sentences for crack cocaine that are three to six times longer than offenses involving equal amounts of powder cocaine. If Kimbrough had possessed powder cocaine, his guidelines range would have been much lower at 96 to 106 months. The court sentenced Kimbrough to 15 years. The Fourth Circuit Court of Appeals vacated his sentence and found that a sentence outside the guideline range is per se unreasonable when it is based on a court disagreeing with the sentencing disparity for crack and powder offenses.

ISSUE
Has the crack/powder sentencing disparity adopted in the U.S. Sentencing Guidelines been rendered advisory by our decision in *Booker*?

HOLDING
It is not abuse of discretion for a District Court to conclude when sentencing a particular defendant that the crack/powder disparity yields a sentence greater than necessary.

RATIONALE
In its 7–2 decision, the Court affirmed the sentence handed down by the district court. The majority opinion, authored by Justice Ginsburg, emphasized that the sentencing guidelines are advisory only and a sentencing judge can decide that a particular sentence within the guidelines is not necessary to serve the objectives of sentencing. The crack/powder cocaine disparity has been controversial and the Sentencing Commission itself recently determined that the disparity does not meet the objectives of the 1986 legislation. Further, the disparity is not consistent with punishing the major traffickers more severely than the low level dealers. It has also fostered a lack of confidence in the criminal justice system. Although Congress had failed to act on the recommendation from the Commission that the ratio be reduced, the Court concluded that under *Booker v. U.S.* (2005), the district court judge is

permitted to tailor a sentence and rejected the argument that the 100 to 1 ratio is an exception.

CASE EXCERPT
"But the 100-to-1 crack/powder ratio, the Commission concluded, significantly overstates the differences between the two forms of the drug. Accordingly, the Commission recommended that the ratio be 'substantially' reduced."

CASE SIGNIFICANCE
The *Kimbrough* decision was the basis for the Supreme Court's holding in the 2009 case *Spears v. U.S*, 555 U.S. 261 (2009). In that case, the District Court had determined that the 100:1 ratio in sentencing between powder and crack cocaine was excessive and sentenced Spears based on a 20:1 ratio. Wrote the *Spears* Court: "That was indeed the point of *Kimbrough*: a recognition of district court's authority to vary from the crack cocaine Guidelines based on a *policy* disagreement with them, and not simply based on an individualized determination that they yield an excessive sentence in a particular case." In 2007, the US Sentencing Commission submitted proposed amendments to the Guidelines that significantly reduced the 100:1 ratio and proposed the changes be made retroactively applicable if Congress did not object. The amendments went into effect in November 2007. In 2010, Congress passed and President Obama signed the Fair Sentencing Act, which reduced the disparity to 18:1.

GALL v. UNITED STATES
552 U.S. 38 (2007)

FACTS
As a college student, Gall was involved in a drug ring distributing Ecstasy, but he left the drug conspiracy after seven months, moved to Arizona, lived a drug-free, crime-free life, and started a business. Three and a half years later, he pleaded guilty to conspiracy to distribute a controlled substance. The presentence investigation recommended a sentence of 30 to 37 months incarceration. The government urged a 30-month sentence, which was the minimum under the federal Sentencing Guidelines. The judge, however, departed from the guidelines and sentenced Gall to 30 months probation. The judge announced that he departed from the guidelines based on the seriousness of the offense

GALL v. UNITED STATES *(cont.)*

and concluding that incarceration was unnecessary because Gall had voluntarily withdrawn from the conspiracy and engaged in exemplary conduct since that time, showing he was no longer a danger to society. The Eighth Circuit Court of Appeals reversed, ruling that sentences falling outside the guidelines must overcome a presumption of unreasonableness. The greater the variation from the guidelines, the need for more compelling justifications. The appellate court ruled that the District Court erred by using Gall's youth as a mitigating factor, placing too much emphasis on his rehabilitation, and undervaluing the seriousness of Gall's crime. Therefore, the judge's departure from the guidelines was unreasonable.

ISSUE

Should Courts of Appeal apply a presumption of unreasonableness to sentences that vary outside the range in the federal Sentencing Guidelines, requiring District Courts to justify departures with a finding of extraordinary circumstances?

HOLDING

Under *Booker v. U.S.* (2005), federal courts have authority to set any reasonable sentence as long as they explain the reasoning. Courts of appeal must review sentences under a deferential abuse-of-discretion standard, taking into account the totality of circumstances, including the extent of the variance from the guideline range, but must give due deference to the District Court's decision that the factors justify the variance.

RATIONALE

The Supreme Court held in this 7–2 decision that appellate courts may take the degree of variance from the guidelines into consideration when they review a sentence, but cannot impose an unreasonableness presumption for sentences outside the guidelines. The guidelines are the starting benchmark, but all the factors should be considered. The judge may not presume that the guideline sentence is reasonable and must make an individualized assessment. In reviewing the sentence, a court of appeals must make sure the district judge did not make significant procedural errors and then impose the abuse-of-discretion standard. In Gall's case, the Supreme Court found that the departure from the guidelines was reasonable.

CASE EXCERPT

"In reviewing the reasonableness of a sentence outside the Guidelines range, appellate courts may therefore take the degree of variance into account and consider the extent of a deviation from the Guidelines. We reject, however, an appellate rule that requires 'extraordinary' circumstances to justify a sentence outside the Guidelines range. We also reject the use of a rigid mathematical formula that uses the percentage of a departure as the standard for determining the strength of the justifications required for a specific sentence."

CASE SIGNIFICANCE

This case was decided the same day as *Kimbrough v. U.S.*, 552 U.S. 85 (2007), in which the Court found that because the federal Sentencing Guidelines are advisory only, the Fourth Circuit Court of Appeals had erred when it held that a sentence outside the guidelines range is per se unreasonable because it was based on a disagreement with the sentencing disparity for crack and powder cocaine offenses. Both decisions are part of a series of cases that more clearly define to what extent judges must adhere to the federal Sentencing Guidelines. In *Rita v. U.S.*, 551 U.S. 338 (2007), the Supreme Court had held that appellate courts can presume that sentences falling within the guidelines are reasonable. In *Gall*, the Court clarified what an appellate court should do when reviewing a sentence outside of the guideline range.

CUNNINGHAM v. CALIFORNIA
549 U.S 270 (2007)

FACTS

John Cunningham was convicted of continuous sexual abuse of a child under the age of fourteen. Under the California Determinate Sentencing law, a judge can choose between a minimum, medium, or maximum sentence for any given crime. Unless there are special circumstances, judges typically impose the medium sentence, which in Cunningham's case would have been 12 years. However, the judge found six special aggravating circumstances and only one mitigating circumstance and sentenced Cunningham to the maximum 16 years incarceration. Under the Court Rules, the aggravating factors had to be established by a preponderance of the evidence. Cunningham appealed, arguing that the judge's sentencing decision violated the Sixth Amendment right to a jury trial because the judge can consider only circumstances that were determined by a jury. He cited *Blakely v. Washington* (2004), in which the Supreme Court decided that under the Sixth Amendment any fact that increases a sentence beyond the statutory maximum must be proved to a jury. The California Court of Appeals upheld his sentence, and the California Supreme Court denied his appeal.

ISSUE

Does the California determinate sentencing law violate the Sixth Amendment right to a jury trial because trial judges and not juries are permitted to find facts not admitted to by the defendant, which can lead to enhanced sentences?

HOLDING

The California determinate sentencing law violates the Sixth Amendment right to a jury trial because trial judges, and not juries, are permitted to find facts not admitted to by the defendant which can lead to enhanced sentences.

RATIONALE

The Court California's determinate sentencing law is similar to the sentencing laws in Washington State that were found in violation of the Sixth Amendment in *Blakely v. Washington* (2004) and the federal Sentencing Guidelines found unconstitutional in *Booker v. U.S.* (2005). The middle term, the medium sentence, is the relevant statutory maximum under California law and not the maximum, upper term. Aggravating circumstances must be found before the upper term can be imposed. Because California law allows those circumstances to be found by a judge by a preponderance of the evidence, the law violates the Sixth Amendment right to a jury as established in the line of cases beginning with *Apprendi v. New Jersey* (2000).

CASE EXCERPT

"Because the DSL authorizes the judge, not the jury, to find the facts permitting an upper term sentence, the system cannot withstand measurement against our Sixth Amendment precedent."

CASE SIGNIFICANCE

This 6–3 decision follows the *Apprendi v. New Jersey*, *Blakely v. Washington*, and *Booker v. United States* line of cases concerning the constitutionality of judicial fact-finding during the sentencing phase of criminal

trials. California claimed that under the state's determinate sentencing law the maximum penalty authorized by the facts of the case was 16 years, not twelve. The state argued that the lower, middle, and upper terms were are all legally authorized sentences a judge could impose based solely on the jury's verdict. In the state's argument, the requirement that a judge impose the middle term in the absence of aggravating or mitigating factors is only a limitation on judge's sentencing discretion. Instead, the majority of the Justices found, according to Justice Ginsburg, that "in all material respects, California's DSL resembles the sentencing systems invalidated in *Blakely v. Washington* and *U.S. v. Booker*."

GRAHAM v. FLORIDA
560 U.S.—(2010)

FACTS

Terrence Graham was 16 years old when he plead guilty in adult court to armed burglary and attempted armed robbery. He was sentenced to concurrent three-year terms of probation and was required to spend the first 12 months in county jail. He received credit for time served and was released after serving six months. Less than six months after his release, Graham, a little less than one month shy of his eighteenth birthday, was tried and convicted as an adult of armed home robbery. He was sentenced to life without the possibility of parole. On appeal, he argued that the imposition of a life without parole sentence on a juvenile violates the cruel and unusual punishment clause of the Eighth Amendment. The Florida appellate court upheld his sentence and the Florida Supreme Court denied review. The US Supreme Court granted certiorari.

ISSUE

Does a life without the possibility of parole sentence for a juvenile convicted of a nonhomicide crime violate the Eighth Amendment?

HOLDING

Yes. The Eighth Amendment does not allow for a juvenile to be sentenced to life without parole for a crime that is not a homicide.

RATIONALE

The six member majority held that the Court's reasoning under its previous decisions *Atkins v. Virginia*

GRAHAM v. FLORIDA *(cont.)*

(2002), *Roper v. Simmons* (2005), and *Kennedy v. Louisiana* (2008) applied. The Court must consider evidence that indicates society's standards and determine whether the punishment violates the Constitution based on the standards set forth in previous cases. The Court found that under both inquiries, the life without parole punishment for a juvenile who committed a nonhomicide crime is not permitted. The Court noted that life without parole is especially harsh for a juvenile, who would on average serve more years and a greater percentage of his life in prison than an adult offender.

CASE EXCERPT

"Terrance Graham's sentence guarantees he will die in prison without any meaningful opportunity to obtain release, no matter what he might do to demonstrate that the bad acts he committed as a teenager are not representative of his true character, even if he spends the next half century attempting to atone for his crimes and learn from his mistakes. The State has denied him any chance to later demonstrate that he is fit to rejoin society based solely on a nonhomicide crime that he committed while he was a child in the eyes of the law."

CASE SIGNIFICANCE

The Court once again applied the evolving standards of decency test and looked at legislation across the United States as well as sentencing practices to conclude that life without parole for juveniles who commit nonhomicide crimes does not have support in this country. The recent decisions in *Atkins, Roper*, and *Kennedy* provided the framework for analyzing Graham's argument. Of course, this decision raises the issue of whether life without the possibility of parole for a juvenile who commits a homicide violates the Eighth Amendment.

DISCUSSION QUESTIONS

1. There are conferences and workshops specifically designed for judges. If you were appointed or elected to serve as a trial judge in criminal cases and had to make difficult sentencing decisions, what kind of training or preparation in sentencing would you want to have?
2. What is the current status of the Supreme Court's position on the proportionality of sentences?
3. What have been the various challenges made to the sexually violent offender statutes that permit certain sex offenders to be civilly committed after they have served their criminal sentence?
4. How did the US Sentencing Guidelines change the way federal judges sentence convicted offenders?
5. How did the Supreme Court explain its reasoning for upholding the constitutionality of the federal Sentencing Guidelines?
6. Why is the *Apprendi v. New Jersey* case significant? How does its holding impact other types of cases, cases outside of New Jersey, and cases not involving hate crimes?
7. How did the Court's decision in *United States v. Booker* (2005) change the way federal judges use the Sentencing Guidelines?
8. What controversy surrounded the sentencing of crack cocaine offenders in federal court and how has the Supreme Court been a part of that controversy?
9. Why is it important that a convicted offender be provided counsel during the sentencing phase of his or her case? You are a criminal defense attorney. Why is sentencing law so important for you to understand?
10. Consult the sentencing laws in your state. Does your state use sentencing guidelines?

CHAPTER TWO

THE DEATH PENALTY

INTRODUCTION

The death penalty has never been a more controversial issue in the United States than it is today. In the past ten years there has been a resurgence of concern about how death penalty law is applied and whether innocent persons have been or are at grave risk of being executed. Much has been written about the history of capital punishment. Dozens of social science research studies have examined such topics as whether the penalty is applied in a discriminatory manner, whether executions deter crime or encourage violence, what the public's opinion is, and the cost of executing a person versus incarcerating them for life. To appreciate fully the depth and complexity of the debate, however, it is essential to become familiar with death penalty law. In the pages of court opinions it is most apparent that constructing a fair and effective process to decide which offenders should be sentenced to death is an extremely difficult task. In *Furman v. Georgia* (1972), Justice Stewart noted that death is different, meaning that it is unlike any other sanction. In recognizing that difference, courts have struggled with, and at times agonized over, the scope the penalty should have.

Until the 1960s, legal challenges to the death penalty focused on the constitutionality of the way the executions were carried out. Until *Furman v. Georgia* in 1972, the Supreme Court had never considered whether the penalty itself was unconstitutional. In that case, the Court effectively struck down every state's death penalty laws for violating the equal protection clause and the Eighth Amendment's prohibition against cruel and unusual punishment. The Court concluded that the laws failed to give juries proper standards or guidelines for making the death versus life judgment, opening the door to arbitrary and capricious decision making. *Furman* is a fascinating and complex case that drove state legislatures to refashion their laws without any assurances the Supreme Court wouldn't strike down the rewritten laws as well. Four years later, in *Gregg v. Georgia* (1972), the Supreme Court made it clear that it did not consider the death penalty to be per se unconstitutional. It upheld the rewritten Georgia capital punishment statute and laid the groundwork for how it would analyze future death penalty cases. The Court further clarified its position in *Woodson v. North Carolina* (1976) when it held that a mandatory death penalty statute was unconstitutional because it failed to allow for a particularized decision, based on the facts of a specific case and the characteristics of an individual defendant. Mandatory death sentences did not permit juries to exercise the guided discretion that *Gregg v. Georgia* considered to be the "heart" of the constitutional requirements.

Since 1976, state and federal appellate courts have considered thousands of cases that have raised various legal challenges to the death penalty. Since the Supreme Court has ruled that the penalty itself is not unconstitutional, the challenges have focused on a myriad of other issues. This chapter highlights the most significant of these challenges, the ones that the Supreme Court has addressed. Because each of the 38 states that currently provide for capital punishment have different statutes, many of the challenges address issues that are specific to a particular state law. In some of these cases, however, aspects of one state's law are similar to capital punishment legislation in other states, which means the Court is addressing issues that impact more than the jurisdiction involved in the case before it. Oftentimes, a state will maintain that its death penalty law is not similar to a law that was declared unconstitutional. When a death-sentenced inmate argues that the law is similar and should share the fate of a law declared unconstitutional in a previous case, courts have to launch a careful legal analysis that may then lead to challenges in other states involving the interpretation of their statutes. Experts in capital punishment law closely follow cases that are decided from jurisdictions throughout the United States. How a South Carolina statute has been interpreted may be very relevant to someone on death row in another state.

A number of the briefs in this chapter are cases that address the aggravating and mitigating factors that juries should be able to consider in making the death penalty decision. This has become an especially difficult area of capital punishment law. Beginning with *Lockett v. Ohio* (1978), the Court concluded that the jury should be able to consider any and all of a defendant's mitigating evidence; however,

in 1993 (*Johnson v. Texas*), the Court decided that the Constitution does not require instructions that advise a jury that it can give full effect to such evidence. In *Godfrey v. Georgia* (1980), an aggravating factor outlined in the Georgia stature was held to be too poorly defined to guide jury discretion, as was a similarly defined factor under the Oklahoma statute in *Maynard v. Cartwright* (1988). In *Tuilaepa v. California* (1994), open-ended factors were determined to be constitutional.

Another important category of Supreme Court cases asks if there are certain convicted offenders who should not be eligible for the death sentence. In *Ford v. Wainwright* (1986), the Court ruled that a prisoner who is insane at the time of his or her scheduled execution cannot be put to death. In *Thompson v. Oklahoma* (1988), the Court decided that the Constitution prohibits executing someone who was 15 years old at the time he or she committed the capital offense, followed soon by the decision that 16-year-olds could be executed (*Stanford v. Kentucky* 1989). *Atkins v. Virginia* (2002) held that executing mentally retarded convicted murderers violates the Eighth Amendment. In *Tison v. Arizona* (1987), the Court stated that if the defendant had not been a major participant in the murder and had not acted with reckless indifference to human life, he or she could not be subject to a death sentence. *Coker v. Georgia* (1977) held that the Constitution prohibits imposing the death penalty on rapists.

In the majority of states with capital punishment, the jury makes the sentencing decision. However, there are a few states that include the trial judge in the process, to a greater or lesser extent. The judge's role in capital punishment sentencing was addressed by the Court in *Spaziano v. Florida* (1984), with the Court holding the Eighth Amendment does not require a judge to accept a jury's recommendation that a defendant in a capital case be sentenced to death as opposed to life. In *Harris v. Alabama* (1995), the Court went on the decide that the Eighth Amendment does not define the weight a sentencing judge must give to an advisory verdict in a capital case. In what may be a far-reaching recent decision, *Ring v. Arizona* (2002), the Court concluded the jury must decide all of the facts that must be established before a death sentence can be imposed, including aggravating factors that allow for the death penalty. What remains to be seen is *Ring's* impact on those states that include the judge in the sentencing decision process.

One of the most important challenges to capital punishment argues that as applied, it discriminates against minority defendants. *McKlesky v. Kemp* (1987) was a major attack on the constitutionality of the death penalty, and many scholars believed that if the Supreme Court ruled in favor of the defendant in that case, the death penalty could not survive anywhere in the United States. The Court did not support the challenge and held that statistical studies alone cannot form the basis of a constitutional violation. A defendant must produce evidence of discrimination in his or her particular case in order to prevail.

Death penalty case law is often dense and technical. Always to be remembered is that in the technicalities lie the lives of actual people. By understanding death penalty law, even to a limited extent, a student better understands how difficult it is to apply a punishment as irrevocable as death in real world situations.

FURMAN v. GEORGIA
408 U.S. 238 (1972)

FACTS

Furman was convicted of murder in Georgia and sentenced to death by a jury. He shot and killed a homeowner during a burglary at night. Furman argued that the death penalty was unconstitutional because it violated the Eighth Amendment's prohibition against cruel and unusual punishment.

ISSUE

Does the death penalty as applied in this case violate the Eighth Amendment?

HOLDING

The imposition and carrying out of the death penalty in this case constitutes cruel and unusual punishment in violation of the Eighth and Fourteenth Amendments.

RATIONALE

Each of the five Justices who voted in the majority wrote their own concurring opinion that outlined their reasons for striking down the Georgia statute.

Justice Douglas: "The Georgia system leaves the determination of which defendants should live or die to the uncontrolled discretion of judges and juries. The state laws provide no standards that govern the selection of the penalty. A defendant can be sentenced to

death on a whim. This unbridled discretion enables the penalty to be applied selectively based on factors such as the defendant's race, socioeconomic status, and membership in unpopular groups."

Justice Brennan: "There are four principles by which to determine whether a punishment is cruel and unusual: 1) if it is unusually severe; 2) if there is a strong probability that it is inflicted arbitrarily; 3) if it is substantially rejected by contemporary society; and 4) if there is no reason to believe that it serves a penal purpose more effectively that a less severe punishment. Applying these principles to capital punishment, the penalty violates the Constitution regardless of how a particular statute is worded or how it operates. The death penalty does not comport with human dignity. It is, therefore, unconstitutional in all circumstances."

Justice Stewart: "The death penalty differs from all other forms of punishment, not in degree but in kind. It is totally irrevocable. It is also unique because it rejects the rehabilitation of the convict as a basic purpose of criminal justice."

Justice White: "The narrow question presented by this case concerns a state statute that delegates to judges and juries when the death penalty should be imposed and those judges and juries have ordered the penalty with such infrequency that the odds are against its imposition with respect to any convicted murderer or rapist. Common sense and experience shows that laws that are seldom enforced are ineffective for controlling human conduct. Unless the death penalty is imposed with sufficient frequency, it will not contribute to deterring crime. Imposing the death penalty so infrequently is pointless and does not serve social or public purposes. A law with such negligible returns is excessive and violates the Eighth Amendment."

Justice Marshall: "Capital punishment under any circumstance violates the Constitution because it is excessive, unnecessary, and abhorrent to currently existing values."

CASE EXCERPT

"Justice Stewart: The Georgia statute results in death sentences that are cruel and unusual in the same way that being struck by lightening is cruel and unusual.... the Eighth and Fourteenth Amendments cannot tolerate the infliction of a sentence of death under legal systems that permit this unique penalty to be so wantonly and so freakishly imposed."

FURMAN v. GEORGIA (cont.)

CASE SIGNIFICANCE

This is the first time the Supreme Court found that capital punishment violated the Constitution. The grounds for the majority's decision, however, were not clear. Only two Justices found the death penalty per se unconstitutional. The other three Justices found the Georgia statute unconstitutional. Because the Georgia statute resembled capital punishment laws in all of the states that provided for the death sentence, the *Furman* decision effectively struck down every death penalty statute in the United States. State legislatures went back to the drawing board to legislate new laws that would correct the deficiencies and address the concerns expressed by the three Justices who focused their opinions on the wording and operation of the Georgia system. The *Furman* decision offered little guidance, although it established the Court would not accept statutes that continued to allow judges and juries to exercise unbridled discretion when making the death v. life decision. The Court wanted standards to guide decision makers and reduce the potential for arbitrary and capricious ("freakish," according to Justice Stewart) death sentences. The significance of *Furman* can only be evaluated in light of the Supreme Court's decision four years later in *Gregg v. Georgia*, 429 U.S. 1301 (1976).

GREGG v. GEORGIA
428 U.S. 153 (1976)

FACTS

Troy Gregg and his companion were convicted of robbing and murdering two men. They were prosecuted under the Georgia death penalty statute that had been revised after the *Furman v. Georgia*, 408 U.S. 238 (1972) decision four years earlier. The new law provided a capital trial should be bifurcated into a guilt/innocence stage and a penalty stage before a judge or a jury. If a defendant is convicted during the first stage, the judge or jury who convicted him should hear additional evidence in extenuation, mitigation, and aggravation of punishment, provided, however, that only aggravating evidence the prosecutor has made known to the defendant prior to trial is admissible. The judge or jury should also hear arguments by both parties regarding the appropriate penalty for the case. The judge is to instruct the jury to consider any mitigating or aggravating circumstances. Before a convicted defendant can be assessed the death penalty, the judge or jury must

find beyond a reasonable doubt one of the ten aggravating circumstances specified in the state statute. That circumstance(s) must be specified. In jury cases, the judge is bound by the jury's recommendation. The statute also provides for a special expedited review to the Supreme Court of Georgia, which is instructed by the statute to consider (1) whether a death sentence was imposed under the influence of passion, prejudice, or any arbitrary factor; (2) whether the evidence supports the jury or judge's finding of a statutory aggravating factor; and (3) whether the death sentence is excessive or disproportionate to the penalty imposed in similar cases. In reaching its decision, the State Supreme Court should consider the complete record of the trial and transcript, along with a separate report prepared by the trial judge in which the judge answers detailed questions about the quality of the defendant's representation; whether race played a role; and whether, in the judge's opinion, there is any doubt about the defendant's guilt or the appropriateness of the sentence. The same jury that convicted Gregg and his companion sentenced them to death after hearing lengthy arguments by the prosecutor and defense counsel during the sentencing stage. The trial judge instructed the jury that it could recommend either a death sentence or life in prison and that in reaching such a recommendation the jury was free to consider the facts presented by the parties on both sides as to the aggravating and mitigating circumstances. The judge also instructed the jury that it could not consider a death sentence unless it first found one of these aggravating circumstances beyond a reasonable doubt: The murder was committed while the offender was engaged in the commission of a capital felony—here the armed robberies of the victims; or the offender committed the murder for the purpose of receiving money and the automobile described in the indictment; or the murders were wantonly and outrageously vile, horrible, and inhuman. The jury found that the first two aggravating circumstances were present beyond a reasonable doubt and assessed the death penalty for both offenders. The Georgia Supreme Court affirmed the convictions and the death sentences.

ISSUE

Is the punishment of death for the crime of murder, under all circumstances, cruel and unusual in violation of the Eighth and Fourteenth Amendments of the Constitution? If the death penalty is not per se unconstitutional, is the Georgia death penalty statute constitutional?

HOLDING

The death penalty for murder is not per se cruel and unusual in violation of the Eighth Amendment. A death penalty statute such as Georgia's is constitutional because it focuses the jury's attention on the particular defendant and crime, the jury must find at least one aggravating circumstance beyond a reasonable doubt and is permitted to consider all mitigating circumstances, and the state supreme court reviews the appropriateness of the sentence.

RATIONALE

Despite the debate about the constitutionality of the death sentence, it was apparent in 1976 that a large proportion of Americans regarded it as appropriate and necessary. The most important indication was that 35 state legislatures enacted new statutes providing for the death penalty after the *Furman* decision. The infrequency of jury verdicts imposing death did not indicate that capital punishment was rejected but reflected the perspective that the penalty of death should be reserved for only the most serious offenders. Although there were no conclusive studies establishing capital punishment to be a deterrent, the Court concluded that it was undoubtedly a deterrent for some types of murders. The death sentence is severe and irrevocable, but "when a life has been taken deliberately by the offender, we cannot say that the punishment is invariably disproportionate to the crime. It is an extreme sanction, suitable to the most extreme of crimes." The *Furman* opinion expressed concern that a death sentence should not be imposed in an arbitrary and capricious manner. That objective can be met by a carefully drafted statute that ensures the judge or jury who is charged with sentencing be given adequate information and guidance, which is best provided by a bifurcated proceeding. In such a proceeding, the sentencer can be apprised of relevant information for making a sentencing decision without compromising the guilt/innocence decision and standards to guide the use of that information. The new Georgia statute focused the jury's attention on the particular nature of the defendant's crime and the defendant's characteristics. The jury must find at least one aggravating circumstance beyond a reasonable doubt before it can impose death and is permitted to consider all mitigating circumstances. The State Supreme Court's review function afforded additional safeguards. The Court stated that the judgment of the Georgia Legislature that capital punishment may be necessary in some cases was not clearly wrong.

CASE EXCERPT

"We hold that the death penalty is not a form of punishment that may never be imposed, regardless of the circumstances of the offense, regardless of the character of the offender, and regardless of the procedure followed in reaching the decision to impose it."

CASE SIGNIFICANCE

This case is significant because it settles once and for all whether the death penalty per se is unconstitutional. The five Justices who comprised the majority decided that a state statute that properly guided a judge's or jury's discretion and provided safeguards that constrained the potential for arbitrariness and capriciousness would be considered constitutional. The *Gregg* case answered any questions that remained after the *Furman* decision in 1972 when five Justices each wrote a concurring opinion and it remained unclear whether a capital punishment sentencing scheme could ever satisfy constitutional muster. The Supreme Court decided another important death penalty cases in 1976: *Jurek v. Texas*, 428 U.S. 262 (1976), in which the Court upheld the constitutionality of the Texas death penalty statute. Texas had constructed a different statutory approach to the concerns raised in Furman. The Court recognized that there is no one way to interject standards and rational decision making into the death sentencing process.

WOODSON v. NORTH CAROLINA

428 U.S. 280 (1976)

FACTS

James Tyrone Woodson and Luby Waxton were convicted of first-degree murder for killing a convenience store cashier during the course of an armed robbery. They also seriously wounded a customer. Under a North Carolina statute that was enacted after *Furman v. Georgia*, 408 U.S. 238 (1972) was decided, Woodson and Waxton were sentenced to death. The North Carolina statute provided that certain types of murders, including felony murders, were first-degree murders punishable by death. All other murders were considered second-degree, punishable for a term of not less than two years nor more that life. In response to Furman, North Carolina had enacted a statute that made a death sentence mandatory for all persons convicted of first-degree murder.

WOODSON v. NORTH CAROLINA *(cont.)*

ISSUE

Does a sentence imposed pursuant to a law that provides for a mandatory death penalty for a broad category of murders constitute cruel and unusual punishment under the Eighth Amendment?

HOLDING

Statutes that authorize the mandatory imposition of the death penalty for the crime of first-degree murder violate the Fourteenth and Eighth Amendments to the Constitution.

RATIONALE

The Court observed that central to applying the Eighth Amendment is the necessity of determining contemporary standards regarding the infliction of punishment. The history of mandatory death penalty statutes in the United States shows the practice of sentencing all persons to death who are convicted of a particular crime has been rejected as unduly harsh and excessively rigid. Although the Supreme Court had not ruled on the constitutionality of mandatory death penalty laws, on several occasions it has commented that society is adverse to them. At the time *Furman v. Georgia* was decided in 1972, mandatory death penalty statutes had been renounced by the state legislatures. After the *Furman* decision, however, several states reversed their prior positions and enacted mandatory capital punishment legislation in an attempt to abide by the constitutional mandates outlined in that case. Proponents of the automatic death penalty laws argued that such laws remedy the inadequacies of the statutes struck down by *Furman* by withdrawing all sentencing discretion from juries in capital cases. The Court stated that "when one considers the long and consistent American experience with the death penalty in first-degree murder cases, it becomes evident that mandatory statutes enacted in response to *Furman* have simply papered over the problem of unguided and unchecked jury discretion." Mandatory statutes do not fulfill *Furman's* requirements that "arbitrary and wanton jury discretion" be replaced with objective standards to guide and standardize jury decision making. Finally, mandatory death penalty laws, in violation of the Eighth Amendment, do not allow for an individualized consideration of relevant aspects of the defendant's character and circumstances of the crime before death can be imposed. The Court noted that the finality of death "differs more from life imprisonment than a 100-year prison term differs from one of only a year or two. Because of that qualitative difference, there is a corresponding difference in the need for reliability in a the determination that death is the appropriate punishment in a specific case."

CASE EXCERPT

"The two crucial indicators of evolving standards of decency respecting the imposition of punishment in our society—jury determinations and legislative enactments—both point conclusively to the repudiation of automatic death sentences."

CASE SIGNIFICANCE

After *Furman* was decided, states reenacted their death penalty laws in light of the constitutional standards the case announced. Several states enacted mandatory death penalty laws that attempted to avoid the issue of jury discretion all together by making a death sentence mandatory for those defendants convicted of certain categories of murder. Woodson struck down those statutes and reversed the death sentences imposed under them. The Court made very clear that particularized consideration of each convicted capital defendant is required by the Constitution. In *Roberts v. Louisiana*, 431 U.S. 633 (1977), the Supreme Court reiterated its position when it struck down a Louisiana statute providing for the mandatory death sentence for murdering a police officer. In *Sumner v. Shuman*, 483 U.S. 66 (1987), the Court ruled that a statute that imposed a mandatory death sentence when a prisoner commits a murder while serving a life sentence without the possibility of parole is unconstitutional.

COKER v. GEORGIA
433 U.S. 584 (1977)

FACTS

Ehrlich Anthony Coker escaped from a Georgia penitentiary where he was serving several sentences for murder, rape, kidnapping, and aggravated assault. While fleeing from authorities, he entered the home of Allen and Elnita Carver through an unlocked kitchen door. He tied up Allen Carver, took his money and the keys to the family car. Brandishing a knife, he raped Elnita Carver. He fled in the Carver's car, taking Elnita Carver with him. He was eventually captured. Elnita Carver was unharmed. Coker was charged with escape, armed robbery, motor vehicle theft, kidnapping, and rape. He was convicted on all counts. During the sentencing phase of his trial, the jury was instructed that it could consider as aggravating circumstances whether the rape was committed by a person with a prior criminal record for a capital felony and whether the rape had been committed during the course of another capital felony, namely an armed robbery. The jury found that the aggravating factors were not outweighed by the mitigating factors and assessed the punishment of death.

ISSUE

Does the Constitution permit imposing capital punishment for the crime of rape?

HOLDING

No. The death sentence is grossly disproportionate and excessive punishment for the crime of rape and is considered cruel and unusual punishment under the Eighth Amendment.

RATIONALE

The Court noted that at no time in the last 50 years have a majority of states permitted the death penalty as a punishment for rape. Prior to *Furman v. Georgia*, 477 U.S. 399 (1986), only 16 states and the federal government authorized capital punishment for rape. After the states rewrote their death penalty statutes to satisfy *Furman's* mandates, only three states provided the death penalty for rape of an adult woman—Georgia, North Carolina, and Louisiana. The North Carolina and Louisiana statutes were struck down under *Woodson v. North Carolina*, 428 U.S. 280 (1976) because they provided for mandatory death sentences. When those two states reenacted their capital punishment laws to abide by *Woodson*, they reenacted the death penalty for murder but not for rape. Georgia was the only jurisdiction that authorized capital punishment when the rape victim was an adult woman, and only two other jurisdictions authorized capital punishment for the rape of a child. Although the attitude of state legislatures did not wholly determine this controversy, the legislative rejection of the death sentence for rape confirmed the Court's judgment that death is a disproportionate penalty for the rape of an adult woman

CASE EXCERPT

Rape is a serious, violent crime that deserves severe punishment; however, "...it does not compare with murder, which does involve the unjustified taking of human life. Although it may be accompanied by another crime, rape by definition does not include the death of or even the serious injury to another person."

CASE SIGNIFICANCE

In the *Coker* decision, the Supreme Court did not address whether capital punishment could be assessed for the rape of a child; however, much of its reasoning suggests that such a punishment would have constitutional problems. That issue was decided by the Supreme Court in *Kennedy v. Louisiana*, 554 U.S. 407 (2008).

LOCKETT v. OHIO
438 U.S. 98 (1978)

FACTS

Lockett was convicted of capital murder and sentenced to death in Ohio. She challenged the constitutionality of the Ohio law on the grounds that the Eighth and Fourteenth Amendments require the sentencing authority be given a full opportunity to consider mitigating circumstances in capital cases and the Ohio statute did not allow for that. The Ohio statute provided that once a defendant was found guilty of aggravated murder with at least one of seven specific aggravating circumstances, the death penalty must be imposed unless the sentencing judge decides at least one of the following mitigating circumstances is present by a preponderance of the evidence: the victim induced or facilitated the offense; the defendant was under duress, coercion, or strong provocation, without which it is unlikely the offense would have been committed; or even though there was insufficient evidence to establish insanity, the offense was primarily the product of the defendant's psychosis or mental deficiency. There was no finding of any of the mitigating factors being present in Lockett's case. Her death sentence was upheld by the Ohio Supreme Court, which concluded that the mitigating circumstances in Ohio's statute are to be liberally construed in favor of the defendant.

ISSUE

Is a capital punishment sentencing statute unconstitutional if it precludes a sentencing authority from considering as mitigating factors any aspect of a defendant's character or record and any of the circumstances of the offense that the defendant places

LOCKETT v. OHIO *(cont.)*

into evidence as a basis for a sentence less than death?

HOLDING

The Eighth and Fourteenth Amendments require that the sentencer not be precluded from considering any aspect of the defendant's character or record and any other evidence he or she offers as mitigating factors.

RATIONALE

The principle of individualized sentencing requires that judges and juries possess the fullest information possible concerning a defendant's life and the circumstances of the crime when reaching a sentencing decision. The Supreme Court's decision in *Woodson v. North Carolina*, 428 U.S. 280 (1976) repudiated mandatory death penalty statutes because they did not allow for such individualized consideration. *Woodson*, however, did not indicate which facets of an offender or his offense is relevant for a capital sentencing hearing. In this case, the Court decided that the Ohio law did not permit individualized consideration of mitigating factors. Only three mitigating factors are specified in the statute. The limited range of mitigating circumstances is incompatible with the Constitution.

CASE EXCERPT

"To meet constitutional requirements, a death penalty statute must not preclude consideration of relevant mitigating factors."

CASE SIGNIFICANCE

This case helped further define the Court's position on what information a judge or jury should be permitted to consider when making a death versus life sentence decision. A statute cannot limit the mitigating evidence a defendant can offer during the sentencing phase of a capital case or a judge or jury can consider in making the sentencing determination.

GODFREY v. GEORGIA

446 U.S. 420 (1980)

FACTS

Godfrey threatened his wife of 28 years with a knife. She announced she was going to leave him and initiated divorce proceedings. She also secured a warrant charging Godfrey with aggravated assault. His wife moved in with her mother. Godfrey tried to convince her to reconcile on several occasions but to no avail. After one such argument over the telephone, Godfrey drove over to his mother-in-law's home with his shotgun. Peering through a window he saw his wife, mother-in-law, and 11-year-old daughter playing cards. He pointed the shotgun at his wife through the window and shot and killed her. He entered the home, striking his fleeing daughter in the head with the gun, and fired the gun at his mother-in-law, killing her. He then called the police and reported what he had done. When they arrived at the scene, he admitted to killing them both. He later told an officer, "I've done a hideous crime, . . . but I have been thinking about it for eight years . . . I'd do it again." Godfrey was convicted on two counts of murder and one of aggravated assault. He was found guilty on all three. During the sentencing phase of his trial, no further evidence was offered to the jury. During closing arguments, the prosecutor stated three times that the case involved no allegation of torture or of an aggravated battery. The trial judge instructed the jury orally and in writing about the standards that must guide their sentencing deliberations in the state of Georgia. He quoted the statutory language of §(b)(7) that said the jury could impose the death sentence if it found that the murders were "outrageously or wantonly vile, horrible and inhuman." The jury sentenced Godfrey to death on both murder convictions. The jury found that each murder met was aggravated under §(b)(7). On appeal to the Georgia State Supreme Court, Godfrey argued that §(b)(7) is unconstitutionally vague. The State Court rejected his allegations.

ISSUE

Was the statutory aggravating circumstance of "outrageously or wantonly vile, horrible or inhuman" so vague and broad in its construction as to violate the Eighth and Fourteenth Amendments to the Constitution?

HOLDING

The statutory aggravating circumstance of "outrageously or wantonly vile, horrible or inhuman" was not so defined as to provide restraint on the arbitrary and capricious infliction of the death penalty and, therefore, violated constitutional requirements.

RATIONALE

In *Gregg v. Georgia*, 428 U.S. 153 (1976), the US Supreme Court upheld the constitutionality of the Georgia death penalty statute. In that opinion, the Court said that the statutory circumstance defined by §(b)(7) was not unconstitutional on its face. The Court opined in Gregg that it could not assume that the Georgia Supreme Court would adopt such an open-ended interpretation of the statute as to permit it to be imposed on any murder case. The question four years later has become whether the State Supreme Court has construed the aggravating circumstance in an unconstitutional manner. A state has a responsibility to tailor and apply its law in a way that avoids the arbitrary and capricious infliction of the death penalty. A state must define the crimes for which death can be imposed in a way that significantly reduces arbitrariness. In this case, the State Supreme Court has upheld a death sentence based on a statute that provides no such restraint. A person of ordinary sensibilities could consider any murder outrageously vile or wanton. The judge's instructions gave the jury no guidance as to the meaning of the aggravating circumstance. In earlier decisions, the Georgia Supreme Court ruled that §(b)(7) required torture, depravity of mind, or an aggravated battery of the victim. The court failed, however, to limit §(b)(7) in such a way in the present case.

CASE EXCERPT

"[It] is of vital importance to the defendant and to the community that any decision to impose the death sentence be, and appear to be, based on reason, rather than caprice or emotion. That cannot be said here. There is no principled way to distinguish this case, in which the death penalty was imposed, from the many cases in which it was not."

CASE SIGNIFICANCE

This is one of several cases that have addressed the importance of the statutory provisions that detail which murders should be considered capital murders. If juries and judges are to guided by laws that ensure the fair application of the death penalty, it is the job of legislatures to carefully craft statutes that are not too broad and ambiguous. It is the job of the state appellate courts to further refine statutory provisions that require more definition and substance so they can provide guidance. It is then up to the trial courts to apply the statutory provisions as they have been interpreted by the state's appellate courts.

PULLEY v. HARRIS
465 U.S. 37 (1984)

FACTS

Harris was convicted of capital murder in California and sentenced to death. Along with several other challenges, Harris alleged that the California statute violated the US Constitution because it failed to require the California Supreme Court to compare Harris's sentence with the sentences imposed in similar death penalty cases to determine whether it was proportionate.

ISSUE

Does the Eighth Amendment require a state appellate court, before it affirms a death sentence, to compare the sentence in the case before it with the penalties imposed in similar cases if requested to do so by the prisoner?

HOLDING

The Constitution does not require that a state appellate court conduct a proportionality review in a death sentence case.

RATIONALE

Traditionally, proportionality has referred to an evaluation of the appropriateness of a sentence for a particular crime. The Supreme Court has on occasion struck down sentences as disproportionate based on the gravity of the offense and the severity of the sentence compared to sentences imposed for other crimes, and compared to sentencing practices in other jurisdictions. The proportionality review sought in this case, however, was somewhat different. The question was whether a death sentence is disproportionate to the punishment imposed on other persons who have been convicted of the same crime. In *Gregg v. Georgia*, 428 U.S. 153 (1976), the Supreme Court upheld the constitutionality of the Georgia capital punishment statute. Both the majority and the concurring opinions in that case mentioned the state's proportionality review acted as an additional safeguard against arbitrary sentencing. Neither opinion, however, declared that proportionality review was essential for a state capital

PULLEY v. HARRIS *(cont.)*

sentencing scheme to be found constitutional. Just because a proportionality review is required in some states does not mean such a review is indispensable. The California statute in the present case was constitutional even without a proportionality review because the jury must find "special circumstances" beyond a reasonable doubt which guides the jury's discretion when making their decision. The jury decision is then reviewed by the trial judge and the State Supreme Court. The California statute provided adequate protection against the arbitrary and capricious administration of the death penalty.

CASE EXCERPT

"There is thus no basis in our cases for holding that comparative proportionality review by an appellate court is required in every case in which the death penalty is imposed and the defendant requests it."

CASE SIGNIFICANCE

The Georgia capital punishment sentencing statute was deemed constitutional in 1976 because the Supreme Court concluded that it successfully limited jury discretion and reduced the opportunity for a jury to make an arbitrary and capricious decision. The 1976 Court specifically pointed to the requirement that the Georgia Supreme Court review each death sentence for evidence of passion, prejudice, or other arbitrary factor; whether the evidence supported the finding of an aggravating circumstance; and whether, considering the crime and the defendant, the death penalty was excessive or disproportionate to the penalty imposed in similar cases. The *Harris* case makes clear that proportionality review, while an appropriate means for limiting arbitrariness, is not constitutionality required. States are free to adopt or reject such a review—as long as there are other safeguards that limit arbitrariness and guide a jury's discretion. This 7–2 decision gives the states the power to enact their own capital sentencing schemes and limits the Court's involvement in determining the details of statutory provisions.

SPAZIANO v. FLORIDA

468 U.S. 447 (1984)

FACTS

Joseph Spaziano was convicted of first-degree murder. The same jury that convicted him served as his sentencing jury. They returned an advisory verdict recommending life imprisonment. The trial judge rejected the jury's recommendation and imposed a death sentence. The Florida State Supreme Court affirmed the conviction but reversed the death penalty because the trial judge considered a confidential portion of a presentence investigation report without letting either party review a copy. The trial court imposed the death penalty upon remand of the case to it. This time, the Florida Supreme Court affirmed the sentence, rejecting Spaziano's argument that the Constitution does not permit the trial judge to override a jury's recommendation for a life sentence.

ISSUE

Does allowing a trial judge to override a jury's recommendation of a life sentence in a capital case violate the Eighth Amendment's prohibition of cruel and unusual punishment?

HOLDING

The Eighth Amendment does not require a trial judge to accept a jury's recommendation that a defendant in a capital case be sentenced to life.

RATIONALE

Spaziano argued that the laws and practice in most states recognized that juries, not judges, are better able to make reliable sentencing decisions in capital cases; therefore, a jury's recommendation of life could not constitutionally be set aside. Thirty of the then-37 jurisdictions with capital punishment gave the life or death decision to the jury. Only three of the remaining seven allowed the trial judge to override a jury's recommendation of life imprisonment. According to Spaziano, a decision to impose death expressed a community's belief that death is the only adequate response to the crime. The jury is in the best position to speak for the community. The Sixth Amendment does not require jury sentencing in any criminal case. Fairness and reliability concerns do not demand jury sentencing in capital cases. The nature and purpose of the punishment of death do not require jury sentencing. The Court concluded there was nothing in the override procedure that resulted in the arbitrary or discriminatory application of the death penalty. Regardless of the jury's recommendation, the judge must conduct an independent review of the evidence and make his or her own findings regarding the aggravating and mitigating circumstances in the case. If the judge imposes death, he or she is required to outline their findings in writing.

CASE EXCERPT

"The fact that a majority of jurisdictions have adopted a different practice, however, does not establish that contemporary standards of decency are offended by the jury override. The Eighth Amendment is not violated every time a State reaches a conclusion different from a majority of its sisters over how best to administer its criminal laws."

CASE SIGNIFICANCE

Unlike some of the Court's previous decisions up to 1984, the Court was not persuaded by the fact that the vast majority of death penalty states give the sentencing decision in capital cases to juries. In only three of the seven states that provide a role for the judge in capital sentencing can the judge refuse a jury's recommendation for life imprisonment. Unlike *Coker v. Georgia*, 433 U.S. 584 (1977) and *Woodson v. North Carolina*, 428 U.S. 280 (1976), the fact that most state legislatures had adopted laws directly opposed to the statute at issue in this case did not convince the Court that contemporary standards of decency meant Florida's jury override provision was unconstitutional. The fact that in most states juries do not traditionally play a significant role in noncapital sentencing was a key component to the Court's holding. Also key was the majority's belief that there was nothing to suggest a judge sentencing was likely to be arbitrary or unfair.

LOCKHART v. MCCREE

476 U.S. 162 (1986)

FACTS

McCree was charged with a capital felony murder. He denied committing the underlying felony, a robbery, and the murder. During the selection of his jury, the trial judge removed for cause any jurors who stated that they could not vote to impose the death penalty regardless of the circumstances. The jury did not impose the death sentence on McCree. Instead he was sentenced to life in prison without parole. McCree argued that by removing jurors who opposed the death penalty from the jury, the court created a jury that was not impartial because it was more predisposed to convict.

ISSUE

Does a judge violate the Sixth Amendment, which requires that a jury be selected from a representative cross-section of the community, when during the guilt/innocence phase of a capital trial she removes for cause prospective jurors who oppose the death penalty and state that their opposition would substantially impair their performance during the sentencing phase?

HOLDING

Neither of the Sixth Amendment requirements that a jury be a cross-section of the community or that it be impartial are violated when a judge removes for cause a prospective juror who opposes the death penalty and states their opposition would make it difficult for them to perform their legal obligations during the sentencing phase of a capital trial.

RATIONALE

Under *Witherspoon v. Illinois*, 391 U.S. 510 (1968), judges are prohibited from removing for cause individuals who state they are opposed to capital punishment and who indicated they had conscientious scruples against inflicting the death penalty. The Constitution, however, does not prohibit the states from death-qualifying juries in capital cases. Jurors who oppose the death penalty under any and all circumstances do not constitute a distinctive group within a community whose exclusion from serving on a capital trial would violate the Sixth Amendment. Jury representativeness cases, whether based on the Sixth Amendment or the equal protection clause of the Fourteenth Amendment have involved groups defined by race, ethnicity, and gender. These groups have been excluded in the past for reasons unrelated to their ability to serve as jurors, raising the possibility their exclusion affected the jury is such a way that a criminal defendant was denied the common-sense judgment of the community. Such exclusion also deprives members of these groups of their rights as citizens to serve on juries in criminal cases. A group defined by a shared attitude that would prevent its members from performing one of their duties as jurors, is not a distinctive group for purposes of the Sixth Amendment's fair cross-section requirement. Not all who oppose the death penalty are removed for cause. Prospective jurors who believe the death penalty is unjust but who state they are willing and able to set their personal beliefs aside in order to apply the law to the facts of a particular case are not removed for cause. The only groups who can be

LOCKHART v. MCCREE *(cont.)*

excluded are those who can and will not obey the law with respect to the sentencing phase of a capital case. Excluding them does not prevent them from serving on juries in noncapital criminal cases. The view that death qualified juries are slanted and more likely to convict is illogical and does not violate the impartiality requirement of the Constitution.

CASE EXCERPT

" 'Death qualification,' unlike the wholesale exclusion of blacks, women, or Mexican-Americans from jury service, is carefully designed to serve the State's concededly legitimate interest in obtaining a single jury that can properly and impartially apply the law to the facts of the case at both the guilt and sentencing phases of a capital trial."

CASE SIGNIFICANCE

Lockhart v. McCree is one of several cases that have created the death-qualified jury doctrine, which governs the jury selection process in capital cases. The doctrine began its evolution in *Witherspoon v. Illinois*, in which the Court ruled on the constitutionality of an Illinois state statute that provided that judges could dismiss a prospective juror in a capital case for cause who stated he had conscientious scruples against capital punishment. The Court held in *Witherspoon* that a death sentence was unconstitutional if it was rendered by a jury chosen by excluding jurors for cause simply because they voiced general objections to the death penalty. The *Witherspoon* Court stated specifically that its ruling was narrow and did not involve the right of the prosecutor to challenge for cause prospective jurors who stated their beliefs about capital punishment would prevent them from making an impartial decision as to the defendant's guilt. Nor did it involve the state's right to exclude from a capital jury any juror who stated they could never vote to impose death or that they would refuse to even consider imposing it. In *Wainwright v. Witt*, 469 U.S. 412 (1985), the Court outlined the proper standard for determining when a prospective juror could be excluded for cause because of his views about the death penalty. When a juror's views would prevent or substantially impair his or her ability to perform their duties in accordance with their juror oath, they may be excluded for cause. In *Lockhart*, the Court further refined the capital trial jury death-qualification doctrine. McCree challenged the doctrine on the grounds there was significant social science

research suggesting death-qualified juries were more likely to convict criminal defendants. His concern was that jurors who were excluded for cause based on an inability to impose a death sentence would be conviction-prone during the guilt/innocence phase of a capital trial. The Court was not persuaded by the body of social science research introduced by McCree. The research did not suggest to the Court that death-qualified juries were not impartial in making decisions about guilt or innocence.

FORD v. WAINWRIGHT
477 U.S. 399 (1986)

FACTS

Alvin Bernard Ford was convicted of capital murder in 1974 and sentenced to death. There was no question that he was competent at the time of his crime, at trial, and at sentencing. While incarcerated, however, he developed a severe mental disorder. At his lawyer's request, he was examined extensively by two different psychiatrists to determine if he was competent to be executed. One of the psychiatrists determined that he was not competent. Defense counsel invoked a Florida statute that outlined the procedures to be used to determine a death-sentenced inmate's competency for execution. Under that statute, the governor appointed three psychiatrists who together interviewed Ford for 30 minutes to determine whether he had the mental capacity to understand the death penalty and why he was to be executed. All three agreed that Ford had a mental disorder but that he was competent for execution. State law provided that the governor had the final decision. Without explanation, the governor signed Ford's death warrant.

ISSUE

Does the Eighth Amendment prohibit executing a death row prisoner who is insane at the time of execution? In order to be constitutionally adequate, must a procedure for determining the sanity of a prisoner who faces execution provide an evidentiary hearing that includes the opportunity to challenge the findings of state-appointed experts and a neutral fact-finder?

HOLDING

The Eighth Amendment prohibits executing a prisoner who is insane at the time of execution. Florida's procedure for determining sanity is unconstitutional because it does not permit the prisoner to present relevant evidence on the issue; it provides no clear mechanism by which the prisoner can challenge the findings of the experts appointed by the state, and the governor cannot act as a neutral fact-finder in making the final decision on the sanity issue.

RATIONALE

The common law barred executing a prisoner who had lost his sanity. The common law has a firm hold on contemporary jurisprudence because no state permits executing the insane. Florida's statutory procedure for determining an inmate's sanity for execution purposes was not adequate because it failed to include the defendant in the process. Any procedure that precludes a death-sentenced inmate or his counsel from presenting evidence on the insanity issue is inadequate. Denying the prisoner or his counsel the opportunity to challenge or impeach the findings of the psychiatrists appointed by the state created the possibility that the ultimate decision, which relied on those reports, would be distorted. Finally, placing the final decision with the governor, who appoints the experts and whose subordinates have been responsible for initiating every stage of the prosecution, did not have the necessary neutrality for making reliable fact-findings.

CASE EXCERPT

"The various reasons put forth in support of the common-law restriction have no less logical, moral, and practical force than they did when first voiced. For today, no less than before, we may seriously question the retributive value of executing a person who has no comprehension of why he has been singled out and stripped of his fundamental right to life. Similarly, the natural abhorrence civilized societies feel at killing one who has no capacity to come to grips with his own conscience or deity is still vivid today."

CASE SIGNIFICANCE

This case is mostly significant for establishing constitutional guidelines to govern the procedures that states develop for determining whether a death-sentenced prisoner is insane. Although it was the first case to bar the execution of insane prisoners, no state had actually sanctioned their execution. The Supreme Court has avoided deciding whether the Constitution permits the government to force an insane death-sentenced inmate to take medication in order to make them sane enough to be executed.

TISON v. ARIZONA
481 U.S. 137 (1987)

FACTS

Armed with guns, Ricky, Raymond, and Donald Tison broke into Arizona State Prison and helped their father Gary Tison and Randy Greenawalt escape. Gary Tison was serving a life sentence for a prison escape during which he had killed a correctional officer. Greenawalt was also a convicted murderer. No shots were fired during the prison break. While on the run, the group's Lincoln automobile had a flat tire, and they decided to steal a car. The three brothers helped their father and Greenawalt flag down a Mazda and abduct a family of four, including a man and women, their two-year-old son, and fifteen-year-old niece. While the family begged not to be murdered, asking only to be left in the desert with some water, Gary Tison told his sons to go and get the water that had been transferred into the Mazda from the Lincoln. Although the brothers' version of events diverges somewhat, they agree that while they were involved in getting the water, they watched their father and Greenawalt repeatedly shoot and kill the family of four. Ricky and Raymond testified they were surprised by the shootings, but did not attempt to aid the victims. The brothers drove away in the Mazda with their father and Greenawalt. The group was apprehended at a police roadblock a few days later. Donald Tison was killed. Gary Tison escaped but died of exposure in the desert. Ricky and Raymond Tison and Randy Greenawalt were captured by the police. Ricky, age 20, and Raymond, age 19, were convicted of capital murder and sentenced to death under Arizona's felony-murder statute and the accomplice liability statute which provided that each participant in the felony is legally responsible for the acts of his accomplices. Ricky and Raymond alleged they should not have been sentenced to death under *Enmund v. Florida*, 458 U.S. 782 (1982), in which the Supreme Court held the Constitution prohibits imposing the death penalty on a defendant who did not take a life, attempted to take a life, or intended to take a life.

ISSUE

Does the Eighth Amendment prohibit imposing the death penalty on a defendant who did not specifically intend to kill the victims or inflict the fatal wounds but whose participation in the crime was major and whose mental state was one of reckless indifference to the value of human life?

TISON v. ARIZONA *(cont.)*

HOLDING

Major participation in a felony combined with reckless indifference to human life is sufficient to satisfy the constitutional requirement that the defendant must be culpable of the killing.

RATIONALE

In *Enmund v. Florida*, the Supreme Court ruled that the Eighth Amendment prohibited imposing the death penalty in those cases where the defendant was a minor accomplice who did not kill or have the intent of participating in or facilitating a murder. The Tisons' situation was different from the facts of the *Enmund* case where the defendant was a lookout for a robbery, was not present when the murders occurred, and did not know that they would take place. The facts supported a finding that the Tison brothers' participation in the crime was major and they both appreciated that their actions might likely result in the taking of an innocent life. Throughout the prison escape, the kidnapping and robbery of the family, and the shoot-out at the police roadblock, the brothers acted in reckless indifference to the value of human life. A review of state statutes indicated that a significant number of state legislatures allowed the death penalty to be imposed for a felony murder where the defendant was a major actor in a crime in which he knew a death was highly likely. A number of state courts have interpreted the *Enmund* decision to permit imposing the death penalty on a defendant who was a substantial participant in a felony under circumstances that were likely to result in a murder. A narrow focus on whether the defendant intended to kill is not a satisfactory means for determining who is the most culpable and dangerous of murderers

CASE EXCERPT

"Some nonintentional murderers may be among the most dangerous and inhumane of all—the person who tortures another not caring whether the victim lives or dies, or the robber who shoots someone in the course of the robbery, utterly indifferent to the fact that the desire to rob may have the unintended consequence of killing the victim as well as taking the victim's property. This reckless indifference to the value of human life may be every bit as shocking to the moral sense as an 'intent to kill.'"

CASE SIGNIFICANCE

Under the felony murder doctrine, a defendant can be convicted of murder even if the killing was unintended. The doctrine holds that if the defendant commits certain predicate felonies, generally those felonies considered dangerous to human life where the danger is foreseeable, during which a person is killed, he may be guilty of a felony murder. In a majority of states with capital punishment, a felony murderer can be sentenced to death even if the facts establish that the killing was unintended. A defendant may also be found guilty of felony murder even if he did not actually commit the murder if he acted as an accomplice in the commission of the felony. In those states that provide for the death penalty, the question then became can a defendant who was an accomplice to a felony murder be sentenced to die if he did not commit the murder himself. Is death a proportionate punishment for the crime he committed? In *Enmund v. Florida* the Supreme Court ruled 5–4 that a participant in a felony murder who does not kill or intend to kill may not be executed. He may still be found guilty of felony murder but is excluded from execution. In *Tison*, also a 5–4 decision, the Court was faced with a different set of facts, and concluded that when the felony murder accomplice is a major actor in the predicate felony and the facts indicate that he recklessly disregarded the value of human life, the death penalty is a proportionate punishment for the crime.

MCCLESKEY v. KEMP
481 U.S. 279 (1987)

FACTS

McCleskey was an African American man convicted of murdering a white police officer during the course of committing an armed robbery in Fulton County, Georgia. McCleskey challenged the death sentence imposed by the jury on the grounds the Georgia capital punishment law violated the Fourteenth Amendment's equal protection clause and the Eighth Amendment's prohibition against cruel and unusual punishment. In support of his claim, McCleskey offered a statistical study done by professors David Baldus, Charles Pulaski, and George Woodworth. The study purported to show there was a disparity in the imposition of the death sentence in Georgia based on the race of the murder victim, and to a lesser extent, the race of the defendant. The study examined over 2,000 murder cases that occurred in Georgia during the 1970s. The raw numbers indicated that defendants charged with killing white persons were sentenced to death in 11 percent of the cases, while defendants charged with killing black persons were sentenced to death in only 1 percent of the cases. The study also divided the cases according to the combination of the race of the defendant and the race of the victim. The researchers found death was imposed in 22 percent of the cases with black defendants and white victims, 1 percent of the cases involving black defendants and black victims, and 3 percent of the cases with white defendants and black victims. The study also looked at data concerning prosecutors' decisions to seek the death penalty. The data indicated that prosecutors sought capital punishment in 70 percent of the cases involving black defendants and white victims, 32 percent of the cases involving white defendants and white victims, 15 percent of the cases involving black defendants and black victims, and 19 percent of the cases with white defendants and black victims. The Baldus study took into account 230 variables that could have explained the disparities on nonracial grounds. The study concluded black defendants who kill white victims have the greatest likelihood of receiving the death penalty. The US District Court concluded that the Baldus study was flawed and suggested the racial disparities could be explained by aggravating factors that were often present in white victim cases and the mitigating factors often present in black victim cases. The Eleventh Circuit Court of Appeals assumed the study was valid, but rejected the claim that there was a constitutional violation.

ISSUE

Does a complex statistical study that indicates a risk that racial considerations enter into capital sentencing decisions establish that an individual defendant's death sentence violates the Fourteenth and Eighth Amendments to the Constitution?

HOLDING

No. A statistical study that indicates a risk that racial considerations enter into capital sentencing decisions does not indicate a violation of the Fourteenth Amendment's equal protection clause because it cannot support an inference that any of the decision makers in a defendant's particular case acted with discriminatory intent. Such a study also fails to establish that the defendant's death sentence was wantonly or freakishly imposed and is disproportionate within the meaning of the Eighth Amendment.

RATIONALE

The Court did not question the validity of the Baldus findings. It began its analysis with a review of the

claim that there was a violation of the equal protection clause. It concluded that a defendant who alleges a violation of that clause must show the existence of purposeful discrimination that had a discriminatory effect on his or her particular case. To prevail under the equal protection clause, McCleskey needed to prove discriminatory purpose. He offered no evidence supporting the inference that racial considerations played a part in his sentence and relied solely on the Baldus study. Although McCleskey argued that the Baldus study compelled an inference that his sentence resulted from purposeful discrimination, he did not argue the facts of his particular case. The Supreme Court accepted statistics as proof of intent to discriminate in limited contexts: an equal protection clause violation in the selection of a jury venire and to prove a statutory violation of Title VII of the Civil Rights Act (employment discrimination). The Court reasoned that the nature of capital sentencing, however, is fundamentally different from both of those contexts. Each sentencing decision is made by a jury unique in its composition, and the Constitution requires that the jury make its decision based on many variables that vary according to a particular defendant and the facts of the case. Discretion is essential to the criminal justice process; therefore, there must be exceptionally clear proof that discretion has been abused. Concerning the Eighth Amendment claim, the Court concluded that McCleskey failed to show that his punishment was disproportionate to the sentences in other murder cases, and he failed to establish that the Georgia system operates in an arbitrary and capricious manner. At most the Baldus study showed a risk that racial prejudice influenced the jury's decision. The question was at what point such a risk violates the Constitution. The Court declined McCleskey's request that it accept the likelihood allegedly shown by the Baldus study as an unacceptable risk that racial prejudice influenced death penalty decisions. "The discrepancy indicated by the Baldus study is 'a far cry from the major systemic defects identified in *Furman*,' *Pulley v. Harris*, 465 U.S. at 54."

CASE EXCERPT

"In light of the safeguards designed to minimize racial bias in the process, the fundamental value of jury trial in our criminal justice system, and the benefits that discretion provides to criminal defendants, we hold that the Baldus study does not demonstrate a constitutionally significant risk of racial bias affecting the Georgia capital sentencing process."

MCCLESKEY v. KEMP *(cont.)*

CASE SIGNIFICANCE

This decision was eagerly awaited by many opponents of the death penalty. If McCleskey's arguments had swayed the majority of the Court instead of only a minority of four, the decision would have had been a major blow to the administration of the death penalty in the United States. In many respects the legal arguments in this case were the last opportunity to strike a fatal on capital punishment. In rejecting McCleskey's equal protection clause claim, the Court refused to accept statistical evidence indicating that racial bias influenced the sentencing of capital defendants in the state of Georgia. It did not matter whether the Baldus study was accurate, because McCleskey failed to show that the individuals involved with seeking the death penalty or imposing the penalty in his case acted with discriminatory purpose. In reaching that conclusion, the Court had to explain why the capital sentencing context differs from other contexts where the Court has accepted statistical evidence to prove intentional discrimination. With this decision, it will be very difficult for a capital murder defendant to gather the evidence to establish that racial bias affected his or her particular case. The Court also ruled against McCleskey's Eighth Amendment claim and reiterated its position that discretion is essential to the criminal justice system and should not be set aside without clear proof of abuse. The Court expressed concern that if McCleskey prevailed on this claim it would open the door to questions about other types of sentences and other types of unexplained sentencing discrepancies.

MAYNARD v. CARTWRIGHT

486 U.S. 356 (1988)

FACTS

Cartwright was a disgruntled ex-employee of Hugh and Charma Riddle. One evening in 1982, he entered their home and shot and killed Hugh Riddle with a shotgun. He shot Charma Riddle, slit her throat, stabbed her twice with a hunting knife the Riddles had given him for Christmas, and then left the house. Charma Riddle survived and called the police. Cartwright was convicted of first-degree murder in an Oklahoma state trial court. The jury imposed the death sentence after it found the existence of two aggravating circumstances outlined in the Oklahoma statutes: first, Cartwright knowingly "created a great

risk of death to more than one person"; second, the murder was "especially heinous, atrocious, or cruel." The Oklahoma Court of Criminal Appeals affirmed the conviction and sentence. Cartwright sought federal habeas corpus relief, arguing his sentence was invalid because it rested in part on an unconstitutionally vague and overbroad aggravating circumstance—that the murder was "especially heinous, atrocious, or cruel." An en banc Tenth Circuit Court of Appeals overturned the sentence on the grounds that the words "heinous," "atrocious," and "cruel" did not offer sufficient guidance to the jury, in violation of the Eighth Amendment. Nor had the Oklahoma Court of Criminal Appeals adopted a limiting construction that remedied the problem.

ISSUE

Is a capital punishment statute constitutional that lists "especially heinous, atrocious, or cruel" as an aggravating circumstance that can support the imposition of a death sentence for murder?

HOLDING

No. A death penalty sentencing statute that allows a death sentence to be imposed based on the aggravating circumstance that a murder is "especially heinous, atrocious, or cruel" is unconstitutionally vague under the Eighth Amendment because the terms of the circumstance do not adequately guide a jury's discretion.

RATIONALE

This case was controlled by the Supreme Court's decision in *Godfrey v. Georgia*, 446 U.S. 420 (1980). The aggravating circumstance at issue there permitted a death sentence to be assessed if the offense "was outrageously or wantonly vile, horrible or inhuman in that it involved torture, depravity of mind, or an aggravated battery to the victim." The Supreme Court ruled that such an aggravating circumstance was unconstitutional because the words, standing alone, provide no restraint on the arbitrary and capricious imposition of the death penalty. The language of the Oklahoma statute suffered from the same infirmity, and the Court noted that the word "especially" provided no additional guidance.

CASE EXCERPT

"The language of the Oklahoma aggravating circumstance at issue—'especially heinous, atrocious, or cruel'—gave no more guidance than the 'outrageously or wantonly vile, horrible or inhuman' language that the jury returned in its verdict in *Godfrey*. The State's contention that the addition of the word 'especially' somehow guides the jury's discretion, even if the term 'heinous' does not, is untenable."

CASE SIGNIFICANCE

This case is one of several cases following *Godfrey v. Georgia*, 446 U.S. 420 (1980), to address vagueness challenges to certain sentencing provisions of death penalty laws. Statutes that provide for a kind of catch all aggravating circumstance, using ambiguous terminology such as "especially heinous" or "outrageously or wantonly vile" have been the basis for many death sentence appeals and the subject of several Supreme Court decisions. In *Walton v. Arizona*, 497 U.S. 639 (1990), the Court considered the constitutionality of the Arizona death penalty statute. The judge found that Walton committed murder "in an especially heinous, cruel, or depraved manner," an aggravating circumstance under state law. Walton challenged the circumstance as a violation of the Eighth Amendment because it failed to channel the sentencer's discretion. The Supreme Court, however, ruled that there was no constitutional problem with the aggravating circumstance as it was applied in Arizona. In a previous decision the Arizona Supreme Court had defined "especially heinous, cruel, or depraved" as a murder committed when the perpetrator inflicts mental anguish or physical abuse before the victim's death and mental anguish includes a victim's uncertainty about his or her ultimate fate. In *Arave v. Creech*, 507 U.S. 463 (1993), the Supreme Court considered an Idaho death sentence based on the aggravating circumstance that the defendant "exhibited utter disregard for human life." The Idaho Supreme Court had previously decided a case that refined "utter disregard" to refer to a killer who is a "cold blooded, pitiless slayer." The U.S. Supreme Court held that in light of the narrow definition given to the phrase "utter disregard" by the state High Court, the aggravating factor is constitutional. Although broadly written aggravating circumstances were shut down in the Godfrey and Maynard cases, as the state courts learned to refine the definitions of those terms, the U.S. Supreme Court adopted a deferential approach and has been willing to find that many of the state court refinements are sufficient to protect the statutes from claims of vagueness.

STANFORD v. KENTUCKY
492 U.S. 361 (1989)

FACTS

Two cases are consolidated in this decision. The first case involved Kevin Stanford, who shot and killed a 20-year-old gas station attendant after he and his accomplice robbed and repeatedly raped and sodomized her. They drove her to a secluded location, and Stanford shot her in the face and in the back of her head. Stanford was 17 years and four months old at the time of his offense. The juvenile court certified him for trial as an adult. In a Kentucky trial court, he was convicted of several crimes, including murder in the first degree, and was sentenced to death and 45 years in prison. The second case involved Heath Wilkins, who was 16 years and six months old when he repeatedly stabbed to death a convenience store clerk and mother of two children during a robbery of the store in Missouri. He was also certified to be tried as an adult. He pleaded guilty to all the charges against him, one of which was first-degree murder. At his punishment hearing, the state and the defendant himself urged that a death sentence be imposed, and it was. Both State Supreme Courts affirmed the Stanford and Wilkins convictions and sentences.

ISSUE

Does it violate the Eighth Amendment to impose the death penalty on a juvenile who was over the age of 16 at the time he or she committed a capital offense?

HOLDING

No. Sentencing a juvenile defendant who is over the age of 16 to death for a capital offense is neither cruel or unusual and, therefore, is not prohibited by the Eighth Amendment.

RATIONALE

Both consolidated cases argued that the death sentence for a juvenile is contrary to the "evolving standards of decency that mark the progress of a maturing society" (*Trop v. Dulles*, 356 U.S. 86 (1958)). To determine what standards have evolved, the Court must look to American society's conception of decency, not just to the judge's own subjective opinions. The Eighth Amendment prohibits only those punishments that are both cruel and unusual. At the time of this decision, of the 37 states with capital punishment laws, 15 did not allow death to be imposed on 16-year-olds and 12 did

STANFORD v. KENTUCKY (cont.)

not allow it to be imposed on 17-year-olds. There was and is no national consensus on this issue. *Stanford* and *Wilkins* next argued that society does not approve of capital punishment for 16- and 17-year-old offenders. Although few juveniles are sentenced to death, their argument supports the argument that juries and judges believe death should rarely be imposed on a juvenile, not that it should never be imposed. Just because 18 has been set by states as the legal age for engaging in various activities does not mean it is the appropriate age in the context of sentencing a convicted capital murderer to a death sentence. Those laws reflect a social judgment that most juveniles are not mature enough to engage in those activities until the age of 18, not that any particular juvenile is not mature enough. Capital sentencing, however, is not about juveniles; it is about a particular juvenile and a particular set of circumstances. The law of capital sentencing requires a particularized decision. One of the mitigating factors that sentencers must consider in many states is the age of the defendant. The judges who certified the juveniles in these two cases to adult court were also required to consider the particulars of the juveniles' backgrounds and maturity levels in making the transfer decisions. Finally, the Court rejected the argument that capital punishment for juveniles fails to deter juveniles who are less developed cognitively than adults and less likely to fear death. The Court concluded there was insufficient socioscientific evidence to support these claims.

CASE EXCERPT

"The battle must be fought, then, on the field of the Eighth Amendment; and in that struggle socioscientific, ethicoscientific, or even purely scientific evidence is not an available weapon. The punishment is either 'cruel and unusual' (i.e., society has set its face against it) or it is not. The audience, in other words, is not this Court but the citizenry of the United States. It is they, not we, who must be persuaded."

CASE SIGNIFICANCE

This 5–4 decision came one year after the Supreme Court decided *Thompson v. Oklahoma*, 487 U.S. 815 (1988)., in which the Court held that it violated the Constitution to execute a convicted murderer who was 15 years old at the time of his offense. Executing juvenile offenders convicted of capital crimes remained an important issue as the juvenile violent crime rate

escalated in the 1990s and many states passed legislation making it easier to certify youths to the adult system. The execution of youths under the age of 18 became a lightning rod for public debate. The Supreme Court revisited the issue and reversed its decision in *Stanford v. Kentucky* in the 2005 case *Roper v. Simmons*, 543 U.S. 551 (2005).

PAYNE v. TENNESEE
501 U.S. 808 (1991)

FACTS

Pervis Tyrone Payne was convicted of murdering 28-year-old Charisse Christopher and her two-year-old daughter and sentenced to death. He was also sentenced to 30 years in prison for assaulting Christopher's three-year-old son with the intent to commit murder. During the sentencing phase of his trial, Payne presented the testimony of four witnesses: his mother and father, who testified their son had no prior criminal record, had never been arrested, and had no drug abuse history; a friend who met Payne at church and testified Payne was a caring person who treated her three children very well; and a psychologist who testified that based on Payne's low score on an IQ test, he was mentally handicapped but was neither psychotic or schizophrenic. The state presented testimony from Charisse Christopher's mother, who described how the murder of her daughter and granddaughter affected her life. During his closing argument, the prosecutor commented on the continuing effect of their deaths on Christopher's three-year-old son who was assaulted and witnessed the murders and the pain experienced by the rest of the family. The Tennessee Supreme Court rejected Payne's argument on appeal in which he argued that the admission of Christopher's mother's testimony and the prosecutor's comments during his closing argument prejudiced his case in violation of the Eighth Amendment as applied in two previous Supreme Court decisions: *Booth v. Maryland*, 482 U.S. 496 (1987) and *South Carolina v. Gathers*, 490 U.S. 805 (1989). In *Booth*, a 5–4 decision, the Court held that the Eighth Amendment prohibits a jury from considering a victim impact statement at the sentencing phase of a capital trial. The Court was clear that the admissibility of a victim impact statement was not to be decided on a case-by-case basis, but that such evidence was per se inadmissible except if and when it related directly to the circumstances of the crime. Two years later in the *Gathers* case (also a 5–4 decision), the Court extended the *Booth* decision and held a prosecutor is not permitted to comment to the sentencing jury about the personal qualities of the victim.

ISSUE

Does the Eighth Amendment bar the admission of victim impact evidence during the penalty phase of a capital trial?

HOLDING

No. The Constitution does not prohibit a state from permitting the admission of victim impact evidence and allowing the prosecutor to comment about the subject. A state may conclude that such evidence about the victim and the impact the murder had on the victim's family is relevant to the jury's decision on the death penalty.

RATIONALE

In both *Booth* and *Gathers*, the Court was concerned that the decision to impose death should be made by a jury based on an individualized determination about the defendant's character and the circumstances of the crime. Evidence about factors unrelated to the defendant's personal responsibility and moral guilt were found to be irrelevant. Victim impact evidence does not address the blameworthiness of the defendant. Information about the victim and his or her family could easily distract a jury from determining whether death was appropriate in light of the defendant's background and the details of the particular crime. Prior to *Payne*, the Court was also concerned that juries might conclude that defendants whose victims were considered assets to their communities would be more likely to receive a death sentence than defendants whose victims were not considered to be important or sympathetic. In contrast to the previous Courts that addressed this issue, the *Payne* Court was concerned with making sure the state has the ability to offer evidence during sentencing to counteract the mitigating evidence a defendant may introduce. Defendants are free to introduce mitigating evidence with few restrictions. Victim impact evidence is designed to show the uniqueness of each victim whose death represents a special loss to society and the victim's family.

CASE EXCERPT

The Supreme Court majority opinion quoted the Tennessee Supreme Court's opinion in this case: "It is

an affront to the civilized members of the human race to say that at sentencing in a capital case, a parade of witnesses may praise the background, character and good deeds of Defendant (as was done in this case), without limitation as to relevancy, but nothing may be said that bears upon the character of, or the harm impose, upon the victims."

CASE SIGNIFICANCE

This case, decided 6–3, is significant because in a rare move it overruled two cases that had been decided only four and two years previously. The Court's majority opinion commented that "...*Booth* deprives the State of the full moral force of its evidence and may prevent the jury from having before it all the information necessary to determine the proper punishment for a first-degree murder." This decision reflects a more conservative Supreme Court. Justice Marshall's dissent noted that "neither the law nor the facts supporting *Booth* and *Gathers* underwent any change in the last four years. Only the personnel of this Court did." This case is also significant because the range of evidence that prosecutors can introduce during the sentencing phase of a capital murder trial grew significantly with this decision. It allows prosecutors to introduce evidence about victims and the impact their deaths have on their loved ones and their communities. Prosecutors can now use sympathy for a victim and his or her family when they argue in favor of death.

HERRERA v. COLLINS
506 U.S. 390 (1993)

FACTS

Lionel Torres Herrera was convicted of the murders of two police officers and sentenced to death. Herrera pleaded guilty to murdering the second officer six months after he was convicted of the first officer's killing. He was unsuccessful in seeking postconviction relief in both state and federal courts. Ten years after his convictions, Herrera filed his second habeas corpus petition in federal court in which he alleged that he was actually innocent of the murders and that his execution would violate the Eighth Amendment's prohibition against cruel and unusual punishment and the due process clause of the Fourteenth Amendment. In support of his claim he submitted three affidavits from affiants who stated that the Herrera's now dead brother told them he had killed both officers, and an affidavit

HERRERA v. COLLINS *(cont.)*

from the deceased brother's son, who was nine years old at the time of the killings, stating that he had witnessed his father shoot the police officers. The federal District Court granted the defendant's request for a stay of execution so that his claim of innocence could be presented to the state court. The Fifth Circuit Court of Appeals, however, vacated the stay on the grounds that the existence of newly discovered evidence relevant to the guilt of a state prisoner was not a ground for federal habeas corpus relief.

ISSUE

Is federal habeas corpus relief available to a defendant on the basis of newly discovered evidence of actual innocence after the defendant has been convicted?

HOLDING

No. Claims of actual innocence based on newly discovered evidence are not sufficient to entitle a defendant to federal habeas corpus relief from a death sentence.

RATIONALE

Writing for the majority, Chief Justice Rehnquist found that the defendant's constitutional claim based on newly discovered evidence of innocence must be evaluated in light of the previous ten years of proceedings. Where it can be shown a defendant was afforded a fair trial that led to his conviction, the constitutional presumption of innocence disappears. Federal habeas corpus relief is not designed to correct errors of fact. It is meant to make certain that people are not convicted in violation of the Constitution. Claims of actual innocence do not state a ground for federal habeas relief, absent an independent constitutional violation that occurred during the course of the state criminal proceeding. Herrera did not seek relief from a procedural error so he could bring an independent claim that challenged either his conviction or sentence. He argued only that there was new evidence that entitled him to habeas relief. Rehnquist argued that to allow Herrera federal habeas relief based on new evidence would require a new trial ten years after the first one, not because of a constitutional violation at the first trial but simply because of a belief that the newly discovered evidence might persuade a jury to find him not guilty. The Majority opinion emphasized that Herrera could still file a request for executive clemency under Texas state law on the grounds of actual innocence.

CASE EXCERPT

"At the conclusion of his trial, the jury found [him] guilty beyond a reasonable doubt. [The defendant] does not appear before us as an innocent man on the verge of execution. He is instead a legally guilty one who, refusing to accept the jury's verdict, demands a hearing in which to have his culpability determined once again."

CASE SIGNIFICANCE

This case makes clear that federal habeas corpus relief is only available if a prisoner alleges there was a procedural violation of constitutional proportions in his case. Claims of innocence based on newly discovered evidence deal with factual errors, not errors that occurred in the trial of a case. Prisoners alleging factual errors must look to some other mechanism, such as a state's clemency process, to gain relief. In this 6–3 decision, Judge Rehnquist wrote the majority opinion. Although Justice O'Connor concurred, in her opinion (joined by Justice Kennedy) she underscored her belief that Herrera was not actually innocent. O'Connor detailed all the evidence that had led to Herrera' conviction and the newly discovered evidence he hoped would prove his innocence. She questioned the credibility of the newly discovered evidence and compared it to the evidence that led to Herrera's conviction. In his concurring opinion, Justice White indicated that while he believed Herrera's claim was not precluded from review by a federal court, Herrera had failed to make a minimal showing that he was entitled to a review.

SIMMONS v. SOUTH CAROLINA
512 U.S. 154 (1994)

FACTS

Jonathan Simmons was convicted of the murder of an elderly woman. Simmons had previously pleaded guilty to first degree burglary and criminal sexual assault. Under South Carolina law, those convictions for violent offenses made him ineligible for parole if he was convicted of another violent crime. Prior to jury selection, the trial judge granted the prosecution's motion to bar the defense from mentioning parole during voir dire and, specifically, from asking jurors whether they understood what is meant by a life sentence under state law. During the penalty phase of the trial, the prosecutor argued Simmons was a future danger to society and urged the jury to consider that when they decided whether he should be sentenced to death or life imprisonment. The judge refused to instruct the jury that Simmons was ineligible for parole. During deliberations, the jury inquired whether a sentence of life imprisonment allowed for parole. The judge told the jury not to consider parole in its deliberations.

ISSUE

Does the Fourteenth Amendment's due process clause require a jury in a capital case where the defendant's future dangerousness is at issue and the only sentencing alternative is life without parole, to be informed of the defendant's ineligibility for parole?

HOLDING

Yes. The due process clause requires that in a death penalty case when the prosecution argues future dangerousness as an issue and by law the defendant is not eligible for parole, the jury must be informed that a life sentence will be a lifetime of incarceration.

RATIONALE

Three times during the course of his client's trial, Simmons's counsel attempted to inform the jury that his client would not be eligible for parole under state law, and the judge refused his motions all three times. The state repeatedly suggested that Simmons would pose a future danger to society if he was not executed. Writing for the Court, Justice Blackmun stated that it was reasonable to conclude that the jury may have believed that if Simmons were sentenced to life, he might someday be released on parole. The jury thus was presented with the false choice between sentencing Simmons to death or to a life sentence that might result in his eventual release. As a result, the state secured a death sentence. The Supreme Court concluded the due process clause was violated because a person cannot be executed based on information he has no opportunity to deny or explain.

CASE EXCERPT

"The State may not create a false dilemma by advancing generalized arguments regarding the defendant's future dangerousness while, at the same time, preventing the jury from learning that the defendant never will be released on parole."

CASE SIGNIFICANCE

As more states create "life without parole" sentences, this decision will significantly impact how juries are instructed during the sentencing phase of capital trials. A jury may conclude the defendant's future dangerousness is not at issue because he will be incarcerated for life and choose not to impose death. The Supreme Court has decided several interesting cases involving the application of *Simmons*. In 2001, the U.S. Supreme Court decided *Shafer v. South Carolina*, 532 U.S. 36, which involved the new death penalty legislation that the South Carolina legislature passed in 1996, after *Simmons* had been decided. According to that law, capital jurors at the sentencing phase were to decide first whether the state had proved beyond a reasonable doubt the existence of any statutory aggravating factors; if the jury failed to agree unanimously on the presence of a statutory aggravator, the judge was to sentence the convicted capital murderer to either life in prison or a minimum 30-year term; and if the jury unanimously found a statutory aggravator, the jury was to recommend either death or a life term without the possibility of parole. Shafer was convicted of capital murder. The trial judge refused to find that Shafer's future dangerousness was not at issue. Because of that finding, he refused to instruct the jury that a life sentence has no possibility of parole. He also refused to allow defense counsel to argue during his closing statement that a life sentence in South Carolina carried no possibility of parole. When the jury asked the judge during deliberations if someone convicted of capital murder would be eligible for parole, the judge responded that parole eligibility was not part of the jury's consideration. The judge did inform the jury that life imprisonment means until the death of the inmate. The jury found a statutory aggravating circumstance and recommended death. On appeal, the South Carolina Supreme Court did not address whether Shafer's future dangerousness was an issue. Instead, the court reasoned that the precedent established in the *Simmons* case did not apply to Shafer because according to the 1996 statute there was a potential alternative—a mandatory minimum of 30 years—to death or life without parole. In essence, the state Supreme Court ruled that *Simmons v. South Carolina* no longer constrained capital punishment sentencing in the state. On appeal, the US Supreme Court relied on the due process clause and overturned the state court. It ruled that even under the new 1996 South Carolina death penalty statute, when future dangerousness is an issue, the jury must be informed a life sentence in that state does not allow for the possibility of parole. The Court also concluded the judge's comments that life imprisonment meant the inmate will die in prison was not sufficient. The Supreme Court was particularly concerned that life without parole statutes are a recent development about which jurors may not be aware. In 2002, the Supreme Court decided *Kelly v. South Carolina*, 534 U.S. 246. Kelly was convicted of murder. Under the 1996 South Carolina statute, his jury was asked to determine if there were any aggravating factors and, if so, recommend a death sentence or life in prison. At the sentencing hearing, the prosecutor presented evidence of a homemade knife that Kelly made in prison and an escape attempt in which he had participated. The prosecutor cross-examined a psychologist about Kelly's sadism and his desire to kill anyone who irritated him. In his closing arguments, the prosecutor described Kelly as "dangerous." Because future dangerousness was an issue, defense counsel asked the judge to instruct the jury that Kelly would be ineligible for parole if he received a life sentence. The judge, however, refused stating that the state's evidence went to Kelly's character, not to his potential for future dangerousness. The jury recommended death. The South Carolina Supreme Court affirmed. The US Supreme Court reversed and remanded, holding that evidence of future dangerousness is evidence with a tendency to prove dangerousness in the future. Even though the prosecutor's comments were directed toward retribution, they were nonetheless arguments that Kelly would be a future danger.

JONES v. UNITED STATES

527 U.S. 373 (1999)

FACTS

In 1995, Louis Jones forcibly abducted Private McBride at gunpoint from Goodfellow Air Force Base in San Angelo, Texas. He sexually assaulted and killed her, leaving her body under a bridge 20 miles outside of San Angelo. He was convicted of capital murder. Jones was sentenced under the 1994 Federal Death Penalty Act (FDPA), which incorporates a complex procedure for determining whether a convicted capital murderer should be punished by death. The act requires that after the defendant is convicted, the jury must respond sequentially to three questions, and imposition of the death penalty requires unanimity on each of the three.

First, the jury determines whether there was a killing or death resulting from the defendant's intentional engagement in life-threatening activities. Second, the jury decides which of the government-imposed aggravating factors, statutory and nonstatutory, were proved beyond a reasonable doubt. Third, if the jury finds at least one aggravating factor, it then determines whether the aggravating factors sufficiently outweigh the mitigating factors to warrant death, or, absent mitigating factors, whether the aggravating factors alone warrant death. The mitigating factors are individually determined by each juror. Unlike aggravating factors, which must be agreed to unanimously beyond a reasonable doubt, a mitigating factor may be considered in the jury's weighing process if any one juror finds the factor proved by a preponderance of the evidence. Under the FDPA, the decision to impose death must be unanimous and the court is required to impose death if the jury recommends it. During Jones's sentencing hearing, the federal District Court provided the jury with four forms on which to record its sentencing decision. Jones requested the jury be instructed that it must sentence him to life without the possibility of parole rather than death if any one of them was not persuaded that justice demands his execution. He also requested an instruction telling the jury that if it was unable to agree on a unanimous decision as to the sentence, the jury should inform the judge, who would then impose a sentence of life imprisonment without release. Jones requested that instruction because he was concerned that jurors would vote for death rather than hold out if they thought the court could impose a sentence less than life in the event of a deadlock. The judge refused and instructed the jury that it could recommend death, life without the possibility of parole, or a lesser sentence, in which event the court would decide what the lesser sentence would be. The jury recommended death. After interviewing members of the jury, Jones moved for a new trial on grounds the court's instructions misled the jury. Specifically, the charge allowed the jurors to believe that a deadlock would result in a court-imposed lesser sentence. To avoid that, he argued, the jurors who favored life imprisonment changed their votes to death. The trial court denied his motion and the Fifth Circuit Court of Appeals affirmed his death sentence. It ruled that the District Court correctly refused to instruct the jury that a deadlock would result in a court-imposed life sentence. Jury deadlock under the FDPA would not occasion a life sentence, opined the Fifth Circuit; instead a deadlock would necessitate a second sentencing hearing before a new jury. The appeals court held that despite what jurors stated in interviews, the jury instructions could not have led a reasonable jury to conclude that a nonunanimous verdict would result in a lesser sentence.

ISSUE

Does the Eighth Amendment require a jury be instructed as to the consequences of a deadlock while deliberating on sentencing in a capital case?

HOLDING

No. An accused facing a possible death sentence is not entitled under the Eighth Amendment to an instruction to the jury as to the effect of a sentencing jury deadlock.

RATIONALE

The Supreme Court first decided that the Fifth Circuit's construction of the FDPA was incorrect. The Court concluded that if the jury does not reach a unanimous verdict, the FDPA does not require a new jury for purposes of considering sentencing. If a jury cannot reach a unanimous sentencing decision, the duty of sentencing falls on the District Court. The Supreme Court concluded the Eighth Amendment does not require that the jury be instructed as to the consequences of its failure to agree on a sentence. Jones's proposed instruction had no bearing on the role of the jury in the sentencing phase of a capital case. The objective of the jury system is to secure unanimity through discussion and argumentation. The government has a strong interest in having the jury express the conscience of the community. A jury instruction like the one Jones proposed might undermine both of those interests. Finally, the Court noted that when Congress drafted the FDPA, it did not require that such an instruction be provided to the jury.

CASE EXCERPT

"The truth of the matter is that the proposed instruction has no bearing on the jury's role in the sentencing process. Rather, it speaks to what happens in the event that the jury is unable to fulfill its role—when deliberations break down and the jury is unable to produce a unanimous sentence recommendation. Petitioner's argument, although less than clear, appears to be that a death sentence is arbitrary within the meaning of the Eighth Amendment if the jury is not given any bit of information that might possibly influence an individual juror's voting behavior. That contention has no merit."

CASE SIGNIFICANCE

This was the first case before the Supreme Court involving the Federal Death Penalty Act of 1994. The FDPA created a complicated sentencing process and the *Jones* decision was an important opportunity for the Court to clarify some of its provisions. Federal death penalty legislation has been in force since 1790. Mandatory death penalties were part of the federal legislation until 1897, when Congress eliminated all mandatory federal death penalties, making such decisions entirely discretionary. The 1897 legislation also abolished the federal death penalty for all but five federal crimes. Between 1927 and 1963, the federal government executed only 34 persons. Following *Furman v. Georgia*, 408 U.S. 238 (1972), Congress did not revise the federal death penalty statute to establish sentencing procedures that met the *Furman* requirements. In 1988, Congress enacted death penalty procedures for certain violations of the continuing criminal enterprise statute, modeling the legislation after the death penalty state statutes that had been passed post-*Furman*. The Supreme Court upheld those procedures as constitutional in 1993. Congress created the first generalized federal death penalty procedures in 1994 in the FDPA. The procedures are similar to those provided for in the continuing criminal enterprise statute and extend to over 40 federal offenses. The FDPA's procedures apply to any federal offense that can lead to the death penalty. The *Jones* case spotlights a concern that has surfaced in other Supreme Court decisions—the adequacy of jury instructions in capital cases and the need for juries to correctly understand the sentencing options from which they may choose. In *Simmons v. South Carolina*, 512 U.S. 154 (1994) the concern was that jurors be informed that a life sentence in South Carolina for capital murder excludes the possibility of parole. The Court concluded that concealing that information from jurors could cause a jury to make a false choice between death and a limited life sentence. A similar argument was made in the *Jones* case; however, the Court split 5–4 in affirming Jones's sentence, ruling that such an instruction was not required.

ATKINS v. VIRGINIA
536 U.S. 304 (2002)

FACTS

Daryl Renard Atkins was convicted of abduction, armed robbery, and capital murder. During the sentencing phase of his case, the defense called Dr. Nelson, a forensic psychologist, who testified that Atkins was mildly mentally retarded. Intelligence tests indicted that Atkins had a full IQ of 59. The jury sentenced him to death, but the Virginia Supreme Court ordered a second sentencing hearing because the trial court had used a misleading verdict form. At the second sentencing hearing, Nelson testified again. This time the state had a rebuttal witness, Dr. Samuel Samenow, who testified that in his opinion Daryl Atkins was not mentally retarded. The second jury also sentenced Atkins to death. The Virginia Supreme Court affirmed the sentence, relying on the US Supreme Court's decision in *Penry v. Lynaugh*, 492 U.S. 302 (1989), in which the Court held that the Constitution does not prohibit the execution of a mentally retarded person.

ISSUE

Are executions of mentally retarded offenders who have been convicted of capital murder prohibited by the Constitution?

HOLDING

Yes. Executing mentally retarded convicted capital murderers violates the Eighth Amendment's prohibition against cruel and unusual punishment.

RATIONALE

The Eighth Amendment specifically prohibits excessive sanctions. Punishment should be graduated and in proportion to the offense. To judge whether a particular punishment is excessive the Court must consider current standards rather than the standards in place at the time the Eighth Amendment was adopted. As the Court noted in *Trop v. Dulles*, 356 U.S. 86 (1958), the amendment draws its meaning from "the evolving standards of decency that mark the progress of a maturing society." The Court has also recognized that the clearest and most reliable objective evidence of current standards is found in legislation. In addition, the Constitution requires the Supreme Court exercise its own judgment and ask whether there is reason to agree or disagree with the judgment of the legislators. When the *Penry* case was decided in 1989, only two states that allowed for capital punishment prohibited executing mentally retarded capital offenders (Georgia and Maryland), which caused the High Court to conclude there was insufficient objective evidence of a national consensus against executing the mentally retarded. Much has changed since then. Since 1990, Kentucky, Tennessee, New Mexico, Arkansas, Colorado, Washington, Indiana, Kansas, New York, Nebraska, South Dakota, Arizona, Connecticut, Florida, North Carolina, and the federal government have enacted laws that prohibit executing the mentally retarded. Other states have considered such legislation. The Court concluded there is no reason for it to disagree with the growing consensus. There are serious questions about whether the justifications for the death penalty, deterrence and retribution, apply to mentally retarded offenders. For retribution, the offender's culpability is key. If mentally retarded offenders have lesser culpability, there is no justification for such a harsh form of retribution. The same impairments that make mentally retarded offenders less culpable also make it less probable that they can evaluate the possibility of being executed and control their conduct based on that information. A possible death sentence does not function as a deterrent. Exempting the mentally retarded from a death sentence will not lessen the penalty's deterrent impact on other offenders. Finally, the Court expressed concern that mentally retarded offenders face a high risk of wrongful execution because they are more prone to confess to crimes they did not commit, are less able to assist their counsel in preparing their defense, and are often poor witnesses with courtroom demeanors that may give the impression they are not remorseful.

CASE EXCERPT

"It is not so much the number of these States that is significant, but the consistency of the direction of change. Given the well-known fact that anticrime legislation is far more popular than legislation providing protections for persons guilty of violent crime, the large number of States prohibiting the execution of mentally retarded persons (and the complete absence of States passing legislation reinstating the power to conduct such executions) provides powerful evidence that today our society views mentally retarded offenders as categorically less culpable than the average criminal. The evidence carries even greater force when it is noted that the legislatures that have addressed the issue have voted overwhelmingly in favor of the prohibition."

CASE SIGNIFICANCE

This is a highly significant case. Just 13 years before this decision, the Supreme Court decided it was not unconstitutional to execute a mentally retarded capital murderer, although the Court also ruled in *Penry* that if the defense requests it, the jury should be instructed to consider mental retardation as a mitigating circumstance when making a sentencing decision. *Atkins* is a rare instance where the Supreme Court has reversed one of its earlier cases. The *Penry v. Lynaugh* case was very controversial when it was decided in 1989, and it became a focal point for groups that oppose capital punishment. Although John Paul Penry did not convince the Court in 1989 that the death sentence was unconstitutional for mentally retarded offenders, he actually won his case on other matters having to do with the way juries reach a death penalty verdict in Texas, where he was convicted. During the same week in 2002 in which the Supreme Court handed down *Atkins v. Virginia*, John Paul Penry was in a Texas trial court facing his third sentencing hearing for the capital murder he had been convicted of in 1980. Without a set of procedures from the state legislature on when and how to determine whether a capital defendant is mentally retarded, the trial judge developed a jury instruction. The jury concluded that Penry was not mentally retarded and sentenced him to die. Importantly, the Court stated in *Atkins* that it is up to the states to develop appropriate methods to enforce its holding. State legislatures must devise procedures for determining if a capital murder defendant is mentally retarded. There were three dissents to the majority opinion. Justices Rehnquist, Scalia, and Thomas opined that the majority's conclusion that there is a growing consensus against executing mentally retarded offenders is a rationalization for the majority's preference rather than an effort to determine the content of an evolving standard of decency. Chief Justice Rehnquist wrote a separate dissenting opinion in which he criticized the Court relying on evidence of foreign laws, the views of professional and religious organizations, and opinion polls that oppose executing the mentally retarded offender. In

Rehnquist's view such information is not relevant. The only relevant evidence is legislation and the practices of sentencing juries in the United States.

RING v. ARIZONA
536 U.S. 584 (2002)

FACTS

At Timothy Ring's trial for murder, armed robbery, and related charges, the judge instructed the jury on alternative charges of premeditated murder and felony murder. The jury deadlocked on premeditated murder, but convicted Ring of a felony murder occurring during the commission of an armed robbery. Under Arizona law, Ring could not be sentenced to death unless further findings were made. According to the statute, the death sentence could be imposed only if the judge found at least one statutorily enumerated aggravating circumstance and no mitigating circumstances sufficient to call for leniency. The trial judge conducted a separate sentencing hearing to determine if any aggravating or mitigating circumstances existed. Based on evidence presented at the sentencing hearing, the judge concluded that Ring was the killer and a major participant in an armed robbery. He found two aggravating factors: Ring committed the offense for pecuniary gain and the offense was especially heinous, cruel, or depraved. The only mitigating factor was that Ring had a minimal criminal history. The judge concluded, however, that this mitigating circumstance did not call for leniency. The judge sentenced Ring to death. On appeal to the State Supreme Court, Ring argued that Arizona's statute violated the Sixth Amendment because it required the judge to make a fact finding that permitted his punishment to be raised to the death penalty. The Arizona High Court upheld Ring's death sentence but noted its concern. Because the US Supreme Court upheld the Arizona death penalty statute in *Walton v. Arizona*, 497 U.S. 639 (1990) and stated in *Apprendi v. New Jersey*, 530 U.S. 466 (2000) that *Walton* remained good law, the Arizona Court felt bound to apply *Walton* and rejected Ring's constitutional attack on the state's sentencing system.

ISSUE

Does a capital sentencing statute that requires the judge to find the existence of an aggravating circumstance

RING v. ARIZONA *(cont.)*

necessary for the imposition of the death sentence violate the Constitution?

HOLDING

No. The Sixth Amendment requires that a jury determine all of the facts that must be established before a death sentence can be imposed, including aggravating circumstances that, if found, allow for the imposition of a death sentence.

RATIONALE

In *Walton v. Arizona*, 497 U.S. 639 (1990), the Supreme Court decided that the Sixth Amendment right to a jury trial does not require that the jury specify the aggravating factors that permit the death penalty to be imposed. The Court ruled the Constitution does not require a jury impose the death sentence or make the factfindings that are a prerequisite for that sentence. Under Arizona law, the aggravating factors were not elements of the offense, rather they were sentencing considerations that guided the judge's choice between life and death. In *Apprendi v. New Jersey*, 530 U.S. 466 (2000), the defendant had been convicted of a second-degree possession of a firearm with a maximum penalty of ten years. The judge found by a preponderance of the evidence that Apprendi's crime had been motivated by racial animus. That finding triggered the New Jersey hate crime enhancement statute and doubled Apprendi's maximum sentence. The Supreme Court held that Apprendi's sentence violated his right to have a jury determine he is guilty of every element of the crime beyond a reasonable doubt. That right included the hate crime aggravating circumstance. The Court reasoned if a law allows a defendant's authorized punishment to be increased contingent on the finding of a fact, that fact must be found by a jury beyond a reasonable doubt. The majority opinion in *Apprendi* stated that *Walton* could be reconciled with *Apprendi*. The key distinction was that a first-degree murder conviction in Arizona carried a maximum penalty of death. Once the jury finds a defendant guilty of the elements of an offense that carries the maximum penalty of death, it may be left to the judge to decide whether death or a lesser punishment should be imposed. The *Ring* Court, in a 7–2 decision, concluded that the *Walton* and *Apprendi* decisions were irreconcilable and overruled *Walton* to the extent it allows a sentencing judge, without a jury, to find aggravating factors necessary to impose a death sentence. The trial judge's finding of

aggravated circumstances in Ring's case exposed him to a greater punishment than what was authorized by the jury's guilty verdict. The Supreme Court decided there are no reasons why capital defendants should be exempted from the constitutional protections of the Sixth Amendment.

CASE EXCERPT

Justice Scalia in his concurrence said that "my observing over the last 12 years the accelerating propensity of both state and federal legislatures to adopt 'sentencing factors' determined by judges that increase punishment beyond what is authorized by the jury's verdict, and my witnessing the belief of a near majority of my colleagues that this novel practice is perfectly OK...cause me to believe that our people's traditional belief in the right of trial by jury is in perilous decline. That decline is bound to be confirmed, and indeed accelerated by the repeated spectacle of a man's going to his death because a judge found that an aggravating factor existed. We cannot preserve our veneration for the protection of the jury in criminal cases if we render ourselves callous to the need for that protection by regularly imposing the death penalty without it."

CASE SIGNIFICANCE

This case is significant because the Court reversed its holding in *Walton v. Arizona*, decided only 12 years earlier. The majority opinion stated that although the *stare decisis* doctrine is fundamentally important to the rule of law, the Court's precedents are not sacrosanct, and prior decisions have been overruled when it was necessary. The Court held that *Walton* and *Apprendi* were irreconcilable and overruled *Walton* to the extent that it allows a sentencing judge, without a jury, to find an aggravating circumstance necessary for imposing the death penalty.

ROPER v. SIMMONS
543 U.S. 551 (2005)

FACTS

Christopher Simmons, a junior in high school, was charged with burglary, kidnapping, stealing, and murder in the first degree for crimes he committed when he was 17 years old. Simmons proposed to commit burglary and murder by breaking and entering, tying up a victim, and throwing the victim off a bridge. He told the companions who joined him that they could "get away with it" because they were minors. Simmons was tried as an adult for capital murder and sentenced to death about nine months later when he was 18. He had no prior criminal history. The Missouri Supreme Court affirmed his death sentence. Simmons petition for federal habeas corpus relief was denied. After the proceedings in his case had run their course, the US Supreme Court held that the Eighth Amendment prohibits the execution of a mentally retarded person in *Atkins* v. *Virginia,* 536 U.S. 304 (2002). Simmons filed a new petition for state postconviction relief, arguing that *Atkins* establishes that the Constitution prohibits executing a juvenile who was under 18 when the crime was committed. The Missouri Supreme Court agreed. The US Supreme Court granted certiorari.

ISSUE
Does the cruel and unusual punishment clause of the Eighth Amendment prohibit the execution of minors?

HOLDING
Yes. The cruel and unusual punishment clause prohibits the execution of offenders who were under the age of 18 when they committed their crime.

RATIONALE
In *Thompson* v. *Oklahoma,* 487 U.S. 815 (1988), the Court ruled that our standards of decency do not permit the execution of an offender under the age of 16 at the time of the crime. The next year, however, in *Stanford* v. *Kentucky,* 492 U.S. 361 (1989), the Court referred to contemporary standards of decency and ruled that the Eighth Amendment does not prohibit the execution of juvenile offenders over 15 but under eighteen. That same day, the Court also held that the Eighth Amendment does not prohibit imposing the death penalty on a mentally retarded murderer in *Penry* v. *Lynaugh,* 492 U.S. 301 (1989). In both *Stanford* and *Penry,* the Court determined there was insufficient evidence of a national consensus in favor of such prohibitions. The Court reasoned that just as the *Atkins* Court reconsidered the issue decided in *Penry,* it had now to reconsider the issue decided in *Stanford.* The data shows that 30 states prohibit the juvenile death penalty. Twelve states reject the death penalty altogether. Eighteen states that maintain it have provisions or judicial interpretations that exclude juveniles. In the 20 states that do not prohibit executing juveniles, the practice is infrequent. The five Justices in

the majority ruled that our standards of decency have evolved to the point that executing minors is prohibited by the Eighth Amendment. The Court also discussed the susceptibility of juveniles to immature and irresponsible behavior and their diminished culpability, making retribution and deterrence inadequate justifications for the death penalty.

CASE EXCERPT
"The number of States that have abandoned capital punishment for juvenile offenders since *Stanford* is smaller than the number of States that abandoned capital punishment for the mentally retarded after *Penry;* yet we think the same consistency of direction of change has been demonstrated."

CASE SIGNIFICANCE
The Court took the opportunity, once again, to narrow the reach of the death penalty. As the Court did in *Atkins v. Virginia* (2002) with respect to mentally retarded murderers, it did not hesitate to reverse its previous precedent that allowed minors between the ages of 16 and 18 to be sentenced to death. In its decision the Court also pointed to international opinion against the death penalty for minors. In their dissents, both Justices O'Connor and Scalia questioned whether there was strong enough evidence that a national consensus had formed opposing capital punishment for minors. Justice Scalia was especially critical of the majority citing international opinion as evidence that executing minors cannot be supported by the Constitution.

ROMPILLA v. BEARD
545 U.S. 374 (2005)

FACTS
Rompilla was found guilty of murdering James Scanlon, stabbing him and then setting his body on fire. The state sought the death penalty, and two public defenders were assigned to Rompilla's case. During the sentencing phase, the state offered evidence to prove three aggravating factors to justify a death sentence: (1) it was a felony murder, (2) it was a murder committed by torture, and (3) Rompilla had a significant history of felony convictions indicating the threat to use violence. The jury found all three aggravating factors existed. In mitigation, Rompilla's attorneys offered the testimony of family members who asked the jury for mercy. The jury acknowledged the mitigating

ROMPILLA v. BEARD *(cont.)*

factors but assigned greater weight to the aggravating factors and sentenced Rompilla to death. On appeal, Rompilla's lawyers argued ineffective assistance by trial counsel for failing to present significant mitigating evidence about their client's childhood, mental capacity and health, and alcoholism. The Pennsylvania Supreme Court affirmed his conviction. The federal district court granted his writ of habeas corpus and ruled Rompilla's trial attorneys were ineffective during the sentencing phase. A split Third Circuit Court of Appeals reversed and found that trial counsel had conducted a reasonable investigation.

ISSUE

Is defense counsel obligated to make reasonable efforts to obtain and review all material they know a prosecutor will use as evidence to prove an aggravating factor during a sentencing hearing in a capital case?

HOLDING

Yes. Even in cases where a capital defendant's family members and the defendant himself suggest that no mitigating evidence is available, defendant's counsel "is bound to make reasonable efforts to obtain and review material that counsel knows the prosecution will probably rely on as evidence of aggravation at the sentencing phase of the trial."

RATIONALE

Ineffective assistance of counsel is evaluated under *Strickland v. Washington*, 466 U.S. 668 (1984), which requires evidence of (1) counsel's deficient performance, and (2) resulting in prejudice to the defendant's case. The performance must be measured against an "objective standard of reasonableness under prevailing professional norms." Defense counsel did not totally ignore their obligations. Rompilla's help was minimal. His answers to their questions indicated a fairly normal childhood, except for quitting school in the ninth grade. Counsel interviewed family members who did not feel they knew Rompilla well since he had spent a lot of time in custody. Three mental health experts looked at Rompilla's mental state at the time of the offense and his competency to stand trial. Their reports revealed nothing useful to Rompilla's case. Based on the investigation, the attorneys decided to go no further.

Appellate counsel suggested that trial counsel should have investigated Rompilla's school records, along with records of his juvenile and adult incarcerations, and evidence of alcohol dependence. The majority of the Supreme Court concluded that trial counsel's performance was not reasonable. Counsel knew the state intended to seek the death penalty based on aggravating factors, including Rompilla's history of violent felony convictions. They knew the state would introduce a prior rape and assault conviction and a transcript of the testimony of the rape victim at the earlier trial. The records of Rompilla's prior conviction and the victim's testimony were public records. Nevertheless, defense counsel did not review the file or transcript prior to Rompilla's trial.

The Supreme Court concluded that counsel's failure compromised their ability to respond to the prosecution's evidence. Without reviewing the file, defense counsel would not know if the prosecution was quoting selectively from the transcript or whether the victim mentioned extenuating circumstances. The majority denied it established a rigid per se rule that requires defense counsel to review every file on any prior conviction. Considering all the circumstances in this case, counsel failed to make reasonable efforts to review a prior conviction file.

There was evidence that counsel's failure prejudiced Rompilla's case. If counsel had reviewed the file, they would have found mitigation evidence about Rompilla's abusive childhood, dependence on alcohol, suggestions from prison mental health experts that he suffered from schizophrenia and other disorders, and test scores showing a third grade cognition level—all of which might have influenced the jury's decision to assess death.

CASE EXCERPT

"This evidence adds up to a mitigation case that bears no relation to the few naked pleas for mercy actually put before the jury, and although we suppose it is possible that a jury could have heard it all and still have decided on the death penalty, that is not the test."

CASE SIGNIFICANCE

This decision emphasizes again that defense counsel has the responsibility to investigate all evidence that could be introduced in mitigation of the death penalty. Trial counsel who fails to do so can later be found ineffective. Although the majority states that it is not imposing a per se requirement that requires defense attorneys to review every file on prior convictions, failure to investigate potential mitigating evidence can lead to a sentence being an ineffective assistance of counsel defense. The dissent argues that the decision in this case actually does establish a per se rule.

BAZE v. REES
553 U.S. 35 (2008)

FACTS

The Kentucky Supreme Court upheld the convictions and sentences of Ralph Baze and Thomas Bowling, each convicted of two counts of capital murder and sentenced to death. After exhausting their appeals, they sued state officials in state court, arguing that Kentucky's lethal injection protocol was unconstitutional. Kentucky used a four-part injection protocol: valium to relax the offender, sodium pentathol to cause unconsciousness, pavulon to stop breathing, and potassium chloride to put the offender into cardiac arrest and cause death. Baze and Bowling argued that there was a significant risk that the protocol may not be followed properly, resulting in significant pain—cruel and unusual punishment prohibited by the Eighth Amendment. The Kentucky Supreme Court ruled that the state's method of execution was constitutional. The US Supreme Court granted certiorari.

ISSUE

Is Kentucky's lethal injection protocol a violation of the Eighth Amendment's cruel and unusual punishment clause?

HOLDING

No. Kentucky's lethal injection protocol does not violate the cruel and unusual punishment clause of the Eighth Amendment.

RATIONALE

At the time of this decision, thirty-six states and the federal government had adopted lethal injection as the exclusive or primary means of execution. Kentucky replaced electrocution with lethal injection in 1998. Baze and Bowling did not contend that lethal injection itself or the proper administration of a particular protocol adopted by Kentucky violated the Eighth Amendment. They claimed that there was a risk that the procedures would not be properly followed, especially that sodium pentathol would not be administered properly, resulting in severe pain when the other drugs are administered. The Court has recognized that subjecting individuals to future harm under some circumstances can be cruel and unusual punishment, however, the risk must be substantial, an "objectively intolerable risk of harm." The Court concluded that an isolated mistake does not raise an Eighth Amendment violation because such an event, while regrettable, does not amount to cruelty. The Court carefully detailed the Kentucky lethal injection protocol and the efforts made by the state to ensure its proper administration. The risk of improper administration was deemed not so substantial or imminent as to amount to an Eighth Amendment violation.

CASE EXCERPT

"Simply because an execution method may result in pain, either by accident or as an inescapable consequence of death, does not establish the sort of 'objectively intolerable risk of harm' that qualifies as cruel and unusual."

CASE SIGNIFICANCE

In this 7–2 opinion, Justice Roberts' majority opinion was joined by Justices Kennedy and Alito. Justices Scalia and Thomas filed concurring opinions, as did Justice Breyer. Justice John Paul Stevens wrote his own separate concurring opinion supporting the decision but stating for the first time his opposition to the death penalty. He wrote, "in sum, just as Justice White ultimately based his conclusion in *Furman* on his extensive exposure to countless cases for which death is the authorized penalty, I have relied on my own experience in reaching the conclusion that the imposition of the death penalty represents 'the pointless and needless extinction of life with only marginal contributions to any discernible social or public purposes.'"

KENNEDY v. LOUISIANA
554 U.S. 407 (2008)

FACTS

Patrick Kennedy was convicted of the rape of his 8-year-old stepdaughter and sentenced to death under the Louisiana statute, enacted in 1995, that permitted capital punishment for the rape of a child under the age of twelve. Kennedy would have been the first person executed for the crime of rape in Louisiana under the 1995. Louisiana was also in the minority of jurisdictions that authorized death for child rape. Kennedy argued that the punishment was unconstitutional

KENNEDY v. LOUISIANA (cont.)

under the Eighth Amendment because it was disproportionate to the offense. The Supreme Court of Louisiana ruled the statute was constitutional. The US Supreme Court granted certiorari.

ISSUE

Does the death penalty for child rape violate the Eighth Amendment's cruel and unusual punishment clause?

HOLDING

Yes. The Eighth Amendment prohibits the execution of offenders for the crime of child rape.

RATIONALE

The Court found that the death penalty for child rape where the crime did not result or was intended to result in death is unconstitutional because it is disproportionate to the crime. In this 5–4 decision, the majority of Justices reviewed the history of the death penalty for the crime of rape. In *Coker v. Georgia*, 433 U.S. 584 (1977), the Supreme Court ruled that the death penalty for the rape of an adult woman is unconstitutional. The Court then looked at the history of the death penalty for child rape. When this case was decided, thirty-six states and the federal government had the death penalty. Only six of those jurisdictions authorized the death penalty for rape of a child. Though a review of national consensus is not shown simply by adding up the number of states with applicable death penalty laws, it was significant to the Court that in 45 jurisdictions, Kennedy could not be executed for child rape. After reviewing the historical background and the death penalty current statutes, the majority ruled that there is a consensus against the death penalty for child rape. The Court acknowledged the seriousness of the offense, but concluded that based on this consensus and its own independent judgment, a death sentence for one who raped but did not kill a child is unconstitutional.

CASE EXCERPT

"The evidence of a national consensus with respect to the death penalty for child rapists, as with respect to juveniles, mentally retarded offenders, and vicarious felony murderers, shows divided opinion but, on balance, an opinion against it."

CASE SIGNIFICANCE

The Supreme Court narrowed the application of the death penalty once again. The majority relied on the lack of a national consensus supporting capital punishment for the crime of child rape, noting that only six states had enacted such punishments and those laws were quite recently enacted. The majority cited both its decisions in *Roper v. Simmons*, 543 U.S. 551 (2005) and *Atkins v. Virginia*, 536 U.S. 304 (2002), in which it had noted a lack of national consensus for capital punishment for murderers under the age of 18 and those who are mentally retarded.

DISCUSSION QUESTIONS

1. Together, how did the *Furman v. Georgia* and *Gregg v. Georgia* decisions reshape death penalty law in the United States?
2. What about mandatory death sentences violates the US Constitution?
3. Trace the line of cases that address under what circumstances and in what manner a sentencing authority must be able to consider all aspects of a defendant's character or record.
4. What important Supreme Court cases discuss removing a juror who is opposed to the death penalty?
5. Create a scenario where a defendant could be considered a minor accomplice in a capital murder and not eligible for the death penalty and a second scenario where the defendant is a major participant and, therefore, eligible for death. Compare your two scenarios with your fellow classmates. At what point does minor participation escalate into major participation, at what point does the line between the two blur?
6. Create two different scenarios involving victim impact evidence in a capital murder case: one for a sympathetic victim and one for a less sympathetic victim. Decide as a prosecutor how you would or would not use the victim evidence for both scenarios, and how as a defense attorney you might respond to that use or the lack thereof. Consider if victim impact evidence were not admissible, would you expect your chances of winning be different—under either scenario?
7. Survey your classmates about a life without parole statute versus the death penalty. Would they be less willing to impose death if life without parole was an alternative?
8. Discuss the Supreme Court's reasoning in *Atkins v. Virginia* (2002), *Roper v. Simmons* (2005), and *Louisiana v. Kennedy* (2008). Do you agree or

disagree with the Court's decisions in each of those cases? Do you agree or disagree with the Court's rationale for deciding those cases? How does the Court's rationale in those two cases compare with its decision and rationale in *Graham v. Florida* (2010) in the sentencing section of this book?

9. Research the history of different methods of execution in the United States and trace how states, over time, have changed their execution protocols.

Are you convinced there is a humane way to execute a person?

10. Analyze the Court's reasoning in the *McCleskey v. Kemp* (1987) decision in light of what we know from the social science research about discrimination and the death penalty. Does the research suggest that there is discrimination? How should the Supreme Court use or rely on empirical research when it interprets the Constitution?

CHAPTER THREE

ACCESS TO COURTS

EX PARTE HULL, *312 U.S. 546 (1941)*

GRIFFIN v. ILLINOIS, *351 U.S. 12 (1956)*

BURNS v. OHIO, *360 U.S. 252 (1959)*

SMITH v. BENNETT, *365 U.S. 708 (1961)*

JOHNSON v. AVERY, *393 U.S. 483 (1969)*

BOUNDS v. SMITH, *430 U.S. 817 (1977)*

MURRAY v. GIARRATANO, *492 U.S. 1 (1989)*

LEWIS v. CASEY, *518 U.S. 343 (1996)*

SHAW v. MURPHY, *532 U.S. 223 (2001)*

INTRODUCTION

The nine cases presented in this chapter address prisoners' access to the courts. The first case, *Ex parte Hull*, decided in 1941, is the leading case that signaled the beginning of an era of judicial intervention in corrections in the United States. The other cases included in this chapter illustrate how inmate access to the courts has evolved over the years.

The US Supreme Court held in *Ex parte Hull* (1941) that inmates had a right to unrestricted access to federal courts. According to the Court, access to the court system is a basic requirement of due process and thus protected by the due process clause of the Fourteenth Amendment. Without access to courts, inmates would have no legal avenue by which to address their sentences or conditions of confinement and would be no more than "slaves of the state."

Defining what access to the courts includes is an evolving process, exemplified by the other cases in this chapter. Three early cases (*Griffin v. Illinois*, *Burns v. Ohio*, and *Smith v. Bennett*) made sure that adequate and effective appellate review was available for indigent prisoners. A 1989 case (*Murray v. Giarratano*), however, makes clear that states are not required by the Constitution to provide counsel for indigent capital prisoners in postconviction proceedings.

In 1969, the Supreme Court held that a prison regulation which prohibited inmates from assisting other inmates in the preparation of legal materials was unconstitutional if no other reasonable alternatives for inmates to obtain access to the courts were available (*Johnson v. Avery*). This decision resulted in correctional administrators either allowing "jailhouse lawyers" to help other inmates or providing some other form of legal assistance. The Court did not wholeheartedly endorse the concept of inmates providing legal aid to other inmates in this case, noting that inmate law clerks "are sometimes a menace to prison discipline" and that prisoners have an "acknowledged propensity . . . to abuse both the giving and the seeking of assistance" (*Johnson v. Avery*, 393 U.S. 483, 488, 490 (1969)).

Until recently, it was assumed by many lower courts that another decision of the Supreme Court discussed in this chapter, *Bounds v. Smith* (1977), required prison administrators to provide inmates with either law libraries or access to a person with legal training. The 1989 decision in *Murray v. Giarratano* noted that administrators must be given "wide discretion" in providing meaningful access to courts. In 1996, in *Lewis v. Casey*, the Supreme Court clarified its earlier decision in *Bounds*, holding that evidence of inadequacies in the delivery of legal services is not enough to justify remedial judicial action. According to the Court, remedies that address deficiencies in law libraries and access to legal materials are justified only when an inmate's efforts to pursue a legal claim are in fact impaired by these deficiencies.

In the last case presented in this chapter, *Shaw v. Murphy* (2001), the Supreme Court concluded that inmate correspondence containing legal advice does not merit enhanced constitutional protection. The Court observed in part how "[p]risoners have used legal correspondence as a means for passing contraband." This case, as well as the previous cases, illustrates how the broad term "access to the courts" continues to be addressed and defined in corrections law.

EX PARTE HULL
312 U.S. 546 (1941)

FACTS
The petitioner in this case was convicted in January 1936 of a sex offense and sentenced to the Jackson, Michigan state prison indeterminately for six months to ten years. He served ten months before being paroled. While on parole, he committed another sex offense, was convicted, and sentenced to Jackson for two and one-half to five years. At a hearing before the Michigan parole board for violating his parole (due to the second conviction), the sentence for his first offense was changed to the maximum term. The prisoner attempted several times to file a petition for a writ of habeas corpus but was prevented by prison officials from filing. A document describing his attempts to file his petition was filed by the prisoner's father with the clerk of the Supreme Court in December 1940. The Court asked for cause as to why the habeas corpus petition was not granted, and the prisoner warden pointed to a regulation requiring that "'all legal documents, briefs, petitions, motions, habeas corpus proceedings and appeals will first have to be submitted to the institutional welfare office and if favorably acted upon be then referred to Perry A. Maynard, legal investigator to the Parole Board, Lansing, Michigan. Documents submitted to Perry A Maynard, if in his opinion are properly drawn, will be directed to the court designated or will be referred back to the inmate.'" The petitioner then challenged the constitutionality of these regulations as a denial of due process.

ISSUE
This case was a motion for leave to file a petition for writ of habeas corpus, and involved three questions: (1) Is the warden's regulation valid? (2) Is the petition for writ of habeas corpus premature? (3) Is the petition sufficient to necessitate an order requiring the warden to answer?

HOLDING
No, on all three questions. The regulation was determined to be invalid, the petition was not premature, but the Court concluded that the showing made by the petition and exhibits was "insufficient to compel an order requiring the warden to answer."

RATIONALE
The Court acknowledged that the reasons for the prison regulation were not without merit, but the right to petition for a writ of habeas corpus could not be abridged by the state. The Court also ruled that the petition was not premature, but in the end, the Court found the petition to fail to substantiate an order requiring the warden to answer it.

CASE EXCERPT
"The state and its officers may not abridge or impair petitioner's right to apply to a federal court for a writ of habeas corpus. Whether a petition for writ of habeas corpus addressed to a federal court is properly drawn and what allegations it must contain are questions for that court alone to determine."

CASE SIGNIFICANCE
This case is important because this was the first time the Supreme Court dealt with an inmate claim. In it, the Court held that inmates have the right not to have their habeas corpus petitions screened by prison officials, but never identified the source or basis of that right. This was left for subsequent cases.

GRIFFIN v. ILLINOIS
351 U.S. 12 (1956)

FACTS
Griffin and Crenshaw were convicted together of armed robbery in Cook County, Illinois. They moved in trial court, immediately after their conviction, to be provided at no cost with a "certified copy of the entire record, including a stenographic transcript of the proceedings," alleging that "they were 'poor persons with no means of paying the necessary fees to acquire the Transcript and Court Records needed to prosecute an appeal.'" Under Illinois law, certified copies of trial proceedings and the stenographer's transcripts are provided for free only to indigent defendants receiving the death penalty. However, these same records are needed by noncapital defendants filing for direct

GRIFFIN v. ILLINOIS *(cont.)*

appellate review. Griffin and Crenshaw maintained that failure to provide them with these documents freely violated their Fourteenth Amendment due process and equal protection rights. Their motion was denied without a hearing, and they then petitioned under the state Post-Conviction Hearing Act for a free transcript. Only state or federal constitutional questions can be raised under the Post-Conviction Hearing Act, and the petitioners alleged various nonconstitutional errors at trial, which they were prevented from appealing because of their lack of funds to purchase transcripts. This petition was also dismissed, affirmed by the Illinois Supreme Court because the charges raised by Griffin and Crenshaw were not "substantial state or federal constitutional questions."

ISSUE

Did Illinois, by requiring indigent defendants not sentenced to death to pay for trial transcripts when filing for appellate review, violate their due process and equal protection rights under the Fourteenth Amendment?

HOLDING

Yes. Petitioners' constitutional rights were violated.

RATIONALE

The Court maintained that "there is no meaningful distinction between a rule which would deny the poor the right to defend themselves in a trial court and one which effectively denies the poor an adequate appellate review accorded to all who have money enough to pay the costs in advance." While states are not required by the US Constitution to provide appellate courts and review, if they do grant appellate review, then they cannot discriminate against poor defendants. The Court noted that appellate review was a fundamental part of Illinois' trial system and thus, indigent defendants were protected at all stages of trial proceedings by the due process and equal protection clauses of the Fourteenth Amendment . The Court agreed with the Illinois State Supreme Court and emphasized that their decision did not mean a stenographer's transcript had to be provided in every case when an indigent defendant could not afford one. Other means could be found to provide "adequate and effective appellate review," such as some other method of reporting trial proceedings.

CASE EXCERPT

"All of the States now provide some method of appeal from criminal convictions, recognizing the importance of appellate review to a correct adjudication of guilt or innocence. Statistics show that a substantial proportion of criminal convictions are reversed by state appellate courts. Thus to deny adequate review to the poor means that many of them may lose their life, liberty or property because of unjust convictions which appellate courts would set aside. Many States have recognized this and provided aid for convicted defendants who have a right to appeal and need a transcript but are unable to pay for it. A few have not. Such a denial is a misfit in a country dedicated to affording equal justice to all and special privileges to none in the administration of its criminal law. There can be no equal justice where the kind of trial a man gets depends on the amount of money he has. Destitute defendants must be afforded as adequate appellate review as defendants who have money enough to buy transcripts."

CASE SIGNIFICANCE

This case established that indigent inmates have the same right to adequate appellate review that other persons have. This includes the right to a transcript or other written report of the trial proceedings.

BURNS v. OHIO

360 U.S. 252 (1959)

FACTS

The petitioner in this case was a convicted burglar serving a life sentence in Ohio. Ohio gives convicted felons whose convictions have been affirmed by the Ohio Court of Appeals the right to apply to the Ohio Supreme Court for appellate review. The State Supreme Court has discretion to grant and hear these appeals. After the petitioner's conviction was affirmed by the state court of appeals, he attempted to file in the state supreme court for leave to appeal in forma pauperis and included an affidavit of poverty. The clerk of the Ohio Supreme Court returned his documents along with a letter regarding the Ohio Supreme Court's determination on several previous occasions that the documents could not be filed with paying a twenty dollar filing fee. The state acknowledged that the clerk's letter was " 'in reality and in effect' the judgement of the [Ohio] Supreme Court," and the US

Supreme Court granted certiorari to hear whether a state's requirement that indigent defendants must pay filing fees before they can file motions for leave to appeal is constitutional.

ISSUE

May a state constitutionally require that an indigent defendant in a criminal case pay a filing fee before permitting him to file a motion for leave to appeal in one of its courts?

HOLDING

No. Since a person who is not indigent may have the Ohio Supreme Court consider his application for leave to appeal from a felony conviction, denial of the same right to this indigent petitioner solely because he was unable to pay the filing fee violated the Fourteenth Amendment.

RATIONALE

Writing for the Court, Chief Justice Warren noted that Ohio attempted to justify the practice at issue and to distinguish this case from *Griffin*, decided three years earlier. Ohio prisoners were entitled to one appellate review of convictions, whereas Illinois had not afforded Griffin and Crenshaw any review. The Court did not agree with this distinction because, as held in *Griffin*, once appellate review is established, indigents cannot be barred from access "to any phase of that procedure because of their poverty." So in the case at hand, Ohio could not afford Burns access to one phase of appellate review but then deny access to the second phase just because of his poverty. The state argued that the second phase was discretionary on the part of the Ohio Supreme Court, but Justice Warren observed that their current practice of requiring filing fees meant that indigent defendants did not "have the same opportunities to invoke the discretion of the Supreme Court of Ohio."

CASE EXCERPT

"The State's action in this case in some ways is more final and disastrous from the defendant's point of view than was the *Griffin* situation. At least in *Griffin*, the defendant might have raised in the Supreme Court any claims that he had that were apparent on the bare record, though trial errors could not be raised. Here, the action of the State has completely barred the petitioner from obtaining any review at all in the Supreme Court of Ohio. The imposition by the State of financial barriers restricting the availability of appellate review for indigent criminal defendants has no place in our heritage of Equal Justice Under Law."

CASE SIGNIFICANCE

In this case the Supreme Court made it clear that a state cannot require a filing fee if doing so prevents indigent inmates from seeking to pursue an appeal.

SMITH v. BENNETT

365 U.S. 708 (1961)

FACTS

This case is a consolidation of two habeas corpus cases brought by Iowa prisoners. Both cases challenged Iowa's statutory provisions requiring indigent defendants to pay filing fees for an application for a habeas corpus writ or for appeals to be docketed in state court. The first petitioner, Smith, had his parole revoked for violation of convictions and was serving the remainder of a ten-year sentence for breaking and entering. He attempted to file a writ of habeas corpus *in forma pauperis*, along with a poverty affidavit, raising questions about the constitutionality of his arrest and parole revocation. His petition was not docketed because he did not pay the four dollar filing fee. He then sought leave to appeal *in forma pauperis* in the Iowa Supreme Court, which was also denied. The second petitioner, Marshall, was also serving ten years for breaking and entering. He had attempted to file a habeas corpus writ *in forma pauperis* in an Iowa District Court, challenging aspects of his guilty plea. Similar to Smith's case, Marshall's petition was not docketed, but the Iowa District Court did examine the petition and said that it would have been denied anyway. He appealed to the Iowa Supreme Court, but that application was denied. The US Supreme Court granted certiorari to address the validity of Iowa's laws requiring indigent prisoners to pay filing fees before applications for habeas corpus writs or allowances of appeals would be docketed.

ISSUE

Is the requirement of Iowa law that necessitates the payment of statutory filing fees by an indigent prisoner of the state before an application for a writ of habeas corpus, or the allowance of an appeal in such proceedings will be docketed, valid, under the equal protection clause of the Fourteenth Amendment?

SMITH v. BENNETT *(cont.)*

HOLDING

No. "[T]o interpose any financial consideration between an indigent prisoner of the [s]tate and his exercise of a state right to sue for his liberty is to deny that prisoner the equal protection of the laws."

RATIONALE

In vacating the Iowa Supreme Court's decisions and remanding both cases, Justice Clark reasoned that because "there is no rational basis for assuming that indigents' motions for leave to appeal will be less meritorious than those of other defendants, there can be no equal justice where the kind of trial a man gets depends on the amount of money he has," and consequently that "[t]he imposition by the State of financial barriers restricting the availability of appellate review for indigent criminal defendants has no place in our heritage of Equal Justice Under Law." The Court emphasized that the decision here applied only to habeas corpus and other civil rights actions involving indigent convicted prisoners.

CASE EXCERPT

"Throughout the centuries, the Great Writ has been the shield of personal freedom insuring liberty to persons illegally detained. Respecting the State's grant of a right to test their detention, the Fourteenth Amendment weighs the interests of rich and poor criminals in equal scale, and its hand extends as far to each. In failing to extend the privilege of the Great Writ to its indigent prisoners, Iowa denies them equal protection of the laws."

CASE SIGNIFICANCE

In this case the Supreme Court again made it clear that a state cannot require a filing fee if doing so prevents indigent inmates from seeking to pursue an appeal.

JOHNSON v. AVERY

393 U.S. 483 (1969)

FACTS

Johnson, , a Tennessee prisoner serving a life sentence, was disciplined for violating a prison regulation which prohibited inmates from assisting other prisoners in preparing writs. The District Court held the regulation void because it had the effect of barring illiterate prisoners from access to federal habeas corpus and

conflicted with 28 U.S.C. 2242. The Court of Appeals reversed, finding that the state's interest in preserving prison discipline and limiting the practice of law to attorneys justified any burden the regulation might place on access to federal habeas corpus.

ISSUE

Does a state regulation absolutely barring inmates from assisting other prisoners in preparing writs violate the Constitution?

HOLDING

Yes. In the absence of some provision by the State of Tennessee for a reasonable alternative to assist illiterate or poorly educated inmates in preparing petitions for postconviction relief, the state may not validly enforce a regulation which absolutely bars inmates from furnishing such assistance to other prisoners.

RATIONALE

In the Majority opinion by Justice Fortas, the Supreme Court noted at the time this decision was rendered that Tennessee did not provide any alternatives to the assistance given by other inmates. The warden where Johnson was imprisoned stated that they did notarize prisoners' petitions for free, but Justice Fortas stated that this "obviously meets only a formal requirement." The warden said inmates were sometimes allowed to look at the Nashville telephone directory's list of attorneys so they could perhaps write to one and interest him in their case, and he had contacted a public defender "on several occasions" for inmates. There was no regular system in place, however, and Tennessee could not show that it had not deprived inmates of access to the writ of habeas corpus. At the time, other states had public defender systems in place that supplied attorneys to consult with inmates regarding their petitions. In one state, senior law students interviewed and advised inmates, and another state had a voluntary program where local attorneys consulted with inmates. Even if states allowed inmate assistance, they were not prohibited from imposing reasonable limitations on that assistance.

CASE EXCERPT

"The State may impose reasonable restrictions and restraints upon the acknowledged propensity of prisoners to abuse both the giving and the seeking of assistance in the preparation of applications for relief: for example, by limitations on the time and location of such activities and the imposition of punishment for the giving or receipt of consideration in connection with such activities. But unless and until the State provides some reasonable alternative to assist inmates in the preparation of petitions for postconviction relief, it may not validly enforce a regulation such as that here in issue, barring inmates from furnishing such assistance to other prisoners."

CASE SIGNIFICANCE

In this case the Supreme Court held that prison authorities must provide inmates with access to courts. Barring fellow inmates from providing legal assistance is not permitted, unless the prison affords inmates "reasonable alternatives." The precise meaning of this phrase was not made clear by the Court until a subsequent case, *Lewis v. Casey* (1996).

BOUNDS v. SMITH
430 U.S. 817 (1977)

FACTS

Respondents, inmates incarcerated in correctional facilities of the Division of Prisons of the North Carolina Department of Correction, filed three separate actions under 42 U.S.C. 1983, all eventually consolidated in the District Court for the Eastern District of North Carolina. Respondents alleged, in pertinent part, that they were denied access to the courts in violation of their Fourteenth Amendment rights by the state's failure to provide legal research facilities. The District Court granted respondents' motion for summary judgment on this claim, finding that the sole prison library in the state was "severely inadequate" and that there was no other legal assistance available to inmates. It held on the basis of *Younger v. Gilmore*, 404 U.S. 15 (1971), that respondents' rights of access to the courts and equal protection of the laws had been violated because there was "no indication of any assistance at the initial stage of preparation of writs and petitions." The court recognized, however, that determining the "appropriate relief to be ordered... presents a difficult problem," in view of North Carolina's decentralized prison system. Rather than attempting "to dictate precisely what course the State should follow," the court "charge[d] the Department of Correction with the task of devising a Constitutionally sound program" to assure inmate access to the courts. It left to the state the choice of what alternative would "most easily and

economically" fulfill this duty, suggesting that a program to make available lawyers, law students, or public defenders might serve the purpose at least as well as the provision of law libraries. The state responded by proposing the establishment of seven libraries in institutions located across the state chosen so as to serve best all prison units. In addition, the state planned to set up smaller libraries in the central prison segregation unit and the women's prison. Under the plan, inmates desiring to use a library would request appointments. They would be given transportation and housing, if necessary, for a full day's library work. In addition to its collection of law books, each library would stock legal forms and writing paper and have typewriters and use of copying machines. The state proposed to train inmates as research assistants and typists to aid fellow prisoners. It was estimated that ultimately some 350 inmates per week could use the libraries, although inmates not facing court deadlines might have to wait three or four weeks for their turn at a library. Respondents protested that the plan was totally inadequate and sought establishment of a library at every prison. The District Court rejected respondents' objections, finding the state's plan "both economically feasible and practicable," and one that, fairly and efficiently run, would "insure each inmate the time to prepare his petitions." Further briefing was ordered on whether the state was required to provide independent legal advisors for inmates in addition to the library facilities. In its final decision, the District Court held that petitioners were not constitutionally required to provide legal assistance as well as libraries. It found that the library plan was sufficient to give inmates reasonable access to the courts and that the US Supreme Court's decision in *Ross v. Moffitt*, 417 U.S. 600 (1974), while not directly in point, supported the state's claim that it need not furnish attorneys to bring habeas corpus and civil rights actions for prisoners. After the District Court approved the library plan, the state submitted an application to the Federal Law Enforcement Assistance Administration (LEAA) for a grant to cover 90 percent of the cost of setting up the libraries and training a librarian and inmate clerks. The state represented to LEAA that the library project would benefit all inmates in the state by giving them "meaningful and effective access to the court[s]...[T]he ultimate result...should be a diminution in the number of groundless petitions and complaints filed...The inmate himself will be able to determine to a greater extent whether or not his rights have been violated," and judicial evaluation

BOUNDS v. SMITH *(cont.)*

of the petitions will be facilitated. Both sides appealed from those portions of the District Court orders adverse to them. The Court of Appeals for the Fourth Circuit affirmed in all respects save one: It found that the library plan denied women prisoners the same access rights as men to research facilities. Since there was no justification for this discrimination, the Court of Appeals ordered it eliminated. The state petitioned for review and we granted certiorari.

ISSUE

Are prison authorities required to assist inmates in the preparation and filing of meaningful legal papers by providing prisoners with adequate law libraries or adequate assistance from persons trained in the law?

HOLDING

Yes. The fundamental constitutional right of access to the courts requires prison authorities to assist inmates in the preparation and filing of meaningful legal papers by providing prisoners with adequate law libraries or adequate assistance from persons trained in the law.

RATIONALE

It is now established beyond doubt that prisoners have a constitutional right of access to the courts. The Court recognized that right more than 35 years ago when it struck down a regulation prohibiting state prisoners from filing petitions for habeas corpus unless they were found "properly drawn" by the "legal investigator" for the parole board. The Court held this violated the principle that "the state and its officers may not abridge or impair petitioner's right to apply to a federal court for a writ of habeas corpus." More recent decisions have struck down restrictions and required remedial measures to insure that inmate access to the courts is adequate, effective, and meaningful. Thus, in order to prevent "effectively foreclosed access," indigent prisoners must be allowed to file appeals and habeas corpus petitions without payment of docket fees. Because it is recognized that "adequate and effective appellate review" is impossible without a trial transcript or adequate substitute, the Court has held that states must provide trial records to inmates unable to buy them. Similarly, counsel must be appointed to give indigent inmates "a meaningful appeal" from their convictions.

CASE EXCERPT

"We hold, therefore, that the fundamental constitutional right of access to the courts requires prison authorities to assist inmates in the preparation and filing of meaningful legal papers by providing prisoners with adequate law libraries or adequate assistance from persons trained in the law... It should be noted that while adequate law libraries are one constitutionally acceptable method to assure meaningful access to the courts, our decision here, as in *Gilmore,* does not foreclose alternative means to achieve that goal."

CASE SIGNIFICANCE

In this case the Supreme Court upheld the right of inmates to meaningful access to the courts. The Court attempts to provide prisons with some flexibility in how they go about providing this access, but access of some kind is required. The various methods suggested by the Court were taken as requirements by most prisons and lower courts, but the subsequent decision in *Lewis v. Casey* (1996) suggests these are just suggestions, not requirements.

MURRAY v. GIARRATANO

492 U.S. 1 (1989)

FACTS

The respondents in this case were a class of indigent Virginia death row inmates who did not have counsel to pursue postconviction proceedings. They filed a 42 U.S.C. 1983 suit against various state officials in the District Court, "alleging that the Constitution required that they be provided with counsel at the state's expense for the purpose of pursuing collateral proceedings related to their convictions and sentences." The District Court concluded that death row inmates required greater assistance than provided for in *Bounds* (access to adequate law libraries or other legal aid). Death row inmates, according to the District Court, had a "limited amount of time to prepare petitions, since their cases are unusually complex, and since the shadow of impending execution interferes with their ability to do legal work." The District Court ruled that "access to a law library or lawbooks, the availability of 'unit attorneys,' and appointment of counsel after a petition is filed" did not constitute meaningful access to the courts in Virginia because the death row inmates were not guaranteed "continuous assistance of counsel." Virginia was ordered to develop programs for counsel to be provided, upon request, to indigent prisoners on death row who wished to pursue habeas corpus in state court. The Court of Appeals affirmed the lower court's decision, and stated that the situations relating to inmates on death row were not clearly in error. The Court of Appeals found that the case was not controlled by *Pennsylvania v. Finley*, 481 U.S. 551 (1987), because *Finley* was not a "meaningful access" case, nor did it address the rule enunciated in *Bounds*, and it did not involve the death penalty.

ISSUE

Does Virginia's process for securing representation for indigent death row inmates seeking state postconviction relief violate the US Constitution?

HOLDING

No. Justice Rehnquist, joined by Justices White, O'Connor, and Scalia, concluded that neither the Eighth Amendment nor the due process clause requires states to appoint counsel for indigent death row inmates seeking state postconviction relief. Justice Kennedy, joined by Justice O'Connor, concluded that Virginia's scheme for securing representation for indigent death row inmates does not violate the Constitution.

RATIONALE

In the Majority opinion written by Chief Justice Rehnquist, the Court stated that *Pennsylvania v. Finley* applied no differently in capital cases than in noncapital cases. The Chief Justice also observed that the *Bounds* and *Finley* decisions were not inconsistent: "The right of access at issue in *Bounds* rests on a constitutional theory considered in *Finley*. Extending *Bounds* would partially overrule the subsequently decided *Finley* and would reject a categorical rule—the usual tack taken in right to counsel cases—for the adoption of a case-by-case determination based on 'factual' findings, which, under a 'clearly erroneous' standard, could result in different constitutional rules being applied in different [s]tates." *Bounds*'s meaningful access requirement can be satisfied in various ways, and state legislatures and prison administrators must be given "wide discretion" to select appropriate solutions from a range of complex options.

CASE EXCERPT

"We have recognized on more than one occasion that the Constitution places special constraints on the procedures used to convict an accused of a capital offense and sentence him to death...These holdings, however, have dealt with the trial stage of capital offense adjudication, where the court and jury hear testimony, receive evidence, and decide the questions of guilt and punishment...We think that these cases require the conclusion that the rule of *Pennsylvania v. Finley* should apply no differently in capital cases than in noncapital cases. State collateral proceedings are not constitutionally required as an adjunct to the state criminal proceedings and serve a different and more limited purpose than either the trial or appeal. The additional safeguards imposed by the Eighth Amendment at the trial stage of a capital case are, we think, sufficient to assure the reliability of the process by which the death penalty is imposed."

CASE SIGNIFICANCE

In this case the Court refused to extend to indigent capital defendants the right to an attorney provided by the state in habeas corpus proceedings. The right to counsel extends only to the first appeal, none as the appeal of right. This is a significant limitation on the ability of indigent inmates to secure habeas corpus relief.

LEWIS v. CASEY
518 U.S. 343 (1996)

FACTS

Respondents, who were inmates of various prisons operated by the Arizona Department of Corrections (ADOC), brought a class action against petitioners, ADOC officials, alleging that petitioners were furnishing them with inadequate legal research facilities and thereby depriving them of their right of access to the courts, in violation of *Bounds v. Smith*. The District Court found petitioners to be in violation of *Bounds* and issued an injunction mandating detailed, system-wide changes in ADOC's prison law libraries and in its legal assistance programs. The Ninth Circuit affirmed both the finding of a Bounds violation and the injunction's major terms.

ISSUE

Were ADOC officials depriving inmates of their right of access to the courts, in violation of *Bounds*?

HOLDING

No. "[T]he success of respondents' systemic challenge was dependent on their ability to show widespread actual injury," and the District Court's "failure to identify anything more than isolated instances of actual

68 SIGNIFICANT CASES IN CORRECTIONS

LEWIS v. CASEY *(cont.)*

injury renders its finding of a systemic *Bounds* violation invalid."

RATIONALE

The Majority opinion by Justice Scalia emphatically stated that *Bounds* did not create an abstract, free-standing right to a law library or legal assistance; rather, the right that *Bounds* acknowledged was the right of access to the courts. Thus, to establish a *Bounds* violation, the "actual injury" that an inmate must demonstrate is that alleged shortcomings in the prison library or legal assistance program have hindered, or are presently hindering, his efforts to pursue a nonfrivolous legal claim. Justice Scalia noted that the actual injury requirement derived from the doctrine of standing, and that "although *Bounds* itself made no mention of an actual injury requirement, it can hardly be thought to have eliminated that constitutional prerequisite." However, statements in *Bounds* suggesting that prison authorities must also enable the prisoner to discover grievances, and to litigate effectively once in court, had no antecedent in pre-*Bounds* cases, and the Court disclaimed those statements in *Lewis v. Casey*. Moreover, *Bounds* did not guarantee inmates the wherewithal to file any and every type of legal claim, but requires only that they be provided with the tools to directly or collaterally attack their sentences, and to challenge the conditions of their confinement. Accordingly, the findings related to actual injury did not support the District Court's order of a system-wide injunction. Justice Scalia wrote that even though this was a class action, all named plaintiffs had to show personal injury.. The District Court found only two instances of actual injury. Both cases involved illiterate and/or non-English speaking prisoners who did not receive adequate legal assistance and ended up having, in one instance, the case dismissed with prejudice, and in the other, the inmate being unable to file a claim. However, these inadequacies were not sufficiently widespread to justify system-wide relief. The Court also relied on the 1987 decision, *Turner v. Safley*, 482 U.S. 78, in concluding that ADOC's restrictions on lockdown inmates were unjustified. The District Court failed to follow *Turner* accord substantial deference to the judgment of prison authorities. The court also failed to leave with prison officials the primary responsibility for devising a remedy. The result of this improper procedure was an inordinately intrusive order.

CASE EXCERPT

"*Bounds* does not guarantee inmates the wherewithal to transform themselves into litigating engines capable of filing everything from shareholder derivative actions to slip-and-fall claims. The tools it requires to be provided are those that the inmates need in order to attack their sentences, directly or collaterally, and in order to challenge the conditions of their confinement. Impairment of any *other* litigating capacity is simply one of the incidental (and perfectly constitutional) consequences of conviction and incarceration."

CASE SIGNIFICANCE

This case provides some clarification regarding the extent of an inmate's right of access to courts. The Court noted that the *Bounds v. Smith* decision did not create a right to a law library of legal assistance, something that was assumed by many lower courts in the years following the *Bounds* decision. Instead, the Court stated that the existing right of access to the courts is different from the right to access to (and use of) a law library. The result has been the dismantling, in many states, of the prison law library system.

SHAW v. MURPHY
532 U.S. 223 (2001)

FACTS

Kevin Murphy, a Montana State Prison inmate law clerk, sent a letter to another inmate assisting him with his defense after he assaulted a correctional officer. The inmate had already asked that Murphy be assigned to his case; however, the request was denied based on policy that forbade high-security inmates like Murphy from meeting with maximum security inmates (in this case Tracy, the other inmate). In accordance with prison policy, Murphy's letter was intercepted. Based on its content, which included accusations that the correctional officer had made homosexual advances, Murphy was charged with insolence, interference with due process hearings, and conduct interfering with security and the orderly operation of the institution. Murphy was found guilty of the first two charges. Murphy sought relief under §1983, alleging First Amendment violations, including the right to provide legal assistance to other inmates. The District Court ruled against Murphy, applying the Supreme Court decision in *Turner v. Safley*, 482 U.S. 78, 1987, that regulations impinging on inmates' constitutional rights must be reasonably related to legitimate penological interests. The Court of Appeals for the Ninth Circuit reversed this decision, finding that prisoners possessed a First Amendment right of association that included providing legal assistance to other inmates, and this right outweighed the government's interests.

ISSUE

Do prison inmates have a special First Amendment right to provide legal assistance to fellow inmates?

HOLDING

No. The Court reversed and remanded the Ninth Circuit's decision, holding that inmates do not possess a special First Amendment right to provide legal assistance to fellow inmates that enhances the protection otherwise available under Turner.

RATIONALE

Applying the four-pronged Turner analysis to the issue at hand, the Court concluded that inmate correspondence containing legal advice does not merit enhanced constitutional protection. Justice Thomas stated that "[a]ugmenting First Amendment protection for inmate legal advice would undermine prison officials' ability to address the 'complex and intractable' problems of prison administration.... [T]he *Turner* factors concern only the relationship between the asserted penological interests and the prison regulation. Moreover, under *Turner* and its predecessors, prison officials are to remain the primary arbiters of the problems that arise in prison management.... If courts were permitted to enhance constitutional protection based on their assessments of the content of the particular communications, courts would be in a position to assume a greater role in decisions affecting prison administration.... Finally, even if we were to consider giving special protection to particular kinds of speech based upon content, we would not do so for speech that includes legal advice."

CASE EXCERPT

"We thus decline to cloak the provision of legal assistance with any First Amendment protection above and beyond the protection normally accorded prisoners' speech. Instead, the proper constitutional test is the one we set forth in *Turner*. Irrespective of whether the correspondence contains legal advice, the constitutional analysis is the same."

CASE SIGNIFICANCE

This case follows precedent established in *Turner v. Safley*, the current standard for determining whether inmates' constitutional rights are violated by prison regulations and laws. In noting how written correspondence containing legal advice could hamper prison officials' ability to manage institutions, Justice Thomas noted that "prisoners have used legal correspondence as a means for passing contraband and communicating instructions on how to manufacture drugs or weapons." In the oral arguments before the Court, the attorney for the petitioners conceded that Murphy could have sent the letter to Tracy's assigned counsel outside the prison, or even to investigative journalists outside the prison, and such means of communication would have been permissible.

DISCUSSION QUESTIONS

1. Identify and discuss the most significant aspect of the Supreme Court's decision in *Ex parte Hull*.
2. Explain how the Supreme Court has expanded access to the courts for indigent prisoners.
3. Some Court watchers observe that the Supreme Court has abridged or reduced prisoners' access to the courts. Do you agree or disagree? Explain your answer.
4. Discuss the various means by which prison administrators can ensure that inmates have reasonable and meaningful access to the courts.
5. If an inmate claims that he or she has been denied access to the courts, what must he or she demonstrate?
6. Which do you think provides inmates with better, more effective legal assistance—a prison law library, a paralegal to help inmates by appointment, or allowing other inmates to help?
7. Why is the decision in *Ex parte Hull* so important to the development of corrections law?
8. Why did the Supreme Court decide in *Murray v. Giarrantano* that indigent capital prisoners are not entitled to counsel provided by the state?
9. What First Amendment rights related to access to courts remain for inmates?
10. If inmates lacked the ability to get into court, how would prisons change from the way they operate today?

CHAPTER FOUR

ACCESS TO THE PRESS, THE OUTSIDE WORLD, AND THE MAIL

PROCUNIER v. MARTINEZ, *416 U.S. 396 (1974)*

PELL v. PROCUNIER, *417 U.S. 817 (1974)*

JONES v. NORTH CAROLINA PRISONERS' LABOR UNION, *INC., 433 U.S. 119 (1977)*

HOUCHINS v. KQED, *INC., 438 U.S. 1 (1978)*

BLOCK v. RUTHERFORD, *468 U.S. 576 (1984)*

TURNER v. SAFLEY, *482 U.S. 78 (1987)*

THORNBURGH v. ABBOTT, *490 U.S. 401 (1989)*

INTRODUCTION

The seven cases in this chapter address prisoners' general access to the outside world with respect to their mail, the media, unions, visitation rights, and the right to marry. The first two cases were both decided in 1974 and concerned California Department of Corrections regulations.

The first case, *Procunier v. Martinez*, centered on regulations regarding mail censorship between inmates and noninmates and using law students and paralegals to conduct attorney-client interviews. Both regulations were found to be unconstitutional because they restricted the rights of noninmates. The next case, *Pell v. Procunier*, focused on California's regulations restricting access to the press and did survive judicial scrutiny. The Supreme Court found that California's policy prohibiting media interviews with specific prisoners, while restricting the rights of both the press and the inmates, was justified because of the reduced rights of inmates and the need for prisons to be able to control access to the outside world for security reasons. This case illustrates the balancing act involved with trying to uphold the individual constitutional rights of inmates on the one hand and legitimate penological concerns on the other. Four years later, the Court again balanced the interests of the media against the interests of prison officials and

found in favor of the prison officials in *Houchins v. KQED, Inc.*, 438 U.S. 1 (1978).

The same kind of balancing act was at issue in 1977 in *Jones v. North Carolina Prisoners' Labor Union, Inc.* Prisoners in North Carolina alleged that their First Amendment freedom to associate rights were violated because of regulations prohibiting inmates from soliciting other inmates to join the North Carolina Prisoners' Labor Union, Union meetings, and bulk mailings of union materials. The Court referred back to *Pell v. Procunier*, noting that "confinement and the needs of the penal institution impose limitations on constitutional rights" (*Pell v. Procunier*, 417 U.S. 817, 822). Because inmate unions can be detrimental to prison order and security, regulations banning such unions are both "reasonable and necessary."

The constitutionality of restrictions on pretrial detainees' access to the outside world have also been addressed by the Court with similar results. In 1984, the Court heard another California case, this time brought by pretrial detainees at the Los Angeles County Central Jail. The detainees who were awaiting trials challenged the constitutionality of jail regulations which denied them contact visits with family and friends, and also regulations which permitted jail employees to search their cells whether the detainees were present or not

(*Block v. Rutherford*, 468 U.S. 576). As this chapter notes, the Supreme Court again deferred to the discretion of prison administrators, seeing the ban on contact visits and the random, irregular cell searches as reasonably related to security concerns of the jail.

The three-member dissenting opinion in *Block v. Rutherford* illustrates the conflict and controversial nature of these issues. The dissent noted that the Court in recent years had "turned a deaf ear to inmates' claims that the conditions of their confinement violate the Federal Constitution." While deferring to prison administrators seems logical to lay persons, dissenting justices caution that the "confidence in the good faith and 'expertise' of prison administrators" may be misguided and may lead to sanctioning prison conditions that are in fact cruel or ill-justified. In this particular case, expert testimony maintained that denial of contact visits weakens family bonds, contributes to the break up of inmates' marriages, and harms mental health. The dissent did not believe that permitting low-risk pretrial detainees who have been incarcerated for more than a month to have occasional contact visits with family would interfere with any substantial state interest in order and security. Further, the dissent pointed to the unnecessary destruction of inmate property when not permitted to observe shakedown searches. Allowing pretrial detainees to observe searches of their cells would pose minimal burdens on jail officials and would reduce the "wanton destruction" of the detainees' possessions. While the decision in this case shows that the unique security needs of the prison outweigh the individual rights of the inmate, a consideration of the dissent's opinion makes clear that many times there are no trouble-free answers.

The next case in this chapter, *Turner v. Safley*, 482 U.S. 78 (1987), concerns both the right to marry and access to mail, and the holding echoes the previous decisions. This case currently stands as the landmark case for establishing standards for restricting prisoners' constitutional rights. In it, the Supreme Court ruled that prison regulations which impinge on inmates' constitutional rights are valid if those regulations are "reasonably related to legitimate penological interests" (*Turner*, at 2254). The four-pronged Turner test consists of the following factors:

1. Existence of valid rational connection between prison regulation and legitimate government interest put forward to justify it;

2. Existence of alternative means of exercising rights remaining open to prison inmates;

3. Impact that accommodation of asserted constitutional rights will have on guards and other inmates and on allocation of prison resources generally; and

4. Absence of ready alternatives as evidence of the reasonableness of the regulation (*Turner*, at 2262).

The last case in this chapter, *Thornburgh v. Abbott*, 490 U.S. 401 (1989), regarded restrictions on receiving certain publications from the outside world and takes us back to the first case in this chapter, *Procunier v. Martinez*. Federal Bureau of Prison inmates and certain publishers claimed that the bureau's regulations excluding 46 publications violated the inmates' First Amendment rights under *Martinez*. The Supreme Court heard this case for the purpose of determining the appropriate standard of review. Applying the *Turner* standard decided in 1987, the Court saw the regulations at issue as legitimately related to penological interests of security. *Thornburgh v. Abbott* offered an opportunity for the Court to overrule *Martinez* in the sense of drawing a distinction between whether mail is incoming or outgoing and whether it is from prisoners or nonprisoners. As the law currently stands, then, the *Martinez* standard, which is less deferential to prison administrators, applies to regulations affecting outgoing personal inmate mail, and the *Turner* reasonableness standard applies to incoming correspondence.

Taken together, these seven cases illustrate the difficulty in protecting individual constitutional rights and allowing administrators to run their prisons safely and efficiently and the precarious balancing act that ensues. This chapter also delineates the evolving conservative nature of the decisions issued by the Supreme Court in recent decades.

PROCUNIER v. MARTINEZ
416 U.S. 396 (1974)

FACTS
The California Department of Corrections issued regulations allowing the censorship of prisoner mail and banning the use of law students and paralegals to conduct attorney-client interviews with inmates. The mail censorship regulations forbade inmate correspondence that "unduly complained, magnified

PROCUNIER v. MARTINEZ *(cont.)*

grievances, expressed inflammatory political, racial, religious or other views or beliefs," or contained matter deemed "defamatory" or "otherwise inappropriate." Prison inmates brought a class-action suit against the corrections department challenging these regulations as violations of the First and Fourteenth Amendments. The district court held that the regulations violated the First Amendment and the Fourteenth Amendment's due process clause and were void for vagueness. The lower court also decided that banning law students and legal paraprofessionals from conducting attorney-client interviews with inmates violated the inmates' right of access to the courts.

ISSUE

Are the California Department of Corrections' regulations concerning mail censorship and attorney-client interviews unconstitutional?

HOLDING

Yes. The Supreme Court held that "censorship of direct personal correspondence involves incidental restrictions on the right to free speech of both prisoners and their correspondents, and is justified if the following criteria are met: (1) it must further one or more of the important and substantial governmental interests of security, order, and the rehabilitation of inmates, and (2) it must be no greater than is necessary to further the legitimate governmental interest involved." Under this two-pronged standard of review, the California Department of Corrections' regulations were "far broader than any legitimate interest of penal administration demands and were properly found invalid by the District Court." The Court also found the ban against law students and paralegals conducting attorney-client interviews was not a justifiable restriction on inmate access to the courts because the ban "created an arbitrary distinction between law students employed by attorneys and those associated with law school programs (against whom the ban did not operate)."

RATIONALE

The Court's opinion in this case began with an explication of the principles that frame an analysis of prisoners' alleged claims of constitutional violations. Justice Powell noted that the duty before the Court in the instant case was to formulate a standard of review for constitutional challenges to prisoner mail censorship that would properly protect rights of inmates while, at the same time, accord deference to prison administrators. The Court noted that both parties' arguments assumed that the decision in this case involved a determination of First Amendment rights for inmates. The Court stated, however, that such a determination was unnecessary: "We have no occasion to consider the extent to which an individual's right to free speech survives incarceration, for a narrower basis of decision is at hand." In reaching a decision, the majority focused on the impermissible restriction of First and Fourteenth Amendment rights of the nonprisoners affected by the censorship regulations. The decision in *Martinez* only addressed mail censorship between inmates and noninmates. Thirteen years later, in *Turner v. Safley*, 482 U.S. 78 (1987), the Supreme Court would address inmate-to-inmate correspondence and would observe that lower courts erred in reading *Martinez* as imposing a strict scrutiny standard of review. *Martinez* "expressly reserved the question of the proper standard of review to apply in cases 'involving questions of `prisoners' rights'" (482 U.S. 78, at 86). While *Martinez* left open the question of the proper standard review, prisoners' rights cases following *Martinez* endorsed the lower reasonableness standard when assessing whether a prison regulation impinges on inmates' constitutional rights. The *Turner* Court would rule explicitly that "when a prison regulation impinges on inmates' constitutional rights, the regulation is valid if it is reasonably related to legitimate penological interests." The *Martinez* Court advocated a standard of review that did not "unnecessarily perpetuate the involvement of the federal courts in affairs of prison administration," and the *Turner* Court observed that any higher standard would result in such needless judicial interference.

CASE EXCERPT

"Censorship of prisoner mail is justified if the following criteria are met. First, the regulation or practice in question must further an important or substantial governmental interest unrelated to the suppression of expression. Prison officials may not censor inmate correspondence simply to eliminate unflattering or unwelcome opinions or factually inaccurate statements. Rather, they must show that a regulation authorizing mail censorship furthers one or more of the substantial governmental interests of security, order, and rehabilitation. Second, the limitation of First Amendment freedoms must be no greater than is necessary or essential to the protection of the particular governmental interest involved. Thus a restriction on inmate correspondence that furthers an important or substantial interest of penal administration will nevertheless be invalid if its sweep is unnecessarily broad."

SIGNIFICANCE

In this case the Court upheld prison regulations affecting inmate mail, on the ground that prison officials must be able to regulate the mail in order to ensure institutional security. This decision follows in a long line of cases restricting the First Amendment rights of inmates in order to ensure a safe and secure prison.

PELL v. PROCUNIER

417 U.S. 817 (1974)

FACTS

Four California prison inmates and three professional journalists filed suit in district court challenging the constitutionality of a regulation, ß415. 071, of the California Department of Corrections Manual. The regulation provided that "[p]ress and other media interviews with specific individual inmates will not be permitted," although media could still interview inmates at random. The regulation was passed after a violent prison episode that prison authorities believed was due in part to the former practice of free face-to-face prisoner-press interviews, which resulted in a small number of inmates gaining disproportionate notoriety and influence among other inmates. The district court held that the regulation prohibiting inmates from having face-to-face communication with journalists unconstitutionally infringed the inmates' First and Fourteenth Amendment freedoms. However, the court granted a motion to dismiss with respect to the claims of the professional journalists, holding that their rights were not infringed because of their otherwise available rights to enter state institutions and interview inmates at random. Further, the court's decision affording inmates' broader access was sufficient to protect the rights of the press. The prison officials and the professional journalists appealed.

ISSUE

Is the California Department of Corrections ban on media-inmate interviews unconstitutional?

HOLDING

No. The challenged regulation did not constitute a violation of inmates' rights of free speech. Likewise,

the regulation did not infringe upon media access to information.

RATIONALE

The Court ruled that freedom of speech and other First Amendment rights of inmates must be balanced against legitimate penological interests of the correctional system. Legitimate interests of the system include confining inmates to deter crime, protecting society by incapacitating criminal offenders for a period of time during which rehabilitation measures can be applied, and maintaining security within correctional institutions. The ban on face-to-face media interviews did not affect alternative channels of communication to which inmates had access. Inmates could correspond by mail with persons, including the media, and they had rights of visitation with family, clergy, attorneys, and friends of prior acquaintance. Visitation rights gave inmates unrestricted opportunity to communicate with the press or public through the prison visitors. Justice Stewart noted that according to prison officials, restricting visitation of inmates to family, friends of prior acquaintance, legal counsel, and clergy permitted inmates to have personal contact with people who would assist in their rehabilitation, but the restrictions would also keep visitations at a manageable level that would not interfere with institutional security. In the words of the Court, "[s]uch considerations are peculiarly within the province and professional expertise of corrections officials, and, in the absence of substantial evidence in the record to indicate that the officials have exaggerated their response to these considerations, courts should ordinarily defer to their expert judgment in such matters." The majority further held that the rights of the media under the First and Fourteenth Amendments were not abridged by the regulation. Under California policy, news media were free to visit both maximum and minimum security areas of correctional institutions and to speak with inmates and, unlike members of the general public, to interview inmates selected at random: "[T]he First Amendment does not guarantee the press a constitutional right of special access to information not available to the public generally."

CASE EXCERPT

"In *Procunier v. Martinez*, we could find no legitimate governmental interest to justify the substantial restrictions that had there been imposed on written communication by inmates. When, however, the

PELL v. PROCUNIER *(cont.)*

question involves the entry of people into the prisons for face-to-face communication with inmates, it is obvious that institutional considerations, such as security and related administrative problems, as well as the accepted and legitimate policy objectives of the corrections system itself, require that some limitation be placed on such visitations. So long as reasonable and effective means of communication remain open and no discrimination in terms of content is involved, we believe that, in drawing such lines, prison officials must be accorded latitude."

SIGNIFICANCE

In this case the Supreme Court held that a prison regulation prohibiting media interviews with inmates does not violate the constitutional rights of either the media or the inmate, so long as alternative means of communication are available. This clearly restricts the First Amendment rights of both media and inmates, but was justified by the Court because of the reduced rights of inmates and the need of the institution to be able to control access to the outside world generally, for security purposes.

JONES v. NORTH CAROLINA PRISONERS' LABOR UNION, INC.
433 U.S. 119 (1977)

FACTS

The North Carolina Prisoners' Labor Union was incorporated in late 1974 with a stated goal of "the promotion of charitable labor union purposes" and the formation of a "prisoners' labor union at every prison and jail in North Carolina to seek through collective bargaining to improve working conditions." It also proposed to work toward altering or eliminating practices and policies of the Department of Correction that it did not approve of, and to serve as a vehicle for presenting and resolving inmate grievances. By early 1975, the union had attracted some prospective 2,000 inmate members in 40 different prison units throughout North Carolina. The State of North Carolina, unhappy with these developments, passed a regulation on March 26, 1975 that prohibited inmate solicitation of other inmates to join the union, meetings between members of the union, and bulk mailings concerning the union from outside sources. The union filed a Section 1983 suit, claiming that the prohibitions violated First Amendment rights

of the union and its members. It also alleged a denial of equal protection under the Fourteenth Amendment because the Jaycees and Alcoholics Anonymous were permitted to have meetings and other organizational rights, such as the distribution of bulk mailing material, that the union was being denied. The district court ruled that since the Department of Correction allowed inmates to join the union, it could not prohibit the solicitation of other inmates to join, either by inmate-to-inmate solicitation or by correspondence. In the issues concerning bulk mailing by the union of literature into the prisons for distribution and meetings of inmate members, the court found that since such meetings and bulk mailing privileges had been permitted the Jaycees, Alcoholics Anonymous, and, in one institution, the Boy Scouts, it concluded that appellants "may not pick and choose depending on [their] approval or disapproval of the message or purpose of the group" unless "the activity proscribed is shown to be detrimental to proper penological objectives, subversive to good discipline, or otherwise harmful."

ISSUE

Is the North Carolina Department of Correction regulation prohibiting inmate solicitation of union membership, union meetings, and bulk mailings a violation of the First and Fourteenth Amendments?

HOLDING

No. The regulations did not violate First Amendment rights or the equal protection clause of the Fourteenth Amendment.

RATIONALE

The Court began its decision by noting that "[t]he District Court, we believe, got off on the wrong foot in this case by not giving appropriate deference to the decisions of prison administrators and appropriate recognition to the peculiar and restrictive circumstances of penal confinement." Accordingly, "confinement and the needs of the penal institution impose limitations on constitutional rights, including those derived from the First Amendment, *Pell v. Procunier*, 417 U.S. 817, 822, perhaps the most obvious of which is associational rights that the First Amendment protects outside of prison walls." The Court noted that the right to a freedom to associate was not abridged without justification. Prison officials contended that a prisoners' union would be detrimental to order and security, and the Court agreed that the regulations at issue "were no broader than necessary to meet the perceived threat of group meetings and organizational activity to such order and security." Thus, a ban on inmate solicitation to join a union and hold group meetings is "rationally related to the reasonable objectives of prison administration." Freedom of speech rights under the First Amendment by banning bulk mailings also were not violated in this case. Justice Rehnquist stated that since "other avenues of outside informational flow by the Union remain available, the prohibition on bulk mailing, reasonable in the absence of First Amendment considerations, remains reasonable." The prohibition on inmate-to-inmate solicitation of membership did not violate First Amendment speech rights because such solicitation is "more than the simple expression of individual views as to the advantages or disadvantages of a union or its views; it is an invitation to collectively engage in a legitimately prohibited activity. If the prison officials are otherwise entitled to control organized union activity within the prison walls, the prohibition on solicitation for such activity is not then made impermissible on account of First Amendment considerations, for such a prohibition is then not only reasonable but necessary." The lower court had reasoned that the ban on bulk mailings and union meetings violated the equal protection clause of the Fourteenth Amendment because the Jaycees, Alcoholics Anonymous, and the Boy Scouts were allowed meet and use bulk mailings. The majority disagreed with this opinion and the lower court's analysis, seeing the lower court as "erroneously treating this case as if the prison environment were essentially a 'public forum.'" Because a prison is not a public forum, prison administrators need only show that there is a rational basis for distinguishing between organizations. Officials provided affidavits indicating that the Jaycees and Alcoholics Anonymous were rehabilitative organizations and were working in conjunction with the goals of the prison. The union, on the other hand, constituted an adversarial organization at odds with institutional goals.

CASE EXCERPT

"An examination of the potential restrictions on speech or association that have been imposed by the regulations under challenge, demonstrates that the restrictions imposed are reasonable, and are consistent with the inmates' status as prisoners and with the legitimate operational considerations of the institution…First Amendment associational rights, while perhaps more directly implicated by the regulatory prohibitions, likewise must give way to the reasonable considerations of penal management. As already noted, numerous associational rights are necessarily curtailed by the realities of confinement. They may be curtailed whenever the institution's officials, in the exercise of their informed discretion, reasonably conclude that such associations, whether through group meetings or otherwise, possess the likelihood of disruption to prison order or stability, or otherwise interfere with the legitimate penological objectives of the prison environment."

SIGNIFICANCE

This is the only case decided by the Supreme Court dealing with inmate unions. Inmate unions were popular in the 1970s, but have largely been abandoned. Consequently, no further cases involving union activities have reached the high court. This case failed to provide clear guidelines on how to resolve alleged First Amendment violations. If a similar case were to be decided today, it is likely the Court would employ (no pun intended) the *Turner v. Safley* test.

HOUCHINS v. KQED, INC.
438 U.S. 1 (1978)

FACTS

On March 31, 1975, KQED, a broadcasting company for licensed television and radio stations in the San Francisco Bay Area, reported the suicide of a prisoner in a section of the Santa Rita county jail. The report included a psychiatrist's statement that conditions in this particular section were responsible for the illnesses of his patient-prisoners there. This section was described as the scene of alleged rapes, beatings, and adverse physical conditions. The report also included a statement from Sheriff Houchins of Alameda County, denying that prison conditions were responsible for prisoners' illnesses. KQED requested permission to inspect and take pictures within the specific area. After permission was denied, KQED and the Alameda and Oakland branches of the National Association for the Advancement of Colored People (NAACP) filed suit alleging that Sheriff Houchins had violated the First Amendment by not permitting media access and failing to provide any effective means by which the public could be informed of jail conditions or of inmate grievances. They asserted that public access to such information was essential in order for NAACP members to

HOUCHINS v. KQED, INC. *(cont.)*

participate in the public debate on jail conditions, and that television coverage of the conditions in the cells and facilities was the most effective way of informing the public of prison conditions. The district court found that the media policy was not necessary to protect inmate privacy or minimize security and administrative problems and ruled in favor of KQED and the NAACP branches. The court of appeals sustained the district court's decision.

ISSUE

Does the news media have a constitutional right of access to a county jail, over and above that of other persons, to interview inmates and make sound recordings, films, and photographs for publication and broadcasting by newspapers, radio, and television?

HOLDING

No. The First Amendment grants no special right of access to the press to government-controlled sources of information.

RATIONALE

The Court reasoned that the importance of acceptable prison conditions and the media's role of providing information afforded "no basis for reading into the Constitution a right of the public or the media to enter these institutions... and take moving and still pictures of inmates for broadcast purposes"; also, "neither the First Amendment nor the Fourteenth Amendment mandates a right of access to government information or sources of information within the government's control." Following precedent established in *Pell v. Procunier*, 417 U.S. 817 (1974) and *Saxbe v. Washington Post Co.*, 417 U.S. 843 (1974), media have no special right of access to correctional institutions that is different from or greater than that given to the general public. The Court noted that the respondents still possessed First Amendment rights to receive uncensored letters from inmates. They also were free to interview legal counsel of inmates and to seek out former inmates, prison visitors, public officials, and institutional personnel. In a footnote, Chief Justice Burger stated that "inmates in jails, prisons, or mental institutions retain certain fundamental rights of privacy; they are not like animals in a zoo to be filmed and photographed at will by the public or by media reporters, however 'educational' the process may be for others."

CASE EXCERPT

"Neither the First Amendment nor the Fourteenth Amendment mandates a right of access to government information or sources of information within the government's control... Until the political branches decree otherwise, as they are free to do, the media have no special right of access to the Alameda County Jail different from or greater than that accorded the public generally."

SIGNIFICANCE

In this case the Supreme Court once again restricted the freedom of the press, by holding that the media have no right of access to specific inmates or prison in general greater than the right of access enjoyed by the general public. In so holding, the Court again balanced the interests of the media against the interests of prison officials, and found in favor of the prison officials.

BLOCK v. RUTHERFORD

468 U.S. 576 (1984)

FACTS

In 1975, pretrial detainees at Los Angeles County's Central Jail brought a class action under due process grounds against the County Sheriff, certain administrators of Central Jail, and the County Board of Supervisors, challenging various policies and practices of the jail and conditions of their confinement. The suit challenged the policy denying pretrial detainees contact visits with their spouses, relatives, children, and friends, and the jail's practice of permitting irregularly scheduled shakedown searches of individual cells in the absence of the cell occupants. The district court sustained both of these challenges, and the court of appeals affirmed the district court's orders requiring that certain pretrial detainees should be allowed contact visits and that inmates be allowed to observe searches of their cells: "The Court of Appeals held that the District Court's order on contact visitation 'fits harmoniously within [the] pattern' of federal cases following Wolfish 'recognizing the important security interests of the [penal] institution but at the same time recognizing the psychological and punitive effects which the prolonged loss of contact visitation has upon detainees. It suggested that a blanket prohibition of contact visits for all detainees would be an 'unreasonable, exaggerated response to security concerns.'"

ISSUE

Do pretrial detainees have a constitutional right to contact visits and to observe shakedown searches of their cells by prison officials?

HOLDING

No. In a 6–3 judgment written by Chief Justice Burger, the Court reversed the lower court's decision, and ruled that the blanket prohibition on contact visits and the observing of cell searches was a reasonable, non-punitive response to legitimate penal interests of security and did not constitute Fourteenth Amendment violations.

RATIONALE

In 1979, the Court decided in *Bell v. Wolfish*, 441 U.S. 520 (1979), the extent of constitutional protection accorded to pretrial detainees. In *Wolfish*, the Court held that when pretrial detainees allege deprivation of liberty without due process, "the dispositive inquiry is whether the challenged condition, practice, or policy constitutes punishment." The Court concluded that if a challenged condition or restriction is "reasonably related to a legitimate governmental objective, it does not, without more, amount to 'punishment.' In the case at hand, the blanket prohibition on contact visits was seen as "an entirely reasonable, nonpunitive response to legitimate security concerns, consistent with the Fourteenth Amendment." The Court pointed to the numerous security problems that contact visits posed, included opportunities to bring in drugs and weapons. "Moreover, to expose to others those detainees who, as is often the case, are awaiting trial for serious, violent offenses or have prior convictions carries with it the risks that the safety of innocent individuals will be jeopardized. Totally disallowing contact visits is not excessive in relation to the security and other interests at stake. There are many justifications for denying contact visits entirely, rather than attempting the difficult task of establishing a program of limited visits such as that imposed here. Nothing in the Constitution requires that detainees be allowed contact visits; responsible, experienced administrators have determined, in their sound discretion, that such visits will jeopardize the security of the facility and other persons." The majority further ruled that "conducting random, irregular 'shakedown' searches of cells in the absence of the cell occupants is also a reasonable response by the jail officials to legitimate security

concerns." The Court reaffirmed its holding in *Wolfish* that "proper deference to the informed discretion of prison authorities demands that they, and not the courts, make the difficult judgments which reconcile conflicting claims affecting the security of the institution, the welfare of the prison staff, and the property rights of the detainees."

CASE EXCERPT

"The question before us, therefore, is narrow: whether the prohibition of contact visits is reasonably related to legitimate governmental objectives. More particularly, because there is no dispute that internal security of detention facilities is a legitimate governmental interest, our inquiry is simply whether petitioners' blanket prohibition on contact visits at Central Jail is reasonably related to the security of that facility. That there is a valid, rational connection between a ban on contact visits and internal security of a detention facility is too obvious to warrant extended discussion…Contact visits invite a host of security problems. They open the institution to the introduction of drugs, weapons, and other contraband. Visitors can easily conceal guns, knives, drugs, or other contraband in countless ways and pass them to an inmate unnoticed by even the most vigilant observers. And these items can readily be slipped from the clothing of an innocent child, or transferred by other visitors permitted close contact with inmates."

SIGNIFICANCE

In this case the Supreme Court held that inmates have no right to either observe searches of their cells or to contact visits. The basis for both holdings was the reduced constitutional rights possessed by inmates, and the need for prison officials to be able to control their institutions as efficiently as possible.

TURNER v. SAFLEY

482 U.S. 78 (1987)

FACTS

Respondent inmates brought a class action challenging two regulations promulgated by the Missouri Division of Corrections (MDC). The first permitted correspondence between immediate family members who are inmates at different institutions within the division's jurisdiction, and between inmates "concerning

TURNER v. SAFLEY *(cont.)*

legal matters," but allowed other inmate correspondence only if each inmate's classification/treatment team considered it to be in the best interests of the parties. The second regulation permitted an inmate to marry only with the prison superintendent's permission, which was given only under "compelling reasons" to do so. Testimony indicated that generally only a pregnancy or the birth of an illegitimate child would be considered "compelling." The Federal District Court found both regulations unconstitutional, and the Court of Appeals affirmed.

ISSUE

(1) Is a prison regulation banning certain correspondence between inmates at different institutions unconstitutional? (2) Is a prison regulation prohibiting inmates from marrying without "compelling reasons" unconstitutional?

HOLDING

No to the first question. Yes to the second question. The lower courts erred in ruling that *Procunier v. Martinez* and its progeny require the application of a strict scrutiny standard of review for resolving respondents' constitutional complaints. Rather, those cases indicate that a lesser standard is appropriate whereby inquiry is made into whether a prison regulation that impinges on inmates' constitutional rights is "reasonably related" to legitimate penological interests. The Missouri inmate correspondence regulation is, on the record here, reasonable and facially valid. The constitutional right of prisoners to marry is impermissibly burdened by the Missouri marriage regulation.

RATIONALE

Writing for the Majority, Justice O'Connor noted that to determine whether a prison regulation is reasonable, the relevant factors to be considered are "(a) whether there is a 'valid, rational connection' between the regulation and a legitimate and neutral governmental interest put forward to justify it, which connection cannot be so remote as to render the regulation arbitrary or irrational; (b) whether there are alternative means of exercising the asserted constitutional right that remain open to inmates, which alternatives, if they exist, will require a measure of judicial deference to the corrections officials' expertise; (c) whether and the extent to which accommodation of

the asserted right will have an impact on prison staff, on inmates' liberty, and on the allocation of limited prison resources, which impact, if substantial, will require particular deference to corrections officials; and (d) whether the regulation represents an 'exaggerated response' to prison concerns, the existence of a ready alternative that fully accommodates the prisoner's rights at *de minimis* costs to valid penological interests being evidence of unreasonableness" (*Turner v. Safley*, 482 U.S. 78, 79). The Missouri inmate correspondence regulation was seen to be "logically related to the legitimate security concerns of prison officials, who testified that mail between prisons can be used to communicate escape plans, to arrange violent acts, and to foster prison gang activity. Moreover, the regulation does not deprive prisoners of all means of expression, but simply bars communication with a limited class of people—other inmates—with whom authorities have particular cause to be concerned. The regulation is entitled to deference on the basis of the significant impact of prison correspondence on the liberty and safety of other prisoners and prison personnel, in light of officials' testimony that such correspondence facilitates the development of informal organizations that threaten safety and security at penal institutions. Nor is there an obvious, easy alternative to the regulation, since monitoring inmate correspondence clearly would impose more than a de minimis cost in terms of the burden on staff resources required to conduct item-by-item censorship, and would create an appreciable risk of missing dangerous communications. The regulation is content neutral and does not unconstitutionally abridge the First Amendment rights of prison inmates."

However, the Court viewed the second marriage regulation differently. "Prisoners have a constitutionally protected right to marry under *Zablocki v. Redhail*, 474 U.S. 374 (1978). Although such a marriage is subject to substantial restrictions as a result of incarceration, sufficient important attributes of marriage remain to form a constitutionally protected relationship." The Court also ruled that the regulation was not reasonably related to legitimate penological objectives. While the officials had maintained that the ban on marriage prevented "love triangles," the Court observed that such a contention was meritless and that "inmate rivalries are likely to develop with or without a formal marriage ceremony. Moreover, the regulation's broad prohibition is not justified by the security of fellow inmates and prison staff, who are not affected where the inmate makes the private decision to marry a civilian. Rather, the regulation represents an exaggerated response to the claimed security objectives, since allowing marriages unless the warden finds a threat to security, order, or the public safety represents an obvious, easy alternative that would accommodate the right to marry while imposing a *de minimis* burden." The regulation also was seen as too broad by refusing permission to marry to all inmates without a compelling reason. The Court pointed to "officials' testimony that male inmates' marriages had generally caused them no problems and that they had no objections to prisoners marrying civilians."

CASE EXCERPT

"As our opinions in *Pell, Bell,* and *Jones* show, several factors are relevant in determining the reasonableness of the regulation at issue. First, there must be a 'valid, rational connection' between the prison regulation and the legitimate governmental interest put forward to justify it ... A second factor relevant in determining the reasonableness of a prison restriction, as *Pell* shows, is whether there are alternative means of exercising the right that remain open to prison inmates ... A third consideration is the impact accommodation of the asserted constitutional right will have on guards and other inmates, and on the allocation of prison resources generally ... Finally, the absence of ready alternatives is evidence of the reasonableness of a prison regulation ... Applying our analysis to the Missouri rule barring inmate-to-inmate correspondence, we conclude that the record clearly demonstrates that the regulation was reasonably related to legitimate security interests. We find that the marriage restriction, however, does not satisfy the reasonable relationship standard, but rather constitutes an exaggerated response to petitioners' rehabilitation and security concerns."

SIGNIFICANCE

In this case the Supreme Court upheld a prison regulation limiting the ability of inmates to communicate via the mails with inmates in other prisons. This follows in a long line of cases limiting the First Amendment rights of inmates. More significantly, in this case the Supreme Court enunciated a new test for determining the constitutionality of a prison regulation which affects the constitutional rights of inmates: Such a regulation is valid if it is "reasonably related" to a "legitimate penological interest."

THORNBURGH v. ABBOTT

490 U.S. 401 (1989)

FACTS

Federal Bureau of Prison regulations permitted federal prisoners to receive publications from the outside, but authorized prison officials to reject incoming publications if they were found to be detrimental to institutional security, violated their First Amendment rights. The regulations permitted an inmate to subscribe to, or to receive, a publication without prior approval but authorized the warden to reject a publication if it was determined to be "detrimental to the security, good order, or discipline of the institution or if it might facilitate criminal activity." Regulations prohibited the warden from rejecting a publication "solely because its content is religious, philosophical, political, social or sexual, or because its content is unpopular or repugnant." The warden was prohibited from establishing an excluded list of publications; each issue of a subscription publication had to be reviewed separately. Respondents, a class of inmates and certain publishers, brought suit against the Federal Bureau of Prisons, claiming that the regulations, both on their face and as applied to 46 specifically excluded publications, violated their First Amendment rights under *Procunier v. Martinez*, 416 U.S. 396 (1974). Without following Martinez, the district court upheld the regulations and did not address the 46 excluded publications, adopting a standard according deference to the judgment of prison administrators. The Court of Appeals, however, followed *Martinez*, ruling that the regulations were facially invalid and remanding the case to the district court for a determination of the constitutionality of the 46 excluded publications. Officials of the Department of Justice and the Bureau of Prisons appealed, and the Court granted certiorari in order to determine the appropriate review standard.

ISSUE

What is the proper standard of review for the Federal Bureau of Prison's regulations restricting inmates' access to outside publications? Are these regulations unconstitutional?

HOLDING

No. In a decision written by Justice Blackmun, the Court agreed with the district court that the proper

THORNBURGH v. ABBOTT *(cont.)*

standard of review in this case was the standard set forth in *Turner v. Safley*, 482 U.S. 78 (1987): whether the regulations are "reasonably related to legitimate penological interests." The Court found the regulations, under this standard, to be facially valid and vacated the decision of the court of appeals. The Court agreed with the appellate court with respect to remanding the case to the district court for a case-by-case review of the validity of the regulations as applied to each of the 46 publications.

RATIONALE

Under the *Turner* standard, correctional administrators are to be accorded "considerable deference in regulating the delicate balance between prison order and security and the legitimate demands of 'outsiders' who seek to enter the prison environment." The underlying objective of the regulations at issue is to protect prison security and is thus a legitimate objective. Further, the regulations permitted "a broad range of publications to be sent, received, and read," so other forms of expression were still open to inmates. The decision in *Martinez* was overruled by this case "to the extent that it might support the drawing of a categorical distinction between incoming correspondence from prisoners (to which *Turner* applied its reasonableness standard) and incoming correspondence from nonprisoners." The less deferential *Martinez* standard, "whereby prison regulations authorizing mail censorship must be 'generally necessary' to protect one or more legitimate governmental interests," pertains to regulations affecting the outgoing personal mail of inmates.

CASE EXCERPT

"In our view, when prison officials are able to demonstrate that they have rejected a less restrictive alternative because of reasonably founded fears that it will lead to greater harm, they succeed in demonstrating that the alternative they in fact selected was not an 'exaggerated response' under *Turner*. Furthermore, the administrative inconvenience of this proposed alternative is also a factor to be considered."

SIGNIFICANCE

In this case the Supreme Court applied the *Turner v. Safley* test to a prison regulation limiting the receipt of periodicals by inmates, and upheld the regulation. This case makes it clear that the *Turner v. Safley* test is an easy test for prison officials to pass, thereby making it easier for them to craft prison regulations which limit inmate rights.

DISCUSSION QUESTIONS

1. Imagine that you are a prison administrator addressing new inmates in an orientation session. How will you explain both the restrictions and freedoms regarding contact with the outside world?
2. What are the four prongs of the *Turner v. Safley* test? How are they applied in that case?
3. Take the issues in each of the cases in this chapter and present the point of view of an inmate toward the issues.
4. As in question 3, take the issues in each of the cases in this chapter, but present the point of view of a corrections administrator toward the issues. Keep in mind legitimate security concerns and explain how each issue specifically affects security of the institution.
5. Imagine that you represent the media. What kind of access to prisoners can you expect to have? Does any limitation on that access affect your performance of your job? If so, in what way?
6. What is the significance of the Supreme Court's decision in *Turner v. Safley*?
7. What rights, if any, do visitors to jails retain?
8. What purpose is served by allowing prison staff to search jail visitors? Should the standards be different for jail and prison visitors? Why or why not?
9. Why is press access to prisons limited? Does this limitation make it more difficult for inmates to communicate with the outside world in a meaningful way?
10. Why is it important for prisons to be able to closely monitor inmate communications with the outside world?

CHAPTER FIVE

CONDITIONS OF CONFINEMENT

LEE v. WASHINGTON, *390 U.S. 333 (1968)*

CRUZ v. BETO, *405 U.S. 319 (1972)*

BELL v. WOLFISH, *441 U.S. 520 (1979)*

RHODES v. CHAPMAN, *452 U.S. 337 (1981)*

O'LONE v. ESTATE OF SHABAZZ, *482 U.S. 342 (1987)*

DESHANEY v. WINNEBAGO COUNTY DEPARTMENT OF SOCIAL SERVICES, *489 U.S. 189 (1989)*

WILSON v. SEITER, *501 U.S. 294 (1991)*

RUFO v. INMATES OF SUFFOLK COUNTY JAIL, *502 U.S. 367 (1992)*

HELLING v. MCKINNEY, *509 U.S. 25 (1993)*

FARMER v. BRENNAN, *511 U.S. 825 (1994)*

JOHNSON v. CALIFORNIA, *543 U.S. 499 (2005)*

CUTTER ET AL. v. WILKINSON, *544 U.S. 709 (2005)*

U.S. v. GEORGIA, *546 U.S. 151 (2006)*

INTRODUCTION

The thirteen cases in this chapter concern several issues affecting prisons and jails: racial segregation; religion; various conditions of confinement, including due process rights in Supermax prisons; overcrowding; and the duty to protect. The first decade of the twenty-first century has given the Court the opportunity to revisit several of the earlier cases discussed here. The cases are presented in chronological order and begin with a 1968 racial segregation case.

In *Lee v. Washington* (1968), the Supreme Court struck down an Alabama law that required segregated prison cells. This was the first time the Court addressed the practice of racial segregation in correctional facilities. The Court ruled that segregation violated the equal protection clause of the Fourteenth Amendment. However, it was also noted that the prohibition against segregation was not absolute and could depend on circumstances. In 2003, the Ninth Circuit ruled that the California prison system practice of making temporary 60-day double-cell assignments based primarily on race was not a violation of equal protection (*Johnson v. State of California*, 321 F. 3d 791,

9th Cir. 2003). This policy objective was made to avoid racial conflict and, applying the *Turner* test discussed in chapter 4 of this volume, the appellate court saw the regulation as reasonably related to legitimate penological concerns. However, the Supreme Court reversed the Ninth Circuit in 2005 in *Johnson v. California*, 543 U.S. 499 (2005), the second segregation case discussed later in this chapter. In holding that strict scrutiny is the proper standard of review, the Supreme Court reaffirmed the *Lee* decision. The Court did not, however, determine whether California's practice in fact violated the equal protection clause of the Fourteenth Amendment. Since 2005, California has amended its practice, phasing out automatic race-based segregation policies and looking closely at other factors contributing to prison violence.

The Supreme Court also cited the *Lee v. Washington* decision in the next case presented in this chapter, *Cruz v. Beto*. The Court noted that prisoners, like all individuals "have the right to petition the Government for redress of grievances" and that "racial segregation, which is unconstitutional outside prisons, is unconstitutional within prisons, save for 'the necessities of prison security and discipline'" (*Lee v. Washington*). *Cruz v. Beto* involved a Buddhist inmate's freedom to practice his religion. In this case, the Court ruled that inmates holding unconventional religious beliefs must have an opportunity to practice their beliefs similar to the opportunity afforded inmates of conventional religious beliefs.

Religious freedoms are guaranteed by the First Amendment and are made applicable to the states by the Fourteenth Amendment. In the other religious freedom case discussed in this chapter, *O'Lone v. Estate of Shabazz* (1987), the Court held that religious rights may be restricted in prisons in the interest of promoting institutional security, discipline, limited resources, and inmate and correctional officer safety. This case was decided one week after the Court's decision in *Turner v. Safley* (see chapter 4), and the Court applied the *Turner* test to the alleged freedom of religion violation in *O'Lone*.

The *Turner* test was overturned in religious freedom cases in 1993 when Congress passed the Religious Freedom Restoration Act (RFRA). RFRA mandated that the "government may substantially burden a person's exercise of religion only if it is in furtherance of a compelling governmental interest; and is the least restrictive means of furthering that compelling governmental interest" (PL 103–141(HR 1308)). The "compelling interest/least restrictive means" is a heightened standard unlike the *Turner* rational basis test. This heightened standard applied to challenges of religious freedoms until 1997, when the Supreme Court overturned RFRA in *City of Boerne v. Flores*, ruling that Congress violated separation of power principles in enacting RFRA. Thus, in 1997, the *Turner* rational basis test was reinstated, although RFRA remained binding for the Federal Bureau of Prisons due to an executive order.

Just three years later, Congress passed the Religious Land Use and Institutionalized Persons Act of 2000 (RLUIPA) which reestablished RFRA's compelling interest/least restrictive means test. In other words, restrictions on religious practices must further compelling government interests such as safety, security, efficiency, and cost effectiveness, and these compelling interests must be satisfied through the least restrictive means possible. Some of the examples of religious practices that RLUIPA protects are kosher diets, allowing Catholic inmates to wear crucifixes, allowing Christian inmates to receive communion wine, not forcing Muslim inmates to handle pork, and allowing

religious texts in prisons. Many states have also passed their own RFRA laws, so state prisons must adhere to those laws and RLUIPA. This means that prison officials have to be more sensitive to inmate religious requests than they would under the *Turner* standard, as long as the religious requests are based on legitimate and sincere religious beliefs.

Muddying the waters still further, the American Correctional Association supports the *Turner* test as one of its legislative priorities, stating on its web site that "[t]he legal standard for establishing the validity of institutional rules on religious faith and practice should be the reasonableness standard provided in *Turner v. Safley* and *O'Lone v. Shabazz*."

Legal challenges to restrictions in state prisons on religious freedoms have been numerous, with several courts addressing the constitutionality of RLUIPA. While most appellate courts upheld RLUIPA's constitutionality, the Sixth Circuit found it unconstitutional (*Cutter et al. v. Wilkinson*, 2003 FED App. 0397P (6th Cir.)). Thus, in 2004, the Supreme Court granted certiorari to hear this case and to address the constitutionality of RLUIPA. As discussed later in this chapter in *Cutter v. Wilkinson* (2005), the Court, in a unanimous verdict, reversed the Sixth Circuit and ruled that RLUIPA "does not, on its face, exceed the limits of permissible government accommodation of religious practices." Security interests of prisons are still paramount, however, and corrections officials can refuse excessive requests for religious accommodations that affect the efficient operations of the institution or that burden other prisoners. The Court also noted in a footnote in *Cutter* that accommodating religious requests does not always result in "benefits" to those inmates making such requests. For example, a Kosher diet in one state means "'a fruit, a vegetable, a granola bar, and a liquid nutritional supplement—each and every meal'" (*Cutter*, fn.10). For the time being, the constitutionality of the RLUIPA remains intact. Inmates can also challenge the totality of the prison's conditions as unconstitutional. This form of suit is known as a "conditions of confinement" lawsuit. The other cases in this chapter concern such conditions of confinement lawsuits, as well as the issue of double-bunking as it applies to overcrowding, and the duty to protect. In 1979, the Supreme Court addressed various conditions of confinement affecting pretrial detainees in *Bell v. Wolfish* (1979). These conditions which inmates claimed violated their constitutional rights included double-bunking, a "publisher-only" rule regarding receipt of books, body-cavity searches, a prohibition against receipt of packages, and a room-search rule. Such conditions were found not to deprive the pretrial detainees of any of their constitutional rights. Double-bunking was also the issue in 1981 in *Rhodes v. Chapman*. Inmates alleged that the double-celling and crowded conditions were cruel and unusual punishment under the Eighth Amendment and made applicable to the states through the Fourteenth Amendment.

While cruel and unusual punishment is prohibited by the Eighth Amendment, exactly what is cruel and unusual has changed as our society has evolved. While the Court ruled that double-bunking, in and of itself, is not cruel and unusual, lower courts had ruled quite differently.

In 1991, the Court again addressed conditions of confinement in *Wilson v. Seiter* and provided definitive guidance on what constitutes cruel and unusual punishment. The Court held that prisoners claiming that conditions of confinement violate the Eighth Amendment's ban on cruel and unusual punishment must show a culpable state of mind amounting to "deliberate indifference" on the part of prison officials. The "deliberate indifference" standard was first applied in 1976 in another case discussed in the next chapter, *Estelle v. Gamble,* when the Supreme Court ruled that correctional administrators could be held liable for injury to an inmate if the administrators displayed "deliberate indifference" to the situation. This is generally a fairly difficult standard for inmate plaintiffs to meet in conditions of confinement cases.

When courts do hold that conditions in prisons and jails are constitutionally deficient, corrections officials and inmates may enter into consent decrees providing for redress of violations within a specified period of time. This was the situation in the next case, *Rufo v. Inmates of Suffolk County Jail* (1992), when the Court ruled that decrees may be modified under certain circumstances.

In 1993, the Supreme Court again applied the deliberate indifference standard to an Eighth Amendment case involving exposure to second-hand cigarette smoke. In *Helling v. McKinney*, the Court ruled that prison authorities' deliberate indifference to an inmate's involuntary exposure to environmental tobacco smoke posed an unreasonable risk to future health and constituted an Eighth Amendment violation.

An emerging area of liability for prison officials is the duty to protect incarcerated inmates from themselves and each other. In a nonprison case included in this chapter, *DeShaney v. Winnebago County Department of Social Services*, the Supreme Court held that the due process clause of the Fourteenth Amendment does not impose a special duty on the state to provide services to the public for protection against private actors. This important case is applicable to corrections law because it suggests that the state does have an affirmative duty to protect those in state custody from a third party. Thus, in another case discussed in this chapter, in 1994 the Supreme Court held that correctional personnel may be liable for failing to prevent harm to an inmate by another inmate but only if it can be demonstrated that employee conduct displayed "deliberate indifference" to the safety of the inmate (*Farmer v. Brennan*). This is the same deliberate indifference standard upheld in previous cases in this chapter. The Court provided guidance in defining "deliberate indifference" as when officials are subjectively aware of the risk of serious harm to an inmate and disregard that risk by failing to take reasonable measures to decrease it. In *Farmer v. Brennan*, the Court rejected an objective test regarding "whether the risk is known or should have been known" as the appropriate test for deliberate indifference.

The subjective test appears to make it harder for inmate plaintiffs to prevail in Eighth Amendment cases. While the Court emphasized that prison officials are not free to disregard obvious risks, they stated that "prison officials may not be held liable if they prove that they were unaware of even an obvious risk or if they responded reasonably to a known risk, even if the harm ultimately was not averted."

How congressional acts affect the rights of prisoners and prison conditions has already been discussed in light of religious freedoms and the RLUIPA. Prison authorities grapple with accommodating another congressional act, the Americans with Disabilities Act (ADA) of 1990. While it is clear that employers, state and local governments, employment agencies, and labor unions may not discriminate under the ADA against disabled but otherwise qualified persons in employment situations, it was not so clear how the ADA applied to incarcerated individuals. Significant numbers of prisoners have vision and hearing problems, mental problems, and physical, learning, and speech disabilities. Aging inmate populations and long prison sentences only exacerbate these conditions. One case discussed in chapter 6 in this volume, *Pennsylvania Department of Corrections v. Yeskey* (1998), did hold that ADA's Title II protections apply to prison inmates and prisons, but the Court declined to consider in that whether the application of the ADA to state prisons was a constitutionally valid exercise of Congress' power. One of the last cases in the chapter, *U.S. v. Georgia* (2006), makes clear that Title II of the ADA, as applied to state prisons, is constitutional with respect to conduct that violates the Fourteenth Amendment. Prior to this decision, the state of Georgia had maintained that state prisons were immune from being sued for damages and that Congress had exceeded its power in authorizing suits against states under the ADA.

LEE v. WASHINGTON
390 U.S. 333 (1968)

FACTS

Alabama law barred the integration of the races in prison cells. Inmates in the Alabama prison system sought an injunction. A special three judge federal district court conceded that while extraordinary circumstances might occasionally require separation of the races for a limited time, complete and permanent separation of the races in all state correctional facilities was unconstitutionally overbroad. The district court struck down the state statute and entered an order directing correctional administrators to begin the desegregation of all state jail and prison facilities. The district court relied on *Brown v. Board of Education*, 347 U.S. 483 (1954), in reaching its decision, stating, "it is unmistakably clear that racial discrimination by governmental authorities in the use of public facilities cannot be tolerated." The court also indicated that "the principle extends to all institutions controlled or operated by the state." The state appealed the decision to the United States Supreme Court.

ISSUE

Is a state statute requiring racial segregation in prisons a violation of the Fourteenth Amendment?

HOLDING

Yes. Mandatory racial segregation in a state prison is unconstitutional.

RATIONALE

The Supreme Court, in a one paragraph per curiam opinion, affirmed the decision of the district court striking down racial segregation in Alabama's prisons and jails. This was the first time the high court addressed the issue of racial segregation in correctional facilities,

although the Court had previously struck down racial segregation in a host of other public facilities.

CASE EXCERPT

"The State's contentions that Rule 23 of the federal rules of civil procedure, which relates to class actions, was violated in this case and that the challenged statutes are not unconstitutional are without merit. The remaining contention of the State is that the specific orders directing desegregation of prisons and jails make no allowance for the necessities of prison security and discipline, but we do not so read the 'Order, Judgment and Decree' of the District Court, which when read as a whole we find unexceptionable."

CASE SIGNIFICANCE

In a concurring opinion, Justice Black emphasized that while racial discrimination is generally prohibited, this general prohibition was not absolute. He conceded that "prison authorities have the right, acting in good faith and in particularized circumstances, to take into account racial tensions in maintaining security, discipline, and good order in prisons and jails." This is an important caveat, as it provided prison officials with a possible justification for racial segregation, if institutional security necessitated it. Defining exactly what sort of situation would constitute the "particularized circumstances" alluded to by Justice Black was left for another day. A number of lower courts have since upheld racial segregation only for brief periods of time and in emergency situations.

CRUZ v. BETO
405 U.S. 319 (1972)

FACTS

In a Section 1983 civil suit, Cruz, a Buddhist inmate in a Texas prison, alleged that he was discriminated against and persecuted for his religious beliefs by prison authorities. Cruz was not allowed to use the prison chapel, and, when he shared his Buddhist religious material with other prisoners, he was placed in solitary confinement on a diet of bread and water for two weeks, without access to newspapers, magazines, or other sources of news. Cruz also was prohibited from corresponding with his religious advisor in the Buddhist sect. In his complaint, Cruz claimed that Texas encouraged inmates to participate in religious programs of other faiths, providing at state expense

Catholic, Jewish, and Protestant chaplains. The state also provided copies of the Jewish and Christian Bibles, conducting weekly Sunday school classes and religious services as well. Cruz claimed that good merit points were given to prisoners as a reward for attending orthodox religious services. These points enhance a prisoner's eligibility for desirable job assignments and early parole consideration. The district court denied relief and refused to hear the case, stating that Cruz's complaint was in an area that should be left "to the sound discretion of prison administration." The Court of Appeals affirmed, and Cruz appealed to the Supreme Court.

ISSUE

Are inmates who hold unconventional religious beliefs still entitled to practice their beliefs in as comparable a situation as those who hold more conventional religious beliefs?

HOLDING

Yes. In a per curiam opinion, the Supreme Court vacated and remanded the case back to the lower courts for hearing, holding that, on the basis of the allegations, Texas discriminated against Cruz by denying him a reasonable opportunity to pursue his Buddhist faith comparable to that offered other prisoners adhering to conventional religious precepts.

RATIONALE

The Supreme Court observed that federal courts do not sit to supervise prisons, "but to enforce the constitutional rights of all 'persons,' including prisoners." Prisoners are subject by necessity to rules and regulations, and prison officials must be given latitude in the administration of prison affairs. However, as the Court ruled in *Johnson v. Avery*, 393 U.S. 483 (1969), prisoners still retain the right "to petition the Government for redress of grievances which, of course, includes 'access of prisoners to the courts for the purpose of presenting their complaints.'" The Court noted that a decision more to the point at hand was the 1964 decision in *Cooper v. Pate*, 378 U.S. 546, where the Court addressed an allegation that a prisoner, because of his religious beliefs, was denied permission to purchase certain religious publications and was denied certain other privileges enjoyed by other inmates. The Court ruled that prisoners are allowed to bring civil actions alleging civil rights violations against prison officials. In a footnote, the Court stated that they were

not suggesting that every religious group in a prison "must have identical facilities or personnel. A special chapel or place of worship need not be provided for every faith regardless of size; nor must a chaplain, priest, or minister be provided without regard to the extent of the demand. But reasonable opportunities must be afforded to all prisoners to exercise the religious freedom guaranteed by the First and Fourteenth Amendments without fear of penalty."

CASE EXCERPT

"If Cruz was a Buddhist and if he was denied a reasonable opportunity of pursuing his faith comparable to the opportunity afforded fellow prisoners who adhere to conventional religious precepts, then there was palpable discrimination by the State against the Buddhist religion, established 600 B.C., long before the Christian era. The First Amendment, applicable to the States by reason of the Fourteenth Amendment, *Torcaso* v. *Watkins,* 367 U.S. 488, 492–493, prohibits government from making a law 'prohibiting the free exercise' of religion. If the allegations of this complaint are assumed to be true, as they must be on the motion to dismiss, Texas has violated the First and Fourteenth Amendments."

CASE SIGNIFICANCE

This is a very important case because it establishes the right of inmates to follow the tenets of unconventional religious movements. The First Amendment right to practice one's religious beliefs is not restricted to conventional, mainstream religions, even in the prison setting. The Court did make clear, however, that what is required is access to places of worship and the opportunity to practice one's faith, not necessarily equal treatment for all religions.

BELL v. WOLFISH

441 U.S. 520 (1979)

FACTS

Respondent inmates brought this class action in Federal District Court challenging the constitutionality of numerous conditions of confinement and practices in the Metropolitan Correctional Center (MCC), a federally operated short-term custodial facility in New York City designed primarily to house pretrial detainees. The District Court, on various constitutional grounds, enjoined the practice of housing two

BELL v. WOLFISH *(cont.)*

inmates in individual rooms originally intended for single occupancy (double-bunking); enforcement of the so-called publisher-only rule prohibiting inmates from receiving hard-cover books that are not mailed directly from publishers, book clubs, or bookstores; the prohibition against inmates' receipt of packages of food and personal items from outside the institution; the practice of body-cavity searches of inmates following contact visits with persons from outside the institution; and the requirement that pretrial detainees remain outside their rooms during routine inspections by MCC officials. The Court of Appeals affirmed these rulings, holding with respect to the double-bunking practice that the MCC had failed to make a showing of "compelling necessity" sufficient to justify such practice.

ISSUE

Are pretrial detainees' conditions of confinement (which include crowded cells, body cavity searches, etc.) constitutionally valid?

HOLDING

Yes. The double-bunking practice does not deprive pretrial detainees of their liberty without due process of law in contravention of the Fifth Amendment, nor do the publisher-only rule, body-cavity searches, the prohibition against the receipt of packages, or the room-search rule violate any constitutional guarantees.

RATIONALE

There is no source in the Constitution for the Court of Appeals' compelling necessity standard. Neither the presumption of innocence, the due process clause of the Fifth Amendment, or a pretrial detainee's right to be free from punishment provides any basis for such standard. In evaluating the constitutionality of conditions or restrictions of pretrial detention that implicate only the protection against deprivation of liberty without due process of law, the proper inquiry is whether those conditions or restrictions amount to punishment of the detainee. If there is no expressed intent to punish, and if the specific restrictions or circumstances are reasonably related to legitimate nonpunitive governmental objectives, then they do not constitute "punishment." However, "arbitrary or purposeless" conditions or restrictions may lead to judicial inferences that "the purpose of the governmental action is punishment that may not constitutionally be inflicted

upon detainees *qua* detainees." In addition to ensuring the detainees' presence at trial, effective management of a detention facility is a valid objective. Accordingly, double-bunking as practiced at the MCC did not, as a matter of law, amount to punishment and hence did not violate respondents' rights under the due process clause of the Fifth Amendment. The conditions at the MCC did not fail to meet the standards required by the Constitution, particularly given that nearly all pretrial detainees were released within 60 days. There must be a "mutual accommodation between institutional needs and objectives and the provisions of the Constitution that are of general application," per *Wolff v. McDonnell*, 418 U.S. 539 (1974), and this principle applies equally to pretrial detainees and convicted prisoners. In the essential interests of maintaining security and preserving order, retained constitutional rights of both convicted prisoners and pretrial detainees may be limited or retracted. "[W]ide-ranging deference" to prison administrators' judgment should be accorded, given the absence of easy solutions to problems arising in day-to-day operations. The publisher-only rule does not violate First Amendment rights of MCC inmates but is a rational response by prison officials to the obvious security problem of preventing the smuggling of contraband in books sent from outside. Moreover, this is a neutral rule, without regard to the content of reading material, and there are alternative means of obtaining reading material. Further, the impact of the rule on pretrial detainees is limited to a maximum period of approximately 60 days. The restriction against receiving packages from outside the facility does not deprive pretrial detainees "of their property without due process of law in contravention of the Fifth Amendment," especially considering that such packages allow for easy smuggling of contraband. Assuming that a pretrial detainee retains a diminished expectation of privacy after commitment to a custodial facility, the room-search rule does not violate the Fourth Amendment but simply facilitates the safe and effective performance of the searches and thus does not render the searches unreasonable within the meaning of that Amendment. Similarly, assuming that pretrial detainees retain some Fourth Amendment rights upon commitment to a corrections facility, the body cavity searches do not violate that Amendment. Balancing the significant and legitimate security interests of the institution against the inmates' privacy interests, such searches can be conducted on less than probable cause and are not unreasonable. All of the above security restrictions and practices were reasonable responses by MCC officials to legitimate security concerns, and, in any event, were of only limited duration so far as the pretrial detainees were concerned.

CASE EXCERPT

"There was a time not too long ago when the federal judiciary took a completely 'hands-off' approach to the problem of prison administration. In recent years, however, these courts largely have discarded this 'hands-off' attitude and have waded into this complex arena. The deplorable conditions and Draconian restrictions of some of our Nation's prisons are too well known to require recounting here, and the federal courts rightly have condemned these sordid aspects of our prison systems. But many of these same courts have, in the name of the Constitution, become increasingly enmeshed in the minutiae of prison operations. Judges, after all, are human. They, no less than others in our society, have a natural tendency to believe that their individual solutions to often intractable problems are better and more workable than those of the persons who are actually charged with and trained in the running of the particular institution under examination. But under the Constitution, the first question to be answered is not whose plan is best, but in what branch of the Government is lodged the authority to initially devise the plan. This does not mean that constitutional rights are not to be scrupulously observed. It does mean, however, that the inquiry of federal courts into prison management must be limited to the issue of whether a particular system violates any prohibition of the Constitution or, in the case of a federal prison, a statute. The wide range of 'judgment calls' that meet constitutional and statutory requirements are confided to officials outside of the Judicial Branch of Government."

CASE SIGNIFICANCE

This is one of the only cases dealing with the rights of pretrial detainees—those housed in local jails. Essentially the Court in this case treated jails much the same as prisons and gave jail officials the same discretion to run the institution as they see fit, even though pretrial detainees still enjoy a presumption of innocence not enjoyed by prison inmates. The Court decided that the interests of institutional security and orderly administration outweighed the rights of pretrial detainees, who are consequently treated as having the same sort of diminished constitutional rights as prison inmates.

RHODES v. CHAPMAN
452 U.S. 337 (1981)

FACTS

Respondents, who were housed in the same cell in an Ohio maximum security prison, brought a class action in Federal District Court under 42 U.S.C. 1983 against petitioner state officials, alleging that double-celling violated the Constitution and seeking injunctive relief. Despite its generally favorable findings of fact, the District Court concluded that the double-celling was cruel and unusual punishment in violation of the Eighth Amendment, as made applicable to the states through the Fourteenth Amendment. This conclusion was based on five considerations: (1) inmates at the prison were serving long terms of imprisonment; (2) the prison housed 38 percent more inmates than its design capacity; (3) the recommendation of several studies that each inmate have at least 50–55 square feet of living quarters as opposed to the 63 square feet shared by the double-celled inmates; (4) the suggestion that double-celled inmates spend most of their time in their cells with their cellmates; and (5) the fact that double-celling at the prison was not a temporary condition. The Court of Appeals affirmed.

ISSUE

Does double-celling violate the constitution?

HOLDING

No. The double-celling in question is not cruel and unusual punishment prohibited by the Eighth and Fourteenth Amendments.

RATIONALE

In reversing the lower courts' ruling that double-celling was cruel and unusual punishment, the Court looked at Eighth Amendment precedents and evolving standards of decency, emphasizing that the Eighth Amendment prohibition is against punishments that are unnecessary and wanton. Included under unnecessary and wanton inflictions of pain would be those conditions or restrictions of confinement that are "totally without penological justification." In the case at hand, double-celling does not rise to that standard of an Eighth Amendment violation. The practice of double-celling was made necessary due to the increase in population and did not result in increased violence, deprivation of food, medical care, or sanitation. The five considerations are insufficient to prove constitutional

RHODES v. CHAPMAN *(cont.)*

violations because there is no evidence of unnecessary or wanton pain "grossly disproportionate to the severity of crimes warranting imprisonment."

CASE EXCERPT

"These general considerations fall far short in themselves of proving cruel and unusual punishment, for there is no evidence that double-celling under these circumstances either inflicts unnecessary or wanton pain or is grossly disproportionate to the severity of crimes warranting imprisonment. At most, these considerations amount to a theory that double-celling inflicts pain. Perhaps they reflect an aspiration toward an ideal environment for long-term confinement. But the Constitution does not mandate comfortable prisons, and prisons of SOCF's type, which house persons convicted of serious crimes, cannot be free of discomfort. Thus, these considerations properly are weighed by the legislature and prison administration rather than a court."

CASE SIGNIFICANCE

This case makes clear that there is no per se rule for when a prison is overcrowded. Double-celling is not, in and of itself, proof of overcrowding; nor is the fact that a prison does not comply with professional correctional standards regarding the minimum number of square feet of space per inmate. The Court instead allows prison officials great leeway.

O'LONE v. ESTATE OF SHABAZZ

482 U.S. 342 (1987)

FACTS

According to prison regulations, inmates at New Jersey's Leesburg State Prison were placed in one of three custody classifications. Maximum security and "gang minimum" security inmates were housed in the main prison building, and those with the lowest classification, full minimum status, lived in a satellite building called "the Farm." In April 1983, the New Jersey Department of Corrections issued Standard 853, which provided that inmates could no longer move directly from maximum security to full minimum status, but instead must first spend a period of time in the intermediate gang minimum status. This change was designed to redress problems that had arisen when inmates were transferred directly from the restrictive maximum security status to full minimum status, with its markedly higher level of freedom. Because of serious overcrowding in the main building, Standard 853 mandated that gang minimum inmates would be assigned to jobs outside the main building. These work details were made up of eight to 15 inmates, supervised by one guard. Standard 853 also required that full minimum inmates work outside the main institution, whether on or off prison grounds, or in a satellite building such as the Farm. The new policies were implemented gradually. In the initial stages of the outside work details for gang minimum prisoners, some Muslim inmates apparently were allowed to work inside the main building on Fridays so that they could attend Jumu'ah, a weekly Muslim service. In March of 1984, this practice ceased in light of the directive that all gang minimum inmates work outside the main building. Subsequently, some inmates assigned to outside work details avoided reporting for their assignments, while others found reasons for returning to the main building during the course of the workday (including their desire to attend religious services). Because details of inmates were supervised by only one guard, the whole detail was forced to return to the main gate when one prisoner desired to return to the facility, thus creating security risks and administrative burdens. The main gate was a high security risk area because it was the site of all incoming foot and vehicle traffic. When an inmate returned, vehicle traffic was delayed while the inmate was logged in and searched. In response to these issues, prison officials made arrangements to keep all inmates on outside work details at their work sites for the whole day. Lunch and medications were brought out to prisoners, and doctor or social worker appointments were scheduled for late afternoons. When these arrangements proved insufficient, officials began to study alternatives. After consulting with the director of social services, the director of professional services, and the prison's imam and chaplain, officials issued a policy memorandum prohibiting inmates on to outside work details from returning to the prison during the day except in the case of emergencies. This policy prevented Muslims from attending Jumu'ah. Muslim inmates filed suit, alleging deprivation of freedom of religion rights under the First Amendment. The district court found no constitutional violation, but the Court of Appeals vacated and remanded, finding that "prison policies could be sustained only if the State showed that the challenged regulations were intended to and did serve the penological goal of security, and that no reasonable method existed by which prisoners' religious rights could be accommodated without creating bona fide security problems. The court also held that the expert testimony of prison officials should be given due weight on, but is not dispositive of, the accommodation issue." Prison officials appealed.

ISSUE

Is the right to freedom of religion violated by prison regulations prohibiting inmates from returning to the building in which religious services are held?

HOLDING

No. In a 5–4 opinion written by Chief Justice Rehnquist, the Court reversed the decision of the Court of Appeals and held that "1. The Court of Appeals erred in placing the burden on prison officials to disprove the availability of alternative methods of accommodating prisoners' religious rights. That approach fails to reflect the respect and deference the Constitution allows for the judgment of prison administrators. 2. The District Court's findings establish that the policies challenged here are reasonably related to legitimate penological interests, and therefore do not offend the Free Exercise Clause. 3. Even where claims are made under the First Amendment, this Court will not substitute its judgment on difficult and sensitive matters of institutional administration for the determinations of those charged with the formidable task of running a prison."

RATIONALE

The Court found that both prison policies were rationally related to legitimate governmental interests in institutional order and security. The policies also reflected goals of rehabilitation as prison officials testified that the outside work details simulated working conditions and responsibilities in society: "Although the policies at issue may prevent some Muslim prisoners from attending Jumu'ah, their reasonableness is supported by the fact that they do not deprive respondents of all forms of religious exercise, but instead allow participation in a number of Muslim religious ceremonies." The Court noted previous decisions establishing that courts must accord appropriate deference to the judgment of corrections administrators "who are actually charged with and trained in the running of the particular institution under examination" (*Bell v. Wolfish*). In *Turner v. Safley* 482 U.S. (1987), decided one week before the instant case, the Court restated the proper standard of review to be applied to prison regulations

that are alleged to impair constitutional rights: "[W]hen a prison regulation impinges on inmates' constitutional rights, the regulation is valid if it is reasonably related to legitimate penological interests." The majority emphasized that they were not minimizing the importance of Jumu'ah to the inmates but could not hold that the Constitution required officials to sacrifice legitimate penological objectives in order to accommodate the inmates. Inmates could still participate in other Muslim religious ceremonies, such as congregating for prayer or discussion during off-work hours and the state-provided imam had free access to the prison. Further, Muslim prisoners were given different meals whenever pork was served, and Muslim prisoners were accommodated during Ramadan, a month-long period of fasting and prayer, with early breakfasts and late dinners. The Court reasoned that the restrictions with respect to Jumu'ah were reasonable in light of the other religious activities in which the prisoners could participate. The application of *Turner* included considering the impact that accommodating the Muslim prisoners' rights would have on other inmates, on prison employees, and on prison resources. Accordingly, the Court accepted prison officials' testimony that if they had to make special arrangements for one group and allow them to avoid a "rigorous work detail," other prisoners would perceive favoritism.

CASE EXCERPT

"We take this opportunity to reaffirm our refusal, even where claims are made under the First Amendment, to 'substitute our judgment on . . . difficult and sensitive matters of institutional administration,' for the determinations of those charged with the formidable task of running a prison. Here the District Court decided that the regulations alleged to infringe constitutional rights were reasonably related to legitimate penological objectives. We agree with the District Court, and it necessarily follows that the regulations in question do not offend the Free Exercise Clause of the First Amendment to the United States Constitution."

CASE SIGNIFICANCE

In this case the Supreme Court applied the *Turner v. Safley* test for the validity of a prison regulation of a regulation impacting inmate religious practices, and upheld the prison's regulation. This case is significant because with it the Court moves away from the "strict scrutiny" test to a form of the "rational basis" test, which is a much easier test for prison officials

O'LONE v. ESTATE OF SHABAZZ *(cont.)*

to pass. Prior to this case, it was thought that prison regulations governing religious practices had to pass the more exacting strict scrutiny test.

DESHANEY v. WINNEBAGO COUNTY DEPARTMENT OF SOCIAL SERVICES
489 U.S. 189 (1989)

FACTS

In 1984, four-year-old Joshua DeShaney became comatose and then profoundly retarded due to traumatic head injuries received when he was subjected to a series of beatings by his father. The Winnebago County Department of Social Services took various steps to protect the child after receiving numerous complaints of the abuse; however, the department did not remove Joshua from his father's custody. Joshua DeShaney's mother subsequently sued the Winnebago County Department of Social Services, alleging that the department had deprived the child of his "liberty interest in bodily integrity, in violation of his rights under the substantive component of the Fourteenth Amendment's Due Process Clause, by failing to intervene to protect him against his father's violence." The district court granted summary judgment for the respondents and the Seventh Circuit Court of Appeals affirmed, ruling in part that the due process clause of the Fourteenth Amendment does not require a state or local governmental entity to protect its citizens from "private violence, or other mishaps not attributable to the conduct of its employees."

ISSUE

Does a state's failure to protect an individual against violence by a private person constitute a violation of the due process clause of the Fourteenth Amendment?

HOLDING

No. The due process clause of the Fourteenth Amendment does not impose a special duty on the state to provide services to the public for protection against private actors.

RATIONALE

The Court rejected the contention that the state's knowledge of Joshua's danger and its willingness to protect Joshua against that danger established a "special relationship" giving rise to an affirmative constitutional

duty to protect. Certain special relationships created or assumed by the state with respect to particular individuals do give rise to an affirmative duty to provide adequate protection under the due process clause. However, that duty comes from limitations imposed by the state on an individual's freedom to act on his own behalf, such as through imprisonment or institutionalization. Joshua was in the custody of his father, a private citizen, and not the state. The Court gave examples of the limited circumstances when states possess affirmative duties of care of particular individuals: "In *Estelle v. Gamble*...we recognized that the Eighth Amendment's prohibition against cruel and unusual punishment, made applicable to the States through the Fourteenth Amendment's Due Process Clause, *Robinson v. California*, 370 U.S. 660 (1962), requires the State to provide adequate medical care to incarcerated prisoners." The state is required to provide involuntarily committed mental patients with "such services as are necessary to ensure their 'reasonable safety' from themselves and others" (*Youngberg v. Romeo*, 457 U.S. 307 (1982). The rationale focused on the fact that the state, by "affirmative exercise of its power" has restrained an individual to the point that the person is unable to care for himself or herself; thus, the state is responsible for providing for basic human needs such as food, clothing, medical care, reasonable safety, and so on. Failure to do so would violate the Eighth Amendment and the due process clause.

CASE EXCERPT

"The Clause is phrased as a limitation on the State's power to act, not as a guarantee of certain minimal levels of safety and security. It forbids the State itself to deprive individuals of life, liberty, or property without 'due process of law,' but its language cannot fairly be extended to impose an affirmative obligation on the State to ensure that those interests do not come to harm through other means. Nor does history support such an expansive reading of the constitutional text. Like its counterpart in the Fifth Amendment, the Due Process Clause of the Fourteenth Amendment was intended to prevent government 'from abusing [its] power, or employing it as an instrument of oppression.'"

CASE SIGNIFICANCE

This case is important for purposes of corrections law because the Court in part addressed the circumstances under which the Constitution imposes upon the state affirmative duties of care and protection with respect to individuals, as discussed above. However, the Court determined that there is no constitutional right to be protected from harm by a third party. The state has no duty to protect individuals who are not in state custody. By implication, this leaves open the possibility that the state has an affirmative duty to protect those in state custody (i.e., prison inmates) from harm by a third party. This implication was dealt with by the Court in a subsequent case, *Farmer v. Brennan* (1994).

WILSON v. SEITER
501 U.S. 294 (1991)

FACTS
Wilson, an Ohio prison inmate, filed suit under 42 U.S.C. Section 1983 against respondents, state prison officials, alleging that certain conditions of his confinement constituted cruel and unusual punishment in violation of the Eighth and Fourteenth Amendments. His affidavits described the challenged conditions and charged that the authorities, after notification, had failed to take remedial action. The District Court granted summary judgment for respondents, and the Court of Appeals affirmed on the ground that the affidavits failed to establish the requisite culpable state of mind on the part of respondents. The US Supreme Court granted certiorari to determine what state of mind applies in Eighth Amendment cases challenging prison conditions.

ISSUE
Is a prisoner claiming that conditions of confinement constitute cruel and unusual punishment required to show a culpable state of mind on the part of prison officials and, if so, what state of mind is required?

HOLDING
Yes. A prisoner claiming that the conditions of his confinement violate the Eighth Amendment must show a culpable state of mind on the part of prison officials, an intent requirement implicit in that Amendment's ban on cruel and unusual punishment. The "deliberate indifference" standard is the required state of mind.

RATIONALE
Prior decisions in *Estelle v. Gamble, Rhodes v. Chapman*, and *Whitley v. Albers* 475 U.S. 312, (1986) mandate that the "unnecessary and wanton infliction of pain" must be established in prison cases alleging Eighth Amendment violations in conditions of confinement. *Whitley* in particular established the necessity of considering whether prison officials have acted with a "sufficiently culpable state of mind." The Court rejected as neither logical nor practical Wilson's suggested distinction between short-term prison conditions requiring official state-of-mind inquiry, versus systemic conditions, where such a culpable state-of-mind inquiry would be immaterial. There is no merit to respondents' contention that the "deliberate indifference standard" should be applied only in cases involving personal, physical injury, and that a malice standard is appropriate in cases challenging conditions. The deliberate indifference standard applied in *Estelle v. Gamble*, to claims involving medical care applies generally to prisoner challenges to conditions of confinement. It is possible that the error was harmless, since the court said that Wilson's affidavits established "[a]t best...negligence." Conceivably, however, the court would have reached a different disposition under the correct standard, and so the case is remanded for reconsideration on that basis. The Court of Appeals erred in failing to consider Wilson's claims under the deliberate indifference standard and applying instead a standard of "behavior marked by persistent malicious cruelty."

CASE EXCERPT
"Assuming the conduct is harmful enough to satisfy the objective component of an Eighth Amendment claim, whether it can be characterized as 'wanton' depends upon the constraints facing the official. From that standpoint, we see no significant distinction between claims alleging inadequate medical care and those alleging inadequate 'conditions of confinement.' Thus, as retired Justice Powell has concluded: 'Whether one characterizes the treatment received by [the prisoner] as inhumane conditions of confinement, failure to attend to his medical needs, or a combination of both, it is appropriate to apply the 'deliberate indifference' standard articulated in *Estelle*.'"

CASE SIGNIFICANCE
This case is important because in it the Supreme Court defines the meaning of "deliberate indifference" for purposes of Section 1983 actions. For an inmate plaintiff to establish deliberate indifference on the part of prison officials, he or she must establish a "culpable state of mind" on the part of these officials. This makes

it difficult for inmate plaintiffs to recover money damages from prison officials, just as it is difficult for inmate plaintiffs to establish a violation of a constitutional right in conditions of confinement cases.

RUFO v. INMATES OF SUFFOLK COUNTY JAIL
502 U.S. 367 (1992)

FACTS

Years after the District Court held that conditions at the Suffolk County, Massachusetts jail were constitutionally deficient, petitioner officials and respondent inmates entered into a consent decree providing for construction of a new jail that, among other things, would provide single occupancy cells for pretrial detainees. Work on the jail was delayed and, in the interim, the inmate population outpaced projections. While construction was still underway, petitioner sheriff moved to modify the decree to allow double-bunking in a certain number of cells, thereby raising the jail's capacity. Relying on federal Rule of Civil Procedure 60(b)—which provides that "upon such terms as are just, the court may relieve a party...from a...judgment...for the following reasons:...(5) it is no longer equitable that the judgment should have prospective operation"—the sheriff argued that modification was required by a change in law, this Court's postdecree decision in *Bell v. Wolfish*, and a change in fact, the increase in pretrial detainees. The District Court denied relief, holding that Rule 60(b)(5) codified the standard of *United States v. Swift & Co.*, 286 U.S. 106 (1932)—"Nothing less than a clear showing of grievous wrong evoked by a new and unforeseen conditions should lead...to [a] change [in] what was decreed after years of litigation with the consent of all concerned"—and that a case for modification under this standard had not been made. The court also rejected the argument that *Bell* required modification of the decree; found that the increased pretrial detainee population was "neither new nor unforeseen"; declared that relief would be inappropriate, even under a more flexible modification standard, because separate cells for detainees were "perhaps the most important" element of the relief sought; and held that, even if the sheriff's double-celling proposal met constitutional standards, allowing modification on that basis would undermine and discourage settlement of

institutional cases. The Court of Appeals affirmed, and the US Supreme Court granted certiorari.

ISSUE

Did the lower courts apply the correct standard in denying the motion to modify the previously agreed to decree?

HOLDING

No. The "grievous wrong" standard of *Swift* "does not apply to requests to modify consent decrees stemming from institutional reform litigation."..."[A] party seeking modification of a consent decree must establish that a significant change in facts or law warrants revision of the decree, and that the proposed modification is suitably tailored to the changed circumstances."

RATIONALE

The *Swift* grievous wrong standard applied to situations where no changes had occurred that required modification of a consent decree, and the *Swift* Court, as well as subsequent decisions, recognized that decrees may be modified in order to adapt to changing circumstances in either fact or law. The need for flexibility and a less stringent standard than the grievous wrong standard is "made all the more important by the recent upsurge in institutional reform litigation, where the extended life of decrees increases the likelihood that significant changes will occur....Modification may be warranted when changed factual conditions make compliance with the decree substantially more onerous, when the decree proves to be unworkable because of unforeseen obstacles, or when enforcement of the decree without modification would be detrimental to the public interest." The Court noted, however, that if a party is relying upon circumstances that were actually anticipated at the time the party entered in the consent decree, then modification should not be granted unless the party could convince the court that it agreed to the original decree in good faith, made reasonable efforts to comply, and thus should be relieved of the terms of the decree under Rule 60(b). In the instant case, the District Court thus should consider whether the increase in population was actually anticipated, according to the record and the decree itself. If it was unanticipated, then relieving officials from the requirement to provide single cells for pretrial detainees will not necessarily violate the decree's remedies for the unconstitutional conditions in the old jail. Further, *Bell* in 1979 made clear that double-celling is not in all cases unconstitutional. Such changes in law, however, fall to the party seeking modification to show that the significant change in law warrants revision. The respondents in this case maintain that *Bell* is factually distinguished from the circumstances at hand, and the Court stated that "if respondents are correct that *Bell* is factually distinguishable and that double-celling at the new jail would violate pretrial detainees' constitutional rights, modification should not be granted" on remand. Proposed modifications may also take into consideration budget constraints.

CASE EXCERPT

"In evaluating a proposed modification, three matters should be clear. Of course, a modification must not create or perpetuate a constitutional violation.... A proposed modification should not strive to rewrite a consent decree so that it conforms to the constitutional floor. Once a court has determined that changed circumstances warrant a modification in a consent decree, the focus should be on whether the proposed modification is tailored to resolve the problems created by the change in circumstances. A court should do no more, for a consent decree is a final judgment that may be reopened only to the extent that equity requires.

Within these constraints, the public interest and '[c]onsiderations based on the allocation of powers within our federal system,' require that the district court defer to local government administrators, who have the 'primary responsibility for elucidating, assessing, and solving' the problems of institutional reform, to resolve the intricacies of implementing a decree modification... Financial constraints may not be used to justify the creation or perpetuation of constitutional violations, but they are a legitimate concern of government defendants in institutional reform litigation, and therefore are appropriately considered in tailoring a consent decree modification."

CASE SIGNIFICANCE

This is an important case because it deals with an issue facing a number of correctional facilities—modification of consent decrees. According to the Supreme Court, a consent decree may be modified, under certain circumstances. This makes it easier for states to seek and obtain modification of consent decrees.

The Prison Litigation Reform Act (1995) has further impacted this issue (see cases below).

HELLING v. MCKINNEY
509 U.S. 25 (1993)

FACTS

McKinney, a Nevada state prisoner, filed suit against prison officials, claiming cruel and unusual punishment, an Eighth Amendment violation, because he was involuntarily exposed to environmental tobacco smoke (ETS) from his cellmate's five-packs-of-cigarettes-a-day habit, as well as other inmates' cigarettes. According to McKinney, this created an unreasonable risk to his health. At a jury trial before a magistrate, the magistrate found that McKinney "had no constitutional right to be free from cigarette smoke: While 'society may be moving toward an opinion as to the propriety of nonsmoking and a smoke-free environment,' society cannot yet completely agree on the resolution of these issues." According to the magistrate, McKinney could present no evidence of medical problems due to cigarette smoke nor could he prove deliberate indifference to serious medical needs. Therefore, the magistrate granted petitioner officials' motion for a directed verdict. The Court of Appeals agreed that there was no constitutional right to smoke-free prison environments but also held that McKinney stated a valid Eighth Amendment cause of action on the allegation of unreasonable risk of harm to future health because of involuntary exposure to high levels of ETS. Scientific evidence supported McKinney's claim, and involuntary exposure to second-hand smoke violate society's current standards of decency. The appellate court held that the magistrate was in error by not permitting McKinney the opportunity to prove that ETS exposure posed unreasonable risk to his future health. The prison officials appealed this decision to the Supreme Court, which had recently decided *Wilson v. Seiter*, holding that Eighth Amendment conditions of confinement cases required proof that officials are deliberately indifferent to those conditions or failure to attend to prisoners' medical needs. The Supreme Court remanded the case back to the Court of Appeals for consideration in light of the *Seiter* decision. The lower court agreed that *Seiter* added a subjective deliberate indifference state of mind component that McKinney would have to prove, but his original objective claim (that it is cruel and unusual punishment to

HELLING v. MCKINNEY *(cont.)*

house an inmate in an environment that exposes him to high levels of ETS, thus posing unreasonable risk to health) had not been invalidated. The Court of Appeals remanded the case for further proceedings and petitioner officials again appealed. The US Supreme Court granted certiorari.

ISSUE

Can a prisoner make an Eighth Amendment claim of cruel and unusual punishment based on risks to his or her future health?

HOLDING

Yes. It was not improper for the Court of Appeals to decide the question whether McKinney's claim could be based on possible future effects of ETS. By alleging that petitioners have, with deliberate indifference, exposed him to ETS levels that pose an unreasonable risk to his future health, McKinney has stated an Eighth Amendment claim on which relief could be granted.

RATIONALE

In affirming the appellate court's decision and remanding this case for further proceedings, the Court referred first back to the rationale in *DeShaney* that individuals in custody are dependent upon the state, by its affirmative exercise of power, for their basic human needs. While McKinney's grievances are centered on the possibility of future medical problems, one of those basic human needs includes "reasonable safety." Numerous cases have ruled that the "Eighth Amendment protects against sufficiently imminent dangers as well as current unnecessary and wanton infliction of pain and suffering." The Court noted further that Eighth Amendment claims in conditions of confinement cases, under *Seiter*, require inquiry into the states of mind of the prison officials. Agreeing with the lower court, the Court stated that McKinney must be provided the opportunity to prove that he had been exposed by prison officials to such levels of ETS that "an unreasonable risk of serious damage to his future health has been created." McKinney must prove both the subjective (deliberate indifference) and objective (unreasonable risk to health) components of alleged Eighth Amendment violations.

CASE EXCERPT

"Determining whether McKinney's conditions of confinement violate the Eighth Amendment requires more than a scientific and statistical inquiry into the seriousness of the potential harm and the likelihood that such injury to health will actually be caused by exposure to ETS. It also requires a court to assess whether society considers the risk that the prisoner complains of to be so grave that it violates contemporary standards of decency to expose anyone unwillingly to such a risk. In other words, the prisoner must show that the risk of which he complains is not one that today's society chooses to tolerate."

CASE SIGNIFICANCE

This is an important case because it has pushed prison officials to eliminate tobacco use in prison. Many prisons have prohibited tobacco use in the wake of this decision, leading to inmate disquiet (as anticipated) and correctional officer upset (not as anticipated). Since the Court held that future harm could form the basis of liability, prison officials are advised to take preventive measures to eliminate potential health risks.

FARMER v. BRENNAN

511 U.S. 825 (1994)

FACTS

Dee Farmer, a preoperative transsexual, was convicted and sentenced to a federal prison for credit card fraud in 1986 at the age of eighteen. For several years before that conviction, Farmer "wore women's clothing, underwent estrogen therapy, received silicone breast implants, and submitted to unsuccessful 'black market' testicle-removal surgery." Farmer claimed to continue to undergo hormone treatment in prison using smuggled drugs and continued to dress in a feminine manner and display "feminine characteristics." Since the federal prison practice was to incarcerate preoperative transsexuals with prisoners of like biological sex, after Farmer's sentence, Farmer was housed in several federal facilities, sometimes in the general male prison population, but more often in segregation. On March 9, 1989, Farmer was transferred for disciplinary reasons from the federal correctional institution in Oxford, Wisconsin to the United States Penitentiary in Terre Haute, Indiana (USP-Terre Haute). Such penitentiaries are typically higher security prisons for "more troublesome prisoners than federal correctional institutes." Farmer initially was placed in administrative segregation at USP-Terre Haute and then in the general population. Within two weeks after being placed in the general population, Farmer alleged that he was beaten and raped by another inmate in Farmer's cell. Farmer filed a pro se claim under *Bivens v. Six Unknown Fed. Narcotics Agents*, 403 U.S. 388 (1971), alleging that several prison officials violated his Eighth Amendment rights. The complaint was late amended and alleged that the named officials either transferred Farmer to the penitentiary or placed Farmer in general population, knowing that USP-Terre Haute "had a violent environment and a history of inmate assaults, and despite knowledge that [Farmer,] as a transsexual who 'projects feminine characteristics,' would be particularly vulnerable to sexual attack by some USP-Terre Haute inmates." Farmer alleged deliberate indifference to his personal safety. The district court ruled that "failure to prevent inmate assaults violates the Eighth Amendment only if prison officials were reckless in a criminal sense, i.e., had actual knowledge of a potential danger, and that respondents lacked such knowledge because petitioner never expressed any safety concerns to them," and the appellate court affirmed. The Supreme Court granted certiorari to define the proper test for determining "deliberate indifference."

ISSUE

May prison officials be found in violation of the Eighth Amendment if they are subjectively aware of the risk of serious harm to an inmate and disregard that risk, failing to take reasonable measures to decrease it?

HOLDING

Yes. A prison official's deliberate indifference to a substantial risk of serious harm to an inmate violates the Eighth Amendment. The Court defined "deliberate indifference" as requiring a showing that officials are subjectively aware of the risk of serious harm and disregard that risk, failing to take reasonable measures to decrease it.

RATIONALE

In vacating and remanding the case for further proceedings, the Court addressed the duty of prison officials to protect prisoners from injury from other prisoners. There are two requirements to be met before officials may be found constitutionally liable under the Eighth Amendment for failing to protect inmates. When the alleged claim is failure to prevent harm, "the inmate must show that he is incarcerated under conditions posing a substantial risk of serious harm." Secondly, "a prison official must have a 'sufficiently culpable state

of mind.' In prison conditions cases that state of mind is one of 'deliberate indifference' to inmate health or safety." In reaching a decision as to the proper test for showing deliberate indifference, the Court noted that under *Estelle*, deliberate indifference is something more than negligence, but "something less than acts or omissions for the very purpose of causing harm or with knowledge that harm will result. Thus, it is the equivalent of acting recklessly. However, this does not establish the level of culpability deliberate indifference entails, for the term recklessness is not self defining, and can take subjective or objective forms." The Court then concluded that "subjective recklessness, as used in the criminal law, is the appropriate test for 'deliberate indifference.'" The Court rejected an objective test regarding "whether the risk is known or should have been known." While the subjective test seems to be a higher hurdle than the objective test rejected by the Court, the Court emphasized that prison officials are not free to disregard obvious risks.

CASE EXCERPT

"Whether a prison official had the requisite knowledge of a substantial risk is a question of fact subject to demonstration in the usual ways, including inference from circumstantial evidence and a factfinder may conclude that a prison official knew of a substantial risk from the very fact that the risk was obvious... Nor may a prison official escape liability for deliberate indifference by showing that, while he was aware of an obvious, substantial risk to inmate safety, he did not know that the complainant was especially likely to be assaulted by the specific prisoner who eventually committed the assault."

CASE SIGNIFICANCE

In this case the Supreme Court determined that prison officials would be liable for third party injuries (i.e., inmate-on-inmate assaults) only if the officials knowingly disregarded an excessive risk of harm. This is a very high standard, which means inmate plaintiffs are unlikely to be successful.

JOHNSON v. CALIFORNIA
543 U.S. 499 (2005)

FACTS

Johnson, a California state prisoner, filed a federal lawsuit alleging that the California Department of

JOHNSON v. CALIFORNIA *(cont.)*

Corrections(CDC) unlawfully used race to assign temporary cell mates for new prisoners in violation of the equal protection clause of the Fourteenth Amendment. The CDC had an unwritten policy of racially segregating new inmates in reception centers and when transferred to new institutions for up to 60 days. The CDC maintained that the necessity of this practice was due to potential racial and gang violence. Inmates were segregated and observed by officials as to whether they posed threats to other inmates. After 60 days, inmates could choose their own cellmates. Johnson, an African-American inmate, was transferred to several correctional facilities over several years of imprisonment, each time double-celled in reception areas with another African-American inmate. He filed a *pro se* suit in 1995, alleging that the policy to racially segregate in reception center violated his Fourteenth Amendment equal protection rights. His complaint was dismissed for failure to state a valid claim, but the Ninth Circuit Court of Appeals reversed the District Court's decision and remanded the case, ruling that Johnson claimed racial discrimination, a Fourteenth Amendment equal protection clause violation. Johnson was appointed counsel and filed an amended claim, seeking damages and/or injunctive relief from three former CDC officials for racial discrimination. After hearing the amended complaint, the District Court found that CDC officials were entitled to qualified immunity because their actions were not clearly unconstitutional. The Court of Appeals affirmed, holding that the proper standard of review of the constitutionality of CDC's policy should not be reviewed under a strict scrutiny standard but rather under the deferential *Turner* standard. Under *Turner*, Johnson had the burden of showing that there was not a "common-sense connection" between the CDC policy and prison violence. The lower court found that this policy could survive the relaxed *Turner* standard, although four judges dissented on the grounds that the Supreme Court mandates a strict scrutiny standard of review on "all racial classifications imposed by the government." The Supreme Court granted certiorari to determine the proper standard of review.

ISSUE

Is a state's policy and practice of temporary racial segregation of state prisoners for up to 60 days subject to a strict scrutiny standard of review for an equal protection challenge to that policy or practice?

HOLDING

Yes. Racial classifications must receive strict scrutiny, even when such policies are neutral and affect all races equally.

RATIONALE

In holding that strict scrutiny is the proper standard of review, the Supreme Court reversed and remanding the case for further proceedings applying the correct legal standard. The Court noted that a heightened standard of review was previously applied to the issue of racial segregation in prisons in *Lee v. Washington* (1968), and it is just as necessary in this case, affording the Court an opportunity to reaffirm the *Lee* decision. While the CDC claimed that at least two other states had a similar policy, the Court stated that they were unable to confirm this, noting that the Federal Bureau of Prisons and all other states manage their prison systems without segregating inmates according to race. The more relaxed *Turner* standard has never been applied to racial classifications, and the Court was not inclined to do so in this case. Thus far, the *Turner* standard has been applied to First Amendment challenges to prison regulations, including limits on freedom of association, inmate correspondence restrictions, inmates' access to courts, restrictions regarding inmates' attendance at religious services, due process claims such as involuntary medicating of mentally ill inmates, and restrictions on inmate marriages. *Turner*, however, "is too lenient a standard to ferret out invidious uses of race." The Court stated that "[g]ranting the CDC an exemption from the rule that strict scrutiny applies to all racial classifications would undermine our 'unceasing efforts to eradicate racial prejudice from our criminal justice system'" (*McCleskey* v. *Kemp,* 481 U.S. 279 1987). Even given the heightened standard does not necessarily invalidate the CDC policy; however, prison officials, on remand, have the burden of proving that the race-based policies further a compelling interest in prison safety and are narrowly tailored to that end: "Prisons are dangerous places, and the special circumstances they present may justify racial classifications in some contexts. Such circumstances can be considered in applying strict scrutiny, which is designed to take relevant differences into account."

CASE EXCERPT

"By insisting that inmates be housed only with other inmates of the same race, it is possible that prison officials will breed further hostility among prisoners and reinforce racial and ethnic divisions. By perpetuating the notion that race matters most, racial segregation of inmates 'may exacerbate the very patterns of [violence that it is] said to counteract.' "

CASE SIGNIFICANCE

This case is important because the Court had the opportunity to continue to apply the *Turner* standard of deference to prison administrators and the rational relationship test, but instead reaffirmed its 1968 *Lee* decision, mandating that all cases involving racial classifications are subject to the heightened strict scrutiny standard of review. Courts must protect individuals against racial discrimination, even in prison. The Court did not, however, determine whether the CDC practice in fact violates the equal protection clause of the Fourteenth Amendment.

CUTTER ET AL. v. WILKINSON
544 U.S. 709 (2005)

FACTS

This case is a combination of three Ohio cases, involving state inmates who alleged that the Ohio Department of Rehabilitation and Corrections violated the Religious Land Use and Institutionalized Persons Act (RLUIPA) for refusing to allow them to practice their religions. The religions at issue were Asatru, a polytheistic religion of Norse origin; the Church of Jesus Christ Christian, a racial separatist religion; Wicca; and Satanism. RLUIPA was passed by Congress in 2000 and reestablished RFRA's compelling interest/least restrictive means test. Section 3 of RLUIPA specifically mandates that "[n]o government shall impose a substantial burden on the religious exercise of a person residing in or confined to an institution" (42 U.S.C. §2000cc-1(a). The Ohio prison officials challenged the constitutionality of RLUIPA, alleging in part that the act violated the establishment clause of the First Amendment by improperly advancing religion. The district court denied the officials' motion to dismiss and ruled in favor of the inmates. In 2003, the Sixth Circuit, without addressing the legitimacy of the religions or the sincerity of the inmates' beliefs, reversed the lower court's decision and found RLUIPA to violate the establishment clause of the First Amendment, ruling that the statute impermissibly "favors religious rights over other fundamental rights without any

showing that religious rights are at any greater risk of deprivation." The Supreme Court granted certiorari to address the constitutionality of RLUIPA.

ISSUE

Did Congress violate the establishment clause by enacting the Religious Land Use and Institutionalized Persons Act of 2000, which requires state officials to lift unnecessary governmental burdens imposed on the religious exercise of institutionalized persons under their control?

HOLDING

No. RLUIPA "does not, on its face, exceed the limits of permissible government accommodation of religious practices."

RATIONALE

In reversing the Sixth Circuit's decision in a unanimous opinion, the Court reasoned that RLUIPA is not unconstitutional, nor does it override security interests of a prison. On its face, Section 3 of RLUIPA is compatible with the establishment clause because it lessens any extraordinary burdens governments might impose on institutionalized persons' private religious exercise. However, courts must also consider the burdens a requested accommodation might impose and such accommodation does not take precedence over a prison's need for safety, discipline, order, and security. The Act's requirements must be administered neutrally among different faiths and not confer a privileged status on any particular religion.

CASE EXCERPT

"We see no reason to anticipate that abusive prisoner litigation will overburden the operations of state and local institutions. The procedures mandated by the Prison Litigation Reform Act of 1995, we note, are designed to inhibit frivolous filings. Should inmate requests for religious accommodations become excessive, impose unjustified burdens on other institutionalized persons, or jeopardize the effective functioning of an institution, the facility would be free to resist the imposition. In that event, adjudication in as-applied challenges would be in order."

CASE SIGNIFICANCE

This case is important because prior to this decision, four circuit courts of appeals had upheld RLUIPA's constitutionality, with the lone exception being the

CUTTER ET AL. v. WILKINSON *(cont.)*

Sixth Circuit. Prison officials have to be more sensitive to inmate religious requests than they would under the *Turner* standard, as long as the religious requests are based on legitimate and sincere religious beliefs. This is sometimes a difficult issue for correctional administrators, and both prison officials and the courts have been compelled to examine newly established religions for sincerity and valid commitment to spiritual beliefs. The Court noted that RLUIPA does not override security interests of a prison. Corrections officials can refuse excessive requests for religious accommodations that affect the efficient operations of the institution or that burden other prisoners.

U.S. v. GEORGIA
546 U.S. 151 (2006)

FACTS

Goodman, a paraplegic since 1992, was transferred to the Georgia State Prison in Reidsville in 1996, after being convicted of aggravated assault, possession of a firearm by a convicted felon, and possession of cocaine with intent to distribute. In 1999, Goodman filed a pro se Sectional 1983 claim against numerous prison officials and also sued under the Americans with Disabilities Act of 1990, challenging conditions of his confinement. Goodman alleged several complains, some serious, some trivial. Of the more serious allegations was the claim that he was confined for 23 to 24 hours per day in a 12x3 foot cell in which he could not turn his wheelchair around. He could not use the toilet and shower without assistance, which was often denied. He claimed that he seriously injured himself on several occasions when he would have to hurl himself on to the toilet. On other occasions, he was forced to sit in his own feces and urine, and prison officials refused to give him cleaning supplies. He also claimed that he had been denied physical therapy and medical treatment, as well as access to prison programs and services because of his disability.

In the ADA discrimination suit, Goodman sought monetary relief from eight prison officials. The district court dismissed the Section 1983 claims for vagueness and granted prison officials summary judgment on the Title II money damages claims because they were barred by state sovereign immunity. The United States intervened on appeal, also suing Georgia and arguing that Title II of the ADA abolishes state sovereign immunity from monetary suits, and the two cases were consolidated. The Eleventh Circuit affirmed the District Court's ruling on the Title II claims but reversed the Section 1983 ruling, finding that Goodman had alleged facts that were sufficient to support three Eighth Amendment claims and should be permitted to amend his complaint. The Supreme Court granted certiorari to decide only whether a disabled inmate in a state prison may sue the state for monetary damages under the ADA with respect to Eighth Amendment claims.

ISSUE

(1) Does Title II of the ADA validly annul state sovereign immunity for suits by prisoners with disabilities challenging discrimination by state prisons? (2) Is Title II of the ADA a proper exercise of Congressional power under Section 5 of the Fourteenth Amendment, as applied to the administration of prison systems?

HOLDING

Yes to both questions. Title II of the Americans with Disabilities Act creates a private cause of action for damages against states for unconstitutional action and is a valid abrogation of state sovereign immunity in cases where conduct violates the Fourteenth Amendment.

RATIONALE

The unanimous Court assumed for purposes of this case that the Eleventh Circuit correctly held that Goodman alleged actual Eighth Amendment violations under Section 1983 and those alleged violations also violated Title II of the ADA. Under the Fourteenth Amendment, the Eighth Amendment applied to states, and Congress can enforce the Amendment against the states by repealing state sovereign immunity and sanctioning private suits. The Court remanded the case to allow Goodman to amend his complaint. Once the complaint is amended, lower courts will have to determine whether the specific alleged conduct did in fact violate Title II of the ADA, the extent to which the conduct also violated the Fourteenth Amendment, and the extent to which sovereign immunity is valid with respect to misconduct violating the ADA but not the Fourteenth Amendment.

CASE EXCERPT

"It is quite plausible that the alleged deliberate refusal of prison officials to accommodate Goodman's disability-related needs in such fundamentals as mobility, hygiene, medical care, and virtually all other prison programs constituted 'exclu[sion] from participation in or…den[ial of] the benefits of' the prison's 'services, programs, or activities.'42 U.S.C. § 12132…Therefore, Goodman's claims for money damages against the State under Title II were evidently based, at least in large part, on conduct that independently violated the provisions of §1 of the Fourteenth Amendment.…In this respect, Goodman differs from the claimants in our other cases addressing Congress' ability to abrogate sovereign immunity pursuant to its §5 powers…Thus, insofar as Title II creates a private cause of action for damages against the States for conduct that *actually* violates the Fourteenth Amendment, Title II validly abrogates state sovereign immunity."

CASE SIGNIFICANCE

The importance of this case lies in the fact that the Supreme Court ruled for the first time that the Americans with Disabilities Act of 1990 applies to state prisoners and protects them from discrimination by prison officials based on their disabilities. This decision upholds the constitutionality of the ADA and makes clear that prisoner plaintiffs are not required to show a history of past unconstitutional conduct in order to state a claim.

DISCUSSION QUESTIONS

1. Should First Amendment religious rights of inmates be recognized and protected? Why or why not?

2. Explain the meaning of the concept of "deliberate indifference."

3. How does the concept of deliberate indifference apply to the constitutional rights of prisoners?

4. Research your state's current policy on tobacco use in prison. Does it comply with the Supreme Court's decision?

5. List and discuss various conditions of prison and jail confinement that pose potential concerns for both inmates and corrections staff.

6. After the Court's decision in *Johnson v. California*, the California Department of Corrections began to phase out race-based segregation policies and to consider other factors that contribute to prison violence. Research and discuss what those other factors may be. In making housing assignments in prison, what should be the most important characteristics prison officials should consider?

7. Question 5 concerned conditions of prison and jail confinement that pose potential concerns for both inmates and corrections staff. Expand your discussion to include additional conditions and concerns at Supermax prisons.

8. What difficulties, if any, do correctional administrators face by the decision in *U.S. v. Georgia* (2006)? Research how your state's prisons accommodate inmates with disabilities.

9. How can prison officials use race to make decisions about inmate housing and living conditions today? Can they consider it at all? Should they be able to?

10. How will the aging inmate population affect what prison administrators must do?

CHAPTER SIX

MEDICAL CARE

ESTELLE v. GAMBLE, *429 U.S. 97 (1976)*

WEST v. ATKINS, *487 U.S. 42 (1988)*

WASHINGTON v. HARPER, *494 U.S. 210 (1990)*

PENNSYLVANIA DEPARTMENT OF
CORRECTIONS v. YESKEY, *524 U.S. 206 (1998)*

MCKUNE v. LILE, *536 U.S. 24 (2002)*

INTRODUCTION

The five cases in this chapter concern medical care of prisoners and inmate rights to treatment. The right to treatment is not mentioned in the text of the Constitution, but courts have made it clear that inmates and those persons under civil commitment do enjoy a right to treatment. The rationale behind mandating such a right for incarcerated persons is that because the state has restricted their liberty, they are unable to obtain medical services on their own initiative. Therefore, the state must accept responsibility for institutionalized persons' medical well-being. However, the medical treatment need not be the best that science has to offer; rather, it is enough if the state provides reasonable care.

The Supreme Court addressed medical care for inmates for the first time in 1976 in *Estelle v. Gamble*, 429 U.S. 97, holding that correctional administrators could be held liable for injury to an inmate if the administrators displayed "deliberate indifference" to the situation. Merely negligent treatment does not constitute deliberate indifference. Instead, there must be evidence similar to recklessness or intentional disregard for the client on the part of the state. This standard has proven to be a fairly difficult one for inmate plaintiffs to meet, but it is a far cry from the days of *Ruffin v. Commonwealth*, 62 Va. 790 (1871) when inmates were seen literally as "slaves of the state."

The second medical treatment case in this chapter was heard by the Supreme Court in 1988 (*West v. Atkins*, 487 U.S. 42) and resolved a conflict between two appellate courts. The Fourth Circuit ruled in this case that private physicians are removed from the purview of Section 1983 if they are professionals acting in accordance with professional discretion and judgment, and that professionals may be liable under Section 1983 only if exercising custodial or supervisory authority. In other cases, the Eleventh Circuit Court of Appeals ruled that private physicians who, under state contracts, provide medical services to inmates act under color of state law for purposes of Section 1983. The Supreme Court ruled that the Fourth Circuit erred in their decision and misread *Estelle v. Gamble*. Custodial and supervisory functions are irrelevant when deciding whether a particular action that has been challenged was performed under color of state law. When a state hires private physicians to provide medical care to inmates, those private physicians are "clothed with the authority of state law." This decision expanded the reach of Section 1983 to cover private parties working on behalf of the state, thereby increasing the opportunity for inmate plaintiffs to sue under Section 1983.

Two years later, the Supreme Court gave prison officials greater power and flexibility with respect to medical treatment for seriously mentally ill inmates. The Court held in *Washington v. Harper* (494 U.S. 210) that an institutionalized person does not have an absolute right to refuse treatment if that refusal poses a danger to that inmate or others and the treatment is in that individual's best medical interest.

In 1990, Congress passed the Americans with Disabilities Act (ADA), which states that a public entity may not discriminate against disabled persons on account of that disability. The Supreme Court ruled in 1998, in *Pennsylvania Department of Corrections v. Yeskey* (524 US 206), that the ADA clearly applies to inmates in state prisons and excluding prisoners with disabilities from "services, programs, or activities" violates the provisions of the ADA.

The last case in this chapter, *McKune v. Lile*, relates to participation in rehabilitation programs, specifically, an intensive therapeutic program for sex offenders. This program required inmate participants to submit sexual history forms and admit responsibility for all sexual misconduct, requirements that the inmate plaintiff saw as abridging his Fifth Amendment right against self-incrimination. Further, by refusing to participate in the program, the inmate faced losing privileges and a possible transfer to a more secure institution. The Supreme Court's decision supported these requirements, however, ruling that the requirements did not compel offenders to incriminate themselves in violation of the Fifth Amendment.

ESTELLE v. GAMBLE
429 U.S. 97 (1976)

FACTS

Gamble, a Texas Department of Corrections inmate, was injured on November 9, 1973 while performing a prison work assignment, when a bale of cotton fell on him while he was unloading a truck. He continued to work but after four hours became stiff and was granted a pass to the unit hospital. The following day, the prison doctor diagnosed Gamble's injury as a lower back strain, prescribed pain reliever and muscle relaxant, and placed Gamble on cell-pass, cell-feed status for two days, allowing him to remain in his cell at all times except for showers. On November 12, Gamble again saw the doctor who continued the medication and cell-pass, cell-feed for another seven days. He also ordered that Gamble be moved from an upper to a lower bunk for one week, but the prison authorities did not comply with that directive. Gamble remained on cell-pass for the rest of the month of November. On December 3, despite Gamble's statement that his back hurt as much as it had the first day, the doctor took him off cell-pass, thereby certifying him as capable of light work. Gamble then went to a prison official and told him that he was in too much pain to work. Gamble was moved to administrative segregation. On December 5, Gamble was taken before the prison disciplinary committee, apparently because of his refusal to work. The committee directed that Gamble be seen by another doctor after hearing his complaint of back pain and high blood pressure. On December 6, Gamble saw a different doctor, who performed a urinalysis, blood test, and checked blood pressure. Blood-pressure medicine and pain relievers were prescribed. For all of December and January, Gamble remained in administrative segregation, refusing to work because of the pain. On January 31, Gamble was brought before the prison disciplinary committee for his refusal to work. He told the committee that he could not work because of his severe back pain and high blood pressure. A prison official testified that Gamble was in "first class" medical condition. The committee, with no further medical examination or testimony, placed him in solitary confinement. Four days later, on February 4, at 8 a.m., Gamble asked to see a doctor for chest pains and "blank outs." It was not until 7:30 that night that a medical assistant examined him and ordered him hospitalized. The following day a doctor performed an electrocardiogram, and one day later Gamble was placed on Quinidine for treatment of irregular cardiac rhythm and moved to administrative segregation. On February 7, Gamble again experienced pain in his chest, left arm, and back and asked to see a doctor. The guards refused. He asked again the next day. The guards again refused. Finally, on February 9, he was allowed to see the doctor, who ordered the Quinidine continued for three more days. On February 11, 1974, Gamble brought a Section 1983 civil rights action against the director of the Department of Corrections, the prison warden, and the medical director of the department, complaining that the treatment he received after the injury constituted cruel and unusual punishment. The complaint was dismissed by the district court dismissed for failure to state a claim upon which relief could be granted. Upon appeal, the appellate court reversed the decision and remanded the case, holding that the alleged insufficiency of the medical treatment required reinstatement of the complaint.

ISSUE

Was Gamble's treatment cruel and unusual punishment in violation of the Eighth Amendment?

ESTELLE v. GAMBLE *(cont.)*

HOLDING

No. In an 8–1 opinion written by Justice Marshall, the Court reversed and remanded this case, holding that deliberate indifference by prison personnel to a prisoner's serious illness or injury constitutes cruel and unusual punishment in violation of the Eighth Amendment. However, Gamble's allegations against the medical director did not suggest deliberate indifference, given that the medical director and other medical personnel saw him on 17 occasions during a three-month span and treated his injury and other problems. Whether or not a constitutional claim existed against the director of the Department of Corrections and the prison warden was not separately evaluated by the appellate court and was ordered to be considered on remand.

RATIONALE

The Court observed that inmates rely on prison authorities to treat their medical needs; "if the authorities fail to do so, those needs will not be met." Failure to treat medical needs can result in unnecessary pain and suffering or even death. Even in the less serious cases of pain and suffering, "[t]he infliction of such unnecessary suffering is inconsistent with contemporary standards of decency as manifested in modern legislation codifying the common-law view that 'it is but just that the public be required to care for the prisoner, who cannot by reason of the deprivation of his liberty, care for himself.'" The Court concluded "that deliberate indifference to serious medical needs of prisoners" constitutes the Eighth Amendment prohibition of "unnecessary and wanton infliction of pain," and that "[t]his is true whether the indifference is manifested by prison doctors in their response to the prisoner's needs or by prison guards in intentionally denying or delaying access to medical care or intentionally interfering with the treatment once prescribed." However, in Gamble's case against the medical director, the Court noted that deliberate indifference was not proved. While the doctor failed to x-ray Gamble or use additional techniques, such failures did not amount to cruel and unusual punishment under the Eighth Amendment but were, at the most, medical malpractice. As such, claims of medical malpractice are to be litigated in state court under the Texas Tort Claims Act.

CASE EXCERPT

"In the medical context, an inadvertent failure to provide adequate medical care cannot be said to constitute 'an unnecessary and wanton infliction of pain' or to be 'repugnant to the conscience of mankind.' Thus, a complaint that a physician has been negligent in diagnosing or treating a medical condition does not state a valid claim of medical mistreatment under the Eighth Amendment. Medical malpractice does not become a constitutional violation merely because the victim is a prisoner. In order to state a cognizable claim, a prisoner must allege acts or omissions sufficiently harmful to evidence deliberate indifference to serious medical needs. It is only such indifference that can offend 'evolving standards of decency' in violation of the Eighth Amendment."

CASE SIGNIFICANCE

This case is very important, not only because it is the first Supreme Court case dealing with prison medical treatment, but because in it the Court enunciated the "deliberate indifference" standard for determining whether a constitutional violation has occurred. Precisely what constitutes deliberate indifference is not entirely clear, and as later cases reveal, the meaning of the term may vary depending upon the situation. This case is also the first Supreme Court case applying the Eighth Amendment to prison conditions.

WEST v. ATKINS
487 U.S. 42 (1988)

FACTS

Quincy West, a prisoner at Odom Correctional Center in Jackson, North Carolina, tore his left Achilles tendon in 1983 while playing volleyball. A physician at Odom examined West and directed that he be transferred to Raleigh for orthopedic consultation at Central Prison Hospital, the acute care medical facility operated by the state. Dr. Samuel Atkins, a private physician under a part-time contract with the state, treated West for several months, placing his leg in a series of casts. West alleged that although Atkins agreed that surgery would be necessary, he refused to schedule it. West further alleged that Atkins discharged him while movement was still difficult and his ankle was still swollen and painful. Because West was a prisoner in close custody, he was not allowed to choose his own physician. West brought a Section 1983 civil suit against the doctor, claiming that Atkins was deliberately indifferent to his serious medical needs, and by failing to provide adequate treatment, was in violation of West's Eighth

Amendment right to be free from cruel and unusual punishment. The district court dismissed the suit, holding that, as a contract physician, Atkins was not acting "under color of state law," a jurisdictional prerequisite for a 1983 action. The court of appeals affirmed.

ISSUE

Is a physician who is under contract with the state to provide medical services to inmates at a state prison hospital on a part-time basis acting under color of state law, within the meaning of 42 U.S.C. § 1983, when he treats an inmate?

HOLDING

Yes. A physician who is under contract with the state to provide medical services to inmates at a state prison hospital on a part-time basis acts under color of state law, within the meaning of §1983, when he treats an inmate.

RATIONALE

The Supreme Court granted certiorari in this case to resolve a conflict between the Fourth Circuit and Eleventh Circuit. The Eleventh Circuit Court of Appeals had ruled in two other cases that private physicians who, under state contracts, provide medical services to inmates act under color of state law for purposes of Section 1983. The Fourth Circuit concluded in this case that private physicians are removed from Section 1983's purview if they are professionals acting in accordance with professional discretion and judgment, and that professionals may be liable under Section 1983 only if exercising custodial or supervisory authority. Justice Blackmun observed that the "traditional definition of acting under color of state law requires that the defendant in a 1983 action have exercised power 'possessed by virtue of state law and made possible only because the wrongdoer is clothed with the authority of state law.'" The Court ruled that the Fourth Circuit erred in their decision and misread the case upon which they relied in reaching their judgment. Implicit in the Court's decision in *Estelle v. Gamble*, custodial and supervisory functions are irrelevant when deciding whether a particular action that has been challenged was performed under color of state law. When a state hires private physicians to provide medical care to inmates, those private physicians are "clothed with the authority of state law." Justice Blackmun stated that the physician's function determines whether his actions are ascribed to the state:

"Contracting out prison medical care does not relieve the State of its constitutional duty to provide adequate medical treatment to those in its custody, and it does not deprive the State's prisoners of the means to vindicate their Eighth Amendment rights." Since states have an obligation to provide adequate medical care to inmates and since North Carolina delegated this obligation to Dr. Atkins, who voluntarily undertook those duties by contract, his delivery of medical duties was fairly attributable to the state and he was acting under color of state law.

CASE EXCERPT

"We now make explicit what was implicit in our holding in *Estelle*: Respondent, as a physician employed by North Carolina to provide medical services to state prison inmates, acted under color of state law for purposes of §1983 when undertaking his duties in treating petitioner's injury. Such conduct is fairly attributable to the State."

CASE SIGNIFICANCE

In this case the Supreme Court held that private physicians under contract with the state could be sued under Section 1983. By expanding the reach of Section 1983 to cover private parties working on behalf of the state, the Court greatly increased the opportunity for inmate plaintiffs to sue under Section 1983. While this may seem an unfortunate decision in that regard, it follows the clear intent of the legislation.

WASHINGTON v. HARPER
494 U.S. 210 (1990)

FACTS

Walter Harper was sentenced to prison in 1976 for robbery. From 1976 to 1980, he was incarcerated at the Washington State Penitentiary. Most of that time, Harper was housed in the prison's mental health unit, where he consented to being given antipsychotic drugs. Harper was paroled in 1980 on the condition that he participate in psychiatric treatment. He continued psychiatric treatment at a psychiatric ward at a Seattle medical center and was later sent to Western State Hospital pursuant to a civil commitment order. In December 1981, Harper's parole was revoked after he assaulted two nurses at a hospital in Seattle. Upon his return to prison, Harper was sent to the Special Offender Center (SOC), a correctional institute

WASHINGTON v. HARPER *(cont.)*

established to diagnose and treat convicted felons with serious mental disorders. At the center, psychiatrists diagnosed Harper as suffering from a manic-depressive disorder. At first, he voluntarily consented to treatment, including taking antipsychotic medications. However, in November of 1982, Harper refused to continue the prescribed medications. The treating physician then sought to medicate Harper against his will, pursuant to SOC Policy 600.30. This policy provides that if a psychiatrist determines that an inmate should be treated with antipsychotic drugs but the inmate does not consent, the inmate may be subjected to involuntary treatment with the drugs only if he suffers from a "mental disorder" and is "gravely disabled" or poses a "likelihood of serious harm" to himself, others, or their property. Only a psychiatrist may order or approve the medication. The inmate in question is also entitled to a hearing before a special committee consisting of a psychiatrist, a psychologist, and the associate superintendent of the center, none of whom may be, at the time of the hearing, involved in the inmate's treatment or diagnosis. If the committee determines by a majority vote that the inmate suffers from a mental disorder and is gravely disabled or dangerous, the inmate may be medicated against his will. The inmate also has certain procedural rights before, during, and after the hearing. He must be given at least 24 hours' notice of the center's intent to convene an involuntary medication hearing, during which time he may not be medicated. In addition, he must receive notice of the tentative diagnosis, the factual basis for the diagnosis, and why the staff believes medication is necessary. At the hearing, the inmate has the right to attend; to present evidence, including witnesses; to cross-examine staff witnesses; and to the assistance of a lay adviser who has not been involved in his case and who understands the psychiatric issues involved. Minutes of the hearing must be kept, and a copy provided to the inmate. The inmate has the right to appeal the committee's decision to the center's superintendent within 24 hours, and the superintendent must decide the appeal within 24 hours after its receipt. The inmate may seek judicial review of a committee decision in state court by means of a personal restraint petition or extraordinary writ. After the initial hearing, involuntary medication can continue only with periodic review. When Harper first refused the medication, a committee, again composed of a nontreating psychiatrist, a psychologist, and the center's associate superintendent, was required

to review his case after the first seven days of treatment. If the committee reapproved the treatment, the treating psychiatrist was required to review the case and prepare a report for the medical director of the Department of Corrections every 14 days while treatment continued. Harper was absent when members of the Center staff met with the committee before the hearing. The committee then conducted the hearing in accordance with the policy, with Harper present and assisted by a nurse practitioner from another institution. The committee found that Harper was a danger to others as a result of a mental disease or disorder, and approved the involuntary administration of antipsychotic drugs. On appeal, the superintendent upheld the committee's findings. Beginning on November 23, 1982, Harper was involuntarily medicated for about one year. Periodic review occurred in accordance with policy. The following year, Harper was transferred to Washington State Reformatory. While there, he took no medication, and as a result, his condition deteriorated. He was transferred back to the Special Offender Center after only one month. Another committee hearing was held in accordance with Policy 600.30, and the committee again approved medication against Harper's will. Harper continued to receive antipsychotic drugs, subject to the required periodic reviews, until he was transferred to Washington State Penitentiary in June 1986. In February 1985, Harper filed a Section 1983 civil suit in state court, claiming that the failure to provide a judicial hearing before the involuntary administration of antipsychotic medication violated due process, equal protection, and free speech clauses of both the federal and state constitutions, as well as state tort law. The trial court ruled against Harper, but the State Supreme Court reversed and remanded, concluding that, under the due process clause of the Fourteenth Amendment, the state could administer such medication to a competent, nonconsenting inmate only if, in a judicial hearing at which the inmate had the full panoply of adversarial procedural protections, the state proved by "clear, cogent, and convincing" evidence that the medication was both necessary and effective for furthering a compelling state interest.

ISSUE

Is a judicial hearing required by the due process clause of the Fourteenth Amendment before the state may treat a mentally ill prisoner with antipsychotic drugs against his will?

HOLDING

No. In an opinion written by Justice Kennedy, the Supreme Court reversed the decision of the Washington Supreme Court, ruling that treating a mentally ill inmate with antipsychotic medication against his or her will without a judicial hearing does not violate due process, but the state must first establish that the inmate is dangerous to himself or others, or is seriously disruptive to the environment and that such treatment is in his "medical interest."

RATIONALE

By enacting the policy at issue, Policy 600.30, the state of Washington created a protected liberty interest on the part of prisoners to be free from "arbitrary administration of antipsychotic medication." The inmate must be found to be mentally ill and seriously disabled or dangerous. The Court stated that Harper also had a significant liberty interest in being free from being given antipsychotic drugs against his will under the due process clause of the Fourteenth Amendment. However, the procedures established by Policy 600.30 met the demands of the due process clause. These procedures included providing notice of the intent to hold the involuntary medication hearing, the right to be present at the hearing, and the right to present and cross-examine witnesses. In assessing whether or not the standards set by policy met due process requirements, the Court applied the standard of reasonableness established in *Turner v. Safley*, 482 U.S. 78 (1987), and *O'Lone v. Estate of Shabazz*, 482 U.S. 342 (1987). That is, if a prison regulation infringes on an inmate's constitutional rights, is the regulation reasonably related to legitimate penological interests? The Court applied the three-pronged *Turner* analysis to the case at hand, finding Policy 600.30 to be a rational means of further the legitimate objectives of the prison system. Harper had suggested that alternative means such as physical restraints or seclusion could be employed in lieu of the medication. The Court stated that Harper failed to show that these alternatives were acceptable, "in terms of either their medical effectiveness or their toll on limited prison resources." The Court acknowledged the serious potential side effects of the drugs being given to Harper, including acute acute dystonia, a severe involuntary spasm of the upper body, tongue, throat, or eyes, akathesia (motor restlessness, often characterized by an inability to sit still); neuroleptic malignant syndrome (a relatively rare condition which can lead to death from cardiac dysfunction); and tardive dyskinesia, involuntary, uncontrollable movements of various muscles, especially around the face. Despite these side effects, the Court stated that the decision to administer the medication was better made by medical professionals than a judge in a judicial hearing. In fact, given the risks involved, inmates' interests are "perhaps better served" by medical decisonmakers. "In sum, we hold that the regulation before us is permissible under the Constitution. It is an accommodation between an inmate's liberty interest in avoiding the forced administration of antipsychotic drugs and the State's interests in providing appropriate medical treatment to reduce the danger that an inmate suffering from a serious mental disorder represents to himself or others. The Due Process Clause does require certain essential procedural protections, all of which are provided by the regulation before us."

CASE EXCERPT

"We hold that, given the requirements of the prison environment, the Due Process Clause permits the State to treat a prison inmate who has a serious mental illness with antipsychotic drugs against his will, if the inmate is dangerous to himself or others and the treatment is in the inmate's medical interest."

CASE SIGNIFICANCE

This case is important because it gives the state the authority to forcibly administer medication, without a judicial hearing. This gives prison officials great power and flexibility in dealing with seriously mentally ill inmates, the number of whom is steadily increasing. The Court did require that certain due process safeguards be in place, however, so the power of prison officials is not arbitrary.

PENNSYLVANIA DEPARTMENT OF CORRECTIONS v. YESKEY

524 U.S. 206 (1998)

FACTS

Ronald Yeskey was sentenced to 18 to 36 months in a Pennsylvania correctional facility. He was also recommended by the sentencing court for placement in a motivational boot camp for first-time offenders. Successful completion of the boot camp would have made him eligible for parole in just six months. Prison officials refused Yeskey's admission to the program because of his medical history of hypertension. Yeskey

PENNSYLVANIA DEPARTMENT OF CORRECTIONS v. YESKEY *(cont.)*

then filed suit alleging that the exclusion violated the Americans with Disabilities Act of 1990 (ADA), Title II of which prohibits a "public entity" from discriminating against a "qualified individual with a disability" on account of that disability. The district court dismissed the suit for failing to state a claim, holding that the ADA does not apply to state prison inmates, but the Third Circuit reversed.

ISSUE

Did the Pennsylvania Department of Corrections' refusal to allow a prison inmate to participate in a motivational boot camp, because of the inmate's history of hypertension, violate the Americans with Disabilities Act prohibiting disability-based discrimination against qualified individuals?

HOLDING

Yes. In a unanimous opinion written by Justice Scalia, the Court affirmed the Third Circuit's ruling, holding that under the ADA no "public entity" may discriminate against qualified disabled individuals due to their disability. Moreover, the Court stated that the ADA's protections covered prisons and prison inmates as well as any other liberated citizen.

RATIONALE

"Title II of the ADA provides that: 'Subject to the provisions of this subchapter, no qualified individual with a disability shall, by reason of such disability, be excluded from participation in or be denied the benefits of the services, programs, or activities of a public entity, or be subjected to discrimination by any such entity' " (42 U.S.C. §12132). Justice Scalia stated that a state prison is a "public entity," according to the statutory definition of public entities, "which includes 'any department, agency, special purpose district, or other instrumentality of a State or States or local government' " (§12131(1)(B)). The Pennsylvania Department of Corrections' case focused on the phrase regarding "benefits of . . . services, programs, or activities of a public entity," contending that prisons do not provide benefits, so the ADA did not apply to prisons. The Court disagreed, noting that prisons in fact do provide many programs, such as educational programs, which can be said to benefit prisoners. Thus, excluding prisoners with disabilities from such programs would violate the provisions of the ADA. The Court concluded that

a plain reading of the text of the ADA did not reveal ambiguities and the ADA clearly applies to inmates in state prisons.

CASE EXCERPT

"We think the requirement of the rule is amply met: the statute's language unmistakably includes state prisons and prisoners within its coverage. There, although the ADEA plainly covered state employees, it contained an exception for " 'appointee[s] on the policy making level' which made it impossible for us to conclude that the statute plainly cover[ed] appointed state judges. Here, the ADA plainly covers state institutions without any exception that could cast the coverage of prisons into doubt."

CASE SIGNIFICANCE

In this case the Supreme Court held that the ADA applies to state prisons. This is significant for prison officials, who must now seek to comply with all of the terms of this act, which requires reasonable accommodations for persons with a variety of disabilities. This will have a major impact on both correctional practices and finances, as the inmate population ages.

MCKUNE v. LILE
536 U.S. 24 (2002)

FACTS

Robert Lile was convicted of rape, aggravated sodomy, and aggravated kidnapping. During his trial, he maintained that the sexual encounter was consensual. A few years before he was to be released from the Kansas Department of Corrections, prison officials ordered him to participate in an 18-month-long intensive sexual abuse treatment program (SATP). Inmates in the program are required to write and sign an Admission of Responsibility form. They accept responsibility for their crime and complete a sexual history in which they detail all their prior sexual misconduct, including activities for which they have not been criminally charged. The information in the SATP can be used against them in future criminal proceedings. Prison officials advised Lile that if he refused to participate in the program his privileges would be reduced, impacting his visitation rights, earnings, work assignments, ability to send money to his family, commissary rights, and access to a personal television. He would also be transferred to a maximum security facility. Lile refused to participate in the SATP because disclosing his criminal history would violate the Fifth Amendment privilege against self-incrimination. He filed a civil rights lawsuit under 42 U.S.C. §1983, seeking an injunction to prevent officials from withdrawing his privileges and transferring him to a different facility. The District Court granted him a summary judgment. The Tenth Circuit Court of Appeals affirmed.

ISSUE

Does it violate the Fifth Amendment to require an incarcerated sex offender to participate in a treatment program that includes admitting to sex related crimes for which the prisoner has not been previously charged if the inmate's refusal to participate results in a lose of certain privileges and the possibility of being transferred to a more secure facility?

HOLDING

No. A prison-based sex offender treatment program that requires offenders to admit to sexual misconduct for which they have not been charged or convicted and provides that if they refuse to participate they lose privileges and may be transferred to a more security facility does not compel offenders to incriminate themselves in violation of the Fifth Amendment.

RATIONALE

The Court stated that "[s]ex offenders are a serious threat in this Nation," and reviewed statistics showing that the number of sex offenders in prison increased at a faster rate than any other category of violent offender between 1980 and 1994. According to various studies, after they are released from prison, sex offenders are very likely to commit another sex crime. However, there is strong agreement among corrections professionals that they can benefit from treatment. Most treatment programs such as the Kansas SATP in the case at hand require sex offenders to confront past misconduct and accept responsibility because the research indicates that offenders who deny their past are likely to fail. The District Court found Kansas's program to be a "valid, clinical rehabilitative program, supported by a legitimate penological objective in rehabilitation." While the Kansas SATP did not offer inmate participants immunity from prosecution based on statements of past conduct, no inmate had to date been prosecuted based on those statements. However, the potential for prosecution remained. This potentiality, according to the treatment professionals, was an important part of

the rehabilitation process because it showed participants how serious society considered these crimes to be. Other jurisdictions with similar programs at the time also refused to grant immunity. The main question then, according to the Court, was whether the Kansas SATP created a compulsion to participate and thus incriminate themselves, thereby encumbering a constitutional right. The Court explained that the program did not compel prisoners to participate and incriminate themselves because nonparticipation consequences —transfer to another unit, more limited work opportunities, limits on certain privileges—are not consequences that compel an inmate to reveal past crimes against his right and desire to remain silent. While such consequences might be unpleasant, such a fact must be understood in the prison context in which those consequences occur. Prisoners do not have the full range of constitutional rights available to free citizens. In *Sandin v. Conner*, 515 U.S. 472 (1995), the Supreme Court ruled that prison conditions do not violate the due process clause unless they constitute "atypical and significant hardships on inmates in relation to the ordinary incidents of prison life." The Kansas SATP, as a prison rehabilitation program rationally related to a legitimate penological purpose, "does not violate the privilege against self-incrimination" if a prisoner who refuses to participate faces consequences that are related to the program's goals and are not atypical and significant hardships in the context of incarceration. Lile's refusal to participate did not extend his prison sentence, result in loss of good-time, or affect his eligibility for parole. Transferring him to another unit was not punishment because space in SATP was limited, and inmates who did not want to participate had to be moved to accommodate those who did want to participate. Admittedly, certain prison privileges were reduced, but the Constitution gives officials autonomy to grant or restrict privileges based on their evaluation of what is best. Further, if Lile prevailed, Justice Kennedy stated that "there would be serious doubt about the constitutionality of the federal sex offender treatment program," which was very similar to the Kansas program. It would also cast doubt on an "accepted feature of federal criminal law, the downward adjustment of a sentence for acceptance of criminal responsibility."

CASE EXCERPT

"The Kansas SATP represents a sensible approach to reducing the serious danger that repeat sex offenders

MCKUNE v. LILE *(cont.)*

pose to many innocent persons, most often children. The State's interest in rehabilitation is undeniable. There is, furthermore, no indication that the SATP is merely an elaborate ruse to skirt the protections of the privilege against compelled self-incrimination. Rather, the program allows prison administrators to provide to those who need treatment the incentive to seek it."

CASE SIGNIFICANCE

At the time this case was decided there were several sex offender prison-based treatment programs that required admitting past misconduct without immunity from prosecution. Although it is a case about the conditions under which a particular offender is incarcerated, it is also a case about sentencing. A convicted and sentenced sex offender was required to participate in a treatment program he believed violated his constitutional rights or face a serious reduction in his living conditions.

DISCUSSION QUESTIONS

1. The lone dissenter in *Estelle v. Gamble* stated that establishing deliberate indifference looks at the subjective motivation of the defendant. Explain this observation, referring, if necessary, to the actual case.
2. What are some crucial issues faced by correctional administrators with respect to providing medical care for inmates? Your discussion should include, but not be limited to, the aging prison population.
3. The dissent in *McKune v. Lile* was of the opinion that the requirements of Kansas' sex offender treatment program required "an impermissible and unwarranted sacrifice from the participants." In the case at hand, the inmate claimed that he was innocent of the crime for which he had been convicted. If you knew that the inmate were actually innocent, would you still agree with the majority opinion? Discuss.
4. Should Congress amend the ADA to exclude prisoners from coverage? Why or why not?
5. Should mentally ill prisoners be committed to hospitals for the mentally ill, rather than prison? Discuss the burdens faced by corrections officials in dealing with the mentally ill.
6. Do you think the standard established in *Estelle v. Gamble* provides inmates with meaningful protection? Why or why not?
7. What area of law did the Court derive the *Estelle v. Gamble* standard from?
8. Why must prisons provide inmates with medical care that is better than the medical care some people in the free world are able to afford?
9. How might prison officials apply the right to forced medical treatment in an inappropriate manner?
10. 10. Do you think inmates should have the right to refuse all medical treatment? Why or why not?

CHAPTER SEVEN

INMATE SEARCHES AND USE OF FORCE

HUDSON v. PALMER, *468 U.S. 517 (1984)*
WHITLEY v. ALBERS, *475 U.S. 312 (1986)*

HUDSON v. MCMILLIAN, *303 U.S. 1 (1992)*

INTRODUCTION

The three cases in this chapter address inmate searches and both deadly and nondeadly use of force and concern Fourth and Eighth Amendment protections.

The first case in this chapter, *Hudson v. Palmer* (468 U.S. 517), was the first time that the Supreme Court addressed whether the Fourth Amendment applies to prison cells. The Court held that the Fourth Amendment did not apply "within the confines of the prison cell." Inmates alleging violations against their Fourth Amendment right to be free from unreasonable searches and seizures are generally unsuccessful, and the Fourth Amendment has obviously limited application to the institutional setting. Inmates are subject to searches of their person, belongings, and cells without a warrant or probable cause. As the Court noted in *Block v. Rutherford* (468 U.S. 576), decided in 1984, the same year that Palmer was decided, the unique security needs of a prison outweigh the individual rights of inmates. (See chapter 4 for the brief and discussion of *Block v. Rutherford*.) In *Palmer*, the Chief Justice stressed that not being able to invoke Fourth Amendment protections did not mean that officials could "ride roughshod over inmates' property rights with impunity." Inmates could still invoke the Eighth Amendment prohibition against cruel and unusual punishment when alleging destruction of personal property.

The Eighth Amendment is also the focus of the two cases in this chapter dealing with use of force. Prison officials are permitted to use reasonable force to maintain discipline and for protection. The force must be reasonable under the circumstances. Thus, officials may be justified in using extreme force, even deadly force, if the situation warrants it. In the first of these two cases, *Whitley v. Albers* (475 U.S. 312), the Court made clear that prison officials will not be liable for the use of deadly force unless it can be shown that the officials acted in a "wanton" manner. This is a difficult standard for inmate plaintiffs to meet. The Court failed to indicate whether this standard applied to all use of force cases, or only to those involving the use of deadly force. This issue was addressed in the second case, *Hudson v. McMillian* (303 U.S. 1), a case involving the use of less than deadly force. Here, the Court held that so long as force is used in a good faith effort to maintain order, liability does not attach. It is only in instances where the inmate can prove a correctional officer acted maliciously that liability will attach.

HUDSON v. PALMER
468 U.S. 517 (1984)

FACTS

Russell Palmer, an inmate at Bland Correctional Center in Bland, Virginia, was the subject of a shakedown search on September 16, 1981, in which Ted Hudson, an officer at the institution, and another officer searched Palmer's prison locker and cell for contraband. During the search, the officers discovered a ripped pillowcase in a trashcan near Palmer's cell bunk. Palmer was charged with destroying state property and

HUDSON v. PALMER *(cont.)*

ordered to reimburse the state. Palmer filed a Section 1983 suit, claiming that Hudson had conducted the search and brought a false charge against him solely to harass him, in violation of his Fourth Amendment protection against unreasonable searches. Palmer also charged that Hudson had violated his Fourteenth Amendment right not to be deprived of property without due process of law by intentionally destroying certain of his noncontraband personal property during the search. Hudson denied the allegations and moved for and was granted summary judgment by the district court. The appellate court affirmed the lower court's decision that Palmer was not deprived of his property without due process. However, the court of appeals reversed and remanded the district court's decision with regard to the alleged Fourth Amendment violation. The court held that prisoners possess limited privacy rights in their cells and are entitled to protection against searches conducted solely to harass or to humiliate. The appellate court remanded the case back to the district court in order to determine the purpose of the search of Palmer's locker and cell.

ISSUE

Did the search of Palmer's locker and cell violate the Fourth Amendment? Did prison officials deprive Hudson of his property in violation of the Fourteenth Amendment?

HOLDING

No to both questions. The Supreme Court held that the Fourth Amendment prohibition against unreasonable searches did not apply "within the confines of the prison cell." The Court found that "the paramount interest in institutional security" outweighed all privacy concerns. The Court further held that "random and unauthorized" deprivations of property did not violate the due process clause, so long as postdeprivation remedies were available.

RATIONALE

This case was the first occasion for the Supreme Court to address whether the Fourth Amendment applies within prison cells. Fourth Amendment protections depend on a justifiable, reasonable, or legitimate expectation of privacy. The Supreme Court noted that privacy was fundamentally incompatible with the maintenance of prison security and surveillance, stating that the "recognition of privacy rights for prisoners

in their individual cells simply cannot be reconciled with the concept of incarceration and the needs and objectives of penal institutions." Chief Justice Burger emphasized, however, that not being able to invoke Fourth Amendment protections did not mean that prison officials could "ride roughshod over inmates' property rights with impunity." Inmates are still protected by the Eighth Amendment prohibition against cruel and unusual punishment and tort and common-law remedies at the state level for addressing allegations of destruction or deprivation of personal property.

CASE EXCERPT

"Notwithstanding our caution in approaching claims that the Fourth Amendment is inapplicable in a given context, we hold that society is not prepared to recognize as legitimate any subjective expectation of privacy that a prisoner might have in his prison cell and that, accordingly, the Fourth Amendment proscription against unreasonable searches does not apply within the confines of the prison cell. The recognition of privacy rights for prisoners in their individual cells simply cannot be reconciled with the concept of incarceration and the needs and objectives of penal institutions."

CASE SIGNIFICANCE

This case went a step beyond the decision in *Parratt v. Taylor*, 451 U.S. 527 (1981), and held that not only depriving an inmate of his personal property was not a violation of the due process clause, but that inmates have no protections under the Fourth Amendment from searches, as they do not have the requisite "reasonable expectation of privacy" in their cells. (See chapter 8 for discussion of *Parratt v. Taylor*.) This gives prison authorities virtually unlimited discretion to conduct warrantless searches of both inmates and their cells.

WHITLEY v. ALBERS

475 U.S. 312 (1986)

FACTS

In 1980, Albers was a prisoner at Oregon State Penitentiary when a riot broke out after officers attempted to move four intoxicated prisoners. One officer was taken hostage, and the inmate leader of the riot demanded that representatives from the media be brought in. The prison officials devised an assault plan to rescue the hostage that required Whitley, the prison security manager, to go into the cellblock unarmed, but to be followed by armed officers. One of the officers was ordered by Whitley to "shoot low" at inmates attempting to climb to the upper tier where the hostage officer was being held. Albers claimed that during the disturbances, he had asked Whitley for a key to the row of elderly prisoners' cells, so that he could move them to a safer area if tear gas was going to be used. Albers alleged that Whitley said that he would be back with the key, but Whitley denied this conversation. When Albers next saw Whitley, he asked him if he had the key. Whitley replied that he did not and proceeded to the upper tier. The armed officer fired two warning shots, and a third shot hit Albers in the left knee as he started up the stairs after Whitley. Whitley filed a § 1983 civil suit in Federal District Court against the prison officials, alleging Eighth and Fourteenth Amendment violations. The District Court found for the prison officials, but the Court of Appeals reversed the District Court and remanded the case for a new trial based on Albers's Eighth Amendment claims.

ISSUE

Is it cruel and unusual punishment under the Eighth Amendment to shoot a prisoner during an attempt to stop a prison riot?

HOLDING

No. "After incarceration, only the 'unnecessary and wanton infliction of pain'... constitutes cruel and unusual punishment forbidden by the Eighth Amendment."

RATIONALE

This case required the Court to establish the standard governing Eighth Amendment cruel and unusual punishments clause in a prison environment. Justice O'Connor stated, "It is obduracy and wantonness, not inadvertence or error in good faith, that characterize the conduct prohibited by the cruel and unusual punishments clause, whether that conduct occurs in connection with establishing conditions of confinement, supplying medical needs, or restoring control over a tumultuous cellblock. The infliction of pain in the course of a prison security measure, therefore, does not amount to cruel and unusual punishment simply because it may appear in retrospect that the degree of force authorized or applied for security purposes was unreasonable, and hence unnecessary in the strict sense." The officer was ordered to "shoot low," and such a command fails to show wantonness or unnecessary

infliction of pain. The Court also noted that Albers was running up the stairs after Whitley, so his actions could reasonably have been seen as threatening the attempt to rescue the hostage. "Under all these circumstances, the shooting was part and parcel of a good-faith effort to restore prison security."

CASE EXCERPT

"Where a prison security measure is undertaken to resolve a disturbance, such as occurred in this case, that indisputably poses significant risks to the safety of inmates and prison staff, we think the question whether the measure taken inflicted unnecessary and wanton pain and suffering ultimately turns on whether force was applied in a good faith effort to maintain or restore discipline or maliciously and sadistically for the very purpose of causing harm... 'Prison administrators... should be accorded wide-ranging deference in the adoption and execution of policies and practices that in their judgment are needed to preserve internal order and discipline and to maintain institutional security.' That deference extends to a prison security measure taken in response to an actual confrontation with riotous inmates, just as it does to prophylactic or preventive measures intended to reduce the incidence of these or any other breaches of prison discipline. It does not insulate from review actions taken in bad faith and for no legitimate purpose, but it requires that neither judge nor jury freely substitute their judgment for that of officials who have made a considered choice."

CASE SIGNIFICANCE

In this case the Court made clear that prison officials will not be liable for the use of deadly force unless it can be shown that the officials acted in a "wanton" manner. This is a difficult standard for inmate plaintiffs to meet. The Court did not make clear, however, whether this standard applied to all use of force cases, or only to those involving the use of deadly force. This issue was addressed in *Hudson v. McMillian* (1992).

HUDSON v. MCMILLIAN
503 U.S. 1 (1992)

FACTS

Hudson, a Louisiana state prisoner, testified that he had been beaten by two correctional officers after an argument with one of the officers, McMillian. Hudson

HUDSON v. MCMILLIAN *(cont.)*

also maintained that the supervisor saw the beating but just told the officers "not to have too much fun." Hudson sustained minor bruising and swelling about the face and a cracked dental plate. Hudson filed a § 1983 civil suit in the Federal District Court, seeking monetary compensation and alleging that his Eighth Amendment rights had been violated. A magistrate tried the case, awarding Hudson eight hundred dollars in damages and finding the officers used unnecessary force, which was condoned by the supervisor. The Fifth Circuit Court of Appeals reversed this finding, ruling that in prison Eighth Amendment excessive use of force cases, prisoners must prove "significant injury" from the excessive force and an "unnecessary and wanton infliction of pain." While the Court of Appeals did agree that the beating by the officers was excessive, unnecessary, and wanton, Hudson's injuries were "minor," requiring no medical attention. Thus, the Eighth Amendment violation was not established.

ISSUE

Is significant injury required in order for an excessive use of force incident to be considered a violation of the Eighth Amendment?

HOLDING

No. The use of excessive physical force against a prisoner may constitute cruel and unusual punishment even though the inmate does not suffer serious injury.

RATIONALE

Justice O'Connor wrote the Majority opinion in this case, as she had in *Whitley v. Albers*. She noted the similarity between the two cases and stated that the "core judicial inquiry" when prison officials are accused of cruel and unusual punishment involving the use of excessive force was established in *Whitley* and centers on whether the "force was applied in a good faith effort to maintain or restore discipline, or maliciously and sadistically to cause harm." The amount of injury sustained by the use of force is only one factor, according to the *Whitley* standard. Other factors include the "the need for application of force, the relationship between that need and the amount of force used, the threat 'reasonably perceived by the responsible officials,' and 'any efforts made to temper the severity of a forceful response.'" If it is shown that the use of force was malicious and sadistic, then contemporary standards of decency have been violated, whether or not there is

a resultant significant injury. The Court allowed that some *de minimus* injuries would not rise to an Eighth Amendment violation, but in the instant case, Justice O'Connor stated that "blows directed at Hudson, which caused bruises, swelling, loosened teeth, and a cracked dental plate, are not *de minimis* for Eighth Amendment purposes. The extent of Hudson's injuries thus provides no basis for dismissal of his § 1983 claim."

In his dissent, Justice Thomas argued that *Wilson v. Seiter*, 501 U.S. 294 (1991), required that an inmate alleging excessive force had to show significant injury in addition to the unnecessary and wanton infliction of pain. The Court did not agree and saw this as a misapplication of *Wilson*, as well as a disregard for all of the Supreme Court's Eighth Amendment cases. *Wilson* itself did not involve an excessive force allegation. Justice Thomas also argued that excessive force claims and conditions of confinement claims are the same in kind, which the Court said "is likewise unfounded. To deny the difference between punching a prisoner in the face and serving him unappetizing food is to ignore the 'concepts of dignity, civilized standards, humanity, and decency' that animate the Eighth Amendment."

CASE EXCERPT

"When prison officials maliciously and sadistically use force to cause harm, contemporary standards of decency always are violated. This is true whether or not significant injury is evident. Otherwise, the Eighth Amendment would permit any physical punishment, no matter how diabolic or inhuman, inflicting less than some arbitrary quantity of injury. Such a result would have been as unacceptable to the drafters of the Eighth Amendment as it is today…That is not to say that every malevolent touch by a prison guard gives rise to a federal cause of action. The Eighth Amendment's prohibition of cruel and unusual punishments necessarily excludes from constitutional recognition *de minimis* uses of physical force, provided that the use of force is not of a sort repugnant to the conscience of mankind."

CASE SIGNIFICANCE

In this case the Supreme Court defined the standard of conduct for cases involving the use of less than deadly force by correctional officers. Here, the Court held that so long as force is used in a good faith effort to maintain order, liability does not attach. It is only in instances where the inmate can prove a correctional officer acted maliciously that liability will attach.

DISCUSSION QUESTIONS

1. In your opinion, what kind of protections should be afforded inmates with respect to cell searches? What recourse should be available to inmates if their personal property is intentionally damaged by corrections officials?

2. What standards did *Whitley v. Albers* establish regarding use of force by correctional officers?

3. The dissent in *Whitley v. Albers* supported allowing civilian juries to decide if a correctional officer's use of force was reasonable, even if no malicious intent was present. Discuss the pros and cons of such an arrangement.

4. Research the use of force policy in your state's department of corrections. Does it meet constitutional standards?

5. What would be an example of an unconstitutional search of an inmate or an inmate's cell?

6. What do you think of Justice Thomas's dissent in *Hudson v. McMillan*? Do you agree with his view of the Eighth Amendment?

7. How has the Supreme Court's interpretation of the Eighth Amendment changed over time?

8. How has the "evolving standards of decency" approach to the Eighth Amendment affected the use of force in corrections over time?

CHAPTER EIGHT

DUE PROCESS AND DISCIPLINE, ADMINISTRATIVE SEGREGATION, AND TRANSFER

WOLFF v. MCDONNELL, *418 U.S. 539 (1974)*

BAXTER v. PALMIGIANO, *425 U.S. 308 (1976)*

HUTTO v. FINNEY, *437 U.S. 638 (1978)*

HEWITT v. HELMS, *459 U.S. 460 (1983)*

HUGHES v. ROWE, *449 U.S. 5 (1980)*

SUPERINTENDENT, *WALPOLE v. HILL, 472 U.S. 445 (1985)*

PONTE v. REAL, *471 U.S. 491 (1985)*

MEACHUM v. FANO, *427 U.S. 215 (1976)*

MONTANYE v. HAYMES, *427 U.S. 236 (1976)*

VITEK v. JONES, *445 U.S. 480 (1980)*

SANDIN v. CONNER, *515 U.S. 472 (1995)*

WILKINSON v. AUSTIN, *545 U.S. 209 (2005)*

INTRODUCTION

This chapter examines the key Supreme Court cases involving inmate discipline. It also looks at related cases that have addressed due process requirements for assignment to administrative segregation and transfer to another facility.

Disciplining prisoners who have violated prison rules or regulations has always been a critical and controversial area for prison managers. Officials must be able to enforce regulations in order to maintain order and to protect the safety of inmates and staff. A prison where regulations are not enforced does not provide a safe and secure living or working environment. Once the daily routine breaks down, no one is certain of what to expect next. Prisoners are subject to a myriad of rules that govern almost every aspect of their lives, and they are not always the most willing rule abiders.

The challenge for officials is to develop a prison disciplinary system that encourages prisoners to obey the rules and provides fair and effective sanctions for rule infractions. Officials provide inmates with rulebooks that outline all the rules they must live by and explain the process by which inmates will be disciplined if they break the rules. Rulebooks are usually printed in more than one language in correctional systems where that is necessary. Unfortunately, there will be prisoners who are illiterate or who do not speak a language in which a rulebook is published. Offenses are generally categorized as serious (major) or less serious (minor); punishments for serious offenses are more severe, while punishments for minor offenses are less severe. Lawsuits decided in the 1960s and early 1970s established that corporal punishment could not be used against prisoners who violate regulations. Since that time, officials have had a limited number of available sanctions. A common punishment for more serious infractions is assignment to punitive or disciplinary segregation for a set period of time. Conditions in punitive segregation cellblocks are restricted and prisoners must stay in their cells. Another important sanction for serious infractions is a reduction in earned good-time credit, which lengthens a prisoner's stay in prison. Less severe punishments include such things as extra work detail and restrictions on recreation and visiting.

Wolff v. McDonnell set forth the due process requirements prisoners must be afforded who face a loss of good time as a disciplinary sanction. Before *Wolff,* prison officials did not have to abide by certain procedures. Some states afforded inmates extensive due process, others did not. *Wolff* is important because it recognized the importance of due process protections for prisoners faced with serious sanctions, like loss of good time. It outlined the essential steps in the process that all state prison systems must follow. The Court in *Wolff* stated specifically that the due process requirements were not mandated by the Constitution; rather, they were mandated because the state of Nebraska had created a liberty interest for prisoners in their good time credits. By state law, those credits could not be taken away without following due process. *Baxter v. Palmigiano* is an important case because the Court refused to extend the *Wolff* due process protections to permit prisoners to bring attorneys to disciplinary hearings. It also refused to extend the privilege against self-incrimination to the disciplinary hearing setting.

The state-created liberty doctrine first mentioned in *Wolff* was later expanded significantly in *Hewitt v. Helms.* Although *Hewitt* was not a case about discipline (it addressed assignment to administrative segregation), the Court took the concept it first recognized in *Wolff* and defined it more clearly. A state creates a liberty interest when it drafts rules, regulations, or statutes that give mandatory directives to officials in mandatory language. Those types of rules trigger due process protections for prisoners. The *Hewitt* case generated thousands of inmate lawsuits that attacked official actions on the grounds that prison regulations were mandatory and inmates were not given their due process rights. In 1995, the Court addressed what the majority of the court considered a situation that had become untenable under *Hewitt.* In *Sandin v. Conner,* the Court ruled that the *Hewitt* definition of a state-created liberty interest was no longer controlling. Instead a liberty interest that triggers due process for an inmate must involve a deprivation or restraint that

is atypical to life in prison or is a significant hardship. *Sandin* is a major departure from previous prisoner due process case law. Its impact on inmate disciplinary systems and the procedures by which inmates are placed in administrative segregation depends on how the lower courts interpret it.

The past few decades of coping with crowded prisons and concomitant prison violence have prompted many states to construct Supermax prisons. About 30 states have Supermax facilities, and there are at least two federal Supermax prisons. Such maximum security institutions are reserved for the "worst of the worst" prisoners and characterized by highly restrictive and harsh conditions, such as extreme isolation in single cells, lights on 24 hours a day, no communication with other inmates, rare to no outside contact, and indefinite periods of confinement. Inmates have a protected liberty interest from being placed in such facilities without due process under *Sandin v. Conner.* A new case in this chapter, *Wilkinson v. Austin* (2005), gave the Supreme Court the opportunity to delineate just what procedures constitute due process rights and protect inmates' liberty interests. The Court upheld the constitutionality of Ohio's informal, nonadversarial model.

Also important to prisoners is the process by which they can be transferred to another facility. Conditions in correctional facilities can differ significantly. Prisoners are aware of those differences either because they have lived in various facilities or by reputation. Many prisoners would prefer to be housed in a prison close to their families and friends. When a prisoner is transferred he or she will be assigned a new job and must readjust to a new social life. He or she may lose their place in school or in a programmatic activity. Transfer can be a traumatic experience. Nonetheless, in *Meachum v. Fano* and *Montayne v. Haymes,* the Supreme Court refused to extend prisoners the right to a hearing before they are transferred. Officials have the discretion to transfer inmates for whatever reasons they deem necessary, even if the motivation is to discipline. The exception to that rule is transfer to a mental health facility. The *Vitek v. Jones* opinion lays out the reasons why transfer to that type of facility is different and why due process must be provided. It also details the specific steps correctional officials must follow.

The Fourteenth Amendment's due process clause does not protect inmates to the same extent that it protects free world citizens who are defendants in a criminal trial. Whether the issue is discipline, transfer, or assignment to administrative segregation, the Court has ruled that prisoner due process is limited. Since *Sandin* it is arguably more limited than it used to be. Despite those limits, it is important to recognize that inmates do have very important due process protections. The Constitution crosses over prison walls and to some degree protects prisoners from arbitrary and capricious official decision making.

WOLFF v. MCDONNELL
418 U.S. 539 (1974)

FACTS

McDonnell, a Lincoln, Nebraska prisoner, filed a § 1983 lawsuit on behalf of himself and other inmates at the Nebraska Penal and Correctional Complex, alleging that prison disciplinary proceedings violated due process under the Fourteenth Amendment, the legal assistance program for inmates was unconstitutional, and regulations regarding correspondence between inmates and their attorneys was unconstitutionally restrictive. The key issue with the disciplinary hearings involved the fact that inmates would lose their good-time credits if found guilty of misconduct. The inmates sought both injunctive relief and damages. The District Court denied the due process claim and found the legal assistance program to meet constitutional standards, but did hold that the inspection of correspondence between attorneys and inmates was unconstitutional. The Court of Appeals, however, reversed the District Court's ruling as to the constitutionality of the due process claim, holding that the procedures required by *Morrissey v. Brewer*, 408 U.S. 471 (1972), and *Gagnon v. Scarpelli*, 411 U.S. 778 (1973), applied to prison disciplinary hearings. *Morrissey* and *Gagnon* had been decided after the District Court's earlier ruling. The specific due process requirements of disciplinary hearings, such as whether or not counsel was to be provided, were to be determined by the District Court on remand The Court of Appeals also ordered that findings of misconduct that were determined at disciplinary proceedings that did not meet the due process requirements outlined by the District Court to be expunged from prison records.

ISSUE

Do inmates have due process rights in prison disciplinary proceedings?

HOLDING

Yes. Due process in prison disciplinary proceedings entails: (1) providing the inmate with written notice of the charges against him or her; (2) providing an opportunity for the inmate to present evidence and witnesses in defense; (3) providing the assistance of staff or a fellow prisoner in compiling evidence if the inmate needs such assistance; and (4) providing to the inmate a written statement from the disciplinary board explaining its findings.

RATIONALE

In writing for the Court, Justice White referred to the Court's consistent holding that some kind of a hearing must be held before individuals are deprived of their property interests. Analagous to property interests are one's liberty interests. In this case, inmates had a state-protected liberty interest in retaining good-time credits. Justice White further explained that "[a] prisoner is not wholly stripped of constitutional protections," but inmates facing prison disciplinary proceedings are not entitled to all of the rights a defendant receives in a criminal proceeding. Prison disciplinary proceedings have to accommodate institutional needs as well as "generally applicable constitutional requirements." Justice White noted that prisoners lose good-time credits if found guilty of serious misconduct, so the procedure for determining serious misconduct has to follow minimal due process requirements, although the full range of procedures required by *Morrissey* and *Gagnon* in probation and parole revocations are not required in a prison setting. The Court did not require that the inmate be allowed to confront or cross-examine witnesses, reasoning that such procedures in prison, "where prison disruption is a serious concern, are discretionary with prison officials." The Court also did not require that inmates be provided with counsel, reasoning that providing counsel would make the proceeding more adversarial and would work against the goals of corrections. The Court did allow that counsel substitutes should be provided in cases where inmates are illiterate or the issues are so complex to make it unlikely that the inmate would be able to present evidence.

CASE EXCERPT

"But though his rights may be diminished by the needs and exigencies of the institutional environment, a prisoner is not wholly stripped of constitutional protections when he is imprisoned for crime. There is no iron curtain drawn between the Constitution and the prisons of this country."

CASE SIGNIFICANCE

In this case the Supreme Court determined that inmates are entitled to due process during a disciplinary hearing. Exactly what constitutes due process in a given situation is not always clear, but here the Court was quite specific in laying out what is considered the minimum due process rights possessed by each inmate. It is important to remember that while this case provides inmates with a number of rights, these rights involve procedural matters and serve merely to bar arbitrary decision making. In reality, prison disciplinary proceedings are still tightly controlled by the prison administration.

BAXTER v. PALMIGIANO
425 U.S. 308 (1976)

FACTS

This case was a consolidation of two cases, one from California and one from Rhode Island. Two prison inmates at the San Quentin, California state prison, filed a § 1983 lawsuit on behalf of themselves and other San Quentin inmates for declaratory and injunctive relief, claiming that prison disciplinary proceedings violated their due process and equal protection rights under the Fourteenth Amendment. The District Court granted relief, and the Court of Appeals affirmed, setting forth various procedures due inmates facing disciplinary hearings. One year later, the Court of Appeals granted a rehearing to modify its earlier opinion in light of the Supreme Court's holding in *Wolff*, which had been decided in the interim. The Court of Appeals held that at a minimum, inmates are due a notice and a right to respond when they are facing loss or suspension of privileges, even if the suspension is only temporary. If inmates were denied the privilege to confront and cross-examine witnesses, then they were to be provided with written reasons for that denial. Further, upholding their earlier opinion, the Court of Appeals stated that inmates had the

right to counsel when they were facing prison discipline for conduct that could also be punished under state criminal law.

The second case involved Palmigiano, a Rhode Island state prisoner, convicted of murder and serving a life sentence at the Rhode Island Adult Correctional Institution. Palmigiano was charged with inciting a disturbance at the prison. At a Disciplinary Board hearing, prison officials told him "that he might be prosecuted for a violation of state law, that he should consult his attorney (although his attorney was not permitted by the Board to be present during the hearing), that he had a right to remain silent during the hearing, but that, if he remained silent, his silence would be held against him." Palmigiano did have a counsel substitute allowed by prison procedures at the hearing, and he remained silent. He was given thirty days in "punitive segregation." Palmigiano then filed a § 1983 lawsuit, requesting injunctive relief and damages and alleging that the disciplinary hearings violated his Fourteenth Amendment due process rights. The District Court denied relief, but the Court of Appeals reversed the lower court's ruling, finding that he was denied due process and that he should have had access to an attorney. The Supreme Court granted certiorari and remanded the case back to the Court of Appeals to reconsider their holding in light of *Wolff*. The Court of Appeals affirmed its original decision but modified it to hold "that an inmate at a prison disciplinary proceeding must be advised of his right to remain silent, that he must not be questioned further once he exercises that right, and that such silence may not be used against him at that time or in future proceedings." The Court of Appeals also ruled that if criminal prosecution is a possibility, then prison officials should consider whether counsel should be brought into the disciplinary hearing, "not because *Wolff* requires it in that proceeding, but because *Miranda v. Arizona,* 384 U. S. 436 (1966) requires it in light of future criminal prosecution." The Supreme Court granted certiorari again and consolidated both cases in its decision.

ISSUE

Do inmates have a constitutional right to counsel during a disciplinary hearing? Is an inmate's silence at a disciplinary hearing sufficient to draw an "adverse inference"?

BAXTER v. PALMIGIANO (*cont.*)

HOLDING

No to both questions. Under the Court's decision in *Wolff*, inmates do not have a right to an attorney in prison disciplinary hearings, and "permitting an adverse inference to be drawn from an inmate's silence at his disciplinary proceedings is not, on its face, an invalid practice."

RATIONALE

The Supreme Court reversed both of the courts of appeals' decisions and took the opportunity to clarify that under *Wolff*, inmates involved in disciplinary proceedings do not have the right to be assisted by counsel. The Court's opinion, written by Justice White, disagreed with both courts of appeals that decisions in two earlier cases (*Miranda* and *Mathis v. United States*, 391 U.S. 1, 1968) required counsel in prison hearings that might lead to state criminal prosecution. The lower courts were reasoning that assistance of counsel was required because inmates' statements at the prison hearings might be used against them at a later date if they were prosecuted for the same actions in criminal court. With respect to permitting unfavorable inferences from inmates remaining silent, the Court distinguished prison disciplinary hearings from criminal prosecution. In the hearing in the Rhode Island prison, Palmigiano was not denied his Fifth Amendment privilege to remain silent, and he was "not, in consequence of his silence, automatically found guilty," even though he was informed that his silence could be used against him. The Court stated that their decision in this case was "consistent with the prevailing rule that the Fifth Amendment does not forbid adverse inferences against parties to civil actions when they refuse to testify in response to probative evidence offered against them: the Amendment 'does not preclude the inference where the privilege is claimed by a party to a civil cause.'"

CASE EXCERPT

"We see no reason to alter our conclusion so recently made in *Wolff* that inmates do not 'have a right to either retained or appointed counsel in disciplinary hearings.'"

CASE SIGNIFICANCE

In this case the Supreme Court refused to provide any additional due process rights to inmates beyond those provided in *Wolff v. McDonnell*. The Court

clearly distinguished between the rights of persons on trial and inmates in a prison disciplinary hearing, and allowed the disciplinary committee to draw an adverse inference from an inmate's silence during the hearing.

HUTTO v. FINNEY

437 U.S. 678 (1978)

FACTS

In 1969, litigation began which challenged the conditions in the Arkansas prison system. In evaluating the diet and sleeping arrangements of the inmates, the physical condition of cells, and the behavior of prison guards, a district court called the conditions which inmates were forced to face "a dark and evil world completely alien to the free world" and a violation of the Eighth and Fourteenth Amendments (*Holt v. Sarver*, 309 F. Supp. 362. 381 (ED Ark. 1970)). Among the rulings in this case was the district court's decision to limit "punitive isolation" to no more than thirty days. The practice in Arkansas prisons concerning punitive isolation involved sentences of indiscriminate periods, sometimes months, in crowded windowless cells. From four to 11 prisoners were crowded into these cells with only a source of water and a toilet that could not be flushed from inside the cell. Prisoners slept on mattresses used by other prisoners suffering from infectious diseases. The petitioners did not object to the district court's decisions regarding the conditions violations but only to the portion concerning the 30-day time limit placed on punitive isolation. The petitioners also challenged the award of attorney's fees to be paid out of Arkansas Department of Correction funds, based on a finding that the petitioners had acted in bad faith in failing to cure the identified violations in earlier remedial rulings. The court of appeals affirmed and assessed additional attorney's fees to cover the appeal.

ISSUE

Was a 30-day limitation on sentences to punitive isolation constitutional? Was the district court's award of attorney's fees to be paid out of department funds based on a finding that petitioners had acted in bad faith constitutional?

HOLDING

Yes to both questions. In a decision written by Justice Stevens, the Court affirmed the Court of Appeals' judgment, holding that punitive isolation for longer than thirty days in Arkansas prisons was a violation of the Eighth Amendment's ban on cruel and unusual punishment, applicable to the states by the Fourteenth Amendment. Further, the award of attorney's fees to be paid out of department funds was also constitutional.

RATIONALE

Justice Stevens noted that the district court conceded that isolation in and of itself was not necessarily unconstitutional and may in fact serve a legitimate interest in administering a prison. However, the totality of the conditions in Arkansas' prisons, including severe risk to inmates' health and safety that accompanied confinement in isolation, did constitute cruel and unusual punishment: "It is plain that the length of confinement cannot be ignored in deciding whether the confinement meets constitutional standards. A filthy, overcrowded cell and a diet of 'grue' might be tolerable for a few days and intolerably cruel for weeks or months." (Note: 'grue' was a mashed paste of potatoes, meat, eggs, oleo, and seasonings baked in four inch squares.) Justice Stevens noted that the district court had the authority to amend earlier remedial orders because the prison system had not complied with those orders. The Court suggested that the 30-day time limit would help to correct the existing conditions of overcrowding, friction, and violence: "Moreover, the limit presents little danger of interference with prison administration, for the Commissioner of Correction himself stated that prisoners should not ordinarily be held in punitive isolation for more than 14 days." The Supreme Court also decided that the award of attorney's fees to be paid out of Department of Correction funds was not an Eleventh Amendment violation and was supported by the district court's finding that petitioners had acted in bad faith. The petitioners also were ordered to pay an additional $2,500 to counsel for the prevailing parties. This order was based on provisions of the Civil Rights Attorney's Fees Awards Act of 1976, which provides that "[i]n any action" to enforce certain civil rights laws (including the law under which this action was brought), federal courts may award prevailing parties reasonable attorney's fees "as part of the costs." Reviewing precedent establishing attorney's fees as one kind of allowable costs, Justice Stevens stated that "[i]t is much too late to single out attorney's fees as the one kind of litigation cost whose recovery may not be authorized by Congress without an express statutory waiver of the States' immunity." The Attorney

General also maintained that attorney's fees should not be awarded because the state of Arkansas and the Department of Corrections were not named as defendants in this case. The Court disagreed. Although the Eleventh Amendment prevented respondents from suing the state by name, their injunctive suit against petitioner prison officials was, for all practical purposes, brought against the state. Absent any indication that petitioners acted in bad faith before the Court of Appeals, the Department of Correction is the entity that should bear the burden of the award.

CASE EXCERPT

"If petitioners had fully complied with the court's earlier orders, the present time limit might well have been unnecessary. But taking the long and unhappy history of the litigation into account, the court was justified in entering a comprehensive order to insure against the risk of inadequate compliance."

CASE SIGNIFICANCE

This case is important because it is one of the first cases in which an entire prison system, rather than a single prison, was declared unconstitutional by a district court. The Supreme Court upheld the power of the district court judge to order widespread reforms to the prison system.

HEWITT v. HELMS
459 U.S. 460 (1983)

FACTS

Inmate Aaron Helms was placed in administrative segregation pending investigation into his role in a prison riot at the Pennsylvania State Prison. Five days after being placed in administrative segregation, a committee reviewed the evidence against Helms, but no finding of guilt was made. After more than seven weeks in administrative segregation pending an investigation, Helms was found guilty of misconduct by a prison hearing committee and sentenced to six months of disciplinary confinement. The finding of guilt was based solely on an officer's report of the statements of an undisclosed informant. Helms filed a Section 1983 suit, alleging that confinement to administrative segregation violated his due process rights under the due process clause of the Fourteenth Amendment. The district court entered summary judgment against Helms, but the Court of Appeals for the Third Circuit reversed.

HEWITT v. HELMS *(cont.)*

The appellate court held that Helms had a protected liberty interest created by Pennsylvania regulations in continuing to reside in the general prison population and that Helms could not be deprived of this interest without a hearing governed by procedures mandated in *Wolff v. McDonnell*, 418 U.S. 539 (1974). The court remanded the case to the district court for an evidentiary hearing regarding the character of the misconduct hearing held by the prison hearing committee.

ISSUE

What limits are placed by the due process clause of the Fourteenth Amendment on the authority of prison administrators to confine inmates to administrative segregation?

HOLDING

In a decision written by Justice Rehnquist, the Court reversed the decision of the court of appeals and held that administrative segregation is not protected by the due process clause of the Fourteenth Amendment. However, in Helms's case, Pennsylvania regulations did create a protected liberty interest in remaining in the general inmate population. That interest is satisfied by an informal, nonadversarial evidentiary review. In such a review hearing, "an inmate must merely receive notice of the charges against him and an opportunity to present his views to the prison official charged with deciding whether to transfer him to administrative segregation."

RATIONALE

Justice Rehnquist noted that the Court has "repeatedly said both that prison officials have broad administrative and discretionary authority over the institutions they manage and that lawfully incarcerated persons retain only a narrow range of protected liberty interests." Prison officials in Pennsylvania use administrative segregation for various reasons, ranging from protecting inmates from each other, breaking up potentially troublesome groups of inmates, or holding inmates for later transfer or classification. However, State Bureau of Corrections regulations governing the use of administrative segregation and procedures to be followed used mandatory language, stating, for example, that certain procedures "shall," "will," or "must" be followed. Such language, the Court concluded, resulted in a state-created liberty interest, necessitating a judgment as to whether the procedures that were followed in Helms's

case satisfied the minimum requirements of the due process clause. The Court reasoned that because of the deference accorded to prison administrators in setting policies and procedures that maintain security, the officials in this case "were obligated to engage only in an informal, nonadversary review of the information supporting respondent's administrative confinement, including whatever statement respondent wished to submit, within a reasonable time after confining him to administrative segregation." In cases of alleged misconduct, a notice of the charges against the inmate must be given, and the inmate must have an opportunity to present his views to the decision maker who must determine if probable cause exists to believe the misconduct occurred. This opportunity may be in the form of a written statement, although the Court noted that oral presentations might be more effective in some cases. A formal hearing and any additional safeguards are not required.

CASE EXCERPT

"[A]dministrative segregation is the sort of confinement that inmates should reasonably anticipate receiving at some point in their incarceration."

CASE SIGNIFICANCE

In this case the Supreme Court determined which rights inmates are entitled to prior to be placed in administrative segregation. There are fewer rights accorded inmates being placed in administrative segregation than there are inmates being placed in punitive segregation. Here, the Court determined that inmates are only entitled to notice of the charges against them and an opportunity to present their case.

HUGHES v. ROWE

449 U.S. 5 (1980)

FACTS

Hughes, an Illinois state prisoner, was charged with violating prison regulations and placed in segregation. A hearing was held two days later, at which Hughes admitted drinking, along with others, a "homemade alcoholic beverage." He was given ten days segregation, demotion in his security grade, and loss of thirty days of good time. Hughes exhausted available administrative remedies and then filed a § 1983 lawsuit against prison officials with a number of complaints, including his initial placement in segregation for two days without a hearing. Prison officials filed no response, and the District Court dismissed the complaint without a hearing for Hughes's failure to state a constitutional claim. Hughes was ordered by that court to pay four hundred dollars in attorney's fees for counsel for the prison officials. The Court of Appeals affirmed the lower court's decision, and the Supreme Court granted certiorari.

ISSUE

Does placing an inmate in segregation without a hearing violate the due process clause? What standard governs ordering inmate plaintiffs to pay defendants' attorney's fees?

HOLDING

The Court held that placing an inmate in segregation without a hearing may violate the due process clause, unless it is an emergency situation. Further, inmate plaintiffs may be ordered to pay defendants' attorney's fees "only if the district court finds that the plaintiff's action was frivolous, unreasonable, or without foundation."

RATIONALE

In a per curiam opinion the Court stated that Hughes's initial segregation without a prior hearing was not due to any emergency conditions, nor was it required because of any security or safety concerns. The District Court improperly dismissed Hughes's complain without an evidentiary hearing, and the Court of Appeals should have reversed that dismissal and remanded the case for a hearing. The Court vacated the award of attorney's fees against Hughes, stating that "[i] n *Christiansburg Garment Co. v. EEOC*, 434 U. S. 412 (1978), we held that the defendant in an action brought under Title VII of the Civil Rights Act of 1964 may recover attorney's fees from the plaintiff only if the District Court finds 'that the plaintiff's action was frivolous, unreasonable, or without foundation, even though not brought in subjective bad faith.'" These standards apply even more to cases where inmate plaintiffs have filed, as in this case, a claim without the assistance of an attorney.

CASE EXCERPT

"Segregation of a prisoner without a prior hearing may violate due process if the postponement of procedural protections is not justified by apprehended emergency conditions."

CASE SIGNIFICANCE

This case stands for the proposition that it is unconstitutional to place an inmate in segregation without a hearing, unless an emergency situation exists. Additionally, this case stands for the proposition that it is proper to assess attorney fees against an inmate plaintiff only if the lawsuit is frivolous—a tough standard to meet.

SUPERINTENDENT, WALPOLE v. HILL

472 U.S. 445 (1985)

FACTS

Crawford and Hill, two Massachusetts state prison inmates, received disciplinary charges for an assault on another inmate. At separate hearings for the inmates, a prison guard testified and submitted a written report. He testified that he found an inmate in a walkway "bleeding from the mouth and suffering from a swollen eye. Dirt was strewn about the walkway," indicative of a fight, and the guard saw three prisoners, including Crawford and Hill, jogging away, with no other inmates present. Crawford and Hill maintained their innocence, and the injured inmate gave written statements that his injuries were not caused by them. The disciplinary board found them both guilty and recommended that they each be given fifteen days in isolation and that they each lose one hundred days of good time credits. After an unsuccessful appeal to the prison superintendent, Crawford and Hill filed a complaint with the Massachusetts Superior Court, alleging a violation of their constitutional rights at the board hearing because of lack of evidence for the board's finding of guilt. The Superior Court granted Crawford and Hill summary judgment, "holding that the board's findings of guilt rested on no evidence constitutionally adequate to support the findings." The Superior Court ordered the restoration of their lost good time credits, and the Massachusetts Supreme Judicial Court affirmed this ruling.

ISSUE

Does a finding by a prison disciplinary board that results in the revocation of an inmate's good time credits violate the due process clause of the Fourteenth Amendment if the decision of the prison disciplinary board is not supported by evidence in the record?

SUPERINTENDENT, WALPOLE v. HILL *(cont.)*

HOLDING

Yes. "Assuming that good time credits constitute a protected liberty interest, the revocation of such credits must be supported by some evidence in order to satisfy the minimum requirements of procedural due process."

RATIONALE

The Court reasoned that the requirement of "some evidence" would "help to prevent arbitrary deprivation without threatening institutional interests or imposing undue administrative burdens." In this case, the state attorney general asked the Supreme Court to first of all, decide whether inmates possessed due process rights to judicial review of disciplinary hearings. If so, then the question becomes what standard of review applies under the due process clause. The Massachusetts Attorney General maintained that the Massachusetts Supreme Judicial Court applied "too strict" a standard. Writing for the Court, Justice O'Connor stated that in the case at hand, "the evidence before the disciplinary board was sufficient to meet the requirements imposed by the due process clause.... The Supreme Judicial Court found that this evidence was constitutionally insufficient because it did not support an inference that more than one person had struck the victim or that either of the respondents was the assailant or otherwise participated in the assault. This conclusion, however, misperceives the nature of the evidence required by the due process clause." While there was no direct evidence implicating Crawford and Hill, and the evidence might be described as "meager," "the record is not so devoid of evidence that the board's findings were without support or otherwise arbitrary."

CASE EXCERPT

"The requirements of due process are satisfied if some evidence supports the decision by the prison disciplinary board to revoke good time credits...We decline to adopt a more stringent evidentiary standard as a constitutional requirement. Prison disciplinary proceedings take place in a highly charged atmosphere, and prison administrators must often act swiftly on the basis of evidence that might be insufficient in less exigent circumstances. The fundamental fairness guaranteed by the Due Process Clause does not require courts to set aside decisions of prison administrators that have some basis in fact."

CASE SIGNIFICANCE

In this case the Supreme Court attempted to balance the liberty interests of inmates against the interests of prison officials. The Court determined that a "modicum" of evidence is required in a prison disciplinary hearing. This simply means there must be some small amount of evidence to support the charge. This is a very easy standard for prison officials to meet.

PONTE v. REAL
471 U.S. 491 (1985)

FACTS

Real, a Massachusetts state prison inmate, was one of several inmates observing a fight between a guard and another inmate. They were ordered to leave the area by the supervising officer. Real reported that as he attempted to leave, another officer stopped him for questioning and a shakedown. The supervising officer saw Real still in the area and despite Real's attempts to explain why he had not left, the supervisor ordered that he be locked up. At Real's disciplinary hearing, the supervising officer offered his version of the situation, and Real offered his version. The disciplinary board denied, without giving a reason, Real's request to call three witnesses he had requested, two other inmates in the area at the time of the dispute and a correctional officer. Real was found guilty by the disciplinary board and lost 150 days of good-time credits. Real then filed a habeas corpus writ in the Massachusetts trial court which ruled that he had been denied due process under the Fourteenth Amendment by being denied the right to call witnesses with no reasons given. This decision was affirmed by the Massachusetts Supreme Judicial Court, holding that "a prison disciplinary hearing which forfeited 'good time' credits of respondent John Real was conducted in violation of the due process clause of the Fourteenth Amendment to the United States Constitution because there did not appear in the administrative record of that hearing a statement of reasons as to why the disciplinary board refused to allow respondent to call witnesses whom he had requested." The Supreme Court granted certiorari.

ISSUE

Does the due process clause of the Fourteenth Amendment require that prison officials' reasons for denying an inmate's witness request appear in the administrative record of the disciplinary hearing?

HOLDING

No. The due process clause of the Fourteenth Amendment does not require that prison officials' reasons for denying an inmate's witness request appear in the administrative record of the disciplinary hearing.

RATIONALE

Writing for the Court, Justice Rehnquist noted that they granted certiorari in this case because the decision by the Supreme Judicial Court of Massachusetts went further than the Court's earlier decision ten years earlier in *Wolff*. The Court vacated the decision and remanded the case back to the Massachusetts Supreme Judicial Court. The Majority opinion did allow that at some point prison officials must state their reasons for not allowing inmates to call witnesses at disciplinary proceedings and that failure to do so violates the due process clause of the Fourteenth Amendment. However, those reasons do not have to be in writing or in any part of the official records of the disciplinary proceedings. The minimum due process requirements mandated by *Wolff* include the "right of an inmate to call and present witnesses and documentary evidence in his defense before the disciplinary board." Both Wolff and Baxter maintained that the right to call witnesses is obviously restricted by the dangers of prison life and penological needs to provide immediate discipline in some cases. Thus, officials could refuse to allow inmates to present witnesses, as well as evidence, at a disciplinary proceeding if allowing such would be overly harmful to the safety of the institution or would in some way interfere with legitimate penological interests.

CASE EXCERPT

"Eleven years of experience since our decision in *Wolff* does not indicate to us any need to now 'prescribe' as constitutional doctrine that the disciplinary board must state in writing at the time of the hearing its reasons for refusing to call a witness. Nor can we conclude that the due process clause of the Fourteenth Amendment may only be satisfied if the administrative record contains support or reasons for the board's refusal. We therefore disagree with the reasoning of the Supreme Judicial Court of Massachusetts in this case."

CASE SIGNIFICANCE

In this case the Supreme Court once again refused to extend the due process rights established in *Wolff v. McDonnell*. This case is symptomatic of the Court's refusal (during this time period) to go beyond the original holding in *Wolff*.

MEACHUM v. FANO

427 U.S. 215 (1976)

FACTS

In 1974, six inmates who were suspected of setting nine serious fires at the Massachusetts Correctional Institutional were placed in administrative segregation. Classification hearings were held before the prison board to determine whether the prisoners should be transferred to another prison such as a maximum security institution where living conditions would be substantially less favorable. Each of the six inmates was notified of the hearings and was informed that officials had information indicating criminal conduct. At the individual hearings, each inmate was represented by counsel. Out of the inmates' presence, Meachum, the prison superintendent, repeated the information given by informants regarding the setting of the fires. Inmates were told of the evidence and allegations against them but were not provided copies of Meachum's testimony. Inmates presented their own testimony and were allowed to present witnesses and written statements from others in their defense. The board recommended one inmate be placed in administrative segregation for 30 days and recommended transfer for the other five. Three inmates were recommended for transfer to Walpole, a maximum security prison with substantially less favorable living conditions. Upon review of the board's recommendation, the acting deputy commissioner for classification and treatment and the commissioner of corrections ordered five of the six inmates to be transferred to Walpole. All but two transfers were carried out. Inmates filed a Section 1983 suit against prison officials, alleging liberty deprivations and deprivation of due process because transfers to a less favorable prison had been ordered without an adequate factfinding hearing. The district court agreed that the classification hearings were constitutionally inadequate and ordered the inmates to be returned to the general prison population at Norfolk until proper notice and hearing. Corrections officials were ordered to circulate regulations governing future transfer hearings involving informant testimony. The court of appeals affirmed, holding that transfers to maximum security institutions involved "a significant modification of the overall conditions of confinement" and that

MEACHUM v. FANO *(cont.)*

this change in circumstances was "serious enough to trigger the application of due process protections."

ISSUE

Does the due process clause of the Fourteenth Amendment entitle a state prisoner to a hearing when he is transferred to a prison the conditions of which are substantially less favorable to the prisoner, absent a state law or practice conditioning such transfers on proof of serious misconduct or the occurrence of other events?

HOLDING

The due process clause of the Fourteenth Amendment does not entitle a state prisoner to a factfinding hearing when he is transferred to a prison the conditions of which are substantially less favorable to him, absent a state law or practice conditioning such transfers on proof of serious misconduct or the occurrence of other specified events.

RATIONALE

Prison officials in Massachusetts are accorded discretion to transfer prisoners for a number of reasons, including but not limited to serious misconduct: "Holding that arrangements like this are within reach of the procedural protections of the Due Process Clause would place the Clause astride the day-to-day functioning of state prisons and involve the judiciary in issues and discretionary decisions that are not the business of federal judges. We decline to so interpret and apply the Due Process Clause." The states are free to follow another course, by statute, rule, or by interpretation of their own constitutions. They may decide that prudent prison administration requires pretransfer hearings. The Court ruled, however, that the due process clause does not impose a nation-wide rule mandating transfer hearings. In his dissent, Justice Stevens agreed with the appellate court that the transfers in this case were enough of a grievous loss of liberty to invoke constitutional protections.

CASE EXCERPT

"[G]iven a valid conviction, the criminal defendant has been constitutionally deprived of his liberty to the extent that the State may confine him and subject him to the rules of its prison system so long as the conditions of confinement do not otherwise violate the Constitution. The Constitution does not require that the State have more than one prison for convicted felons; nor does it guarantee that the convicted prisoner will be placed in any particular prison if, as is likely, the State has more than one correctional institution. The initial decision to assign the convict to a particular institution is not subject to audit under the Due Process Clause, although the degree of confinement in one prison may be quite different from that in another."

CASE SIGNIFICANCE

This case is significant because in it the Supreme Court refused to extend due process protections to inmates being transferred from one prison to another in the same state. The decision to transfer an inmate is within the discretionary authority of the state prison officials. This means inmates can be transferred at will from one prison to another by prison authorities.

MONTANYE v. HAYMES

427 U.S. 236 (1976)

FACTS

On June 7, 1972, Haymes was removed from his assignment as inmate clerk in the law library at the Attica Correctional Facility. Following his removal, Haymes circulated among other inmates a document that he prepared and at the time signed by 82 other prisoners. Among other things, each signatory complained that he had been deprived of legal assistance as the result of the removal of Haymes and another inmate from the prison law library. The document, which was addressed to a federal judge, was seized and held by prison authorities. On June 8, Haymes was advised that he would be transferred to Clinton Correctional Facility, which was a maximum security institution like Attica. He was transferred the following day with no loss of good time, segregated confinement, loss of privileges, or any other disciplinary measures. On August 3, Haymes filed a petition complaining that the seizure of the document not only violated a prison regulation making any communication to a court privileged and confidential, but also infringed his federally guaranteed right to petition the court for redress of grievances. The petition also asserted that Haymes's transfer to another institution was to prevent him from pursuing his remedies and also was in reprisal for his having rendered legal assistance to various prisoners as well as having, along with others, seeking to petition the court for redress. The district court dismissed the case, holding that the rule against giving legal assistance without consent was reasonable, and that the seizure of Haymes's document was not a constitutional violation. The court also ruled that the transfer did not violate Haymes's rights. The Court of Appeals for the Second Circuit reversed and ruled that there were two unresolved issues of material fact: whether Haymes's removal to Clinton was punishment for a disobedience of prison rules and, if so, whether the effects of the transfer were sufficiently burdensome to require a hearing under the due process clause of the Fourteenth Amendment.

ISSUE

Does the due process clause of the Fourteenth Amendment require hearings in connection with transfers, whether or not they are the result of the inmate's misbehavior or may be labeled as disciplinary or punitive?

HOLDING

The due process clause of the Fourteenth Amendment does not require a hearing in order to transfer a state prisoner to another institution in the state whether or not such transfer resulted from the prisoner's misbehavior or was disciplinary or punitive, if, under state law, the prisoner did not have the right to remain at any particular prison and no justifiable expectation that he would not be transferred unless found guilty of misconduct, and the transfer of prisoners is not conditional upon or limited to the misconduct.

RATIONALE

This case was decided the same day as *Meachum v. Fano*, and Justice White noted that the Court's decision in *Meachum* required a reversal in this case. Unlike the appellate court in *Meachum*, however, the lower court in this case did not hold that "every disadvantageous transfer must be accompanied by appropriate hearings." The Second Circuit would exempt administrative transfers from due process protections and would hold that only "disciplinary transfers having substantial adverse impact on the prisoner were to call for procedural formalities." The Supreme Court disagreed, stating that the due process clause does not require hearings before transferring a prisoner to another facility.

CASE EXCERPT

"As long as the conditions or degree of confinement to which the prisoner is subjected is within the sentence imposed upon him and is not otherwise violative of the Constitution, the Due Process Clause does not, in itself, subject an inmate's treatment by prison authorities to judicial oversight. The Clause does not require hearings in connection with transfers, whether or not they are the result of the inmate's misbehavior or may be labeled as disciplinary or punitive."

CASE SIGNIFICANCE

This case was heard and decided at the same time as *Meachum v. Fano*. The Court again held that inmates may be transferred to a different prison without any due process protections. Here the transfer was punitive in nature; in *Meachum* the transfer was to a prison with less favorable conditions. Taken together, these two cases make clear that prison officials may transfer inmates within a state prison system at will.

VITEK v. JONES
445 U.S. 480 (1980)

FACTS

Jones was transferred from a state prison to a mental hospital pursuant to a Nebraska statute that provided if a designated physician or psychologist finds a prisoner has a mental disease or defect which cannot be properly treated in prison, the Director of Correctional Services may transfer the prisoner to a mental hospital. In an action against the state brought by Jones and other inmates challenging on due process grounds the procedures by which Nebraska statutes permit transfers from the prison complex to a mental hospital, the district court held that Jones's transfer was unconstitutional, ruling that transferring Jones to a mental hospital without adequate notice and opportunity for a hearing deprived him of liberty without due process of law contrary to the Fourteenth Amendment. The court ruled further that such transfers must be accompanied by adequate notice, an adversary hearing before an independent decision-maker, a written statement by the factfinder of the evidence relied on and the reasons for the decision, and the availability of appointed counsel for indigent prisoners. The court permanently enjoined the state from transferring to the mental hospital without following the prescribed procedures.

VITEK v. JONES *(cont.)*

ISSUE

Does the involuntary transfer of a Nebraska state prisoner to a mental hospital implicate a liberty interest that is protected by the due process clause of the Fourteenth Amendment, entitling the inmate to certain procedural protections, including notice, an adversary hearing, and provision of counsel, before he is transferred involuntarily to a state mental hospital for treatment of a mental disease or defect?

HOLDING

In a decision written by Justice White, the Court affirmed with modification the judgment of the district court. The Court held that the involuntary transfer of a prisoner to a mental hospital involves a liberty interest that is protected by the due process clause of the Fourteenth Amendment. Such a transfer must include appropriate procedural protections, including notice and an adversary hearing.

RATIONALE

The Court determined involuntary commitment to a mental hospital is not what prisoners can expect when they are sentenced to prison and involves consequences beyond the range of what can be expected with incarceration. The Court ruled that appropriate procedural protections include notice and an adversary hearing. The Court did not decide that counsel must be provided to indigent prisoners whom the state seeks to treat as mentally ill. Four Justices, however, concluded that counsel was appropriate because are likely to be unable to understand or exercise their rights.

CASE EXCERPT

"Involuntary commitment to a mental hospital is not within the range of conditions of confinement to which a prison sentence subjects an individual. While a conviction and sentence extinguish an individual's right to freedom from confinement for the term of his sentence, they do not authorize the State to classify him as mentally ill and to subject him to involuntary psychiatric treatment without affording him additional due process protections. Here, the stigmatizing consequences of a transfer to a mental hospital for involuntary psychiatric treatment, coupled with the subjection of the prisoner to mandatory behavior modification as a treatment for mental illness, constitute the kind of deprivations of liberty that requires procedural protections."

CASE SIGNIFICANCE

This case provides inmates being transferred from a prison to a mental hospital certain due process rights. This does not mean the transfer will not take place, but it does mean the state must provide a bare minimum in the way of protection of due process rights. Unlike transfers to other prison facilities, even those that are more restrictive or have harsher living conditions, transfers to prison mental health facilities are protected by the Fourteenth Amendment due process clause. Inmates have to the right to a hearing, notice of the hearing, and an impartial decision maker.

SANDIN v. CONNER
515 U.S. 472 (1995)

FACTS

While being escorted to a program area, Conner was subjected to a strip search, during which he made "angry and foul" comments to the officer. Eleven days later he was served with a disciplinary report and charged with "high misconduct" for using physical interference to impair a correctional function and a "low moderate misconduct" for using abusive or obscene language and for harassing employees. When he appeared before the disciplinary committee, Conner requested witnesses. His request was denied because the witnesses were deemed unavailable. He was found guilty of the charges and given 30 days to serve in punitive segregation. Conner filed a lawsuit alleging that the failure to allow his witnesses violated his due process rights. The Court of Appeals concluded that Conner had a liberty interest in remaining out of punitive segregation, and there was a disputed question about whether he received the due process rights he was entitled to according to *Wolff v. McDonnell.* The appellate court ruled that the department of correction's prison regulations instructed disciplinary committees to find guilt only when a charge is supported by substantial evidence. In other words, a committee cannot impose punitive segregation without first finding substantial evidence that a disciplinary rule had been violated. This regulation, decided the Court of Appeals, created a liberty interest for the prisoner, and, therefore, Conner was entitled to call witnesses.

ISSUE

Are prisoners entitled to due process rights based on liberty interests created by prison regulations or state statutes that impose mandatory directives on prison officials?

HOLDING

Under certain circumstances, states may create liberty interests for prisoners that are protected by the due process clause; however, these interests are generally limited to freedom from restraint which impose atypical and significant hardship on the prisoner in relation to the ordinary incidents of prison life.

RATIONALE

In *Wolff v. McDonnell* the Court held that the Constitution itself does not create a liberty interest in good-time credits, but that the state's statutory provisions did create such an interest. Because a liberty interest was created by state law, a prisoner was entitled to certain due process protections before his good time could be forfeited as a disciplinary punishment. In *Hewitt v. Helms*, the Court rejected the claim that the inmates' right to remain out of administrative segregation entitled them to due process protections under the Constitution. The Court, however, following the *Wolff* rationale, found that the state's prison regulations used mandatory language that prohibited officials from placing inmates in administrative language without first making certain findings. These mandatory directives created a protected liberty interest for prisoners and entitled them to limited due process protections. *Hewitt* produced undesirable results. It provided a disincentive for states to codify their prison regulations and procedures for fear that they have created liberty interests that, if not strictly followed, result in prisoners successfully challenging official actions. Second, *Hewitt* led the federal courts to become involved in the day-to-day operations of prisons. Courts have been called upon in hundreds of cases to determine whether prison regulations and procedures have created liberty interests. Under certain circumstances, states may create liberty interests that must be protected with procedures that meet due process requirements. Generally, however, these interests will be limited to freedom from the kind of restraint that is atypical of prisoners should expect from being incarcerated and which impose significant hardships compared to the ordinary circumstances prisoners experience as a result of imprisonment. In this case, Conner's confinement in punitive segregation did not present the type of atypical, significant deprivation in which a state might have created a liberty interest. At the time of his confinement, conditions in punitive segregation were similar to conditions in administrative segregation and protective custody. Neither the due process clause of the Constitution nor state prison regulations created a protected liberty interest for Conner that would entitle him to the type of procedure set forth in *Wolff*. Assignment to punitive segregation for 30 days based on misconduct was within the range of confinement to be expected for someone serving a 30-year-to-life prison sentence.

CASE EXCERPT

"[T]he search for a negative implication from mandatory language in prisoner regulations has strayed from the real concerns under girding the liberty protected by the Due Process Clause. The time has come to return to the due process principles we believe were correctly established and applied in *Wolff* and *Meachum*."

CASE SIGNIFICANCE

This is a significant case in the area of due process rights for prisoners. In *Hewitt v. Helms*, the Supreme Court expanded the ability of inmates to argue that they had a state-created liberty interest that needed due process protection. *Hewitt* was more important than the facts of the particular case, which involved the placement of a prisoner in administrative segregation. *Hewitt* was more important because it recognized that states create liberty interests when they use mandatory language in their prison regulations or in statutes. A statute or regulation that requires officials "shall" or "will" take a particular action triggers the due process clause. Failure to follow the mandatory language is a failure to meet an obligation and negates the legality of the official action. The Supreme Court believed that the *Hewitt* decision encouraged prison officials to write less careful regulations without words such as "must," "shall," or "will." Secondly, *Hewitt*, determined the Court, encouraged inmates to scour prison regulations, looking for mandatory language to use as the basis for lawsuits arguing that officials failed to follow the regulations as written. At times, the lawsuits challenged such actions as officials serving a substitute sack lunch during institutional lockdowns. In *Sandin*, the Court ruled that state-created liberty interests are limited, and that mandatory language in a regulation or statute is not the test for determining whether a liberty interest exists. The test is whether the restraint imposed by the regulation is somehow atypical of what prisoners can expect as a result of incarceration

SANDIN v. CONNER *(cont.)*

and is a significant hardship relative to the ordinary hardships experienced while imprisoned. Under the facts presented in *Sandin*, the Court concluded there was nothing atypical about being assigned to punitive segregation for 30 days, nor was it a significant hardship relative to the other hardships in prison. The significance of this case will more apparent as the lower courts interpret the opinion in the context of lawsuits where inmates allege they have a state-created liberty interest and were denied due process.

WILKINSON v. AUSTIN

545 U.S. 209 (2005)

FACTS

In 1998, Ohio opened a Supermax prison, the Ohio State Penitentiary (OSP), designed for Level 5 prisoners, the most dangerous and violent prisoners in the state. Conditions include extreme isolation, confinement for twenty-three hours per day, lights on in cells at all times, limited communication, and rare opportunities for outside visitation. Placement at OSP is indefinite. When OSP first opened, there was no policy to govern placement, with the result that some inmates who were not high-security risks were sent there. A policy, referred to as the "Old Policy" was eventually formulated but assignment problems persisted. The "New Policy" was created in 2002 and gave more guidance regarding factors to consider when assigning inmates to OSP and providing inmates with more procedural protections against improper assignment. According to the new policy, inmates can be placed at OSP upon entry into the Ohio prison system if they were convicted of certain crimes, such as organized crimes. Alternatively, an inmate may be transferred to OSP if he poses high security risks, such as leading a prison gang. The process involves a three-tier classification review. Inmates are reviewed for placement, beginning with a three-page document detailing the inmate's history of violence, escape attempts, gang activity, underlying offense, and any other pertinent factors. A classification committee reviews the form, and holds a hearing, notifying the inmate in writing at least 48 hours before the hearing. The inmate is provided with written notice as to the conduct or offense triggering the review for placement, as well as the three-page document. The inmate has the right to be present at the hearing but

may not call witnesses. If the Committee recommends placement at OSP, the decision and reasons are documented, along with a summary of information presented at the hearing. This documentation is sent to the warden of the inmate's current prison, or in the case of a newly admitted prisoner, to some other designated official. The warden or other designated official has to agree with the proposed placement at OSP, and if agreement is given, the form is then forwarded to the Ohio Bureau of Classification for a final decision. The inmate is also provided with a copy of the recommendations and reasons and given 15 days to file any objections with the bureau. After 15 days, the bureau reviews the form and makes a final decision. At this point, if the inmate is placed in the OSP, he is reviewed again within 30 days after placement. If the reviewer, an OSP staff member, determines that the inmate is inappropriately placed, then the warden is so informed. If the OSP warden agrees, a recommendation for transfer to a lower security prison is sent to the bureau. If the reviewer determines that the inmate's placement is appropriate, then the inmate remains at OSP and is reviewed at least annually, following the same three-tier review process.

Austin, along with a class of current and former OSP inmates, sued prison officials, alleging that the old policy violated due process. Before the trial was held, Ohio created the new policy with the three-tier classification procedure, and the lower courts evaluated the new policy for constitutional adequacy. The District Court found that inmates possessed a liberty interest in avoiding assignment to OSP and that they had been denied due process rights because many inmates had not been given notice and adequate opportunities to be heard before transfer to OSP. Inmates were not given sufficient notice of the reasons for their retention at OSP, nor sufficient opportunity to understand those reasons and evidence. While the new policy provided more procedural protections, those protections did not meet procedural due process requirements, given the severity of conditions in the Supermax prison. Thus, the District Court ordered several modifications, including substantive modifications narrowing the grounds for recommending OSP placement, as well as providing inmates with an exhaustive list of grounds justifying such placement, and the opportunity to present evidence and call witnesses at the Classification Committee hearing, provided that so doing would not be unduly hazardous or burdensome. In addition, Ohio would be required to notify inmates twice a year in writing and orally of their progress toward a reduction in their security levels, as well as notifying inmates specifically what conduct was necessary for such reductions. Ohio appealed, maintaining that inmates lacked a liberty interest in avoiding OSP placement and even if there was a liberty interest, the new policy was constitutionally adequate as it stood. The Court of Appeals, however, agreed with the District Court's decision that inmates possessed a liberty interest in avoiding OSP placement and also upheld the procedural modifications. The Court of Appeals ruled that the substantive modifications exceeded the lower court's authority and set those aside. The Supreme Court granted certiorari to decide what process is due an inmate when considered for OSP placement.

ISSUE

Do inmates have a protected liberty interest in avoiding assignment to OSP? If so, does the process by which Ohio assign prisoners to its supermaximum security institution afford them adequate due process under the Fourteenth Amendment?

HOLDING

Yes to both questions. Inmates have a protected liberty interest in avoiding assignment at OSP. The procedures set forth in Ohio's new policy are sufficient to satisfy the Fourteenth Amendment's due process requirements.

RATIONALE

The Court concluded that the due process clause itself does not require procedural protection to inmates facing assignment to the OSP. Based on the precedent it had established in *Sandin v. Conner*, 515 U.S. 472 (1995), however, assignment to the OSP amounts to an atypical and significant hardship in relation to the ordinary experiences that make up life in prison, which creates a liberty interest that needs due process protections. After detailing the restrictions placed on OSP inmates, the Court ruled that the procedures Ohio had implemented met constitutional requirements and did not require the modifications ordered by the District Court. The Court noted that due process must be flexible and reflect the circumstances where security is the dominant consideration. OSP inmates have notice, the opportunity to respond, and the right to be present at the classification hearing. There are multiple levels of review. Concerning the right to call witnesses, the Court noted, "[w]ere Ohio

to allow an inmate to call witnesses or provide other attributes of an adversary hearing before ordering transfer to OSP, both the State's immediate objective of controlling the prisoner and its greater objective of controlling the prison could be defeated." The Court stressed the importance of deferring to the expertise of prison administrators.

CASE EXCERPT

"OSP's harsh conditions may well be necessary and appropriate in light of the danger that high-risk inmates pose both to prison officials and to other prisoners. That necessity, however, does not diminish our conclusion that the conditions give rise to a liberty interest in their avoidance."

CASE SIGNIFICANCE

This case helped clarify the *Sandin v. Conner* (1995) decision and what amounts to an atypical and significant hardship in prison, creating a liberty interest that must be protected by due process. It is now clear that placement in a Supermax facility or cell block similar to the OSP triggers due process. The decision also makes clear that as atypical and significant as that hardship is, the due process that must be afforded to an inmate is flexible and must be balanced with the security and control issues faced by prison officials. Inmates do not have the right to call witnesses. They do not have the right to the type of extensive documentation the District Court required. The past two decades have seen an increase in Supermax prisons, with about 30 states operating such facilities, as well as two federal Supermax prisons. These prisons have arisen in part due to the increase in prison violence and gangs. The harsh conditions of such facilities give rise to protected liberty interests on the part of inmates and cause prison administrators to engage in a balancing act: protecting those liberty interests, preserving prison security and safety, and coping with restricted budgets.

DISCUSSION QUESTIONS

1. Identify the Supreme Court cases that have addressed disciplining prisoners. How has the Court's perspective on prison discipline changed over time?
2. How does the Court analyze the difference between transferring a prisoner to another facility

versus transferring a prisoner to a mental institution? Explain why the difference results affects due process rights.

3. How does *Baxter v. Palmigiano* distinguish between the due process rights that should be afforded to prisoners involved in disciplinary proceedings and free world criminal defendants?

4. What is a state-created liberty interest, which Supreme Court case defined that concept in 1983, and which more recent case redefined the concept?

5. Check the website for your state's correctional system and locate the rules or handbook that explains the inmate disciplinary system. Identify the specific rules that track the Court's decision in *Wolff v. McDonnell* (1974).

6. Explain the rationale that the State of California offered in defense of its policy to segregate inmates by race as they were admitted into the reception areas of institutions. How does the Supreme Court address the state's rationale?

7. Conditions in administrative segregation units and supermaximum security cellblocks are harsh. From an inmate's perspective, explain why officials should carefully follow the rules and regulations that govern an inmate's assignment to that status.

8. Prisoners assigned to Supermax facilities are generally considered the "worst of the worst." From an administrator's perspective, explain why due process protections must be flexible and limited when it comes to assigning inmates to this status.

9. Check the website for your state's correctional system and identify the rules that govern how and when inmates are classified and reclassified into different security levels. Identify the various security levels.

10. Discuss the importance of properly disciplining and classifying prisoners. How do the disciplinary and classification systems contribute to the goals of rehabilitation, the safety and security of an institution, and the general living environment inside an institution?

CHAPTER NINE

LIABILITY AND DAMAGES

PARRATT v. TAYLOR, *451 U.S. 527 (1981)*

HARLOW v. FITZGERALD, *457 U.S. 800 (1982)*

SMITH v. WADE, *461 U.S. 30 (1983)*

CLEAVINGER v. SAXNER, *474 U.S. 193 (1985)*

DANIELS v. WILLIAMS, *474 U.S. 327 (1986)*

RICHARDSON v. MCKNIGHT, *521 U.S. 399 (1997)*

ALI v. FEDERAL BUREAU OF PRISONS, *552 U.S. 214 (2008)*

MINNECI v. POLLARD, *132 S.CT. 617 (2012)*

INTRODUCTION

Most prisoner lawsuits are filed under the federal Civil Rights Act, 42 U.S.C. §1983, which was passed by Congress in 1871. These lawsuits are often referred to as Section 1983 cases and are tried in federal district courts. Section 1983 states: "Every person who, under color of any statute, ordinance, regulation, custom, or usage, of any State or Territory or the District of Columbia, subjects, or causes to be subjected, any citizen of the United States or other person within the jurisdiction thereof to the deprivation of any rights, privileges, or immunities secured by the Constitution and laws, shall be liable to the party injured in an action at law, suit in equity, or other proper proceeding for redress."

A prisoner who files a §1983 lawsuit must allege that his or her rights under federal law or the US Constitution were violated by persons who were "acting under color of law." Section 1983 has generated many lawsuits and is, obviously, not limited to prisoners. For many years inmates were not even permitted to allege violations of their rights under §1983. In 1964, however, the US Supreme Court decided in *Cooper v. Pate*, 378 U.S. 546, that prisoners can file lawsuits against correctional officials using the statute. With that decision came a flood of prisoner lawsuits based on §1983.

Prisoners file §1983 lawsuits to complain about specific prison practices, regulations, or about the conditions under which they live. These are civil lawsuits, not criminal. Inmates who believe their rights have been violated file the lawsuits; the state is not prosecuting a crime. Sometimes prisoners seek money damages from prison officials. Money damages can be compensatory, meaning they compensate an inmate for his loss, or they can be punitive, which are awarded by the court to punish officials for violating a prisoner's rights. Instead of or in addition to damages, prisoners often seek injunctive relief that requires officials to take a particular action to remedy a situation.

This chapter looks at the most significant Supreme Court cases that address the liability of correctional officials in a §1983 lawsuit. Just because a prisoner alleges and the evidence establishes that a federal right was violated does not mean that prison officials are civilly liable for the violation. The doctrine of immunity can protect a defendant from suit. A limited number of government officials have absolute immunity from civil lawsuits. Their conduct is irrelevant; they cannot be sued. Absolute immunity is designed to free officials to make difficult and controversial decisions without constant fear of being sued. Judges have absolute immunity from civil lawsuits in performing their duties as judges. Absolute immunity is not available to correctional officials. *Cleavinger v. Saxner* (1985) made clear that members of prison disciplinary committees are not entitled to absolute immunity, even though they are acting in a quasi-judicial capacity.

Qualified immunity, on the other hand, is available to many government officials, including correctional officers and administrators. As *Harlow v. Fitzgerald* (1982) held, when performing discretionary functions (and most law enforcement and correctional officials perform functions that require them to exercise discretion), government officials are not civilly liable for their actions if they did not ignore or disregard a clearly established right under a statute or the Constitution of which a reasonable person in their position would have known. For a prisoner to establish liability requires a showing that an official purposely ignored a right about which he or she should have been aware. There is no liability if the right the prisoner seeks to protect is not already clearly established. A qualified immunity defense is far from absolute, but it does offer protection from suit for officials in some situations.

In a deeply divided decision in *Richardson v. McKnight* (1997), the Supreme Court ruled that prison officials employed by private prison firms are not entitled to qualified immunity even though they are responsible for prisoners incarcerated by the state and the private firms are subject to a host of state and federal statutes, regulations, and state and federal Constitutions. The Court concluded that §1983 was not intended to protect private correctional employees, therefore, they do not enjoy the benefits of qualified immunity. This decision may have significant ramifications for the future of private prisons.

Another important question decided by the Supreme Court addressed the §1983 liability of prison officials whose negligence caused harm to a prisoner. The Court decided in *Parratt v. Taylor* (1981) and *Daniels v. Williams* (1986) that not all official actions resulting in loss are actionable in a lawsuit under the Civil Rights Act. Mere negligence does not violate the Constitution, even if it causes injury. In the other extreme, however, prison officials can be held liable for punitive damages under §1983 if their conduct involved a callous or reckless indifference to a prisoner's rights or to the safety of others.

Liability issues involve some of the most complicated legal issues, including who can be considered a "person" under the Civil Rights Act. In *Monell v. Department of Social Services*, 436 U.S. 658 (1978), the Court ruled that municipalities, counties, and other units of local government are persons and can

be sued under §1983. In *Will v. Michigan Department of State Police*, 491 U.S. 58 (1989), however, the Court decided that a state or a state agency is not a person under §1983. Neither can state officials be sued under the statute in their capacity as representatives of the state; they must be sued in their personal capacities. The state's attorneys generally defend correctional officials who are sued in their personal capacities and will assume responsibility for damages that are awarded. If an official acted intentionally or maliciously, or committed an offense against a prisoner, state law usually permits a state to elect not to defend the employee or indemnify them for money damages.

Another important issue raised by §1983 is the requirement that conduct be under color of state law. Employees of state and local government entities act under color of state law while they are on the job, even if their actions were prohibited by their employer's rules or regulations. In *Preiser v. Rodriguez*, 411 U.S. 475 (1973), the Court found that a private physician under contract with North Carolina to provide medical services at a state prison was also acting under color of law when he was treating an inmate and, therefore, could be sued under the Civil Rights Act. It was the doctor's function within the state agency, not the terms of his employment that determined his status.

In addition to §1983, prisoners can file civil lawsuits under tort law where they are incarcerated. A tort is a personal or property damage claim and is governed by state law. Prisoners are not limited to alleging violations of their federal rights in state tort lawsuits. They can also allege violations under state law and the state Constitution. Mere negligence may not be sufficient for a §1983 lawsuit, but it is actionable under tort law. Traditionally prisoners have preferred §1983 claims. The lawsuits are filed in federal court, which has earned the reputation of being more open-minded to civil rights claims. In addition, under 42 U.S.C. §1988, a successful prisoner plaintiff is entitled to have has his or her attorneys' fees paid by the defendant. Interestingly, in recent years prisoners in some states are finding it more beneficial to file their lawsuits in state court alleging tort claims and violations of the state Constitution. As federal judges render more conservative decisions in prisoners' rights cases, there has been a shift to the state courts in jurisdictions where the law and the bench seem more amenable than the traditional route through the federal court system.

PARRATT v. TAYLOR
451 U.S. 527 (1981)

FACTS
Taylor, an inmate in a Nebraska prison, ordered some hobby materials by mail. After being delivered to the prison, the packages containing the materials were lost when the normal procedure for receipt of mail packages was not followed. Taylor brought an action against prison officials in Federal District Court under 42 U.S.C. Section 1983 to recover the value of the hobby materials, claiming that the prison officials had negligently lost the materials and thereby deprived Taylor of property without due process of law in violation of the Fourteenth Amendment. The District Court entered summary judgment for Taylor, holding that negligent actions by state officials can be a basis for an action under Section 1983, that the prison officials were not immune from liability, and that the deprivation of the hobby materials implicated due process rights. The Court of Appeals affirmed.

ISSUE
Did the loss of these hobby materials constitute a violation of the due process clause of the Fourteenth Amendment, and thereby give respondent sufficient grounds for relief under 42 U.S.C. Section 1983?

HOLDING
No. A plaintiff must establish the conduct was engaged by a person "acting under color of law" and that the conduct deprived the inmate of a Constituional right. There was no evidence the loss of hobby materials violated due process.

RATIONALE
In any Section 1983 action the inquiry must focus on whether the essential elements to a Section 1983 action are present: (1) whether the conduct was committed by a person acting under color of state law; and (2) whether the conduct deprived a person of rights, privileges, or immunities secured by the Constitution or laws of the United States. Although Taylor was deprived of his property under color of state law, he did not sufficiently allege a violation of the due process clause. The deprivation was not the result of an established procedure, but as the result of the unauthorized failure of state officials to follow established state procedure. Moreover, Nebraska has a tort claims procedure which provides a remedy to persons who have suffered a tortious loss at the hands of the state, but Taylor did not use it. Such procedure could have fully compensated him for his property loss and was sufficient to satisfy the requirements of due process. In response to the inmate's argument in favor of a section 1983 claim, the Court wrote that under this rationale a party involved in nothing more than an automobile accident with a state official could allege a constitutional violation under § 1983.

CASE EXCERPT
"To accept respondent's argument that the conduct of the state officials in this case constituted a violation of the Fourteenth Amendment would almost necessarily result in turning every alleged injury which may have been inflicted by a state official acting under 'color of law' into a violation of the Fourteenth Amendment cognizable under §1983. It is hard to perceive any logical stopping place to such a line of reasoning."

SIGNIFICANCE
In this case the Supreme Court determined that not every negligent act by a prison official or correctional officer constitutes a violation of a constitutional right. Rather, it must be established that something more than negligence is involved. This case limits the liability of correctional personnel in cases of mere negligence.

HARLOW v. FITZGERALD
457 U.S. 800 (1982)

FACTS
In respondent's civil damages action in Federal District Court based on his alleged unlawful discharge from employment in the Department of the Air Force, petitioners, White House aides to former President Nixon, were codefendants with him and were claimed to have participated in the same alleged conspiracy to violate respondent's constitutional and statutory rights as was involved in *Nixon v. Fitzgerald*, 457 U.S. 731(1982). After extensive pretrial discovery, the District Court denied the motions of petitioners and the former president for summary judgment, holding that petitioners were not entitled to absolute immunity from suit. Independently of the former president, petitioners appealed the denial of their immunity defense, but the Court of Appeals dismissed the appeal.

HARLOW v. FITZGERALD (cont.)

ISSUE
Are governmental officials entitled to absolute immunity?

HOLDING
No. Government officials whose special functions or constitutional status requires complete protection from suits for damages—including certain officials of the executive branch, such as prosecutors and similar officials and the president—are entitled to the defense of absolute immunity. However, executive officials in general are usually entitled to only qualified or good-faith immunity. Public policy does not require a blanket recognition of absolute immunity for presidential aides. Petitioners are entitled to application of the qualified immunity standard that permits the defeat of insubstantial claims without resort to trial.

RATIONALE
The recognition of a qualified immunity defense for high executives reflects an attempt to balance competing values: not only the importance of a damages remedy to protect the rights of citizens, but also the need to protect officials who are required to exercise discretion and the related public interest in encouraging the vigorous exercise of official authority. Federal officials seeking absolute immunity from personal liability for unconstitutional conduct must bear the burden of showing that public policy requires an exemption of that scope. The rationale of *Gravel v. United States*, 408 U.S. 606 (1972),—which held the speech and debate clause derivatively applicable to the legislative acts of a senator's aide that would have been privileged if performed by the senator himself—does not mandate derivative absolute immunity for the president's chief aides. Under the functional approach to immunity law, immunity protection extends no further than its justification warrants. While absolute immunity might be justified for aides entrusted with discretionary authority in such sensitive areas as national security or foreign policy, a special functions rationale does not warrant a blanket recognition of absolute immunity for all presidential aides in the performance of all their duties. To establish entitlement to absolute immunity, a presidential aide first must show that the responsibilities of his office embraced a function so sensitive as to require a total shield from liability. He then must demonstrate that he was discharging the protected function when performing the act for which liability

is asserted. Under the record in this case, neither petitioner has made the requisite showing for absolute immunity. However, the possibility that petitioners, on remand, can satisfy the proper standards is not foreclosed. The previously recognized subjective aspect of qualified or good-faith immunity—whereby such immunity is not available if the official asserting the defense "took the action with the malicious intention to cause a deprivation of constitutional rights or other injury"—frequently has proved incompatible with the principle that insubstantial claims should not proceed to trial. Henceforth, government officials performing discretionary functions generally are shielded from liability for civil damages insofar as their conduct does not violate clearly established statutory or constitutional rights of which a reasonable person would have known.

CASE EXCERPT
"Where an official could be expected to know that certain conduct would violate statutory or constitutional rights, he should be made to hesitate; and a person who suffers injury caused by such conduct may have a cause of action. But where an official's duties legitimately require action in which clearly established rights are not implicated, the public interest may be better served by action taken 'with independence and without fear of consequences.'"

SIGNIFICANCE
While this case did not involve prison officials, the principle of the case applies. Here the Supreme Court established a new test for the good-faith defense available to public officers (including prison officials): A public official is not liable if his or her conduct does not violate clearly established constitutional or statutory rights of which a reasonable person would have known. This is a relatively clear and easy to apply test.

SMITH v. WADE
461 U.S. 30 (1983)

FACTS
Respondent, while an inmate in a Missouri reformatory for youthful first offenders, was harassed, beaten, and sexually assaulted by his cellmates. He brought suit under 42 U.S.C. Section 1983 in Federal District Court against petitioner, a guard at the reformatory, and others, alleging that his Eighth Amendment rights

had been violated. Because of petitioner's qualified immunity, as a prison guard, from 1983 liability, the trial judge instructed the jury that respondent could recover only if petitioner was guilty of "gross negligence" or "egregious failure to protect" respondent. The judge also charged the jury that it could award punitive damages in addition to actual damages if petitioner's conduct was shown to be "a reckless or callous disregard of, or indifference to, the rights or safety of others." The District Court entered judgment on a verdict finding petitioner liable and awarding both compensatory and punitive damages. The Court of Appeals affirmed.

ISSUE

Did the District Court for the Western District of Missouri apply the correct legal standard in instructing the jury that it might award punitive damages under 42 U.S.C. Section 1983?

HOLDING

Yes. A jury may be permitted to assess punitive damages in a 1983 action when the defendant's conduct involves reckless or callous indifference to the plaintiff's federally protected rights, as well as when it is motivated by evil motive or intent.

RATIONALE

Punitive damages are available in a proper case under Section 1983. While there is little in the legislative history of the Civil Rights Act concerning the damages recoverable for liability created by the statute, the availability of punitive damages was accepted as law by nearly all state and federal courts at the time it was enacted. The common law, both in 1871 and currently, allows recovery of punitive damages in tort cases not only for actual malicious intent, but also for reckless indifference to the rights of others. Neither the policies nor the purposes of Section 1983 require a departure from the common-law rule. The contention that an actual-intent standard is preferable to a recklessness standard because it is less vague is unpersuasive. The threshold standard for allowing punitive damages for reckless or callous indifference applies even in a case like this. There is no merit to the claim that actual malicious intent should be the standard for punitive damages because the deterrent purposes of such damages would be served only if the threshold for those damages is higher in every case than the underlying standard for liability in the first instance.

CASE EXCERPT

"As a general matter, we discern no reason why a person whose federally guaranteed rights have been violated should be granted a more restrictive remedy than a person asserting an ordinary tort cause of action."

SIGNIFICANCE

In this case, the Supreme Court made it clear that punitive damages may be awarded in addition to compensatory damages, but only if a correctional officer has acted with reckless disregard or indifference to the rights and safety of inmates. This is a fairly tough standard for an inmate plaintiff to meet, but not as tough as requiring proof of actual intent or malice.

CLEAVINGER v. SAXNER
474 U.S. 193 (1985)

FACTS

Respondent federal prison inmates were found guilty by the prison's discipline committee, composed of petitioner prison officials, of encouraging other inmates to engage in a work stoppage and of other charges, and were ordered to be placed in administrative detention and to forfeit a specified number of days of good time. On appeals to the warden and the regional director of the Bureau of Prisons, respondents were ordered released from administrative detention and all material relevant to the incident in question was ordered expunged from their records. They were later paroled and released. But in the meantime, they brought suit in Federal District Court against petitioners, alleging a violation of various federal constitutional rights and seeking declaratory and injunctive relief and damages. After initially dismissing the complaint on the ground that petitioners were entitled to absolute immunity from liability, the District Court, on reconsideration, reinstated the suit. The case was tried to a jury, which found that petitioners had violated respondents' Fifth Amendment due process rights, and awarded damages. The Court of Appeals affirmed, rejecting petitioners' claim for absolute immunity.

ISSUE

Are members of a prison's discipline committee, which hears cases in which inmates are charged with rules infractions, entitled to absolute, as distinguished from qualified, immunity from personal damages liability for actions violative of the United States Constitution?

CLEAVINGER v. SAXNER *(cont.)*

HOLDING

No. Petitioners are entitled to only qualified immunity.

RATIONALE

The Court noted that the discipline committee members are not judges and do function independently. They are employees of the Bureau of Prisons and they are the direct subordinates of the warden who reviews their decision. They work with the fellow employee who lodges the charge against the inmate upon whom they sit in judgment. Furthermore, the Court does not equate this discipline committee membership to service upon a traditional parole board. The board is a "neutral and detached" hearing body. To be sure, the line between absolute immunity and qualified immunity often is not an easy one to perceive and structure. That determination in this case, however, is not, in the opinion of the Court, difficult, and it readily concludes that committee members fall on the qualified-immunity side of the line.

CASE EXCERPT

"We do not perceive the discipline committee's function as a 'classic' adjudicatory one, as petitioners would describe it. Surely, the members of the committee, unlike a federal or state judge, are not 'independent'; to say that they are is to ignore reality. They are not professional hearing officers, as are administrative law judges. They are, instead, prison officials, albeit no longer of the rank and file, temporarily diverted from their usual duties."

SIGNIFICANCE

This case makes it clear that members of a prison disciplinary board enjoy only qualified immunity, rather than absolute immunity. This is the same type of immunity accorded other correctional officers.

DANIELS v. WILLIAMS
474 U.S. 327 (1986)

FACTS

Daniels brought an action in Federal District Court under 42 U.S.C. Section 1983, seeking to recover damages for injuries allegedly sustained when, while an inmate in a Richmond, Virginia jail, he slipped on a pillow negligently left on a stairway by respondent sheriff's deputy. Daniels contends that such negligence deprived him of his liberty interest in freedom from bodily injury "without due process of law" within the

meaning of the due process clause of the Fourteenth Amendment. The District Court granted respondent's motion for summary judgment, and the Court of Appeals affirmed.

ISSUE

Does the due process clause of the Fourteenth Amendment apply to negligent acts by state officials causing unintended injury to or loss of life, liberty, or property?

HOLDING

No. The due process clause is not implicated by a state official's negligent act causing unintended loss of or injury to life, liberty, or property.

RATIONALE

The due process clause was intended to secure an individual from an abuse of power by government officials. The Constitution does not supplant traditional tort law. While the due process clause addresses some aspects of the relationship between jailers and inmates, its protections are not triggered by lack of due care by the jailers. It is true that jailers owe a special duty of care under state tort law to those in their custody, but the due process clause is not implicated. *Parratt v. Taylor* was overruled to the extent that it stated otherwise.

CASE EXCERPT

"Far from an abuse of power, lack of due care suggests no more than a failure to measure up to the conduct of a reasonable person. To hold that injury caused by such conduct is a deprivation within the meaning of the Fourteenth Amendment would trivialize the centuries-old principle of due process of law."

SIGNIFICANCE

This case follows *Parratt v. Taylor* in holding that a negligent act cannot be the basis for a lawsuit alleging a violation of a constitutional right. What is unsettled is whether other types of negligent actions might provide the basis for liability. This case involved what the Court termed "mere" negligence, leaving open the possibility that violations involving "gross" negligence might give rise to liability.

RICHARDSON v. MCKNIGHT
521 U.S. 399 (1997)

FACTS

Ronnie Lee McKnight, a prisoner at Tennessee's South Central Correctional Center (SCCC), filed a Section

1983 suit against two correctional officers, Darryl Richardson and John Walker, alleging that the guards injured him by placing him in extremely tight physical restraints, thereby unlawfully "subject[ing]" him "to the deprivation of" a right "secured by the Constitution" of the United States. Richardson and Walker sought to have the case dismissed, asserting a qualified immunity from §1983 lawsuits. However, Tennessee had privatized the management of SCCC, and consequently a private firm, not the state government, employed the guards. The court held that the law did not grant the guards immunity because they worked for a private company rather than the government and denied their motion to dismiss. The guards appealed to the Sixth Circuit Court of Appeals, which also ruled against them. The appellate court concluded, primarily for reasons of public policy, that privately employed prison guards were not entitled to the immunity provided their governmental counterparts.

ISSUE

Are prison guards who are employees of a private prison management firm entitled to qualified immunity from suit by prisoners charging a violation of 42 U.S.C. §1983?

HOLDING

In a 5–4 opinion written by Justice Breyer, the Court affirmed the lower court's judgment and held that prison guards employed by a private firm are not entitled to qualified immunity from suit by prisoners charging a Section 1983 violation.

RATIONALE

Section 1983 seeks "to deter state actors from using the badge of their authority to deprive individuals of their federally guaranteed rights." Section 1983 imposes liability only where a person acts "under color" of a state "statute, ordinance, regulation, custom, or usage." The Court concluded that neither history nor purpose shows there is something special about the job or the organizational structure of the private prison industry, which is subject to the ordinary competitive pressures that help private firms adjust their behavior in response to the incentives that tort lawsuits provide, the kinds of pressures not always present in government departments. For those reasons, private prison guards, unlike those who work in public prisons, do not enjoy immunity from suit in a §1983 case. Performance of a governmental function does not automatically support immunity for a private person, especially one who

performs a job without government supervision or direction. Special immunity for government employees protects the public "from unwarranted timidity on the part of public officials." In the case of private prisons, competitive marketplace pressures on the private company serve to protect the public: "A firm whose guards are too aggressive will face damages that raise costs, thereby threatening its replacement by another contractor, but a firm whose guards are too timid will face replacement by firms with safer and more effective job records." The private prison in the this case was legally required to carry insurance and renew its contract after its first three years of operation. Comprehensive insurance coverage for private employees reduces fears of unwarranted liability. The Court suggested that since private companies do not have the civil service restraints, they can offer higher pay or added benefits. Although lawsuits may distract private employees from their duties, this risk is not sufficient grounds for qualified immunity.

CASE EXCERPT

"In other words, marketplace pressures provide the private firm with strong incentives to avoid overly timid, insufficiently vigorous, unduly fearful, or 'non arduous' employee job performance."

SIGNIFICANCE

In this case the Supreme Court determined that correctional officers working in private prisons do not enjoy qualified immunity. Correctional officers in state and federal prisons do enjoy qualified immunity, because they are state agents. But here the Court was unwilling to extend the benefits of the qualified immunity defense to correctional officers not working directly for the state or federal prison systems. This decision exposes correctional officers in private prisons, of which there are many, to an increased likelihood of liability.

ALI v. FEDERAL BUREAU OF PRISONS, ET AL.

552 U.S. 214 (2008)

FACTS

Abdus-Shahid M. S. Ali, a prisoner at the United States Penitentiary (USP) in Atlanta, was transferred to USP Big Sandy. Before he was transferred, he packed two duffle bags with his personal items which were inventoried, packaged, and shipped to Big Sandy. His bags

ALI v. FEDERAL BUREAU OF PRISONS, ET AL. *(cont.)*

arrived at Big Sandy a few days after he did, and after inspecting them he noticed that several items were missing. He reported that the missing items included copies of the Qur'an, a prayer rug, and religious magazines worth $177. The Big Sandy staff told him that he had been given everything that was sent. He was advised to file an administrative claim. Ali filed an the claim which the BOP denied because Ali had signed a receipt form that certified the accuracy of the inventory, thereby relinquishing future claims for missing or damaged property. He then filed a lawsuit under the Federal Tort Claims Act (FTCA). The BOP argued that his FTCA claim was barred by an exception in section 2680 (c) because it was a property claim against law enforcement officers. The District Court dismissed his case and the Eleventh Circuit affirmed.

ISSUE

Does 28 U.S.C. section 2680 (c) which preserves sovereign immunity under the Federal Tort Claims Act for claims arising in respect to the assessment of any tax or customs duty, or the detention of property by any other law enforcement officer, apply to only law enforcement officers enforcing customs or excise laws?

HOLDING

The text and structure of Section 2680 (c) "any other law enforcement officer" includes all law enforcement officers and is not limited to only officers enforcing customs and excise laws; therefore, the BOP is protected by sovereign immunity for prisoners' claims involving lost or damaged property detained by BOP officers.

RATIONALE

Read naturally, the majority held, the word "any" has an expansive meaning. There was no indication that Congress intended to limit the expansive language. The natural meaning, therefore, is that Congress meant to preserve sovereign immunity for claims arising from the detention of property by any law enforcement officer, with nothing to indicate that immunity should be limited to only detentions involving excise or customs enforcement. If Congress intended such a limit, it could have easily written language to the effect such as "any law enforcement officer acting in a customs or excise capacity."

CASE EXCERPT

"Petitioner's argument is inconsistent with the statute's language. The phrase 'any other law enforcement officer' suggests a broad meaning. We have previously noted that '[r]ead naturally, the word "any" has an expansive meaning, that is, one or some indiscriminately of whatever kind.'"

CASE SIGNIFICANCE

This case settled a split in the Circuit Courts. Six circuits construed the statute to include all law enforcement officers and five others held that it was limited to officers performing customs or excise work. As a result of the statutory construction decided upon by the majority in this case, BOP prisoner lawsuits under the FTCA for lost, stolen, or damaged property that was detained by BOP employees will be dismissed because the federal government has not waived sovereign immunity for those claims. Prisoners can continue to seek administrative resolution of their claims.

MINNECI v. POLLARD
132 S.Ct. 617 (2012)

FACTS

Richard Pollard was a prisoner in a federal facility operated by Wackenhutt Corrections Corporation, a private company. He filed a lawsuit against several Wackenhutt employees, including a security officer, food services supervisor, and members of the medical staff, alleging that they deprived him of adequate medical care in violation of the Eighth Amendment. Pollard had slipped and fallen on a cart in the doorway of the prison butcher shop. The medical staff determined that he had several broken bones, took him to an outside clinic for further evaluation, and arranged surgery. He claimed that when he was taken to the clinic, the guards forced him to put on a jumpsuit that hurt his arm and wear arm restraints that caused pain. The medical staff failed to put his arm in a splint and provide necessary physical therapy. Guards failed to provide reasonable alternatives for him to receive his meals so he had to auction off his personal items in order to be able to buy food in the commissary. He was deprived of basic hygiene care, sufficient medicine, and was forced to return to work before he was healed. The District Court dismissed his claim after deciding that the Eighth Amendment does not provide for a

Bivens action against a privately managed prison's personnel (*Bivens v. Six Unknown Narcotics Agents*, 403 U.S. 388 (1971)). The Ninth Circuit Court of Appeal reversed and decided that a *Bivens* action does exist.

ISSUE
Can employees of private prison companies be sued in a *Bivens* type action for violating the constitutional rights of inmates?

HOLDING
Employees of private prison companies cannot be sued in a *Bivens* type action for violations of inmates' constitutional rights where the conduct is of a type that typically falls within the scope of traditional state tort law.

RATIONALE
In *Bivens*, the Supreme Court held that federal agents who violate a person's constitutional rights can be held liable in federal court for damages. *Bivens* actions are similar to section 1983 lawsuits against state and local government officials and their agents. In *Correctional Services Corp. v. Malesko*, 534 U.S. 61 (2001), the Court ruled that a prisoner housed in a federal community corrections facility under contract with the federal Bureau of Prisons could not sue the Correctional Services Corporation under *Bivens*. Malesko sued the corporation claiming he had a heart condition and had permission to use the elevator. When an officer required him to use the stairs, he had a heart attack. The Supreme Court decided that a *Bivens* type lawsuit against the corporation can only be filed against an individual, not a private entity. In *Minneci,* the Court decided that because Pollard's claim fell within the scope of traditional state tort law, he had an alternative process to protect his rights. He alleged injuries that involve improper medical care, a traditional area of state tort law. The Court dismissed concerns that state tort law is inadequate or varies too significantly from state to state to protect the constitutional interests at stake in Minneci's claim.

CASE EXCERPT
"The question is whether, in general, state tort law remedies provide roughly similar incentives for potential defendants to comply with the Eighth Amendment while also providing roughly similar compensation to victims of violations. The features of the two kinds of actions just mentioned suggest that, in practice, the answer to this question is 'yes.' And we have found nothing here to convince us to the contrary."

CASE SIGNIFICANCE
Minneci is one of several cases where the Supreme Court has decided questions involving liability issues and private prison operations. In *Richardson v. McKnight*, 521 U.S. 399 (1997), the Court ruled that private prison employees do not have qualified immunity protections. In *Correctional Services Corp. v. Malesko*, 534 U.S. 61 (2001), the Court ruled that a *Bivens* type action cannot be brought against a private prison corporation. That 2001 decision left open the issue eventually decided in *Minneci*—can a *Bivens*-type lawsuit be brought against private prison employees? Although the Court decided that it could not, it based its decision on the grounds that the inmate had a traditional tort suit alternative. The issue yet undecided is can a *Bivens* or section 1983 lawsuit be brought against a private prison employees if the violation does not have a traditional tort remedy available, such as a violation of an inmate's right to access the courts.

DISCUSSION QUESTIONS

1. Explain how and why the Supreme Court has applied the provisions of Section 1983 to corrections personnel.
2. What is the difference between absolute and qualified immunity?
3. What are the implications of the Supreme Court decision in *Richardson v. McKnight* regarding private prisons?
4. What does "acting under color of law" mean in Section 1983 lawsuits against correctional officers?
5. Why must an inmate establish more than mere negligence to prevail in a section 1983 lawsuit?
6. Explain the Supreme Court's decision in *Minneci v. Pollard* and why the Court decided private prison employees are not liable under a *Bivens*-type lawsuit.
7. Examines the Supreme Court's approach to private prisons and private prison employees as it has evolved in its decisions in *Richardson v. McKnight*, *Correctional Services Corp. v. Malesko*, and *Minneci v. Pollard*.

8. Analyze the Surpeme Court's decision in *Cleavinger v. Saxner*. Do you think disciplinary hearing officers should be protected by more than qualified immunity?

9. What is the purpose of allowing inmates to recover punitive damages in a section 1983 lawsuit? Identify situations where you think an award of punitive damages would be appropriate.

10. Read the dissenting opinions in the *Richardson v. McKnight* case and discuss the dissenting Justices' positions.

CHAPTER TEN

HABEAS CORPUS AND THE PRISON LITIGATION REFORM ACT

INTRODUCTION

This chapter looks at cases involving habeas corpus and the Prison Litigation Reform Act. When convicted offenders are not successful in overturning their convictions through the appeal process, sometimes they are able to challenge their convictions through a petition for a writ of habeas corpus. Habeas corpus is a civil lawsuit that is referred to as a collateral attack because it seeks to have the defendant released through a different and separate procedure from the appeal process. In Article I, Section 9, the Great Writ is enshrined in the US Constitution and permits individuals who believe they are wrongfully held in custody by the government to ask a court to consider whether their detention is legal. Federal habeas corpus law has expanded significantly since the 1940s to allow more and more inmates to petition for writs, crowding federal court dockets with cases that are seldom successful. In similar fashion, after the Supreme Court ruled that prisoners could sue prison officials under 42 U.S.C. §1983, prisoners flooded federal courts with lawsuits alleging their constitutional rights were violated by prison officials. As different as federal habeas and prisoners' rights cases are, they both consume a large portion of federal court time and are quite costly to the government. In response to these concerns, during the 1990s Congress passed legislation to curtail both types of lawsuits.

Federal habeas corpus is only available to prisoners who claim that a federal constitutional right was violated during the investigation or prosecution of their case, with the exception of violations of the Fourth Amendment right against unreasonable searches and seizures. The Supreme Court decided in *Stone v. Powell*, 428 U.S. 465 (1976), that such claims cannot be reviewed under federal habeas if they were fully considered by a state appellate court. Federal habeas corpus is not limited to inmates convicted in federal court of a federal crime. It is also available to prisoners convicted under state laws, however, state inmates must first exhaust the appeal process in their states of conviction and any state habeas corpus process that may also be available.

Federal habeas corpus law generates controversy not just because many prisoners apply for writs, it allows federal judges to second-guess decisions made by state court trial and appellate judges. Habeas petitions are often filed years after a conviction and keep convictions from being finalized. One of the most serious concerns is that prisoners have abused the system by filing an endless succession of writs. On the other hand, federal habeas law has allowed important federal constitutional rights to be vindicated in cases where state courts have failed or refused to recognize a violation occurred. Without the federal habeas process, the state court decisions would have been left standing.

In an effort to curb abuse of the writ, the Supreme Court ruled in *McCleskey v. Zant* that courts have the discretion to deny successive petitions for writs, especially if prisoners raise issues they failed to raise in their first petition. Petitioners must prove they did not deliberately or negligently fail to raise an issue in the first petition. Called the cause and prejudice rule, prisoners must also prove that failure to raise the issue probably affected the outcome of the case.

In 1996, Congress passed the Antiterrorism and Effective Death Penalty Act (AEDPA) and imposed significant limitations on federal habeas corpus. One of the most important provisions limits a prisoner's right to file a second habeas petition. A claim presented in a second or successive application should be dismissed unless it relies on a new constitutional law that has been made retroactive by the Supreme Court to cases on collateral review and that was previously unavailable. A second application is also permitted if the facts upon which the claim are predicated could not have been discovered previously through the exercise of due diligence and, if proven, would be sufficient by clear and convincing evidence to persuade reasonable fact finders that the applicant should be found not guilty. A three-judge panel of US Circuit Court judges must approve the filing of a second petition. The AEDPA also imposes a one-year deadline for filing an application for a writ. Finally, the act provides that a writ should not be granted with respect to any claim that has already been adjudicated on the merits in state court proceedings. The Supreme Court upheld the constitutionality of the habeas corpus provisions of the AEDPA in *Felker v. Turpin*.

Congress enacted the Prison Litigation Reform Act (PLRA) in 1996 to address two concerns: (1) the large number of prisoners' rights lawsuits, and (2) federal judges who intervened in the operation of state prison systems and ordered extensive, expensive reforms. One of the act's most important provisions requires prisoners to exhaust any remedies available through their inmate grievance systems before they can file a lawsuit. The hope is that many grievances can be resolved internally and not require court resources. Each state creates its own grievance system; some systems are considered better designed and organized and more responsive to inmate complaints, than others. In *Booth v. Churner,* the Supreme Court decided that the PLRA requires exhaustion even in those situations where a prisoner is seeking money damages through a grievance system that does not provide for such damages. In *Porter v. Nussle,* the Court concluded the exhaustion requirement is comprehensive and includes all inmate lawsuits, whether they address general living conditions or particular incidents, excessive force or some other wrong. The Court is clear that whatever the issue and however their state's grievance process is designed, prisoners must exhaust that system before they can file suit.

The PLRA also imposed substantial restrictions on the attorney fees that can be awarded to successful prisoner-plaintiffs under 42 U.S.C. §1988. In *Martin v. Hadix,* the Court ruled that the PLRA's cap applied to cases that were pending when the statute was enacted; however, the fee limits do not apply for postjudgement monitoring services performed before the statute's effective date. The issue of attorney fee limits is important because prisoner's rights cases can be expensive to litigate and very few if any money damages are usually awarded. Much of the relief is injunctive in nature. Fee caps may well impact the interest attorneys have in representing inmates.

In *Miller v. French,* the Court grappled with a section of the PLRA that seeks to curtail federal court involvement in prison operations. The Court decided that a provision in the act that places an automatic stay on court orders dealing with prison reform is constitutional when it is requested by the state. A stay temporarily suspends any reform efforts a court has already ordered. The Court concluded that such a stay is mandatory when requested. A state requests an automatic stay in connection with a request for the permanent termination of court orders that mandate changes in certain areas of prison operations in order to meet constitutional standards.

Just like the AEDPA, there are many provisions of the PLRA that the Supreme Court has yet considered but which have been addressed by the federal appellate courts. Both statutes are long and complex, raising as many legal issues as they attempt to resolve.

PRICE v. JOHNSTON

334 U.S. 266 (1948)

FACTS

In 1938, the petitioner was sentenced to 65 years for four counts of bank robbery and was committed to the federal penitentiary at Alcatraz. Over a period of time, he had filed three petitions for writs of habeas corpus, alleging unlawful imprisonment. All three were unsuccessful, and he began a fourth proceeding, for the first time alleging that the prosecution had used false testimony knowingly. The government did not address this new allegation but asked that the petition be denied on the grounds that the new allegation was known to the inmate when he filed the earlier writs and that a fourth petition is an abuse of the writ of habeas corpus. The district court dismissed the petition, although the court did not state any reasons for its dismissal. On appeal, a panel of the Ninth Circuit Court of Appeals ordered up the original files in the petitioner's three previous habeas corpus applications and directed that the prisoner be brought before the court to argue his appeal. The case was then assigned to be heard before the entire circuit court. The petitioner prisoner moved for an order directing his appearance before this court, a motion which was subsequently denied. The majority opinion of the appellate court "held that circuit courts of appeals are without power to order the production of a prisoner for the argument of his appeal in person." The circuit court affirmed the order of the district court, and the Supreme Court granted certiorari.

ISSUE

Is the appearance of a prisoner before a circuit court of appeals to argue his case necessary for the exercise and agreeable to the usages and principles of law for a habeas corpus writ? Is a dismissal of a habeas corpus writ without a hearing or without stating reasons for dismissal justified based on lack of merit or on prisoner's abuse of the writ?

HOLDING

The petitioner's "fourth petition for a writ of habeas corpus, alleging the knowing use of false testimony to obtain his conviction, was improperly dismissed by the District Court" and the Court remanded the case back to the District Court. "[A] circuit court of appeals has power, exercisable in the sound discretion of the court, to issue an order, in the nature of a writ of habeas corpus, commanding that a prisoner be brought before the court for the purpose of arguing his own appeal in a case involving his life or liberty."

RATIONALE

The Court decided that circuit courts of appeals have the power under §262 of the Judicial Code to issue a writ of habeas corpus commanding that a prisoner be brought to the courtroom to argue his own appeal. Although that power had been assumed, the Court stated, "[w]e now translate that assumption into an explicit holding." The Court emphasized that circuit courts of appeals have discretion to issue such a writ, "to be exercised with the best interests of both the prisoner and the government in mind." The Court emphasized that "Section 262...does not justify an indiscriminate opening of the prison gates to allow all those who so desire to argue their own appeals." Noting that the purpose of a habeas corpus proceeding is to make sure that a person is not unjustly imprisoned, the Court reasoned that if there is a justifiable explanation as to why a prisoner was not able to assert his rights or was not aware of the significance of relevant facts, then it would be unreasonable to deny that prisoner the opportunity to obtain relief. It is not necessary that the burden be on the inmate to affirmatively allege in the first instance that he had new information "or had adequate reasons for not raising sooner the issue of the knowing use of false testimony." It was sufficient if he presented an allegation and supporting facts which would entitle him to relief. Prisoners are not trained in the law and often act as their own attorneys in habeas corpus proceedings, making it impossible to impose on them the same high standards placed on licensed attorneys. The Court stated that if the government decided to only claim that the prisoner had abused the habeas corpus writ, then the government had to make that claim clearly and give specific details. Once that abuse has been alleged, the prisoner had the burden of answering that allegation and proving that he had not abused the writ. If his answer was inadequate, then the court may dismiss the petition.

CASE EXCERPT

"If it is apparent that the request of the prisoner to argue personally reflects something more than a mere desire to be freed temporarily from the confines of the prison, that he is capable of conducting an intelligent and responsible argument, and that his presence in

PRICE v. JOHNSTON *(cont.)*

the courtroom may be secured without undue inconvenience or danger, the court would be justified in issuing the writ. But if any of those factors were found to be negative, the court might well decline to order the prisoner to be produced."

CASE SIGNIFICANCE

The Judiciary Act of 1789 first empowered federal courts to issue writs of habeas corpus to prisoners "in custody, under or by colour of the authority of the United States." The right to federal habeas corpus petitions was extended to prisoners in state custody in 1867 by congressional act. *Price v. Johnston*, the case at hand, was decided in 1948 and is an important analysis of the writ of habeas corpus. As Judge Murphy observed, "[t]he writ of habeas corpus has played a great role in the history of human freedom. It has been the judicial method of lifting undue restraints upon personal liberty. But in recent years the increased use of this writ, especially in federal courts, has created many procedural problems which are not easy of solution. This case involves some of those problems. Because of the importance of the writ and the necessity that it not lose its effectiveness in a procedural morass, we have deemed it wise to deal with this case at length and to set forth fully and explicitly the answers to the matters at issue." The two dissenting opinions agreed with the lower courts' conclusions that the claims made in the fourth habeas corpus petition were meritless. The dissents also were in serious opposition to the issue regarding the presence of a prisoner in a circuit court to argue his case on a habeas corpus petition. Justice Jackson stated that "[t]his is one of a line of cases by which there is being put into the hands of the convict population of the country new and unprecedented opportunities to re-try their cases, or to try the prosecuting attorney or their own counsel, and keep the Government and the courts litigating their cases until their sentences expire or one of their myriad claims strikes a responsive chord or the prisoner make the best of an increased opportunity to escape. I think this Court, by inflating the great and beneficent writ of liberty beyond a sound basis, is bringing about its eventual depreciation." One month after the Court decided *Price*, Congress enacted 28 U.S.C. 2244, addressing the issue of repetitive federal habeas corpus petitions: "No circuit or district judge shall be required to entertain an application for a writ of habeas corpus to inquire into the detention of a person pursuant to a judgment of a court of the United States, or of any State, if it appears that the legality of such detention has been determined by a judge or court of the United States on a prior application for a writ of habeas corpus and the petition presents no new ground not theretofore presented and determined, and the judge or court is satisfied that the ends of justice will not be served by such inquiry" (28 U.S.C. 2244).

ROSE v. LUNDY
455 U.S. 509 (1982)

FACTS

Lundy, a Tennessee state prisoner, was convicted on charges of rape and crime against nature. His convictions were affirmed by the state court of criminal appeals, and the Tennessee Supreme Court denied review. He then filed an unsuccessful petition for post-conviction relief in the county criminal court. Lundy next petioned for a writ of habeas corpus in a federal district court alleging "(1) that he had been denied the right to confrontation because the trial court limited the defense counsel's questioning of the victim; (2) that he had been denied the right to a fair trial because the prosecuting attorney stated that Lundy had a violent character; (3) that he had been denied the right to a fair trial because the prosecutor improperly remarked in his closing argument that the state's evidence was uncontradicted; and (4) that the trial judge improperly instructed the jury that every witness is presumed to swear the truth." The district court decided that it could not review the last two grounds because Lundy had not exhausted state remedies on those claims, but the district court also stated that "in assessing the atmosphere of the cause taken as a whole, these items may be referred to collaterally." After reviewing the state trial transcript , the district court identified ten instances of prosecutorial misconduct, five more in addition to the ones raised by Lundy at the state court level. The district court granted Lundy's petition for a writ of habeas corpus, and the circuit court affirmed this decision. The state appealed, arguing that the Supreme Court should apply a " 'total exhaustion rule' requiring district courts to dismiss every habeas corpus petition that contains both exhausted and unexhausted claims."

ISSUE

Does the exhaustion rule in Title 28 U.S.C. §§ 224(b) and (c) require a federal district court to dismiss a petition for a writ of habeas corpus containing any claims that have not been exhausted in the state court?

HOLDING

Yes. Title 28 U.S.C. §§ 2254(b) and (c) provide that a state prisoner's application for a writ of habeas corpus in a federal district court based on an alleged federal constitutional violation will not be granted unless the applicant has exhausted the remedies available in the state courts.

RATIONALE

The Court reversed the judgment of the lower courts in an opinion written by Justice O'Connor. The Court noted that "[T]he exhaustion doctrine existed long before its codification by Congress in 1948;" however, whether the doctrine applied to "mixed" petitions containing both unexhausted and exhausted claims had not been addressed by the Court until this case. The purpose of the exhaustion doctrine is "to protect the state courts' role in the enforcement of federal law and prevent disruption of state judicial proceedings." In effect, the State is given first opportunity to rule upon and correct alleged violations of federal rights of inmates. In addition, if federal courts do address habeas petitions fully exhausted in state courts, there will be a complete factual record assisting federal courts in their review. "Rather than increasing the burden on federal courts, strict enforcement of the exhaustion requirement will encourage habeas petitioners to exhaust all of their claims in state court and to present the federal court with a single habeas petition. To the extent that the exhaustion requirement reduces piecemeal litigation, both the courts and the prisoners should benefit, for as a result the district court will be more likely to review all of the prisoner's claims in a single proceeding, thus providing for a more focused and thorough review."

CASE EXCERPT

"A rule requiring exhaustion of all claims in state courts promotes comity and furthers the purposes underlying the exhaustion doctrine, as codified in §§2254(b) and (c), of protecting the state courts' role in the enforcement of federal law and preventing disruption of state judicial proceedings."

CASE SIGNIFICANCE

In 1948, Congress codified the exhaustion doctrine in 28 U.S.C. 2254. The statute, however, did not address the problem of "mixed" petitions that contain both exhausted and unexhausted claims. This was the dilemma presented in the instant case, and the Court ruled that such a petition must be dismissed until all of the claims had been heard in state court. At the time of this case, eight appellate courts did allow district courts to review the exhausted claims of mixed habeas corpus petitions. Only the Fifth and Ninth Circuit Courts of Appeals followed the conservative "total exhaustion" rule that was subsequently mandated by the Supreme Court here.

MCCLESKEY v. ZANT

499 U.S. 467 (1991)

FACTS

In 1978, McCleskey was convicted of murder and sentenced to death. He had confessed to police that he, along with three other armed men, committed robbery of a furniture store in Georgia. During the robbery, an off-duty police officer was shot and killed by one of the men. At trial, however, McCleskey renounced his confession and denied all involvement. The prosecution introduced overwhelming testimony and evidence, which included the testimony of Evans, who had been in an adjacent jail cell. According to Evans, McCleskey "admitted shooting the officer during the robbery and boasted that he would have shot his way out of the store even in the face of a dozen policemen."

For over ten years, McCleskey sought to obtain direct and collateral relief in the courts. He first filed a direct appeal to the Georgia State Supreme Court, alleging in part that the prosecutor did not disclose Evans's statements to the defense. The Georgia Supreme Court found this failure on the prosecutor's part not indicative of McCleskey's innocence and found that McCleskey had received a fair trial, upholding his conviction and sentence. The US Supreme Court denied certiorari in this instance. McCleskey then began seeking postconviction relief and filed for state habeas corpus relief, claiming among other challenges that his statements to Evans were elicited in a situation created by the state to induce him to make incriminating statements without the assistance of counsel in violation of *Massiah v. United States*, 377 U.S. 201 (1964), and the Sixth Amendment. The state habeas corpus court denied relief, the Georgia Supreme Court denied his application for a certificate of probable cause, and the US Supreme Court denied certiorari in this second instance. He then filed his

MCCLESKEY v. ZANT *(cont.)*

first federal habeas petition, which did not include his *Massiah* claim, and the district court granted relief, finding that Evans had been impermissibly promised favorable treatment and his testimony may have influenced the jury's verdict. The appellate court reversed the district court's decision to grant the writ, and the Supreme Court granted certiori to only address the constitutionality of capital sentencing proceedings in Georgia, denying relief again to McCleskey. The fourth attempt at relief was a second state habeas corpus petition which was dismissed by the state trial court and denied by the state supreme court. In 1987, McCleskey filed a second federal habeas petition, including a *Massiah* challenge. The challenge was based on a transcript of statements Evans made to police two weeks before the trial. This document detailed efforts used by Evans to get McCleskey to talk about the crime. At a hearing on this second habeas hearing, a jailer came forth and testified that the state had requested that Evans be jailed next to McCleskey. Based on the document and the jailer's testimony, the district court granted relief to McCleskey under *Massiah*, finding a relationship between Evans and the state. The court of appeals reversed the district court on grounds that the district court abused its discretion. The appellate court based its decision on the "the doctrine of abuse of the writ, which defines the circumstances in which federal courts decline to entertain a claim presented for the first time in a second or subsequent habeas corpus petition." The circuit court also found that any *Massiah* violation amounted to harmless error. The Court granted certiorari to address alleged violations by the circuit court's analysis of the abuse of the habeas corpus doctrine. The Court also asked the parties in this case to address the question involving whether a state must "demonstrate that a claim was deliberately abandoned in an earlier petition for a writ of habeas corpus in order to establish that inclusion of that claim in a subsequent habeas petition constitutes abuse of the writ."

ISSUE

Does McCleskey's failure to include his *Massiah* claim in his first federal habeas corpus petition constitute abuse of the habeas corpus writ?

HOLDING

Yes. McCleskey's failure to raise his *Massiah* claim in his first federal habeas petition constituted abuse of the writ.

RATIONALE

The Supreme Court affirmed the appellate court, agreeing that McCleskey abused the writ of habeas corpus. In an opinion by Justice Kennedy, the Court acknowledged confusion regarding the proper application of the abuse of the writ doctrine and sought to clarify standards for determining abuse. The Court looked in part at the 1948 decision *Price v. Johnston*, 334 U.S. 266. In *Price*, the district court and court of appeals dismissed the prisoner's fourth habeas petition without a hearing on the ground that the claim was not raised in earlier habeas actions. In reversing and remanding the case, the Court stated that the government must plead an abuse of the writ, and the burden then shifts to the petitioner to show that the new claim does not constitute abuse. The district court in *Price* failed to give the petitioner an opportunity to explain the basis for raising his claim late. Once the explanation is given in trial court, the court may dismiss it if it proves to be inadequate. But if a petitioner "present[s] adequate reasons for not making the allegation earlier, reasons which make it fair and just for the trial court to overlook the delay," he must be given the opportunity to develop these matters in a hearing.

Congress enacted 28 U.S.C. 2244 one month after *Price*, allowing a district court to dismiss a successive petition new grounds. Then in 1963, the Supreme Court decided *Sanders v. United States* 373 U.S. 1, formulating basic rules regarding the doctrine of writ abuse. In 1966, Congress again amended the habeas corpus statute, in an effort to "alleviate the increasing burden on federal courts caused by successive and abusive petitions by 'introducing a greater degree of finality of judgments in habeas corpus proceedings.'" A new paragraph to Section 2244 addressed what was referred to as "repetitive applications" by state inmates:

"(b) When after an evidentiary hearing on the merits of a material factual issue, or after a hearing on the merits of an issue of law, a person in custody pursuant to the judgment of a State court has been denied by a court of the United States or a justice or judge of the United States release from custody or other remedy on an application for a writ of habeas corpus, a subsequent application for a writ of habeas corpus on behalf of such person need not be entertained by a court of the United States or a justice or judge of the United States unless the application alleges and is predicated on a factual or other ground not adjudicated on the hearing of the earlier application for the writ, and unless the court, justice, or judge is satisfied that the applicant has not on the earlier application deliberately withheld the newly asserted ground or otherwise abused the writ."

Justice Kennedy stated that this paragraph establishes subsequent petitions need not be heard by federal courts unless prisoners satisfy two conditions. "First, the subsequent petition must allege a new ground, factual or otherwise. Second, the applicant must satisfy the judge that he did not deliberately withhold the ground earlier or 'otherwise abus[e] the writ.'"

In 1976, Rule 9(b) of the Rules Governing Habeas Corpus Proceedings addressed the issue of new grounds being raised in successive petitions and again stated that failing to raise those new grounds in earlier petitions could be construed as an abuse of the writ.

CASE EXCERPT

"Thus, for example, if a prisoner deliberately withholds one of two grounds for federal collateral relief at the time of filing his first application, in the hope of being granted two hearings, rather than one, or for some other such reason, he may be deemed to have waived his right to a hearing on a second application presenting the withheld ground. Nothing in the traditions of habeas corpus requires the federal courts to tolerate needless, piecemeal litigation, or to entertain collateral proceedings whose only purpose is to vex, harass, or delay."

CASE SIGNIFICANCE

Recent cases before the Court have addressed abuses of the writ of habeas corpus in a range of circumstances. The decision in *McCleskey* is one more "attempt to define the doctrine of the writ of abuse with more precision." In this case, the Court adopted the cause-and-prejudice standard utilized in procedural default analysis as the standard to be used in determining if a habeas petition has been abused through inexcusable neglect: "The cause and prejudice analysis we have adopted for cases of procedural default applies to an abuse-of-the-writ inquiry in the following manner. When a prisoner files a second or subsequent application, the government bears the burden of pleading abuse of the writ. The government satisfies this burden if, with clarity and particularity, it notes petitioner's prior writ history, identifies the claims that appear for the first time, and alleges that petitioner has abused the writ. The burden to disprove abuse then becomes petitioner's. To excuse his failure to raise the claim earlier, he must show cause for failing to raise it and prejudice therefrom as those concepts have been

defined in our procedural default decisions." The adoption of the cause and prejudice standard is not without controversy. The three-member dissenting opinion in McCleskey saw the majority decision as a drastic departure from "the norms that inform the proper judicial function." In the dissent's viewpoint, the Court abandoned longstanding legal principles in adopting the "strict liability" cause and prejudice standard. The cause component of this standard imposes a strict liability standard in that cause for failing to present a federal claim in state proceedings can be established only "when some objective factor external to the defense impeded counsel's efforts to comply with the State's procedural rule... The majority's adoption of the cause-and-prejudice test is not only unwise, but also manifestly unfair. The proclaimed purpose of the majority's new strict liability standard is to increase to the maximum extent a petitioner's incentive to investigate all conceivable claims before filing his first petition."

REED v. FARLEY

512 U.S. 339 (1994)

FACTS

The Interstate Agreement on Detainers (IAD) is a compact among 48 states, the District of Columbia, and the federal government. It enables a state to gain custody of a prisoner incarcerated in another jurisdiction in order to try him on criminal charges. The IAD provides that the trial of a transferred prisoner "shall be commenced within one hundred and twenty days of the arrival of the prisoner in the receiving State, but for good cause shown in open court, the court having jurisdiction of the matter may grant any necessary or reasonable continuance." The IAD also states that when a trial does not occur within the time prescribed, the charges shall be dismissed with prejudice. Reed was transferred in April, 1983 from a federal prison in Indiana to Indiana state custody after an IAD detainer was lodged by Indiana officials. Reed's trial on the state charges was originally scheduled 19 days beyond the 120-day IAD period and was later postponed for an additional 35 days. Reed filed several wide ranging pretrial motions that contained a few general references to the IAD time limit, but he did not specifically object to his trial date until four days after the 120-day period expired. The trial court denied Reed's petition for discharge for the reasons that the judge had previously been unaware

REED v. FARLEY (*cont.*)

of the 120-day limitation and Reed had not objected earlier to the trial date or requested a speedier trial. After his trial and conviction in October 1983, Reed unsuccessfully pursued an appeal and sought postconviction relief in Indiana's courts. He then petitioned for a federal writ of habeas corpus under the Sixth Amendment speedy trial right. The District Court denied relief, and the Court of Appeals for the Seventh Circuit affirmed.

ISSUE

Were Reed's Sixth Amendment rights violated, even though he did not object to the court's schedule until after the IAD time limit had lapsed? What is the appropriate standard for evaluating alleged federal statutory violations under habeas corpus review?

HOLDING

No to the first question. For the second question, "a fundamental defect which inherently results in a complete miscarriage of justice, [or] an omission inconsistent with the rudimentary demands of fair procedure" is the required standard for granting habeas corpus review of federal law.

RATIONALE

The Court's opinion was written by Justice Ginsberg, who began by noting that "[A] state prisoner may obtain federal habeas corpus relief 'only on the ground that he is in custody in violation of the Constitution or laws or treaties of the United States.' (28 U.S.C. 2254(a))." While the IAD is state law, it is also a "congressionally sanctioned interstate compact with the Compact Clause," and therefore is also federal law. Reed had two pretrial hearings where he failed to object to the trial date, and, in fact, indicated that he preferred to be tried after he was released from federal custody, which would be after the 120-day deadline. Further, a "showing of prejudice is required to establish a violation of the Sixth Amendment Speedy Trial Clause, and that necessary ingredient is entirely missing here."

CASE EXCERPT

"[H]abeas review is available to check violations of federal laws when the error qualifies as 'a fundamental defect which inherently results in a complete miscarriage of justice, [or] an omission inconsistent with the rudimentary demands of fair procedure.' ". . . "Reed's case similarly lacks 'aggravating circumstances'

rendering 'the need for the remedy afforded by the writ of habeas corpus . . . apparent.' "

CASE SIGNIFICANCE

The Supreme Court heard this case in order to resolve the conflict among the lower courts regarding the availability of habeas review for state prisoners of IAD speedy trial claims. Some lower courts of appeal had found that IAD speedy trial claims were not available for habeas review because those alleged violations did not constitute a " 'fundamental defect which inherently results in a complete miscarriage of justice,' under *Hill v. United States*, 368 U.S. 424, 428 (1962)." Other courts found that habeas review was not available for alleged IAD speedy trial violations unless actual prejudice could be shown. This case follows Court precedent in ruling that the "fundamental defect" test of *Hill v. United States*, 368 U.S. 424, 428 (1962) is the appropriate standard for evaluating alleged federal statutory violations under habeas corpus review.

FELKER v. TURPIN
518 U.S. 651 (1996)

FACTS

A Georgia jury convicted Felker of murder, rape, aggravated sodomy, and false imprisonment. Felker was sentenced to death on the murder charge. In 1984, the state supreme court affirmed the conviction and death sentence and the US Supreme Court denied certiorari. In 1992, a state trial court denied collateral relief, the state supreme court declined to issue a certificate of probable cause to appeal the denial, and the US Supreme Court again denied certiorari. In 1996, Felker filed a petition for a writ of habeas corpus in a district court, alleging several violations regarding his trial and conviction. The district court denied the petition, the appellate court affirmed the lower court's decision, and the Supreme Court denied certiorari. Felker was scheduled to be executed between May 2 and 9 in 1996. On April 29, 1996, he filed a second petition for collateral relief, which the state trial court denied on May 1, and the state supreme court denied certiorari on May 2. On April 24, 1996, the president signed the Antiterrorism and Effective Death Penalty Act of 1996 into law. Title I of this act contained a series of amendments to existing federal habeas corpus law. Pertinent to Felker's case, Title I requires that all motions for filing a second or successive habeas appeal from a district court be reviewed by an appellate panel whose decision shall not be appealable by writ of certiorari to the Supreme Court. On May 2, 1996, Felker filed a stay of execution application and leave to file a second or successive federal habeas petition in circuit court. The court of appeals denied both motions the day they were filed, concluding that Felker's claims had not been presented in his first habeas petition, and that they did not meet the standards of the act, nor would they have satisfied pre-act standards for obtaining review on the merits of second or successive claims. Felker then filed a pleading in the Supreme Court styled a "Petition for Writ of Habeas Corpus, for Appellate or Certiorari Review of the of the United States Circuit Court for the Eleventh Circuit, and for Stay of Execution." On May 3, the Supreme Court granted his stay application and petition for certiorari in order to decide which provisions of Title I of the act applied to a petition for habeas corpus, whether the application of the act suspended the writ of habeas corpus in this case, and whether Title I of the act constituted an unconstitutional restriction on the jurisdiction of the Supreme Court.

ISSUE
Do the Title I provisions of the Antiterrorism and Effective Death Penalty Act of 1996, preventing the Supreme Court from reviewing an appellate review panel's denial of leave to file a second habeas petition unconstitutionally suspend the habeas writ and restrict the Court's authority to entertain original habeas petitions?

HOLDING
No. The act's creation of an appellate panel, charged with reviewing all second or successive habeas applications, is not unconstitutional. Further, the act does not preclude the Court from entertaining original habeas petitions.

RATIONALE
Chief Justice Rehnquist, writing for the Court, observed that before a petitioner can file a second habeas petition in district court, the act requires the petitioner to obtain leave from the court of appeals. Previously, the district court would have performed this "screening function." Transferring habeas review from the district court to an appellate panel is just a shift in habeas "gatekeeping" duties, and as such is neither an unconstitutional suspension of the habeas writ which would violate the exceptions clause of Article III, nor a deprivation of the Court's appellate jurisdiction.

CASE EXCERPT
"The Act does remove our authority to entertain an appeal or a petition for a writ of certiorari to review a decision of a court of appeals exercising its "gatekeeping" function over a second petition. But since it does not repeal our authority to entertain a petition for habeas corpus, there can be no plausible argument that the Act has deprived this Court of appellate jurisdiction in violation of Article III, Section(s) 2."

CASE SIGNIFICANCE
This case challenges provisions of Title I of the Antiterrorism and Effective Death Penalty Act of 1996, which substantially changed standards for claims under habeas relief. These new restrictions are designed to prevent abuse of the habeas corpus writ. Other titles of the AEDPA addressed victim restitution, international terrorism, and weapons and explosives, as well as various miscellaneous items. As the Court noted in 1991 in *McCleskey v. Zant* 499 U.S. 467, 489, "[t]he doctrine of abuse of the writ refers to a complex and evolving body of equitable principles informed and controlled by historical usage, statutory developments, and judicial decisions." The Court ruled in the instant case that the new provisions in the Act "are well within the compass of this evolutionary process and do not amount to a 'suspension' of the writ." The Chief Justice observed that the writ of habeas corpus is quite different today from the writ as it was known to the framers of the Constitution. Originally, the Great Writ was available only to federal prisoners, not state prisoners. The kinds of cases that could be reviewed by the habeas corpus writ were also more limited. In 1867, "Congress made the writ generally available in 'all cases where any person may be restrained of his or her liberty in violation of the constitution, or of any treaty or law of the United States.'" By 1942, Supreme Court decisions allowed that a final judgment of conviction in a state court could be subject to habeas review. (See, e. g. , *Waley v. Johnston*, 316 U.S. 101 (1942), and *Brown v. Allen*, 344 U.S. 443 (1953).)

MARTIN v. HADIX
527 U.S. 343 (1999)

FACTS
Male and female prisoners in the Michigan prison system filed two separate class action lawsuits against prison officials, one in 1977 and one in 1980, claiming

MARTIN v. HADIX *(cont.)*

that the conditions of their confinement violated the due process clause of the US Constitution. The inmates and officials entered into consent decrees to remedy the situation. In 1987, the District Court ruled that the inmate plaintiffs were entitled to attorney's fees for postjudgment monitoring of prison officials' compliance with the decrees. The court established specific market rates for awarding fees. By April 26, 1996, the effective date of the Prison Litigation Reform Act of 1995 (PLRA), the market rate was $150 per hour. The PLRA limited the size of fees that may be awarded to attorneys who litigate prisoner lawsuits to a maximum hourly rate of $112.50. When first presented with the issue, the District Court concluded that the PLRA cap did not limit attorney's fees for services performed in these cases prior to, but that were still unpaid by, the PLRA's effective date. The Court of Appeals affirmed. Next, fee requests were filed with the District Court for services performed between January 1, 1996, and June 30, 1996, a period encompassing work performed both before and after the PLRA's effective date. The District Court reiterated its earlier conclusion. The Court of Appeals held that the PLRA's fee limitation does not apply to cases pending on the enactment date because if it did, it would have an impermissible retroactive effect, regardless of when the work was performed.

ISSUE

Does the federal Prison Litigation Reform Act of 1995 limit an attorney's fees for postjudgment monitoring services that were pending when the act became effective? Does the PLRA limit an attorney's fees for postjudgment monitoring services performed after the act became effective?

HOLDING

The Prison Litigation Reform Act of 1995 limits attorney's fees for postjudgment monitoring services performed after the Act's effective date but does not limit fees for monitoring performed before that date.

RATIONALE

The opinion was written by Justice O'Connor who began by noting that the basic question presented here is "[w]hen should a new federal statute be applied to pending cases?... The Court first looked to "whether Congress has expressly prescribed the statute's proper reach," citing *Landgraf* v. *USI Film Products*, 511 U.S. 244, 280 (1994). Without direction from Congress,

the Court next determines if applying the statute in a particular instance would have a retroactive effect and attach new legal consequences to events that were completed before the act was enacted. If it would have a retroactive effect, then it would be considered not to apply in that instance. Accordingly, retroactivity would attach to monitoring that had been performed before the PLRA was enacted, so the attorney's fees provisions in the PLRA would not apply to that work. No retroactivity problem applies to work done after the PLRA was enacted (April 26, 1996). Thus, "any expectation of compensation at the pre-PLRA rates" after April 26, 1996 would be irrational.

CASE EXCERPT

"There is no manifest injustice in telling an attorney performing postjudgment monitoring services that, going forward, she will earn a lower hourly rate than she had earned in the past. If the attorney does not wish to perform services at this new, lower, pay rate, she can choose not to work. In other words, as applied to work performed after the effective date of the PLRA, the PLRA has future effect on future work; this does not raise retroactivity concerns."

CASE SIGNIFICANCE

Section 803 of the PLRA specified that attorney's fees shall only be awarded to the extent that they are "directly and reasonably incurred in proving an actual violation of the plaintiff's rights" or in enforcing the relief ordered for the violation. The amount of the fee must be "proportionately related to the court ordered relief for the violation" (Sec. 803)(d)(1)(A). Because the "temporal application" of the statute was not clearly specified in the legislation, lower courts have been in conflict over when to apply the new fee standards. As Justice Scalia noted in a separate concurring opinion in this case, the rule of law is that "in absence of contrary indication, a statute will not be construed to have retroactive application, see *Landgraf* v. *USI Film Products*, 511 U.S. 244, 280 (1994)." However, the question presented, according to Justice Scalia, then becomes, "retroactive in reference to what?" This question accounted for the conflicts in lower court decisions. In the present case before the Court, the five options for judging retroactivity were: (1) at the time of the alleged violation upon which the fee-imposing suit was based; (2) when the lawyer undertook to prosecute the suit for which attorney's fees were provided; (3) at the time of the filing of the suit in which the fees were imposed;

(4) when the legal work was done for which the fees were payable; or (5) when the actual award of fees in the case was rendered. In this case, all nine Justices agreed that the PLRA should not apply to services performed before the law's effective date. However, the Court split over whether the new fee limits contained in the law apply to work performed after April 26, 1996, in cases that were begun before that date. A 7–2 majority said that the new limits do apply to such cases.

MILLER v. FRENCH
530 U.S. 327 (2000)

FACTS
In 1975, inmates at the Pendleton Correctional Facility in Indiana filed a class action lawsuit. After a trial, the District Court found the conditions of confinement violated Eighth Amendment prohibitions against cruel and unusual punishment and issued an injunction to remedy the Eighth Amendment violations. Ongoing injunctive relief, with various modifications, remained in effect. In 1996, Congress enacted the Prison Litigation Reform Act of 1995, which sets a standard for the entry and termination of prospective relief in civil actions challenging prison conditions. The PLRA provides that a motion to terminate such relief "shall operate as a stay" of that relief, or a discontinuance of the relief, beginning 30 days after the motion is filed and ending when the court rules on the motion. In 1997, the State of Indiana filed a motion to terminate the remedial order against the correctional facility. Under the PLRA, the motion stayed the court's original remedial order. The prisoners of Pendleton moved to enjoin or prohibit the operation of the automatic stay, arguing that the automatic stay provision of the PLRA violated due process and the separation of powers doctrine. The District Court enjoined the stay. In affirming, the Court of Appeals found that the provision prevented courts from exercising their equitable powers to prohibit the stay, but concluded that the statute was unconstitutional on separation of powers grounds.

ISSUE
Does the Prison Litigation Reform Act of 1995's automatic stay provision prevent courts from exercising their equitable powers to enjoin such a stay? Does the provision violate the constitutional separation-of-powers doctrine?

HOLDING
Yes to the first question. No to the second. Congress clearly intended to make operation of the PLRA's automatic stay provision mandatory, precluding courts from exercising their equitable power to enjoin the stay. Further, the PLRA does not violate separation of powers principles.

RATIONALE
In an opinion written by Justice O'Connor, the Court engaged in a lengthy analysis of the language of the automatic stay provision of the PLRA. Clearly, Congress meant the automatic stay provision to be mandatory, and "[a]ny construction that preserved courts' equitable discretion to enjoin the automatic stay would effectively convert the PLRA's mandatory stay into a discretionary one." Thus, following congressional intent meant finding that courts could not prohibit a stay of relief that had been ordered in civil actions challenging conditions of confinement upon a motion to terminate such relief. The next issue was whether or not the automatic stay provision was actually constitutional. The Court reasoned that it did not violate separation of powers principles because those principles mainly concern structural constrains on judicial actions.

CASE EXCERPT
"The PLRA does not deprive courts of their adjudicatory role, but merely provides a new legal standard for relief and encourages courts to apply that standard promptly. Through the PLRA, Congress clearly intended to make operation of the automatic stay mandatory, precluding courts from exercising their equitable powers to enjoin the stay. And we conclude that this provision does not violate separation of powers principles."

CASE SIGNIFICANCE
Portions of Section 802 of the PLRA were challenged in this case. Section 802 amended Sec. 3626, Title 18, U.S.C., concerning appropriate remedies with respect to prison conditions. In this section, the act states that the "court shall not grant or approve any prospective relief unless the court finds that such relief is narrowly drawn, extends no further than necessary to correct the violation of the Federal right, and is the least intrusive means necessary to correct the violation of the Federal right." Sec. 802 of the PLRA allows for preliminary injunctive relief with respect to prison conditions, but likewise such relief "must be narrowly

MILLER v. FRENCH *(cont.)*

drawn, extend no further than necessary to correct the harm the court finds requires preliminary relief, and be the least intrusive means necessary to correct that harm," and "[p]reliminary injunctive relief shall automatically expire 90 days after its entry, unless the court makes the findings under required for prospective relief and makes the order final before the expiration of the 90-day period" (Sec. 802 (a)(2)). When prospective relief is ordered, such relief shall be terminated upon the motion of any party "2 years after the date the court granted or approved the prospective relief, 1 year after the date the court has entered an order denying termination of prospective relief under this paragraph; or in the case of an order issued on or before the date of enactment of the Prison Litigation Reform Act, 2 years after such date of enactment" (Sec. 802(b)(1)(A)i-iii)). However, if the court finds that the prospective relief was not narrowly drawn or extended further than necessary to correct the federal violation, or was not "the least intrusive means" necessary to correct that violation, then the defendant is entitled to immediate termination of the prospective relief. Section 802 further mandates that courts shall not enter or approve consent decrees unless they comply with the above limitations on relief. Accordingly, the act defines the term "relief" to mean "all relief in any form that may be granted or approved by the court, and includes consent decrees but does not include private settlement agreements." "Prospective relief" refers to all relief other than compensatory monetary damages. Subsection f of section 802 spells out in detail the role of the special master, including method of appointment, compensation, and limitations on powers and duties. Section 802 applied to all prospective relief whether that relief was "originally granted or approved before, on, or after the date of the enactment of this title." Congress lawfully imposed deadlines for federal judges to review states officials' motions to discontinue court monitoring and supervision of state prison conditions. The "clear intent" of Congress to make the provision mandatory and not discretionary was not so clear to two of the four dissenting Justices. Justice Breyer, joined by Justice Stevens, opted for a more flexible interpretation of this section of the PLRA: "The upshot is a statute that, when read in light of its language, structure, purpose, and history, is open to an interpretation that would allow a court to modify or suspend the automatic stay when a party, in accordance with traditional equitable criteria, has demonstrated a need for such

an exception. That interpretation reflects this Court's historic reluctance to read a statute as depriving courts of their traditional equitable powers. It also avoids constitutional difficulties that might arise in unusual cases. I do not argue that this interpretation reflects the most natural reading of the statute's language. Nor do I assert that each individual legislator would have endorsed that reading at the time. But such an interpretation is a reasonable construction of the statute. That reading harmonizes the statute's language with other basic legal principles, including constitutional principles. And, in doing so, it better fits the full set of legislative objectives embodied in the statute than does the more rigid reading that the majority adopts." The Prison Litigation Reform Act, Title VIII, was signed by President Clinton on April 26, 1996; the PLRA, one of several riders, was attached to the Balanced Budget Downpayment Act, II (HR 3019, Omnibus Appropriations Bill). At Senate hearings before the bill was passed, Senator Kennedy expressed his concern that the PLRA was not just an attempt to reduce frivolous inmate lawsuits but rather "a far-reaching effort to strip Federal courts of the authority to remedy unconstitutional prison conditions." Senator Kennedy called the act "patently unconstitutional and a dangerous legislative incursion into the work of the judicial branch." He noted that it received only a single hearing in the Judiciary Committee. At that hearing, Associate Attorney General John Schmidt had expressed concern with aspects of the act limiting the power of the federal courts to remedy constitutional and statutory violations in prisons. According to Senator Kennedy, Schmidt noted that Section 802, calling for termination of relief two years after an order is issued, would result in unnecessary litigation and "periodic disruption of ongoing remedial efforts." Senator Simon also expressed concern about the PLRA, and offered a copy of Associate US Attorney General John Schmidt's July 27, 1995 testimony before the Judiciary Committee. Schmidt observed that the bill would make it "virtually impossible for States to enter into consent decrees even when the consent decree may well be in the State's best interest for both fiscal and policy reasons." The PLRA was thus viewed as creating new and burdensome standards of review and would prohibit courts from placing population caps on prisons, thus exacerbating the problem of prison overcrowding. Senator Dole, who introduced the PLRA, stated that the act would "work to restrain liberal Federal judges who see violations of constitutional rights in every prisoner complaint and who have used these complaints to micromanage State and local prison systems."

BOOTH v. CHURNER
532 U.S. 731 (2001)

FACTS

The Prison Litigation Reform Act of 1995 requires a prisoner to exhaust "such administrative remedies as are available" before suing over prison conditions. Booth, an inmate at the State Correctional Institution at Smithfield, Pennsylvania, initiated a suit in District Court, claiming that corrections officers violated his Eighth Amendment right to be free from cruel and unusual punishment in various ways. Booth sought both injunctive relief and monetary damages. At the time of Booth's suit, Pennsylvania provided an administrative grievance and appeals system, which addressed Booth's complaints but had no provision for recovery of money damages. After the prison authority denied his administrative grievance, Booth did not seek administrative review. Subsequently, the District Court dismissed the complaint for failure to exhaust administrative remedies. In affirming, the Court of Appeals rejected Booth's argument that the exhaustion requirement was inapplicable because the administrative process could not award him the monetary relief he sought (money being the only relief still sought at this point).

ISSUE

Must prisoners who seek only monetary damages in suits over prison conditions still exhaust all administrative remedies before going to court, even if monetary damages are not available under the particular administrative process?

HOLDING

Yes. The Prison Litigation Reform Act requires administrative exhaustion prior to inmate's filing of civil rights lawsuit even where the grievance process does not permit award of money damages and the inmate seeks only money damages, as long as the grievance tribunal has authority to take some action in response to inmate's complaint.

RATIONALE

In an opinion by Justice Souter, the Court reasoned that "[T]he meaning of the phrase 'administrative remedies available' is the crux of the case, and up to a point the parties approach it with agreement." Neither party denied that some remedy was assumed by the PLRA's requirement of an "available remedy," and neither party argued that exhaustion of administrative procedures was required when such procedures lacked authority to provide relief or any other action. The Court noted that the "dispute here, then, comes down to whether or not a remedial scheme is 'available' where, as in Pennsylvania, the administrative process has authority to take some action in response to a complaint, but not the remedial action an inmate demands to the exclusion of all other forms of redress." In looking both at the statutory context of the phrase and statutory history leading to the passage of the Prison Litigation Reform Act, Justice Souter observed that by Congress imposing a broader exhaustion requirement by the PLRA made it unlikely that "it meant to give prisoners a strong inducement to skip the administrative process simply by limiting prayers for relief to money damages not offered through administrative grievance mechanisms."

CASE EXCERPT

"We think that Congress has mandated exhaustion clearly enough, regardless of the relief offered through administrative procedures."

CASE SIGNIFICANCE

Section 803 of the Prison Litigation Reform Act, passed in 1996, amended sections of the Civil Rights of Institutionalized Persons Act. In particular, suits by prisoners with respect to prison conditions may not be brought "until such administrative remedies as are available are exhausted." Additionally, the "failure of a State to adopt or adhere to an administrative grievance procedure shall not constitute the basis for an action." If the court deems any action to be frivolous or malicious, or "to fail to state a claim upon which relief can be granted, or to seek monetary relief from a defendant who is immune from such relief," the court may dismiss the underlying claim without first requiring that administrative remedies be exhausted (Sec. 803)(c)(1)(2). In the case at hand, Booth bypassed administrative avenues because the remedies available at the time did not include monetary relief. The Court ruled, however, that whether the relief sought was available or not, inmates still must exhaust these avenues. Since this case was filed, Pennsylvania's grievance mechanism does include monetary awards. The PLRA was a

BOOTH v. CHURNER *(cont.)*

broad, controversial attempt by Congress to constrain prison litigation. However, courts have addressed a plethora of cases challenging various sections of the PLRA since it was passed.

ARTUZ v. BENNETT
531 U.S. 4 (2000)

FACTS

In 1984, Bennett was convicted of attempted murder, criminal possession of a weapon, reckless endangerment, criminal possession of stolen property, and unauthorized use of a motor vehicle. Bennett moved *pro se* to vacate his judgment of conviction in 1995. A New York trial court orally denied Bennett's motion. Despite several written requests, Bennett claimed that he never received a copy of a written order of the denial. In 1998, Bennett filed a federal habeas corpus petition alleging violations of his rights to present witnesses in his defense and to a fair trial, to be present at all material stages of the trial, and to the effective assistance of counsel. The Federal District Court dismissed Bennett's federal habeas corpus petition as untimely under the Antiterrorism and Effective Death Penalty Act of 1996 (AEDPA), which set a one-year period of limitation on federal habeas corpus applications by state prisoners. The Court of Appeals reversed, holding that Bennett's habeas petition was not time-barred because his 1995 motion was still pending, since he had never received notification of the state's decision regarding it. Thus, the time for appealing the denial of that motion had not yet expired. Also, in response to petitioner's objection, the court found that the 1995 motion was a "properly filed" application, even though the claims contained in the motion were procedurally barred under two New York statutory provisions. The Supreme Court granted certiorari to address this point.

ISSUE

Is an application for state postconviction relief properly filed within the meaning of the Antiterrorism and Effective Death Penalty Act of 1996 even if it does not comply with all mandatory state law procedural requirements that would bar review of the merits of the application?

HOLDING

Yes. An application for state postconviction relief containing procedurally barred claims is properly filed within the meaning of the Antiterrorism and Effective Death Penalty Act of 1996.

RATIONALE

The Court's decision was written by Justice Scalia, who stated that an application is considered to be filed "when it is delivered to, and accepted by, the appropriate court officer for placement into the official record." Further, that delivery and acceptance must comply with filing laws and rules such as requirements concerning "the form of the document," time limits regarding delivery, and the payment of filing fees.

CASE EXCERPT

"By construing 'properly filed application' to mean application 'raising claims that are not mandatorily procedurally barred,' petitioner [confuses] the difference between an 'application' and a 'claim.' The state procedural bars at issue set forth conditions to obtaining relief, rather than conditions to filing."

CASE SIGNIFICANCE

This case deals with statutory language and meaning of the term "properly filed" for purposes of habeas corpus writs. The statutory provision at issue (Section 2244(d)(2) of Title 28 U.S.C.) states that "[t]he time during which a properly filed application for State postconviction or other collateral review with respect to the pertinent judgment or claim is pending shall not be counted toward any period of limitation under this subsection." Is an application containing procedurally-barred claims still properly filed? In this case, there were two New York state procedural bars at issue. The state provisions barred claims for relief that could have been raised on direct appeal but were not or that were "previously determined on the merits upon an appeal from the judgment" of conviction. Justice Scalia noted that these provisions deal only with conditions to obtaining relief and not with conditions related to filing. Thus, applications "have been properly delivered and accepted so long as the filing conditions have been met."

DUNCAN v. WALKER
533 U.S. 167 (2001)

FACTS

During 1992, Walker received several convictions for robbery. After pursuing various state remedies for relief, Walker's last conviction became final in April 1996, but before the April 24, 1996 date of the

Antiterrorism and Effective Death Penalty Act of 1996. Walker filed a petition for a writ of habeas corpus on April 10, 1996. This petition was dismissed by the district court on the grounds that it was not evident that Walker had exhausted state remedies. Over a year later, on May 20, 1997, Walker filed another petition for habeas corpus without having returned to state court. The district court dismissed this petition because it had not been filed "within a 'reasonable time' from AEDPA's effective date." The circuit court reversed the district court's decision, finding that Walker's first federal habeas petition was an application for other collateral review that did not count toward the limitation period under §2244(d)(2) and made his current petition timely. The Supreme Court granted certiorari in order to resolve the conflict between the lower appellate courts regarding whether a federal habeas petition is an "application for State postconviction or other collateral review" within the meaning of §2244(d)(2). Specifically, 28 U.S.C. §2244(d)(2) provides that the time during which an "application for State postconviction or other collateral review" is pending does not count toward the limitation period for filing federal habeas petitions.

ISSUE
Is a federal habeas corpus petition an "application for State postconviction or other collateral review" within the meaning of provision 28 USC section 2244(d)(2)?

HOLDING
A federal habeas corpus petition is not an "application for State postconviction or other collateral review" within the meaning of 28 USC section 2244(d)(2). "As a result, §2244(d)(2) did not toll the limitation period during the pendency of respondent's first federal habeas petition."

RATIONALE
Writing for the Court, Justice O'Connor observed at the outset that "Congress placed the word 'State' before 'postconviction or other collateral review' without specifically naming any kind of 'Federal' review.... [A] comparison of the text of §2244(d)(2) with the language of other AEDPA provisions supplies strong evidence that, had Congress intended to include federal habeas petitions within the scope of §2244(d)(2), Congress would have mentioned 'Federal' review expressly." Both words were specifically used to refer to "state and federal proceedings" in other sections of AEDPA, and the Court pointed to the well-established presumption

that "Congress acts intentionally and purposefully in the disparate inclusion or exclusion."

CASE EXCERPT
"We find no likely explanation for Congress' omission of the word 'Federal' in §2244(d)(2) other than that Congress did not intend properly filed applications for federal review to toll the limitation period. [I]f the statute were construed so as to give applications for federal review the same tolling effect as applications for state collateral review, then [section] 2244(d)(2) would furnish little incentive for individuals to seek relief from the state courts before filing federal habeas petitions."

CASE SIGNIFICANCE
As the dissent noted, "[t]he federal habeas corpus statute limits the period of time during which a state prisoner may file a federal habeas petition to one year, ordinarily running from the time the prisoner's conviction becomes final in the state courts." The time period that properly filed applications for State postconviction relief or other collateral review are still pending do not count toward the one-year limitation period. The purpose to excluding the time period of pending applications is to give state prisoners adequate time to file federal habeas petitions. The question in this case was whether the phrase "other collateral review" included federal habeas corpus proceedings. While the majority answered in the negative, the two-member dissent, written by Justice Breyer and joined by Justice Ginsberg, disagreed, believing that other collateral review should include federal habeas corpus proceedings. This case is another example of the complexities involved in determining Congressional intent and in construing statutory language whenever amendments to statutes are enacted by Congress. The effects of the Court's ruling in the instant case can pose a significant restriction on seeking habeas relief for state prisoners. In 1982, the Court ruled in *Rose v. Lundy* (455 U.S. 509), covered earlier in this section, that district courts cannot reach the merits of habeas petitions containing both exhausted and unexhausted claims. In 1995, a study by the US Department of Justice Department found that 63 percent of habeas petitions are dismissed, and well over half of those (57 percent) are dismissed for failure to exhaust state remedies. Therefore, a federal court may be required to dismiss a state prisoner's habeas petition for the sole reason that the prisoner has not exhausted state collateral relief for every claim presented in the federal petition. The prisoner must

DUNCAN v. WALKER *(cont.)*

then return to state court to pursue state remedies. If he loses, he may again file a petition for a writ of habeas corpus in federal court, but he may find that time has run out. The dissenting opinion observed that, with the AEDPA, Congress "gave state prisoners a full year (plus the duration of state collateral proceedings) to file a federal habeas corpus petition. Congress would not have intended to shorten that time dramatically, at random, and perhaps erase it altogether, 'den[ying] the petitioner the protections of the Great Writ entirely,'... simply because the technical nature of the habeas rules led a prisoner initially to file a petition in the wrong court. The majority's argument assumes a congressional desire to strengthen the prisoners' incentive to file in state court first. But that is not likely to be the result of today's holding. After all, virtually every state prisoner already knows that he must first exhaust state-court remedies; and I imagine that virtually all of them now try to do so. The problem arises because the vast majority of federal habeas petitions are brought without legal representation.... Prisoners acting *pro se* will often not know whether a change in wording between state and federal petitions will be seen in federal court as a new claim or a better way of stating an old one; and they often will not understand whether new facts brought forward in the federal petition reflect a new claim or better support for an old one. Insofar as that is so, the Court's approach is likely to lead not to fewer improper federal petitions, but to increased confusion, as prisoners hesitate to change the language of state petitions or add facts, and to greater unfairness. And it will undercut one significant purpose of the provision before us—to grant state prisoners a fair and reasonable time to bring a first federal habeas corpus petition."

PORTER v. NUSSLE

534 U.S. 516 (2002)

FACTS

In 1999, Nussle, a Connecticut prisoner, filed a Section 1983 federal civil suit, alleging "a sustained pattern of harassment and intimidation" by correctional officers, including a brutal beating in violation of the cruel and unusual punishment clause of the Eighth Amendment. Nussle did not first file a grievance under the applicable Connecticut Department of Correction procedures. Based on the Prison Litigation Reform Act of

1995, the district court dismissed the suit, finding that the PLRA directs that "[n]o action shall be brought with respect to prison conditions under section 1983... or any other Federal law, by a prisoner... until such administrative remedies as are available are exhausted." In reversing the district court's decision, the appellate court held that administrative exhaustion is not required for a claims of assault or excessive force under Section 1983. Citing legislative history, the appellate court found that the phrase "prison conditions" covers only conditions affecting prisoners generally, not single incidents that immediately affect only particular prisoners. Noting that other circuit courts of appeal have held that inmates alleging assaults by prison officers must exhaust administrative remedies before filing civil rights actions, the Supreme Court granted certiorari to resolve this conflict.

ISSUE

Does the Prison Litigation Reform Act of 1995 require that all inmates seeking redress for general prison circumstances or particular episodes, including allegations of excessive force or some other wrong, exhaust any applicable administrative remedies before filing suit?

HOLDING

Yes. The PLRA's exhaustion requirement applies to all inmate suits about prison life, whether they involve general circumstances or particular episodes, and whether they allege excessive force or some other wrong.

RATIONALE

Nussle and the appellate court believed excessive force claims to be exempt from the exhaustion provision. The Court acknowledged that excessive force claims have been distinguished from "conditions of confinement claims" in other decisions (see e.g., *Hudson v. McMillian*, 503 U. S. 1 (1992); *Farmer v. Brennan*, 511 U. S. 825 (1994)). However, all of the cases making such a distinction involve "proof requirements" regarding the level of injury a prisoner must show or a particular mental state that must be shown. In a unanimous opinion written by Justice Ginsberg, the Court noted that proof requirements are the inquiry when the case has reached judicial scrutiny; in the case at hand, the inquiry was only whether the prison grievance process must be exhausted before a case comes to the court. The Court ruled that it was, stating that "exhaustion is now required for all 'action[s] … brought with respect to prison conditions.' "

CASE EXCERPT

"Even when the prisoner seeks relief not available in grievance proceedings, notably money damages, exhaustion is a prerequisite to suit.... And unlike the previous provision, which encompassed only §1983 suits, exhaustion is now required for all 'action[s] brought with respect to prison conditions,' whether under §1983 or 'any other Federal law.' "

CASE SIGNIFICANCE

As the Court noted in this unanimous opinion, usually when plaintiffs file civil rights suits under 42 U.S.C. §1983, they are not required to exhaust state administrative remedies. However, the law is different for prisoners. In 1980, Congress passed an exhaustion provision for state prisoners filing Section 1983 suits. Under 42 U.S.C. §1997e(a)(1), part of the Civil Rights of Institutionalized Persons Act, district courts had the discretion to stay a state prisoner's §1983 action "for a period not to exceed 180 days" while the prisoner exhausted available "plain, speedy, and effective administrative remedies." Generally, district courts did not require this exhaustion when prisoners sued for damages and the prisoner grievance systems did not offer monetary relief. In 1995, Congress revised the exhaustion provision as part of Section 803 of the Prison Litigation Reform Act. In particular, suits by prisoners with respect to prison conditions may not be brought "until such administrative remedies as are available are exhausted." Additionally, the "failure of a State to adopt or adhere to an administrative grievance procedure shall not constitute the basis for an action." If the court deems any action to be frivolous or malicious, or "to fail to state a claim upon which relief can be granted, or to seek monetary relief from a defendant who is immune from such relief," the court may dismiss the underlying claim without first requiring that administrative remedies be exhausted. As the Court noted, and as decided in 2001 in *Booth v. Churner* (532 U.S. 731), exhaustion in cases covered by §1997e(a) is now mandatory: "All 'available' remedies must now be exhausted; those remedies need not meet federal standards, nor must they be 'plain, speedy, and effective.' " The Court noted that this exhaustion provision includes such advantages as giving correctional officials the "time and opportunity" to handle grievances internally, to take corrective

action , to filter out frivolous or groundless claims, and to establish an administrative record so that if cases are brought to the court, facts are clearly established in the record.

BOUMEDIENNE v. BUSH

553 U.S. 723 (2008)

FACTS

In 2002, Boumedienne and five other Algerian natives were captured in Afghanistan because they were suspected of plotting to bomb the US embassy. The United States classified them as enemy combatants in the war on terror and shipped them to the US military prison in Guantanamo Bay Naval Base, located on land that the United States leases from Cuba. Boumedienne filed a petition for a writ of habeas corpus, alleging violations of the due process clause, various statutes and treatises, the common law, and international law. The District Court dismissed the case on the grounds that he had no right to habeas corpus because he was a detainee at an overseas military base. The US Court of Appeals for the D.C. Circuit affirmed. The Supreme Court reversed in the case *Rasul v. Bush*, 542 U.S. 466 (2004), which held that the habeas corpus statute extends to noncitizen detainees at Guantanamo. Congress enacted the Military Commissions Act of 2006 (MCA) which eliminated federal court jurisdiction to hear habeas applications from detainees who had been designated as enemy combatants. The detainees argued that the MCA did not apply to their petitions, but if it did it was unconstitutional under the suspension clause, Article I, section 9. The suspension clause in the Constitution states the writ of habeas corpus cannot be suspended, unless in "Cases of Rebellion or Invasion of the public Safety may require it." The DC Circuit court ruled in the government's favor. The Supreme Court granted certiorari.

ISSUE

Does the Military Commissions Act of 2006 strip federal courts of jurisdiction over habeas petitions filed by foreign citizens at the US Naval Base at Guantanamo Bay? If so, is the MAC a violation of the Constitution's suspension clause?

HOLDING

Petitioners have the constitutional privilege of habeas corpus and are not barred from seeking the writ or

BOUMEDIENNE v. BUSH (cont.)

invoking the suspension clause's protections because they are designated as enemy combatants or because of they are detained at the Guantanamo Bay Naval Base. The Military Commissions Act is an unconstitutional suspension of that right.

RATIONALE

The Supreme Court reasoned that if the MCA is considered constitutional its legislative history requires that the detainees' cases be dismissed. However, the Court concluded that because the procedures provided in the Detainee Treatment Act of 2005 are not adequate substitutes for the habeas writ, the Military Commissions Act is an unconstitutional suspension of the writ. The detainees were not barred from seeking habeas or invoking the suspension clause merely because they had been designated as enemy combatants or held at Guantanamo Bay. The Court decided that the United States, by virtue of its complete jurisdiction and control, maintains de facto sovereignty over Guantanamo Bay so that that the aliens detained as enemy combatants on that territory are entitled to the writ of habeas corpus protected in Article I, Section 9 of the US Constitution.

CASE EXCERPT

"Our opinion does not undermine the Executive's powers as Commander in Chief. On the contrary, the exercise of those powers is vindicated, not eroded, when confirmed by the Judicial Branch. Within the Constitution's separation-of-powers structure, few exercises of judicial power are as legitimate or as necessary as the responsibility to hear challenges to the authority of the Executive to imprison a person. Some of these petitioners have been in custody for six years with no definitive judicial determination as to the legality of their detention. Their access to the writ is a necessity to determine the lawfulness of their status, even if, in the end, they do not obtain the relief they seek."

CASE SIGNIFICANCE

This is a controversial 5–4 decision rendered during the height of the war on terrorism. It extends the writ of habeas corpus to enemy combatants in that war detained for indefinite periods of time at Guantanamo Bay. Critics contend that Congress had already given Guantanamo Bay prisoners more rights than any other prisoners of war and that the Supreme Court should have waited to see how the Military Commissions

Act operated before deciding this case. Supporters of the decision contend that it is an important step in the United States staying true to its constitutional foundations.

BROWN v. PLATA
131 S.Ct. 1910, 563 U.S.—(2011)

FACTS

California's prison system was designed to hold 80,000 inmates but had more than doubled in population size by 1996. Two federal class action lawsuits had been filed by groups of inmates in separate locations to address numerous prison conditions that allegedly resulted from the overcrowding. *Coleman v. Brown* (docket no. 2:90-cv-00520-LKK-JFM (E.D. Cal.)) was filed in 1990. The District Court in that case found that prisoners with serious mental illness did not receive adequate care. The court-appointed special master oversaw efforts to improve mental health care, but reported after 12 years that the care was continuing to deteriorate due to the overcrowding. In the second class action lawsuit, *Plata v. Brown* (docket no. 3:01-cv-01351-TEH (N.D. Cal.)), filed in the District Court in 2001, the state conceded that prison medical care violated prisoners Eighth Amendment rights and agreed to a remedial plan. When the state failed to comply, the court-appointed receiver in that case reported that the deficiencies continued and they were caused by overcrowding. The plaintiff classes in the *Coleman* and *Plata* cases moved their respective District Courts to convene a three-judge panel under the provisions of the Prison Litigation Reform Act in order to order reductions in the prison population. The judges in both cases granted the request and a consolidated hearing was held before a three-judge panel. That panel heard extensive testimony, made finding of fact, and in 2009 ordered California to reduce its prison population to 137.5 percent of design capacity within two years. Finding that the prison population would have to be reduced if capacity could not be increased with construction, the panel ordered California to submit a compliance plan for approval.

ISSUE

Did the three-judge panel err in finding that overcrowding was the primary cause of the constitutional violations? Is the court-mandated population limit necessary in order to remedy the prisoners' constitutional rights as authorized by the PLRA? Was the relief ordered by the three-judge court narrowly drawn, extending no further than is necessary, and the least intrusive means necessary to correct the violation?

HOLDING

The court below did not err in concluding that overcrowding in California prisons was the primary cause of the violations of prisoners' constitutional rights to adequate health care. The evidence supported the conclusion of the three-judge panel that a population limit was necessary to remedy the overcrowding problem. The relief ordered by the three-judge court was narrowly drawn, extended no further than necessary to correct the violation, and was the least intrusive means necessary to correct the violation.

RATIONALE

The Court reviewed the evidence offered before the three-judge panel that showed the extent of continuing Eighth Amendment violations over many years. It commented on the degree of overcrowding and how reports by several California state agencies had highlighted the severity of the situation. The Justices also reviewed the reports written by the special master and the receiver in which they detailed efforts to improve the delivery of health care to inmates and how they were adversely impacted by overcrowding. The Court supported the finding of the lower courts that overcrowding was the primary cause of the constitutional violations and concluded that California had had a reasonable amount of time to remedy the violations and failed to do so. A population limit was necessary to remedy the situation because all other remedies tried to that point had failed. Because of the state budget crisis, the Justices concluded it was unlikely that California would be able to construct new facilities. The relief ordered by the three-judge panel was the most narrow, least intrusive relief necessary.

CASE EXCERPT

"The Court cannot ignore the political and fiscal reality behind this case. California's Legislature has not been willing or able to allocate the resources necessary to meet this crisis absent a reduction in overcrowding. There is no reason to believe it will begin to do so now, when the State of California is facing an unprecedented budgetary shortfall. As noted above, the legislature recently failed to allocate funds for planned new construction. *Supra,* at 1937–1938. Without a reduction in overcrowding, there will be no efficacious remedy for the unconstitutional care of the sick and mentally ill in California's prisons."

CASE SIGNIFICANCE

This case was a controversial 5–4 decision with Justice Scalia commenting in his dissent that the order to reduce the prison population was "the most radical injunction issued by a court in our Nation's history." California had to quickly develop a plan to release approximately 37,000 inmates. This was the first time the Supreme Court had addressed a prisoner population reduction order from a three-judge panel under the PLRA. It had to interpret the key provisions of the PLRA that permitted a three-judge panel to mandate a reduction. The majority carefully explained the evidence presented during a 14-day trial and the reports issued by the special master and receiver, and how the evidence supported the panel's finding that overcrowding was the primary cause of the inadequate health care—a finding required by the PLRA. Then the Supreme Court explained the evidence it relied on to support the panel's finding that a population reduction was necessary to remedy the problems.

DISCUSSION QUESTIONS

1. How do the PLRA and the AEDPA attempt to limit lawsuits filed by prisoners?
2. Welcome to the procedurally complicated world of federal habeas corpus law. In general terms, describe the goals of federal habeas corpus law and the basic requirements.
3. Why did the Supreme Court rule that the AEDPA habeas corpus provisions are constitutional?
4. In what cases, using what rationale, did the Supreme Court conclude that the PLRA exhaustion requirement is comprehensive with no exceptions?
5. Do you agree with the Supreme Court's decision in *Brown v. Plata* (2011) and its interpretation of the PLRA?
6. Explain why the Supreme Court upheld the right for detainees suspected of terrorism and held at Guantanamo Bay to petition for a writ of habeas corpus.

7. Do you think the Great Writ should be available to detainees held at Guantanamo Bay?

8. Check various websites to see how California responded to the Supreme Court's decision to uphold the population reduction ordered by the three-judge panel.

9. What advantages and disadvantages do you see in requiring prisoners to exhaust their administrative remedies before they can file a lawsuit?

10. How has the war on terror and the efforts to try "enemy combatants" affected Supreme Court decisions regarding habeas corpus?

CHAPTER ELEVEN

PAROLE

INTRODUCTION

The fifteen cases briefed in this chapter involve legal issues pertaining to parole. Parole is the early release of a prisoner subject to conditions and normally under supervision by a parole officer. The goals of parole are at least twofold: to aid the reintegration of the parolee into the community while, at the same time, protecting the public by monitoring the parolee's behavior. Historically, courts in this country have held that the decision to grant or deny parole or a pardon is a matter of executive discretion, implying that courts should not interfere in administrative decision making. While there is no constitutional right to parole or sentence commutation, the Supreme Court has held that when parole is a possibility, correctional administrators must accord inmates due process. This merely requires that the parole board holds a hearing and provides the inmate with written reasons for its decision to grant or deny parole.

Parole revocations are another matter entirely. Revoking parole was the issue in 1972, when the Supreme Court decided *Morrissey v. Brewer*, the first case in this chapter. A parole revocation means that parole is cancelled and the offender is returned to prison, typically because the parolee has violated one or more conditions of parole or has committed a new crime. The Court held in this landmark case that due process required that parole revocation procedures include at a minimum: "(a) written notice of the claimed violations of parole; (b) disclosure to the parolee of evidence against him; (c) opportunity to be heard in person and to present witnesses and documentary evidence; (d) the right to confront and cross-examine adverse witnesses (unless the hearing officer specifically finds good cause for not allowing confrontation); (e) a 'neutral and detached' hearing body such as a traditional parole board, and (f) a written statement by the fact finders as to the evidence relied on and reasons for revoking parole." The Court reasoned that once an inmate has been paroled, to withdraw that parole entails a "grievous loss of freedom," meriting due process protections.

Morrissey did not address whether the due process rights applied to probation revocation hearings, but this issue was decided the following year in *Gagnon v.*

Scarpelli, 411 U.S. 778 (1973), and is discussed in the next chapter. The Court also did not reach the question of whether the parolee is entitled to legal representation or appointment of legal representation if the parolee is indigent.

The Supreme Court has decided several important cases since *Morrissey* that address the reach of due process in the area of both parole and similar early release programs. For example, the Court ruled that a preparole conditional supervision program is sufficiently like parole so that participants in the program are entitled to the same due process protection as in *Morrissey* (*Young v. Harper*, 520 U.S. 143).

Timing of a revocation hearing is one of the due process protections. The second case briefed in this chapter, *Moody v. Daggett*, established that a parolee recommitted for conviction of a crime committed while on parole is not entitled to a prompt hearing for the revocation of the parole from the original sentence.

The Supreme Court has clearly established that revocation hearings do not merit the same level of constitutional protections as do criminal trials. As mentioned earlier, release on parole is subject to various conditions. One of the most common conditions of parole is a consent to search condition. This condition generally covers searches conducted by parole officers and often allows searches by police officers as well. The scope of the search usually includes the offender's person and property. At issue in *Pennsylvania Board of Probation and Parole v. Scott* was whether a search of a parolee's residence must be based on reasonable suspicion even when the parolee had consented to warrantless searches as a condition of parole, and whether the exclusionary rule of the Fourth Amendment applied to parole revocation hearings. The Court ruled that the exclusionary rule does not apply to revocation hearings, but did not address directly the level of suspicion that must be present prior to a search. However, based on this ruling, even if suspicionless searches are illegal, any evidence obtained during the search would be admissible in a revocation proceeding. The most recent case to address searches of parolees is the last case in this chapter, *Samson v. California*. The Court made clear in Samson that suspicionless searches of parolees do not violate Fourth Amendment protections because of the significantly diminished expectation of privacy that a parolee possesses. Particularly salient to this case was the fact that under California law, all parolees sign a document stating they agree to "search and seizure by a parole officer or other peace officer at any time

of the night or day, with or without a search warrant or with or without cause." California law further finds that such searches are reasonable as long as they are not "arbitrary, capricious or harassing."

Also at issue in a number of cases is the wording of state statutes, which may grant to inmates rights not accorded them under the federal Constitution. In 1979, in *Greenholtz v. Inmates of Nebraska Penal and Correctional Complex*, the Court held that under the Constitution inmates are not entitled to parole and that a discretionary parole release determination does not entitle inmates to due process rights. However, the wording of a Nebraska statute providing for parole did create entitlement to due process as a "state-created liberty interest." Such liberty interests are created when state agencies choose to limit discretionary actions through statutes, rules, or regulations, resulting in limitations that must be followed and invoke due process protections. The *Greenholtz* Court noted, however, that the procedures followed in Nebraska, giving inmates the opportunity to be heard at parole hearings and informing them of reasons they fail to qualify for parole, constitute all of the process due under these circumstances.

In this case, the Court distinguished parole release hearings as markedly different from parole revocation hearings because parole release involves a conditional liberty that one would like to have whereas terminating parole involves taking away a liberty that one already has. Thus, the due process protections are also markedly different. Accordingly, a decision by the Ohio Adult Parole Authority to rescind a parole release order without a hearing did not violate due process because the inmate had not yet been released from prison (*Jago v. Van Curen*). Likewise, inmates do not have protected life or liberty interests in clemency proceedings, hearings allowed in some states to determine whether or not a sentence should be amended (*Ohio Adult Parole Authority v. Woodard*).

Another case briefed in this chapter, *Board of Pardons v. Allen*, is similar to *Greenholtz*. In 1986, the Court ruled that, like the Nebraska statute in *Greenholtz*, a Montana statute's use of the mandatory word "shall" created a presumption that parole release would be granted when certain specific findings were made. This statutory language created a liberty interest in parole, triggering due process protections.

While the use of mandatory language in state statutes and regulations can create protected rights, a frequent practice does not. In 1981, the Court held in

Connecticut Board of Pardons v. Dumschat that a state's practice of granting approximately three-fourths of the applications for commutation of life sentences did not create either a liberty interest or an entitlement so as to require the parole board to explain its reasons for denying an application for commutation.

Another important issue surrounding parole involves the application of new statutes affecting parole considerations and the ex post facto clause. Sections 9 and 10 of Article I of the Constitution forbid states from passing any ex post facto laws, laws which change the legal consequences of an event or action that has already happened. In 1798, the Supreme Court ruled that "the Clause is aimed at laws that "retroactively alter the definition of crimes or increase the punishment for criminal acts" (*Calder v. Bull*, 3 Dall. 386, 391–392). Four cases in this chapter address retroactive application of state statutes affecting parole. In the first case, *Weaver v. Graham*, the Court ruled that a Florida statute reducing the amount of "gain time" prisoners could earn for good conduct and obedience to prison rules was unconstitutional as an ex post facto law if it was applied to prisoners whose crime were committed before the statute's enactment. Likewise, another statute in Florida that canceling early release credits to prison inmates after they were released, resulting in their rearrest and reincarceration, violated ex post facto law (*Lynce v. Mathis*). However, retroactive application of a 1981 California statute reducing the frequency of suitability hearings for parole for prisoners who had been convicted of committing multiple murders was not a violation of the ex post facto clause (*California Department of Corrections v. Morales*). Similarly, a Georgia law extending the time between parole considerations for all prisoners serving life sentences could be applied retroactively without violating ex post facto law (*Garner v. Jones*). Taken together, these cases illustrate that in order to survive a challenge that retroactive application of a statute violates ex post facto law, it must be shown that the statute does not lengthen an inmate's sentence or affect the inmate's ultimate date of release.

One last area relating to parole that has been addressed by the Supreme Court is the issue of liability when parolees commit new crimes. In 1980, the Court found valid a California statute granting absolute immunity to public officials that make parole release determinations (*Martinez v. California*). In this case, a family had sued the state, claiming that the authorities who paroled a sex offender were liable for damages after the parolee murdered their daughter. Five years

before being paroled, the offender had been evaluated as a "Mentally Disordered Sex Offender not amenable to treatment." The Supreme Court recognized the difficulty in deciding when to parole an inmate and noted that any parole release decision involves a measure of risk. However, subjecting such decisions to judicial review would impermissibly hinder states in implementing parole programs. Thus, the Court upheld California's statute that said that public officials were not liable for "[a]ny injury resulting from determining whether to parole or release a prisoner or from determining the terms and conditions of his parole or release or from determining whether to revoke his parole or release."

MORRISSEY v. BREWER
408 U.S. 471 (1972)

FACTS

Morrissey was convicted in 1967 after pleading guilty to falsifying checks. After being paroled from the Iowa State Penitentiary, Morrissey bought a car under an assumed name, gave false statements concerning his address and insurance company after a minor accident, obtained credit under an assumed name, and failed to report his place of residence to his parole officer. These actions constituted violations of his parole, so the parole officer recommended that Morrissey's parole be revoked. Morrissey was arrested as a parole violator seven months after his release. The Iowa Board of Parole revoked his parole and returned Morrissey to the penitentiary. Morrissey filed suit, claiming that since he had received no hearing prior to the revocation of his parole, he was denied due process. Morrissey was joined by another inmate, Booher, whose case was much the same.

ISSUE

Does the due process clause of the Fourteenth Amendment require that a state afford a parolee due process rights prior to revoking his parole?

HOLDING

Yes. While a parole revocation does not call for the full array of rights that are due a defendant in a criminal proceeding, a parolee's loss of liberty does require an informal hearing to ensure that the revocation is based on verified facts. The parolee is entitled to an informal hearing before an impartial hearing officer

MORRISSEY v. BREWER *(cont.)*

near the place of the alleged violation or arrest within a reasonably prompt period of time. At the hearing, the parolee is entitled to the minimum due process requirements, including a notice in writing of the alleged violations, disclosure of the evidence against the parolee, the opportunity to be heard in person and to present evidence and witness, and the right to confront and question adverse witnesses (unless the hearing officer specifically finds good cause for not allowing confrontation). A written statement by the fact finders giving the evidence and reasons relied on for parole revocation must also be provided.

RATIONALE

Writing for the majority, Chief Justice Burger stated that "[i]mplicit in the system's concern with parole violations is the notion that the parolee is entitled to retain his liberty as long as he substantially abides by the conditions of his parole. The first step in a revocation decision thus involves a wholly retrospective factual question: whether the parolee has in fact acted in violation of one or more conditions of his parole. Only if it is determined that the parolee did violate the conditions does the second question arise: should the parolee be recommitted to prison or should other steps be taken to protect society and improve chances of rehabilitation?" Addressing the second question, the Court noted that this decision depends in part on facts but is also predictive and discretionary. The Court noted that a parolee's liberty is valuable and termination of parole is a "grievous loss." Thus, the loss of that liberty is protected by the due process clause of the Fourteenth Amendment calls for some orderly process, however informal. The informal hearing must assure that finding a violation of parole is based on verified facts. The Court addressed the two important stages of the revocation process: the arrest and preliminary hearing, and the revocation hearing. The purpose of a preliminary hearing is to determine whether or not probable cause or reasonable grounds exist to substantiate the claim that the individual has violated parole conditions. The parolee should be given written notice about the preliminary hearing, including a statement of the alleged violations. The parolee may appear at the hearing and speak in his own behalf; he may bring letters, documents, or individuals who can give relevant information to the hearing officer. Upon the parolee's request,

anyone who has given adverse information on which the revocation is to be based should be available for questioning in the parolee's presence, unless the hearing officer determines an adverse risk of harm if the informant's identity were to be disclosed.

The Court noted that the second stage of the revocation process should be a revocation hearing, if desired by the parolee, before the final decision is made: "This hearing must be the basis for more than determining probable cause; it must lead to a final evaluation of any contested relevant facts and consideration of whether the facts as determined warrant revocation. The parolee must have an opportunity to be heard and to show, if he can, that he did not violate the conditions, or, if he did, that circumstances in mitigation suggest that the violation does not warrant revocation." The Court suggested that this hearing should be held within two months of a parolee being taken into custody. The majority opinion acknowledged each state's duty and responsibility to write procedures for parole revocations and then set forth minimum requirements to satisfy due process protections: "(a) written notice of the claimed violations of parole; (b) disclosure to the parolee of evidence against him; (c) opportunity to be heard in person and to present witnesses and documentary evidence; (d) the right to confront and cross-examine adverse witnesses (unless the hearing officer specifically finds good cause for not allowing confrontation); (e) a 'neutral and detached' hearing body such as a traditional parole board, members of which need not be judicial officers or lawyers; and (f) a written statement by the factfinders as to the evidence relied on and reasons for revoking parole."

CASE EXCERPT

"The revocation of parole is not part of a criminal prosecution and thus the full panoply of rights due a defendant in such a proceeding does not apply to parole revocations. Parole arises after the end of the criminal prosecution, including imposition of sentence... Revocation deprives an individual, not of the absolute liberty to which every citizen is entitled, but only of the conditional liberty properly dependent on observance of special parole restrictions."

CASE SIGNIFICANCE

This case is important because it is a landmark case in which the Supreme Court ruled that due process applies to the parole system. Prior to this decision, states were virtually free to revoke parole at will. Most states did hold both probation and parole hearings, and some states provided "trial-type rights including representation by counsel." However, not all states held hearings and procedures that were followed in hearings varied widely from state to state. For example, California's parole revocation hearings were described as "secretive affairs conducted behind closed doors and with no written record of the proceedings." *Morrissey* did not explicitly address whether the due process rights would also apply to probation revocation hearings, although the question would be answered the next year in *Gagnon v. Scarpelli*, 411 U.S. 778 (1973). The Court also did not reach the question of whether the parolee is entitled to legal representation or appointment of legal representation if the parolee is indigent. The question of legal representation led Justices Brennan and Marshall to concur with the majority in the result of the decision but to write separately to state that they would support entitlement to an attorney, including the appointment of an attorney if the parolee is indigent. Justice Douglas dissented in part, writing that he would not specify precise procedures to follow in parole revocations but would hold the following three requirements: (1) a hearing in front of someone other that a parole officer; (2) a due process notice and a due process hearing of the alleged parole violations including the opportunity to be confronted by one's accusers and to present evidence and argument on one's own behalf; and (3) allowing the parolee to remain free pursuant to the results of the hearing. Some controversy arises as to whether or not *Morrissey* requires a two-stage parole revocation process. Many states have merged the preliminary hearing with the final hearing, at which the six enumerated due process protections are provided. To date, most challenges in lower courts to the combined hearing have been unsuccessful. The decision in *Morrissey v. Brewer* also is typically relied upon by inmates seeking due process protections in parole release decisions, revocation of good-time credits, and discretionary prison transfers. While the Court has not equated denial of release on parole or discretionary prison transfers to entail the same "grievous loss of liberty" that a parole revocation entails, limited due process protection is attached to the possibility of loss of good-time credit, but only if there is a state-created liberty interest in good time.

MOODY v. DAGGETT
429 U.S. 78 (1976)

FACTS
In 1962, Moody was convicted of rape on an Indian reservation and sentenced to 10 years. In 1966, Moody was released on parole. While still on parole, he killed two people on the Fort Apache Indian Reservation. At trial, he pleaded guilty and was convicted of manslaughter and second-degree murder, receiving concurrent 10-year sentences for these offenses. After his incarceration, the United States Board of Parole issued a parole violator warrant against Moody, citing his two crimes as a violation of his 1966 parole rules. This warrant was not executed, however, but was lodged with prison officials as a detainer, with the intention of executing the warrant after Moody had finished his second sentence. Moody asked that the warrant be executed immediately so that he could serve that sentence simultaneously with his current sentences. The board refused, and Moody brought suit against the board, petitioning for a writ of habeas corpus, and sought to have the parole violator warrant dismissed because he had not been afforded a prompt hearing at which the issues related to his parole revocation could be addressed.

ISSUE
Is a federal parolee imprisoned for a crime committed while on parole constitutionally entitled to a prompt parole revocation hearing when a parole violator warrant is issued and lodged with the institution of his confinement but not served on him?

HOLDING
No. A federal parolee imprisoned for a crime committed while on parole is not constitutionally entitled to an immediate parole revocation hearing when a parole violator warrant has been issued and lodged with the institution of his confinement as a "detainer," but not executed.

RATIONALE
The Court noted that *Moody* did not present the issue of "whether a *Morrissey*-type hearing will ever be constitutionally required in the present case, but whether a hearing must be held at the present time, before the parolee is taken into custody as a parole violator. We hold that there is no requirement for an immediate

MOODY v. DAGGETT (cont.)

hearing." Moody's loss of liberty at the present time was not due to the outstanding parole violator warrant but to his convictions for two homicides. Moody argued that by not executing the parole violator warrant promptly, he was prevented from the possibility of serving his original sentence for the rape conviction concurrently with his present sentences. Additionally, his eligibility for parole on the present sentences would be delayed, and his classification was adversely affected. He also claimed that delaying the hearing could result in a loss of mitigating evidence. The Court reasoned that the Parole Commission still had the discretion, even after Moody completed the homicide sentences, to dismiss the warrant or hold a hearing and decide not to revoke his parole. If parole revocation was ordered, the Commission had the power "to grant, retroactively, the equivalent of concurrent sentences and to provide for unconditional or conditional release upon completion of the subsequent sentence." As the *Morrissey* Court noted, "A parole hearing is predictive in nature: a decision is made as to the ability of the individual to live in society without committing antisocial acts" (408 U.S. 471 at 480). One of the most pertinent factors in making this decision is the institutional record of the inmate. Thus, it would be more appropriate, in Moody's case, to hold his hearing after he served the intervening sentence. In fact, to hold the hearing shortly after Moody's conviction for the double homicides, as Moody wanted, would almost guarantee a decision to revoke parole. Moody claimed that the pending warrant and detainer affected his prison classification and prevented him from being qualified for institutional programs, thereby violating due process rights. The Court was unsympathetic, noting that "every state action carrying adverse consequences for prison inmates" does not automatically activate due process rights. For example, no due process rights attach when a state prisoner is subjected to a discretionary transfer to another prison, even if the transfer involves a "grievous loss" upon the inmate. Likewise, federal prison officials control prisoner classification and who is eligible for rehabilitative programs, and federal prisoners have "no legitimate statutory or constitutional entitlement sufficient to invoke due process."

CASE EXCERPT

"As a practical matter, in cases such as this, in which the parolee has been convicted of an offense plainly constituting a parole violation, a decision to revoke parole would often be foreordained, so that, given the predictive nature of the parole revocation hearing, it is appropriate that such hearing be held at the time at which prediction as to the parolee's ability to live in society without committing antisocial acts is both most relevant and most accurate—at the expiration of the parolee's intervening sentence."

CASE SIGNIFICANCE

The central issue in this case is whether a parolee, recommitted for conviction of a crime committed while on parole, is still entitled to a prompt hearing for the revocation of the parole from the original sentence. Before this decision, the Circuit Courts of Appeals were divided on this issue. Three appellate courts had held that a parolee convicted of a crime committed while on parole was entitled, through due process, to a prompt parole revocation hearing after the issuance of a parole violator warrant and detainer. Other circuit courts had held that there were no due process requirements. The decision in *Morrissey* had been handed down four years earlier, mandating specific due process protections in a prompt revocation hearing, but the instant case involved whether a hearing must be held at the present time, before the parolee is taken into custody as a parole violator. The dissenting opinion maintained that the critical question in this case is whether the timing of a parole revocation hearing is part of the due process protections to which a parolee is constitutionally entitled. The dissent was of the opinion that an incarcerated parolee possesses a due process right to a reasonably prompt revocation hearing, akin to the already established right of a prisoner to a prompt trial on a second criminal charge, but the majority rejected that argument.

GREENHOLTZ v. INMATES OF NEBRASKA PENAL AND CORRECTIONAL COMPLEX

442 U.S. 1 (1979)

FACTS

Inmates at the Nebraska Penal and Correctional Complex who had been denied parole brought a class action in Federal District Court, claiming that the parole board's procedures for determining parole suitability denied them procedural due process. Under Nebraska statutes, once an inmate has served his minimum term, less good-time credits, he becomes eligible for discretionary parole. There are two stages to this process: an initial hearing and a final hearing. Initial review hearings are held at least once a year for every inmate. The initial hearing is informal, involving the Board of Parole reviewing the inmate's preconfinement and postconfinement record, interviewing the inmate, and considering any documents presented in support of an inmate's release. If the board decides that the inmate is not a good candidate for release, parole can be denied at this point, and the reasons for denial are stated. If the board determines that the inmate is a likely candidate for release, a final hearing is scheduled. At the final hearing, the inmate may present evidence, call witnesses, and be represented by counsel. If parole is denied, the board produces a written document stating the reasons for denial. The inmates claimed in part that the Nebraska statutes and procedures denied them procedural due process.

ISSUE

Does the due process clause of the Fourteenth Amendment apply to discretionary parole determinations made by the Nebraska Board of Parole? Since Nebraska statutes give parole candidates certain rights in the procedures, does this entitle them to due process? Does the Nebraska law regarding parole determination procedures meet constitutional requirements?

HOLDING

No, yes, and yes. The mere possibility of release on parole, unlike parole revocation, does not create an entitlement to due process. The language and structure of the Nebraska statute does create a "liberty interest," entitling inmates to some constitutional protection. The procedures established by the Nebraska law meet constitutional requirements and provide all the process that is due the inmates.

RATIONALE

The Court noted that the "Due Process Clause applies when government action deprives a person of liberty or property" and that alleged violations of due process require analysis of the nature of the individual's liberty or property interest at stake. Accordingly, a valid conviction deprives an inmate of liberty and there is no constitutional right of a convicted person to be released before that valid sentence expires. The majority noted that the inmates relied heavily on the due process standards enumerated in *Morrissey*

v. Brewer. However, *Morrissey* involved a parole revocation decision and "parole release and parole revocation are quite different. There is a crucial distinction between being deprived of a liberty one has, as in parole, and being denied a conditional liberty that one desires." Since the Nebraska statute creates a "statutory expectation" of release, some measure of constitution protection is required, leading the Court to consider whether procedures in addition to the one or two board hearings every year for eligible inmates were mandated. The process followed by the Nebraska Board of Parole was deemed as meeting due process requirements: "The Nebraska procedure affords an opportunity to be heard, and when parole is denied it informs the inmate in what respects he falls short of qualifying for parole; this affords the process that is due under these circumstances. The Constitution does not require more."

CASE EXCERPT

"[T]here is no constitutional or inherent right of a convicted person to be conditionally released before the expiration of a valid sentence. Decisions of the Executive Branch, however serious their impact, do not automatically invoke due process protection; there simply is no constitutional guarantee that all executive decision making must comply with standards that assure error-free determinations."

CASE SIGNIFICANCE

This case is important because it afforded the Court the opportunity to examine the applicability of *Morrissey v. Brewer* and *Gagnon v. Scarpelli* to parole release decisions. In addition, the Court addressed the creation of "state-created liberty interests" in the Nebraska statute. The Court made clear that discretionary parole release decisions are not the same thing as revocations of conditional liberty such as parole or probation revocations. The nature of the interest of parole release is a conditional liberty that one wishes to have; the nature of the interest involved in parole revocation is a liberty that one already possesses. The Court emphasized that the parole-release decision is more subtle than parole termination. Parole revocation involves first determining whether the parolee did in fact violate a parole condition and secondly, whether the parolee should be incarcerated again. Parole release turns on both factual and subjective evaluations by Board members, much "like a prisoner-transfer decision." The Nebraska statute

GREENHOLTZ v. INMATES OF NEBRASKA PENAL AND CORRECTIONAL COMPLEX *(cont.)*

required the parole board to take into account the following factors when making parole release decisions: "(a) Personality, including maturity, stability, sense of responsibility and any apparent development in personality which may promote or hinder conformity to law; (b) Adequacy of the inmate's parole plan; (c) Ability and readiness to assume obligations and undertake responsibilities; (d) Intelligence and training; (e) Family status, including relatives who display an interest or other close and constructive associations in the community; (f) Employment history, occupational skills, and stability of past employment; (g) The type of residence, neighborhood or community in which the offender plans to live; (h) Past use of narcotics, or past habitual and excessive use of alcohol; (i) Mental or physical makeup, including disability or handicap which may affect conformity to law; (j) Prior criminal record, including nature and circumstances, recency, and frequency of previous offenses; (k) Attitude toward law and authority; (l) Conduct in the facility, including opportunities for self-improvement, misconduct within six months prior to his hearing or reconsideration for parole release, loss or restoration of good time or other term reductions at the time of hearing or reconsideration; (m) Offender's behavior and attitude during any previous experience of probation or parole and the how recent this experience was; and (n) Any other factors determined by board to be relevant" (Neb. Rev. Stat. 83–1,114 (2) (1976)). The statute also provided that the board would meet and counsel offenders concerning their progress and prospects for future parole. Allegations were apparently made that there had been eight cases of denial of parole over a two-year period where the letters of denial did not include reasons that parole was denied. The representative from the Parole Board testified that this was not standard practice. The Court observed in a footnote that nothing indicated that the inmates could not have received written reasons for denial if they had requested such statements. Further, a direct challenge to this departure from standard practice would not necessarily have produced the relief sought. The Court concluded that the present procedure was constitutionally adequate since there was no claim made that inmates were seriously hindered from preparing for their hearings.

MARTINEZ v. CALIFORNIA

444 U.S. 277 (1980)

FACTS

A California parolee, Thomas, was originally convicted of attempted rape in 1969. After a time in a state mental hospital as a "Mentally Disordered Sex Offender not amenable to treatment," he was sentenced to one to twenty years imprisonment, with the recommendation that he not be paroled. After five years, Thomas was paroled into the care of his mother. Five months after his release, Thomas tortured and killed a 15-year-old girl. The girl's family brought suit against the state, claiming that the state authorities who released Thomas were liable in damages for the harm he caused. The family maintained that because of Thomas's history and mental health evaluations, the parole officials were aware, or should have been aware, that his release "created a clear and present danger." In their suit, the family stated that the decision to release Thomas was "negligent, reckless, willful, wanton and malicious."

ISSUE

Does the Fourteenth Amendment, which protects deprivation of life by the state without due process of law, invalidate a California statute granting absolute immunity to public employees who make parole release determinations? Are such officials absolutely immune from liability in an action brought under the federal Civil Rights Act of 1871?

HOLDING

No to the first question. The second question was not addressed. The Court ruled that "the state statute is valid when applied to claims arising under state law." With respect to the second issue, the appellants did not allege a claim for relief under federal law.

RATIONALE

The California statute at issue stated that "[n]either a public entity nor a public employee is liable for: (a) Any injury resulting from determining whether to parole or release a prisoner or from determining the terms and conditions of his parole or release or from determining whether to revoke his parole or release." In a unanimous decision, the Court reasoned that the statute merely provided the defense to potential state tort law liability and did not deprive the appellants' decedent of her life without due process of law because it condoned a parole decision that led indirectly to her death. Further, even if the statute could be characterized as a deprivation of property, the state's interest in fashioning its own rules of tort law was paramount to any discernible federal interest, except perhaps an interest in protecting the individual citizen from wholly arbitrary or irrational state action. The Court noted that the statute was not irrational, because the California Legislature could reasonably conclude that judicial review of parole decisions "would inevitably inhibit the exercise of discretion." The Court did not address the second question regarding absolute immunity under federal law (Section 1983), because the family did not allege a claim under federal law. If they had, the claim undoubtedly would have proved unsuccessful, as the Court noted that "[u]nder the particular circumstances where the parolee was in no sense an agent of the parole board, and the board was not aware that appellants' decedent, as distinguished from the public at large, faced any special danger, appellants' decedent's death was too remote a consequence of appellees' action to hold them responsible under Section 1983." The parolee could not be characterized as a state agent nor his action as a state action, which would be a requirement for civil liability under federal law.

CASE EXCERPT

"The statute neither authorized nor immunized the deliberate killing of any human being. It is not the equivalent of a death penalty statute which expressly authorizes state agents to take a person's life after prescribed procedures have been observed. This statute merely provides a defense to potential state tort-law liability. At most, the availability of such a defense may have encouraged members of the parole board to take somewhat greater risks of recidivism in exercising their authority to release prisoners than they otherwise might. But the basic risk that repeat offenses may occur is always present in any parole system."

CASE SIGNIFICANCE

The crucial issue in this case centers around the validity of a state statute that gives public employees absolute immunity from liability for an injury or death resulting from a parole release decision. The Court recognized that any decision to parole an inmate carries with it a measure of risk, but judicial review of

a parole officer's decisions "would inevitably inhibit the exercise of discretion." States could be hindered in implementing parole programs if their decisions were subject to such review. Thus, a state statute that provides absolute immunity for parole officials "rationally furthers a policy that reasonable lawmakers may favor."

CONNECTICUT BOARD OF PARDONS v. DUMSCHAT
452 U.S. 458 (1981)

FACTS

Dumschat, a Connecticut state prisoner serving a life term, applied several times for commutation of his sentence. The Connecticut Board of Pardons rejected each application without explanation. Dumschat sued the board in Federal District Court, stating that it was in violation of the due process clause of the Fourteenth Amendment by not providing him with a written statement of reasons for denying commutation. On the day of the district court's decision, Dumschat's sentence was commuted to time served and he was released. A move to dismiss the suit as moot was filed by the Board of Pardons. However, the lower court allowed other inmates to join this case in a class-action suit. Since the board had granted approximately three-fourths of all applications for commutation of life sentences, the District Court held that all prisoners serving life sentences in Connecticut state prisons were entitled to a written statement of reasons for denial of commutation. The District Court "held that all prisoners serving life sentences in Connecticut state prisons have a constitutionally protected expectancy of commutation and therefore that they have a right to a statement of reasons when commutation is not granted." The appellate court affirmed this decision and on appeal, the Supreme Court vacated and remanded the case to the appellate court for reconsideration in light of the recent decision in *Greenholtz*. The Court of Appeals reaffirmed its original decision, holding that the case at hand was markedly different from *Greenholtz*. The Court of Appeals noted no liberty interest created by the wording of a state statute, as in the Nebraska statute. However, the practice of commuting sentences in Connecticut did, in the appellate court's opinion, create a constitutionally protected liberty interest. The appellate court further interpreted *Greenholtz* to hold

CONNECTICUT BOARD OF PARDONS v. DUMSCHAT *(cont.)*
that a brief statement of reasons for denial of parole, or, in this case, commutation, was constitutionally necessary. The Supreme Court granted certiorari.

ISSUE

Does the fact that the Connecticut Board of Pardons granted approximately three-fourths of the applications for commutation of life sentences create a constitutional "liberty interest" or "entitlement" in life-term inmates so as to require the board to provide reasons for denying an application for commutation?

HOLDING

No. "The power vested in the Connecticut Board of Pardons to commute sentences conferred no rights on respondents beyond the right to seek commutation." Further, "statistical probabilities" by themselves do not give rise to constitutional protections.

RATIONALE

In reversing the Court of Appeals' decision, the Court noted that, while state statutes can create rights that are subject to due process protections, no right to commutation exists. With respect to the Connecticut practice of granting commutations in approximately three-fourths of applications, "[n]o matter how frequently a particular form of clemency has been granted, the statistical probabilities standing alone generate no constitutional protections; a contrary conclusion would trivialize the Constitution. The ground for a constitutional claim, if any, must be found in statutes or other rules defining the obligations of the authority charged with exercising clemency."

CASE EXCERPT

"A decision whether to commute a long-term sentence generally depends not simply on objective factfinding, but also on purely subjective evaluations and on predictions of future behavior by those entrusted with the decision. A commutation decision therefore shares some of the characteristics of a decision whether to grant parole. Far from supporting an 'entitlement,' *Greenholtz* therefore compels the conclusion that an inmate has 'no constitutional or inherent right' to commutation of his sentence."

CASE SIGNIFICANCE

The importance of this case involves whether or not a practice of granting commutations by a state can be seen as a state-created liberty interest. The Nebraska statute at issue in *Greenholtz* created a liberty interest in parole because it "expressly mandated that the Nebraska Board of Parole 'shall' order the inmate's release 'unless' it decided that one of four specified reasons for denial was applicable." In the case at issue here, Connecticut's commutation statute contained no such language and thus created no constitutional entitlement to commutation. Even though Connecticut granted a majority of the requested commutations, "[a] state cannot be required to explain its reasons for a decision when it is not required to act on prescribed grounds."

JAGO v. VAN CUREN
454 U.S. 14 (1981)

FACTS

Van Curen pleaded guilty to embezzlement and related crimes, and was sentenced in Ohio to not less than six nor more than 100 years in prison. He would become eligible for parole in 1976. In 1974, Ohio enacted a statute that allowed for early parole—"shock parole," for first-time offenders who had served more than six months for nonviolent crimes. Van Curen was interviewed in 1974 by a panel representing the Ohio Adult Parole Authority (OAPA), and was recommended for early parole. The recommendation was approved and he was notified of his imminent release. Shortly after the initial interview, however, OAPA was informed that Van Curen had lied in his interview concerning the amount of money he had embezzled and on his parole plan concerning the fact that he intended to live with his homosexual lover (he claimed he would live with his half-brother). OAPA immediately rescinded its decision to grant Van Curen shock parole and formally denied parole at a later hearing. Van Curen was never afforded the opportunity to explain the false statements he made in the interview or on the parole plan. Subsequently, he filed a petition for a writ of habeas corpus, claiming that his Fourteenth Amendment due process rights were violated by rescinding his parole without a hearing.

ISSUE

Should procedural due process be accorded an inmate in rescinding a parole recommendation?

HOLDING

No. In an unsigned (per curium) opinion, the Court held that "[t]he Due Process Clause of the Fourteenth

Amendment was not violated by the Ohio Adult Parole Authority's rescission, without a hearing, of its decision to grant respondent early parole." No protected "liberty" interest in early parole was created by Ohio law.

RATIONALE
The Court noted previous decisions in which they recognized the need to balance the limited protected interests of prisoners against the deference to be accorded penal administrators in the operation of their prison systems. This case did not give rise to the type of important right meriting constitutional protection. Were the Court to rule otherwise would "subject to judicial review a wide spectrum of discretionary actions that traditionally have been the business of prison administrators rather than of the federal courts."

CASE EXCERPT
"We do not doubt that respondent suffered 'grievous loss' upon OAPA's rescission of his parole. But we have previously 'reject[ed]...the notion that any grievous loss visited upon a person by the State is sufficient to invoke the procedural protections of the Due Process Clause.'"... "In this case, as in our previous cases, '[t]he question is not merely the 'weight' of the individual's interest, but whether the nature of the interest is one within the contemplation of the 'liberty or property language of the Fourteenth Amendment.'"

CASE SIGNIFICANCE
This case is important because it follows precedents established in *Greenholtz* and *Dumschat* and sheds further light on the nature of the interest of parole and prerelease expectations of parole. Because he had already been notified of his parole release and steps had been taken toward that release, Van Curen felt that he had a protected liberty interest in parole and that he was entitled to certain due process rights under the Fourteenth Amendment, namely a hearing to explain his false statements. The appellate court agreed with Van Curen, finding the liberty interest to arise from a "mutually explicit understanding" of release on parole. The lower court relied on the 1972 Supreme Court decision in *Perry v. Sindermann*, 408 U.S. 593. The Supreme Court disagreed with the reasoning applied by the lower court, noting that *Sindermann* applies more to protection of property interests that arise through mutually explicit understandings rather than

liberty interests. The Court noted that their previous reasoning in *Greenholtz* and *Dumschat* made clear that liberty interests and not property interests are involved, and no protected liberty interest exists until actual release from prison.

WEAVER v. GRAHAM
450 U.S. 24 (1981)

FACTS
In 1976, Florida prisoner Weaver pleaded guilty to second-degree murder that occurred in January of that year. Weaver was convicted and sentenced to prison for 15 years, less time already served, on May 13, 1976. The state statute in place on both the date the crime occurred and the date he was sentenced provided a formula for deducting gain-time credits from the sentences "of every prisoner who has committed no infraction of the rules or regulations of the division, or of the laws of the state, and who has performed in a faithful, diligent, industrious, orderly and peaceful manner, the work, duties and tasks assigned to him." According to the formula, gain-time credits were to be calculated by the month and were to accumulate at an increasing rate the more time the prisoner had already served. This formula was repealed in 1978, and a new formula implemented on January 1, 1979, which reduced the gain time that could be credited to inmates. The state applied the new formula not only to prisoners sentenced for crimes committed since its enactment in 1978, but also to all other prisoners, including Weaver, whose offenses took place before that date. Weaver, acting pro se, sought a writ of habeas corpus from the Supreme Court of Florida on the ground that the application of the new statute to him was an ex post facto law prohibited by the United States and the Florida Constitutions. He alleged that the new formula would extend his required time in prison by over two years, or approximately 14 percent of his original 15-year sentence. The State Supreme Court summarily denied Weaver's petition, relying on its decision in a companion case raising the same issue where it reasoned that "gain time allowance is an act of grace rather than a vested right and may be withdrawn, modified, or denied."

ISSUE
Is the altering of gain time for good conduct unconstitutional as an ex post facto law when applied to

WEAVER v. GRAHAM *(cont.)*

inmates whose crimes were committed before the statute's enactment?

HOLDING

Yes. The Florida statute reducing the amount of gain time for good conduct and obedience to prison rules deducted from a convicted prisoner's sentence is unconstitutional as an ex post facto law as applied to petitioner, whose crime was committed before the statute's enactment.

RATIONALE

For a criminal or penal law to be ex post facto, it must be retrospective, that is, it must apply to events occurring before its enactment, and it must disadvantage the offender affected by it. Even if a statute merely alters penal provisions accorded by the grace of the legislature, it violates the ex post facto clause if it is both retrospective and more onerous than the law in effect on the date of the offense. The new Florida statute substantially altered the punishment attached to a crime already completed by reducing the gain time available under the old statute. Thus, the Court reasoned that this was a retrospective law which could be constitutionally applied to Weaver and other similarly situated prisoners if it was not to their detriment.

CASE EXCERPT

"On its face, the statute reduces the number of monthly gain-time credits available to an inmate who abides by prison rules and adequately performs his assigned tasks. By definition, this reduction in gain-time accumulation lengthens the period that someone in petitioner's position must spend in prison. In *Lindsey v. Washington*, we reasoned that '[i]t is plainly to the substantial disadvantage of petitioners to be deprived of all opportunity to receive a sentence which would give them freedom from custody and control prior to the expiration of the 15-year term.' Here, petitioner is similarly disadvantaged by the reduced opportunity to shorten his time in prison simply through good conduct."

CASE SIGNIFICANCE

This case is important because it clarifies that states cannot enhance the amount of punishment imposed on offenders by altering the formula used to calculate mandatory reductions to the prison terms of inmates who comply with prison rules and regulations. The

Florida law effectively eliminated the lower end of the possible range of prison terms. During this "get tough on crime" era, some state legislatures have enacted legislation making it more difficult for incarcerated offenders to gain parole. This case establishes that the ex post facto clause protects prisoners during the parole process as well as during sentencing. *Weaver* was followed by *Miller v. Florida*, 482 U.S. 423 (1987), which held that a state could not alter the formula for establishing the presumptive sentencing range for certain sexual offenses. In that case, Miller's presumptive sentencing range was three and one-half to four and one-half years at the time he committed his crime. Before his sentencing, however, the state legislature passed a law that increased his presumptive sentencing range to five and one-half to seven years.

BOARD OF PARDONS v. ALLEN
482 U.S. 369 (1986)

FACTS

In 1984, Allen and Jacobsen, Montana State Prison inmates, were denied parole and subsequently brought a class action suit on behalf of all present and future inmates of the Montana State Prison who were or might become eligible for parole. The complaint charged the State Board of Pardons with violating civil rights and, specifically, not applying statutory criteria in determining parole eligibility, thereby denying due process protection to the inmates. The complaint also stated that the board did not adequately explain its reasons for parole denial.

ISSUE

Do inmates have a liberty interest in parole release that is protected under the due process clause of the Fourteenth Amendment?

HOLDING

Yes. The Montana statute clearly created a liberty interest in parole release that is protected by the due process clause of the Fourteenth Amendment.

RATIONALE

The Court reasoned that although, as in *Greenholtz*, the release decision according to the Montana law is "necessarily subjective and predictive" and the Board's discretion "very broad," nevertheless, the Montana statute, like the Nebraska statute, uses mandatory language ("shall") to create a presumption that parole would be granted when the required findings were made. The Montana statute stated, in part: "(1) Subject to the following restrictions, the board shall release on parole any person confined in the Montana state prison or the women's correction center when in its opinion there is reasonable probability that the prisoner can be released without detriment to the prisoner or to the community. (2) A parole shall be ordered only for the best interests of society and not as an award of clemency or a reduction of sentence or pardon. A prisoner shall be placed on parole only when the board believes that he is able and willing to fulfill the obligations of a law-abiding citizen." The Board of Pardons attempted to distinguish the Montana statute from the Nebraska statute because Montana mandated release on parole "when" certain findings were made and Nebraska mandated release "unless" certain findings were made. The Court rejected this argument, however, noting the similarities between the two statutes in terms of the required findings. Both statutes required the state parole boards to assess the parolee's ability to lead a law-abiding life and the impact of the release on the community. Further, both statutes placed equal discretion on the parole boards.

CASE EXCERPT

"In *Greenholtz*, the Court determined that a scheme awarding officials this type of discretion does not create a liberty interest in parole release. But the term discretion may instead signify that 'an official must use judgment in applying the standards set him [or her] by authority'; in other words, an official has discretion when the standards set by a statutory or regulatory scheme 'cannot be applied mechanically.' The Court determined in *Greenholtz* that the presence of official discretion in this sense is not incompatible with the existence of a liberty interest in parole release when release is *required* after the Board determines (in its broad discretion) that the necessary prerequisites exist."

CASE SIGNIFICANCE

This case follows *Greenholtz* and further informs states as to the type of statutory language that create "state-created liberty interests." The dissent relied on the decision in *Connecticut Board of Pardons v. Dumschat* that "an entitlement is created by statute only if 'particularized standards or criteria' constrain the...relevant decisionmakers." The dissent could find no such constraints and, in addition, questioned the correctness of the *Greenholtz* decision, characterizing it as an "aberration" that should be reexamined. Since *Greenholtz*, lower appellate courts have generally found liberty interests to exist when statutes or regulations use mandatory language or explicitly create a presumption of release. Additionally, if statutes or regulations use highly structured guidelines to constrain the exercise of discretion, courts will find a liberty interest to exist. Courts have been divided when confronted with statutes that provide that "an individual shall not be released unless or shall be released only when certain conditions are met." Most courts find that statutes with such language do set forth criteria that must be met before release on parole, but the statutes do not *require* release upon the requisite findings. Provisions that state that a parole board "may," rather than "shall," release a prisoner on parole do not create liberty interests in parole.

CALIFORNIA DEPARTMENT OF CORRECTIONS v. MORALES

514 U.S. 499 (1995)

FACTS

In 1980, Morales was sentenced to 15 years to life for the murder of his wife and became eligible for parole in 1990. Under the law in place in 1980, Morales was entitled to annual suitability hearings for parole, once he neared his eligibility date. In 1981, however, the California statute was amended to allow the Board of Prison Terms to decrease the frequency of suitability hearings for up to three years for a prisoner convicted of more than one offense involving the taking of a life, if the board finds that it is not reasonable to expect that parole would be granted at a hearing during those intervening years and states the reasons for such a finding. At Morales's 1989 suitability hearing, he was found unsuitable for parole for several reasons, including the fact that he had committed his crime while on parole for an earlier murder. Morales would have been entitled to annual suitability hearings under the law in place when he murdered his wife, but following the terms of the 1981 amendment, the board scheduled Morales's next hearing for 1992. Morales then filed a federal habeas corpus petition, asserting that as applied to him, the 1981 amendment constituted an ex post facto law barred by the United States Constitution. The District Court denied the petition,

CALIFORNIA DEPARTMENT OF CORRECTIONS v.
MORALES *(cont.)*

but the Court of Appeals reversed, holding that the retrospective law made a parole hearing less accessible to Morales, thereby increasing his sentence in violation of the ex post facto clause. The Supreme Court granted certiorari.

ISSUE

Does the 1981 amended law regarding suitability hearings eligibility violate the ex post facto clause in regard to prisoners who committed their crimes before 1981?

HOLDING

No. The Supreme Court ruled that the amended California statute did not violate the ex post facto clause.

RATIONALE

The Supreme Court noted previous decisions in which it had held, in accord with the original understanding of the Constitution, that the ex post facto clause is aimed at laws that "retroactively alter the definition of crimes or increase the punishment for criminal acts." California's 1981 amendment to parole laws did not increase Morales's punishment in that his sentence and procedure for securing reductions in that sentence were unaffected. While the amendment affected the timing of subsequent suitability hearings after the initial hearing, that was only after the board had made specific findings. The amendment did not cause an increase in confinement, especially since it only affected prisoners who had taken more than one life, and that class of prisoners was unlikely to be released on parole in the first place.

CASE EXCERPT

"Even if a prisoner were denied an expedited hearing, there is no reason to think that such postponement would extend any prisoner's actual period of confinement. According to the California Supreme Court, the possibility of immediate release after a finding of suitability for parole is largely theoretical; in many cases, the prisoner's parole release date comes at least several years after a finding of suitability."

CASE SIGNIFICANCE

Article I, 10, of the Constitution forbids states from passing any "ex post facto law," laws which change

the legal consequences of an event or action that has already happened. In 1798, the Supreme Court ruled that "the Clause is aimed at laws that 'retroactively alter the definition of crimes or increase the punishment for criminal acts'" (*Calder v. Bull*, 3 Dall. 386, 391–392 (1798)). Previous cases that the Court had found to violate the ex post facto clause involved new sentence enhancement laws that were applied to crimes already committed. The California amendment did not enhance Morales's sentence or his initial parole eligibility date, and the amendment's purpose was to extend the scheduling of "costly and time-consuming" parole suitability hearings for prisoners who have little or no chance of making parole. Morales maintained that the ex post facto clause prohibited "any legislative change that has any conceivable risk of affecting a prisoner's punishment." The Court was unconvinced and observed that there could be countless changes that might "create some speculative, attenuated risk of affecting a prisoner's actual term of confinement by making it more difficult for him to make a persuasive case for early release, but that fact alone cannot end the matter for ex post facto purposes."

LYNCE v. MATHIS

519 U.S. 433 (1997)

FACTS

In 1986, Lynce was sentenced to 22 years in a Florida state prison for attempted murder. He was released in 1992 on the basis of the determination that he had accumulated five different types of early release credits, which totaled 5, 668 days and included 1,860 days of provisional credits awarded as a result of prison overcrowding. These early release credits had been authorized by the Florida legislature in a series of statutes beginning in 1983. Shortly after Lynce was paroled, Florida's attorney general issued an opinion interpreting a 1992 statute as having retroactively canceled all provisional credits awarded to inmates convicted of murder or attempted murder. Lynce was rearrested and returned to custody, with a new release date of May 19, 1998. In 1994 he filed a petition for a writ of habeas corpus, alleging that canceling retroactively the provisional credits violated the ex post facto clause. Following Eleventh Circuit and Florida precedent, the District Court dismissed his petition for lack of probable cause on the basis that revocation of provisional credits was for the sole purpose of alleviating prison overcrowding and was thus procedural, not creating any substantive rights. The Eleventh Circuit also denied his petition for lack of probable cause. The Court noted a different conclusion in a similar case in the Tenth Circuit and granted certiorari to resolve the conflict.

ISSUE

Is the ex post facto clause violated by a state statute canceling early release credits to prison inmates after they have been released?

HOLDING

Yes. The Court ruled that the 1992 statute canceling provisional release credits violated the ex post facto clause of the Federal Constitution.

RATIONALE

The Court stated that in order to sustain an ex post facto clause violation, a law must affect events that occurred before the law was enacted and it must adversely impact the offender affected by it, either by altering the definition of criminal conduct or increasing the punishment for the crime: "In this case the operation of the 1992 statute to effect the cancellation of overcrowding credits and the consequent reincarceration of petitioner was clearly retrospective. The narrow issue that we must decide is thus whether those consequences disadvantaged petitioner by increasing his punishment." Lynce pointed to an earlier decision in which the Court found a statute that retroactively decreased good time credits violated the ex post facto clause. Lynce reasoned that the overcrowding credits in his case were similar to good time because they were contingent upon good behavior. The respondents reasoned otherwise, suggesting that it was overcrowding in the prison system that gave rise to the award of overcrowding credits. The Court noted that both arguments were faulty because they looked at subjective intent instead of the consequences of the statutes: "[I]n this case, the fact that the generous gain time provisions in Florida's 1983 statute were motivated more by the interest in avoiding overcrowding than by a desire to reward good behavior, is not relevant to the essential inquiry demanded by the Ex Post Facto Clause: whether the cancellation of 1,860 days of accumulated provisional credits had the effect of lengthening petitioner's period of incarceration."

CASE EXCERPT

"Respondents...argue that the 1992 statute does not violate the Ex Post Facto Clause because, like the California amendment at issue in *Morales*, it 'create[d] only the most speculative and attenuated possibility of producing the prohibited effect of increasing the measure of punishment for covered crimes.' Given the fact that this petitioner was actually awarded 1,860 days of provisional credits and the fact that those credits were retroactively canceled as a result of the 1992 amendment, we find this argument singularly unpersuasive."

CASE SIGNIFICANCE

Appellate courts were in conflict at the time of this decision over the constitutionality of state statutes revoking inmates' provisional early release credits when the purpose of those credits was solely to alleviate prison overcrowding. In this case, Lynce had been awarded the overcrowding credits and already released from prison when a new Florida statute amended the applicability of early release credits, canceling eligibility of offenders convicted of murder or attempted murder. Because Lynce fell into this classification, he was rearrested and placed in custody. The legislative history of Florida's amendments with respect to early release credits illustrates the difficulty in managing burgeoning prison populations. In 1983, the Florida state legislature passed the Correctional Reform Act, revising Florida's sentencing laws and providing early release credits. The Act also provided procedures when a state of emergency existed in the correctional system, defined as whenever the inmate population exceeded 98 percent of its lawful capacity. Under such emergency conditions, "the sentences of all inmates in the system who are eligible to earn gain time shall be reduced by the credit of up to 30 days gain time in 5 day increments as may be necessary to reduce the inmate population to 97 percent of lawful capacity." In 1987, the legislature changed the definition of the state of emergency from 98 percent to 99 percent of lawful capacity and implemented a new overcrowding credit, administrative gain time, for some inmates, depending on the offense. The state repealed the administrative gain time provision the following year and replaced it with a provisional credits system—the only difference being that the state of emergency existed when the inmate population reached 97.5 percent of lawful capacity. The legislature expanded the list of crimes that would make offenders ineligible for the credits and cancelled

LYNCE v. MATHIS *(cont.)*

the provisional overcrowding credits for certain classes of inmates. At that time, credits for 2,789 inmates still in custody were canceled, and rearrest warrants were issued for 164 offenders who had been released. Other states have implemented similar mechanisms to deal with overcrowding and face similar issues when statutes are revised and retroactively applied. Two years before *Lynce v. Mathis* was decided, the Supreme Court had decided another ex post facto clause challenge in *California Department of Corrections v. Morales*, concerning a state amendment that decreased the number of parole hearings for certain classes of offenders. The Court in *Morales* found no ex post facto clause violation, holding that the amended law did not lengthen an inmate's sentence or affect his ultimate date of release. Thus, the two cases involve very different issues. The *Lynce* opinion was unanimous, although Justice Thomas, joined by Justice Scalia, wrote a separate opinion, concurring in part and concurring in the judgment.

YOUNG v. HARPER
520 U.S. 143 (1997)

FACTS
In 1990, after serving 15 years of a life sentence for two murders, Oklahoma state prisoner Harper was recommended for parole by the Pardon and Parole Board and released under Oklahoma's Preparole Conditional Supervision Program. At the time of this case, Oklahoma operated two conditional release programs: parole and preparole conditional supervision. Preparole conditional supervision took effect whenever state prisons became overcrowded. Eligibility for preparole was after serving 15 percent of a sentence, whereas parole eligibility came after one-third of a sentence had been served. The Pardon and Parole Board made the determinations for release on preparole, while the governor had the final approval for parole decisions, based on the board's recommendation. Harper spent five "apparently uneventful months" on preparole supervision, but the governor denied him parole. In 1991, his parole officer telephoned him to inform him of the governor's decision, and he had to return back to prison that day. Harper petitioned for a writ of habeas corpus, alleging a denial of due process due to his summary return to prison and deprivation of liberty. The district court denied his petition, but the

Tenth Circuit Court of Appeals reversed, holding that preparole was so closely akin to parole and probation that program participants were entitled to "at least" those due process procedural protections as described in *Morrissey v. Brewer*.

ISSUE
Is Oklahoma's Preparole Conditional Supervision Program sufficiently like parole so that participants are entitled to *Morrissey* due process protections as set forth in the Fourteenth Amendment?

HOLDING
Yes. The Court ruled that Oklahoma's preparole conditional supervision program, as it existed when Harper was released, was equivalent to parole and therefore he was entitled to procedural due process safeguards.

RATIONALE
The Court reasoned that the conditions of the preparole conditional supervision program made it equivalent to parole as understood in *Morrissey*. The petitioners maintained that preparole's purpose of reducing prison overcrowding, and the facts that preparolees continued to serve their sentences and receive earned credits, remaining within the custody of the Department of Corrections sufficiently differentiated the program from parole. In addition, preparolees were aware that they could be transferred to a higher security level if the governor denied parole. But the Court referred to these as "phantom differences"; "Other differences identified by petitioners—that participation in the Program was ordered by the Board, while the Governor conferred parole; that escaped preparolees could be prosecuted as though they had escaped from prison, while escaped parolees were subject only to parole revocation, and that a preparolee could not leave Oklahoma under any circumstances, while a parolee could leave the State with his parole officer's permission—serve only to set preparole apart from the specific terms of parole as it existed in Oklahoma, but not from the more general class of parole identified in *Morrissey*. The Program appears to have differed from parole in name alone."

CASE EXCERPT
"Petitioners contend that reincarceration of a preparolee was nothing more than a 'transfe[r] to a higher degree of confinement' or a 'classification to a more supervised prison environment,'...which,

like transfers within the prison setting, involved no liberty interest. In support of their argument that preparole was merely a lower security classification and not parole, petitioners identify several aspects of the Program said to render it different from parole. Some of these do not, in fact, appear to distinguish the two programs. Others serve only to set preparole apart from the specific terms of parole as it existed in Oklahoma, but not from the more general class of parole identified in *Morrissey*. None of the differences—real or imagined—supports a view of the Program as having been anything other than parole as described in *Morrissey*."

CASE SIGNIFICANCE

This case involves another mechanism by which states may reduce prison overcrowding, Oklahoma's preparole program, and it raises the issue of what constitutional protections attach to such a mechanism. The petitioners in this case believed that preparole should be differentiated from parole and therefore not subject to due process protections as set forth in *Morrissey v. Brewer*. They believed that the controlling case should be *Meachum v. Fano*, 427 U.S. 215 (1976), in which the Court determined that discretionary intrastate prison transfer were "too ephemeral and insubstantial to trigger procedural due process protections" (Id., at 228). One of the ways in which the petitioners sought to distinguish preparole from parole was by looking at the purposes of the two systems. The purpose of preparole was to reduce prison overcrowding, while parole was a way to aid inmate reintegration into society. The Court disagreed that the purposes were so clear-cut and diverse. According to a 1990 Oklahoma statute, parole also could be used to reduce prison overcrowding, and the preparole "[p]rogram's requirement that its participants work or attend school belies the notion that preparole was concerned only with moving bodies outside of teeming prison yards." The petitioners did point to several other differences between preparole and Oklahoma's parole system, such as the different branches responsible for conferring or ordering preparole or parole and how escapes were punished. While the Court agreed that these were real differences, the way preparole was handled was not different from the parole system at issue in *Morrissey*. Thus, *Morrissey* was the controlling case. By applying *Morrissey*, the Court implicitly noted that it is not the purpose or intent of the interest at stake that should be the controlling factor but rather the nature of the interest.

PENNSYLVANIA BOARD OF PROBATION AND PAROLE v. SCOTT
524 U.S. 357 (1998)

FACTS

In 1983, Keith Scott pleaded nolo contendere (no contest) to a charge of third-degree murder and was sentenced to a prison term of 10 to 20 years, beginning on March 31, 1983. On September 1, 1993, Scott was released on parole. Scott was required to sign a form, acknowledging that he would follow these conditions, including any special conditions. The conditions included a requirement that he neither own nor possess any weapons and an agreement, stating in part, "I expressly consent to the search of my person, property and residence, without a warrant by agents of the Pennsylvania Board of Probation and Parole. Any items, in [sic] the possession of which constitutes a violation of parole/reparole shall be subject to seizure, and may be used as evidence in the parole revocation process." About five months later, after obtaining an arrest warrant based on evidence that Scott had violated several conditions of his parole by possessing firearms, consuming alcohol, and assaulting a coworker, three parole officers arrested him at a local diner. Before being transferred to a correctional facility, Scott gave the officers the keys to his residence. The officers entered the home, which was owned by his mother, but did not perform a search for parole violations until Scott's mother arrived. The officers neither requested nor obtained consent to perform the search, but Scott's mother did direct them to his bedroom. In a sitting room adjacent to Scott's bedroom, the officers found four shotguns, a semi-automatic rifle, a compound bow, and three arrows. Scott's mother told the agents that the weapons belonged to her husband, and her husband testified to this at the revocation hearing. Scott testified at the revocation hearing that he did not know that the firearms were in the house and that before his release from prison, he had told his mother and stepfather to get rid of them, and his mother had told him that they had been removed. At his parole violation hearing, Scott objected to the introduction of the evidence obtained during the search of his home on the ground that the search was unreasonable under the Fourth Amendment. He also claimed that his prior consent to a warrantless search was invalid because it was obtained involuntarily, as a requirement of parole eligibility. The hearing examiner, however, rejected

PENNSYLVANIA BOARD OF PROBATION AND PAROLE v. SCOTT *(cont.)*

the challenge and admitted the evidence. At the revocation hearing, Scott's parole agent represented the board and acted as prosecutor. His responsibilities included cross-examining Scott and his witnesses and presenting a closing argument that parole violations had been established. The Pennsylvania Board of Probation and Parole found sufficient evidence in the record to support the weapons and alcohol charges and recommitted Scott to serve 36 months' back time. On appeal, the Commonwealth Court reversed the parole revocation decision and remanded the case for a new hearing. The Pennsylvania Supreme Court affirmed the lower court, holding that Scott's consent to warrantless searches did not extend to searches conducted without at least "reasonable suspicion," and the exclusionary rule should apply to parole revocation hearings when parole officers are aware that the subject of their search is a parolee. The Supreme Court granted certiorari.

ISSUE

Does the federal exclusionary rule prohibiting the introduction of evidence seized in violation of the Fourth Amendment's protections against unreasonable search and seizure apply to parole revocation hearings?

HOLDING

No. The federal exclusionary rule applies only to criminal trial proceedings and thus not to parole revocation hearings.

RATIONALE

In reversing the decision of the Pennsylvania Supreme Court, the majority emphasized that it has not extended the exclusionary rule beyond criminal trials, noting the costs associated with the rule and downplaying the rule's benefits, especially in parole revocation hearings. As parole is a "variation on imprisonment of convicted criminals" and parole revocation deprives a parolee "only of the conditional liberty properly dependent on observance of special parole restrictions," the Court stated that applying the exclusionary rule to revocation hearings would significantly alter the revocation process, transforming hearings "from a predictive and discretionary effort to promote the best interests of both parolees and

society into trial-like proceedings less attuned to the interests of the parolee." The purpose of the rule is deterrence of unlawful police conduct in the investigation and prosecution of crime, while the purpose of parole is different—to rehabilitate the offender while at the same time protecting the community. Since extension of the exclusionary rule to revocation hearings would not serve these dual purposes, and would in fact hamper the effective administration of a parole system, it has no place in such proceedings. Parole officers, according to the Court, are deterred from violating their parolees' Fourth Amendment rights due to their departmental training, discipline, and possible civil liability actions. Although parole officers may act like police officers "in some instances" and "seek to uncover evidence of illegal activity, they…are undoubtedly aware that unconstitutionally seized evidence…could be suppressed in a criminal trial."

CASE EXCERPT

"The exclusionary rule is instead a judicially created means of deterring illegal searches and seizures. *United States v. Calandra*, 414 U.S. 338, 348 (1974). As such, the rule does not 'proscribe the introduction of illegally seized evidence in all proceedings or against all persons,' *Stone v. Powell*, supra, at 486, but applies only in contexts 'where its remedial objectives are thought most efficaciously served,' *United States v. Calandra*, supra, at 348….Moreover, because the rule is prudential rather than constitutionally mandated, we have held it to be applicable only where its deterrence benefits outweigh its 'substantial social costs,' *United States v. Leon*, 468 U.S. , at 907."

CASE SIGNIFICANCE

This case is important because it continues the Supreme Court's trend in limiting the reach of the exclusionary rule and was seen as a major victory for probation and parole officers. The Court here refused to apply the exclusionary rule to a revocation hearing. The effect of this decision is that it leaves offenders in the community with virtually no Fourth Amendment protections. State parole authorities must have greater legal latitude since they deal with individuals who, in light of past criminal activities, are more likely than average citizens to offend again. At the time of this case, lower courts were in conflict over whether a search of a parolee must be based on reasonable suspicion, even when the parolee consents to the search. The Supreme Court had granted certiorari in *Scott* to determine this very issue in addition to the applicability of the exclusionary rule to parole revocation hearings. Scott had been required to sign a Conditions Governing Parole/Reparole form, acknowledging in part that he would "expressly consent to the search of my person, property and residence, without a warrant by agents of the Pennsylvania Board of Probation and Parole." The Court, however, chose not to address the larger question of whether a parolee could consent to any search, despite the fact that the Court had asked the parties to brief and argue that issue in addition to the exclusionary rule issue. Writing for the majority, Justice Thomas did not explain why the Court chose not to resolve this issue, only noting the argument of lack of jurisdiction in a footnote. The Court stated that the jurisdiction question did not need to be resolved, as the Court clearly had jurisdiction on the exclusionary rule question and a ruling on that question was enough to decide the case. Thus, the Court left the question of reasonable suspicion and consent unsettled. The Court's ruling on the inapplicability of the exclusionary rule to revocation proceedings indirectly does answer this question. Even if suspicionless searches are illegal, evidence obtained would not be excluded from the proceedings. In dissent, Justice Souter criticized the majority opinion for characterizing the parole officer-parolee relationship as nonadversarial, particularly in instances such as this case, where the parole officers went to Scott's house to search only after they had already arrested him. The dissent reasoned that in a situation such as this one, the deterrent purpose of the exclusionary rule should apply because the revocation hearing is likely to be the only forum in which the illegally obtained evidence will ever be offered. Parole officers realize that a criminal trial is unlikely and that all they need to do to have their client returned to prison is to find evidence of a parole violation. Justice Souter characterized as "hollow" the Court's argument that parole officers are deterred from constitutional violations because of their departmental training and discipline. Some lower courts had held that the exclusionary rule applies to parole revocation hearings in large part because parole officers today are more akin to law enforcement than social workers and hence involved in investigation of criminal activity with the intent to incarcerate the parolee.

OHIO ADULT PAROLE AUTHORITY v. WOODARD
523 U.S. 272 (1998)

FACTS
Ohio prisoner Woodard received the death penalty for aggravated murder committed in the course of a carjacking. His conviction and sentence were affirmed on appeal in 1994, and he was subsequently scheduled for execution. Under the Ohio Constitution, the governor has the power to grant clemency and the Ohio Adult Parole Authority must conduct clemency hearings within 45 days of scheduled executions. The authority holds the clemency hearing and makes recommendations to the governor. Woodard was informed of his clemency hearing and given the opportunity to participate in a voluntary prehearing clemency interview, at which legal counsel was not allowed. Woodard objected to the short notice of the interview and requested that his attorney be allowed to attend and participate in the interview and hearing. The parole authority did not respond, and Woodard sued, alleging that the clemency process violated his due process rights under the Fourteenth Amendment and his Fifth Amendment right to remain silent. The District Court rejected Woodard's suit, and the Sixth Circuit affirmed the district court's decision in part and reversed in part, holding that a "second strand" of due process analysis applied to post conviction proceedings, including clemency hearings, and that some sort of minimal due process was required. The Circuit Court agreed with Woodard that the voluntary prehearing clemency interview was an unconstitutional violation of the inmate's interest in avoiding making incriminating statements in post conviction proceedings. The Supreme Court granted certiorari.

ISSUE
Does an inmate have a protected life or liberty interest in clemency proceedings? Does the option of voluntarily participating in an interview as part of the clemency process violate an inmate's Fifth Amendment rights?

HOLDING
No to both questions. The Court stated that "[w]e reaffirm our holding in *Dumschat* that 'pardon and

OHIO ADULT PAROLE AUTHORITY v. WOODARD *(cont.)*

commutation decisions have not traditionally been the business of courts; as such, they are rarely, if ever, appropriate subjects for judicial review.'...The Due Process Clause is not violated where, as here, the procedures in question do no more than confirm that the clemency and pardon power is committed, as is our tradition, to the authority of the executive." Secondly, Ohio did not violate Woodard's Fifth Amendment privilege against compelled self-incrimination by giving him the option of voluntarily participating in a clemency interview without the benefit of counsel or a grant of immunity for any statements.

RATIONALE

The Court reversed the appellate court's decision, ruling that "Ohio's clemency procedures do not violate due process." The ultimate decision for clemency rested with the governor, whose broad executive discretion "need not be fettered by the types of procedural protections sought by respondent." There is no substantive expectation of clemency and under *Connor*, "...the availability of clemency, or the manner in which the State conducts clemency proceedings, does not impose 'atypical and significant hardship on the inmate in relation to the ordinary incidents of prison life.'" Further, voluntary participation in a clemency interview does not violate Fifth Amendment rights because inmate testimony is not "compelled."

CASE EXCERPT

"Procedures mandated under the Due Process Clause should be consistent with the nature of the governmental power being invoked. Here, the executive's clemency authority would cease to be a matter of grace committed to the executive authority if it were constrained by the sort of procedural requirements that respondent urges. Respondent is already under a sentence of death, determined to have been lawfully imposed. If clemency is granted, he obtains a benefit; if it is denied, he is no worse off than he was before."

CASE SIGNIFICANCE

The importance of this case lies in establishing what, if any, procedural protections are constitutionally attached to clemency hearings and prehearing interviews: "Clemency, while not required by the Due Process Clause, [is] a significant, traditionally available remedy for preventing miscarriages of justice when judicial process [has been] exhausted." Woodard argued that inmates on death row have a "continuing life interest in clemency broader in scope than the 'original' life interest adjudicated at trial and sentencing"; thus death row inmates were entitled to additional due process protection in clemency hearings. The Court relied in part on its earlier rulings in *Dumschat* and *Greenholtz* in deciding this case. The majority noted that the analysis in *Dumschat* was on the nature of the interest or benefit being sought. *Dumschat* involved sentence commutation, the nature of which was described as a "unilateral hope." Similarly, "[a] death row inmate's petition for clemency is also a 'unilateral hope.' The defendant in effect accepts the finality of the death sentence for purposes of adjudication, and appeals for clemency as a matter of grace." Woodard claimed that because of the state law providing for clemency review, he possessed state-created liberty interests and was entitled to due process, just as the mandatory language of the Nebraska statute created protected liberty interests in parole release as decided by *Greenholtz*. The Court rejected this claim, noting that the ultimate decision to grant clemency rested with the governor.

GARNER v. JONES
529 U.S. 244 (2000)

FACTS

While serving a life sentence for murder in Georgia, Robert Jones escaped from prison and committed a second murder in 1982. Jones was sentenced to a second life term. At the time of Jones's second offense, Georgia law required the state Board of Pardons and Paroles to consider inmates serving life sentences for parole after seven years and if it was not granted at that time, that it be reconsidered every three years thereafter. After Jones was incarcerated but before his first parole hearing, the board amended its rule to require that parole reconsideration take place only once every eight years. Jones was initially considered for parole in 1989, seven years after his 1982 conviction, and parole was denied. Following the amended rule, the board scheduled Jones for parole reconsideration eight years later, in 1997. In 1991, the Eleventh Circuit Court of Appeals ruled that such board actions violated the ex post facto clause and could not be applied retroactively, allowing Jones to be reconsidered for parole in 1992 and again in 1995. Parole was denied both times. In 1995 the Parole Board determined that the Supreme Court decision in *California Dept. of Corrections v. Morales*, 514 U.S. 499 allowed for retroactive adjustments in parole and Jones was scheduled for reconsideration in 2003 (eight years later), rather than 1998. Jones filed suit against the board members, claiming that retroactive application of the amended rule violated the ex post facto clause.

ISSUE
Is the ex post facto clause violated when retroactively applying a Georgia law permitting the extension of intervals between parole considerations?

HOLDING
No. The Court held that the retroactive application of the Georgia provision permitting extension of intervals between parole considerations did not necessarily violate the ex post facto clause.

RATIONALE
The Court reasoned that the key element in deciding whether an increase in time between holding parole hearings violates the ex post facto clause is whether the increase "creates a significant risk of prolonging respondent's incarceration." The Court observed that such a risk had not been demonstrated and reversed and remanded the appellate court's decision. The respondent contended that the Parole Board would not exercise its discretion in deciding how often to reconsider inmates for parole, but the majority stated that the new rules did not support that contention. The lower court had deemed Georgia new amendments to scheduled parole hearings to be inadequate "because, unlike the statute in *Morales*, it does not require the Board 'to make any particularized findings' and is not 'carefully tailored.'" The majority maintained, however, that the "decision in *Morales* did not suggest all States must model their procedures governing consideration for parole after those of California to avoid offending the Ex Post Facto Clause.... We also observed that the Ex Post Facto Clause should not be employed for 'the micromanagement of an endless array of legislative adjustments to parole and sentencing procedures.'"

CASE EXCERPT
"The law changing the frequency of parole reviews is qualified in two important respects. First, the law vests the Parole Board with discretion as to how often to set

an inmate's date for reconsideration, with eight years for the maximum.... Second, the Board's policies permit expedited parole reviews in the event of a change in their circumstance or where the Board receives new information that would warrant a sooner review."

CASE SIGNIFICANCE
The amended Georgia law had two important qualifications that enabled the law to survive the ex post facto clause challenge, as noted above. The law gives the Parole Board discretion in setting new parole review hearings, with a maximum of eight years, and the law allows for expedited reviews upon the receipt of new information or a change in the inmate's circumstances. The Supreme Court, however, did not conclusively state that the Georgia law did not lengthen Jones's period of incarceration. The Court of Appeals had disregarded the internal policy statement of the board as part of its determination as to whether a significant risk of increased punishment was created by the new rule, and Jones maintained that he had not been allowed adequate discovery to show that his incarceration had been increased by the amendment. Accordingly, the Supreme Court remanded this case for further proceedings. This case can perhaps be viewed as another example of the trend toward toughening parole laws. In the dissent by Justice Souter, joined by Justices Ginsburg and Stevens, Justice Souter pointed to the Georgia State Board of Pardons and Paroles official website which states that the Georgia board has consistently amended its policies in order "to increase time served in prison." The new rule applies to the "entire class of life-sentenced prisoners, and the natural inference is that the rule affects prisoners throughout the whole class. This is very different from the situation in *Morales*, in which it was shown that 85% of the affected class were found unsuited for parole upon reconsideration. *Morales*, supra, at 511. At some point, common sense can lead to an inference of a substantial risk of increased punishment, and it does so here." The dissent also found no merit in the suggestion that the new rule in Georgia was to save costs and time in scheduling hearings for inmates with little or no chance of making parole, as was the justification for the amendment in California. In Georgia, "one board member examines an inmate's file without a hearing and makes a decision, and no specific findings are required to deny parole, [so] any interpretation of the rule change as a measure to conserve resources is weak at best, and insufficient to counter the inference of a substantial

GARNER v. JONES *(cont.)*

risk that the prisoners who will get subsequent mandatory parole considerations years after the reviews that the old rule would have guaranteed will in fact serve longer sentences."

SAMSON v. CALIFORNIA
547 U.S. 843 (2006)

FACTS

In 2002, Samson, a California state parolee, was stopped by a police officer and asked if he had an outstanding warrant. Samson replied that there was not an outstanding warrant, which the officer confirmed by radio. The officer then searched Samson, finding a plastic bag containing methamphetamine. Samson was then arrested and charged with possession of said drug. Under California law, prisoners eligible for release on parole "shall agree in writing to be subject to search or seizure by a parole officer or other peace officer at any time of the day or night, with or without a search warrant and with or without cause." At his trial, Samson's counsel moved to suppress the methamphetamine evidence, alleging an unlawful, suspicionless search. The trial court denied this motion and a jury subsequently convicted Samson. The California appellate court affirmed the trial court's conviction, holding that suspicionless searches of parolees are lawful and reasonable under the Fourth Amendment "as long as it is not arbitrary, capricious, or harassing," and finding that the search in Samson's case was none of those. The Supreme Court granted certiorari.

ISSUE

Is a suspicionless search of a released prisoner by a police officer a violation of the Fourth Amendment?

HOLDING

No. The Fourth Amendment does not prohibit a police officer from conducting a suspicionless search of a parolee. Parolees possess significantly reduced privacy rights, and in California, parolees sign agreements that they are "subject to search or seizure by a parole officer or other peace officer.... with or without a search warrant and with or without cause."

RATIONALE

The Court reasoned that California's parole search condition was accepted by Samson and that acceptance diminished significantly any expectation of privacy he might have had. Further, a state's interests in reintegrating parolees are aided by the "ability to conduct suspicionless searches." The Court noted the high number of inmates in California that are on parole, as well as the high recidivism rate, and agreed that the state's ability to supervise its parolees and protect the public would be seriously hindered were the state to be required to base searches of parolees on individualized or reasonable suspicion: "Imposing a reasonable suspicion requirement, as urged by petitioner, would give parolees greater opportunity to anticipate searches and conceal criminality."

CASE EXCERPT

"That some States and the Federal Government require a level of individualized suspicion is of little relevance to our determination whether California's supervisory system is drawn to meet its needs and is reasonable, taking into account a parolee's substantially diminished expectation of privacy... The concern that California's suspicionless search system gives officers unbridled discretion to conduct searches, thereby inflicting dignitary harms that arouse strong resentment in parolees and undermine their ability to reintegrate into productive society, is belied by California's prohibition on 'arbitrary, capricious or harassing' searches."

CASE SIGNIFICANCE

The Supreme Court, in *Griffin v. Wisconsin*, (1987) upheld warrantless searches of probationers based on less than probable cause under the "special needs of law enforcement" exception to the warrant requirement. Under this exception, the requirement of a warrant and probable cause are determined to interfere too greatly with the government's objective of protecting the public and supervising the parolee. Courts must balance the degree of intrusion into an individual's right to privacy with the burden on the government. The Court in *Pennsylvania Board of Probation and Parole v. Scott*, a case presented earlier in this chapter, held that the exclusionary rule does not apply to parole revocation proceedings and involved a warrantless search of Scott's home. The instant case, *Samson v. California*, makes clear that suspicionless searches of a parolee's person by a police officer are constitutionally valid as well, as long as they are not arbitrary, capricious, or harassing. The Court emphasized a parolee's severely diminished privacy expectation, although some observers, including the three-member dissent in this case, see

Samson as an "unprecedented curtailment of liberty." The dissent stated that "[t]he suspicionless search is the very evil the Fourth Amendment was intended to stamp out." While the search in *Griffin* was based on reasonable suspicion, the *Samson* decision does not even mandate reasonableness. Warrantless, suspicionless searches of probationers and parolees are seen as necessary restrictions to protect the community and reflect the public's punitive attitudes toward these intermediate sanctions. Further, substantially greater discretion is now accorded probation and parole officers, as well as law enforcement officials.

DISCUSSION QUESTIONS

1. In *Morrissey v. Brewer*, the Supreme Court did not decide whether a parolee is entitled to legal representation or appointment of legal representation if the parolee is indigent at a revocation. Do you think parolees should be entitled to an attorney at revocation hearings? Discuss.
2. Discuss the distinctions made by the Supreme Court between parole release hearings and parole revocation hearings. Explain why due process applies at revocation hearings but not at parole release hearings.
3. A unanimous Court ruled in *Martinez v. California* 444 U.S. 277 that parole officials in California are not liable for crimes committed by inmates on parole. Do you agree with this decision? Why or why not?
4. Based upon your reading of the briefs in this chapter, what considerations should be made by parole officials before granting parole?
5. Explain what is meant by the following statement: In *Young v. Harper* (520 U.S. 143 (1997)), the Supreme Court relied on the nature of the interest at stake, rather than the intent or purpose of the interest, in applying *Morrissey* due process protections.
6. At issue in *Ohio Adult Parole Authority v. Woodard* (523 U.S. 272 (1998)) were Ohio's clemency proceedings. Explain what these proceedings are. Research your own state's procedures, if any, regarding clemency and commutations of sentences.
7. Do you agree with the Court's controversial decision in *Pennsylvania Board of Probation and Parole v. Scott*, 524 U.S. 357 (1998)? Why or why not?
8. Discuss both the majority and dissenting opinions in *Pennsylvania Board of Probation and Parole v. Scott*.
9. Several cases briefed in this chapter can be seen as part of a national trend toward toughening parole laws. Identify these cases and explain in what way they are part of the "get-tough-on-crime" trend.
10. Defend the argument that suspicionless searches of parolees are necessary to promote reintegration and to prevent recidivism. Next, defend the argument that suspicionless search are counterproductive to the tenets of rehabilitation and reintegration.

CHAPTER TWELVE

PROBATION

EX PARTE UNITED STATES (KILLITS),
242 U.S. 27 (1916)

MEMPA v. RHAY, *389 U.S. 128 (1967)*

GAGNON v.. SCARPELLI, *411 U.S. 778 (1973)*

CABELL v.. CHAVEZ-SALIDO, *454 U.S. 432 (1982)*

BEARDEN v.. GEORGIA, *461 U.S. 660 (1983)*

MINNESOTA v.. MURPHY, *465 U.S. 420 (1984)*

BLACK v.. ROMANO, *471 U.S. 606 (1985)*

GRIFFIN v.. WISCONSIN, *483 U.S. 868 (1987)*

FORRESTER v.. WHITE, *484 U.S. 219 (1988)*

ALDEN v.. MAINE, *527 U.S. 706 (1999)*

INTRODUCTION

Like offenders on parole, offenders on probation are under community supervision. Unlike parole, however, probation is a sentence releasing the convicted criminal offender into the community, under the supervision of a probation officer, and in place of any period of incarceration. In 1943 the Supreme Court described the purpose of probation as "…namely to provide an individualized program offering a young or unhardened offender an opportunity to rehabilitate himself without institutional confinement under the tutelage of a probation official and under the continuing power of the court to impose institutional punishment for his original offense in the event that he abuse this opportunity" (*Roberts v. United States*, 320 U.S. 264 at 272 (1943)). In a dissenting opinion to this case, Justice Frankfurter referred to probation as a "testing period" (*Roberts v. United States* at 276.)

This chapter begins with *Ex Parte United States (Killits)*, 242 U.S. 27, a case heard by the Supreme Court in 1916, and involving a type of probation system but without state law establishing such a system. Judge Killits, a lower court judge in Ohio, had suspended the prison sentence of a convicted embezzler, pointing to the circumstances of the crime, the offender's background, the willingness of his employers to forgive him, and the support of his friends, church,

and community. Such reasons are among the factors considered today in deciding whether a sentence to a period of probation is more appropriate than a prison sentence. In 1916, judicial discretionary power did not extend to permanent suspensions of sentences. The Supreme Court did allow that one way to remedy the situation was for legislatures to establish systems of probation or other mechanisms which would allow the exercise of judicial discretion.

All states today have some system of probation. According to a recent publication by the Bureau of Justice Statistics, "Probation and Parole Statistics," by the end of 2001, approximately 4 million adults were on probation in the United States. The remaining nine cases briefed in this chapter concern various rights of probationers or significant issues affecting probation officers.

In 1967, the Court ruled that under the Sixth Amendment, applied through the due process clause of the Fourteenth Amendment, a felony probationer is entitled to be represented by appointed counsel at a combined probation revocation and sentencing hearing (*Mempa v. Rhay*, 389 U.S. 128). It is important to note that the Court did not rule in this case that individuals have the right to counsel at a probation revocation hearing; it is only when deferred sentencing is being imposed at a probation revocation hearing that the right to counsel exists.

Recall from chapter 11 that in 1972, the Supreme Court decided in *Morrissey v. Brewer* (408 U.S. 471) that parole revocation procedures require specific due process protections. The following year, the Court ruled that the same due process procedures apply to probation revocation hearings (*Gagnon v. Scarpelli*, 411 U.S. 778 (1973)). The Court reasoned that despite minimal differences between parole and probation, revocation of either status entails a significant loss of liberty. The Court was reluctant in Gagnon to decide that indigent probationers and parolees are entitled to appointed counsel at revocation proceedings primarily because this right would change the nature of the nonadversarial proceeding into an adversarial process. The Court concluded that the right to counsel for an indigent probationer or parolee should be decided on a case by case basis.

A common condition for probationers is a requirement that they make restitution, if appropriate, and/or pay fines. In 1983, the Supreme Court ruled that indigent probationers can not have their probation revoked solely because of their inability to pay the fines or restitution (*Bearden v. Georgia*, 461 U.S. 660). If a probationer has made genuine attempts to find a job and pay his fines but is unable to do so, a sentencing court must consider alternative forms of punishment other than incarceration. If alternative forms will not accomplish the purposes of punishment and deterrence, then the probationer may be imprisoned. On the other hand, if a probationer simply refuses or does not make genuine efforts to acquire the money to pay fines or make restitution, then probation may be revoked and the probationer sentenced to prison. While *Bearden* mandates that alternatives to incarceration should be considered in certain circumstances, the Court ruled in 1985 that the procedures to be followed in revocation hearings as established by *Morrissey* and *Gagnon* do not include requiring a consideration of alternatives to incarceration (*Black v. Romano*, 471 U.S. 606).

While on probation, individuals obviously have limited constitutional rights, and probation officers supervising probationers can follow somewhat broader procedures than can police officers. Two cases briefed in this chapter illustrate these facts. In 1984, in *Minnesota v. Murphy,* 465 U.S. 420, the Court held that the Fifth and Fourteenth Amendments did not prohibit the introduction into evidence of a probationer's admissions to a probation officer in a subsequent

criminal prosecution. This case involved a probationer who admitted to his probation officer that he had committed a rape and murder seven years prior. He was subsequently arrested and indicted. He tried unsuccessfully to suppress the confession he made to the probation officer on the grounds that he had not been given his Miranda warnings. The Supreme Court reasoned that there was nothing preventing him from claiming the privilege against self-incrimination, nor did his probation officer need to give him Miranda warnings because he was not in custody or under arrest when he met with the officer. In dissent, Justice Marshall observed, "[i]t is to be hoped...that persons currently on probation who are no longer represented by counsel will somehow be informed of the central principle established by the Court's decision: that a probationer has a right to refuse to respond to a question the answer to which might expose him to criminal liability unless he is granted immunity from the use of his answer against him in a subsequent criminal prosecution." Three years later, in 1987, the Court upheld a Wisconsin law that permitted any probation officer to search a probationer's home without a warrant but based on "reasonable suspicion" (*Griffin v. Wisconsin*, 483 U.S. 868). This decision recognizes a "special needs" exception to Fourth Amendment requirements that searches be based on probable cause and with a warrant. The Court observed that warrantless searches are permitted when "special needs, beyond the normal need for law enforcement, make the warrant and probable-cause requirement impracticable." Accordingly, the operation of a probation system presents such special needs.

Three other cases briefed in this chapter affect probation officers rather than probationers. The Court has upheld a California statute that requires probation officers to be American citizens (*Cabell v. Chavez-Salido*, 454 U.S. 432 (1982)). In *Forrester v. White*, 484 U.S. 219 (1988), the Court held that a judge does not have absolute immunity from damages for his decision to demote and fire a court employee, specifically a probation officer. In this case, the probation officer had sued, alleging sex discrimination in violation of the equal protection clause of the Fourteenth Amendment. On the other hand, the Court has also held that nonconsenting states can not be sued by private parties in state courts (*Alden v. Maine*, 527 U.S. 706 (1999)). This case concerned a group of probation officers who had sued the state of Maine for overtime pay and damages under the Fair Labor Standards Act.

The Court pointed to earlier decisions noting that the principle of state sovereignty means that a state can not be sued by its own citizens without the state's consent.

EX PARTE UNITED STATES (KILLITS)
242 U.S. 27 (1916)

FACTS
The accused, a bank officer, pleaded guilty to several counts of embezzlement. He was sentenced to five years imprisonment, the shortest term under the statute which could have been imposed. Over the objection of the US district attorney, the court (the Honorable John Killits, judge of the District Court for the Northern District of Ohio) ordered that the sentence be suspended permanently, dependent upon the offender's good behavior. The district attorney moved to set this order aside because it was not merely a temporary suspension of the sentence to enable legal proceedings pending or contemplated to be revised, or application for pardon to be made, or any other legal relief against the sentence. As a permanent suspension based upon considerations unrelated to the legality of the conviction or the duty to enforce the sentence, the suspension was essentially a refusal to carry out the statute.

ISSUE
Can courts permanently suspend sentences under inherent judicial power or common law?

HOLDING
No. Such a suspension—the legal equivalent of an absolute and permanent refusal to impose any sentence under the statute—was beyond the power of the court. Courts have no inherent constitutional power to diminish or prevent penalties provided by law. Further, "at common law, while the courts exercised a discretion to suspend either imposition or execution of sentence temporarily for purposes and in ways consistent with the due enforcement of the penal laws, so as to facilitate action by the pardoning power and avoid miscarriages of justice, they neither possessed nor claimed the power of permanent refusal to enforce them."

RATIONALE
In a decision written by Chief Justice White, the Court held that "such a suspension — the legal equivalent of an absolute and permanent refusal to impose any sentence under the statute -- was beyond the power of the court." Courts have no inherent constitutional power to diminish or prevent penalties provided by law. Further, "at common law, while the courts exercised a discretion to suspend either imposition or execution of sentence temporarily for purposes and in ways consistent with the due enforcement of the penal laws, so as to facilitate action by the pardoning power and avoid miscarriages of justice, they neither possessed nor claimed the power of permanent refusal to enforce them." The district court reasoned that a permanent suspension was warranted because of the circumstances of the crime, the offender's background, the willingness of his employers to forgive him, and the support of his friends, church, and community. All of the offender's supporters were "unanimous in the belief that the exposure and humiliation of his conviction are a sufficient punishment, and that he can be saved to the good of society if nothing further is done with him." The Supreme Court was unsympathetic and stated that "we are admonished that no authority exists to cure wrongs resulting from a violation of the Constitution in the past, however meritorious may have been the motive giving rise to it, by sanctioning a disregard of that instrument in the future." Chief Justice White allowed that one way to remedy the situation was through applying for a pardon, or, in the future, legislatures can establish systems of probation or other mechanisms which would allow the exercise of judicial discretion. Absent such laws, judicial discretionary power does not extend to permanent suspensions of sentences.

CASE EXCERPT
"[T]he possession by the judicial department of power to permanently refuse to enforce a law would result in the destruction of the conceded powers of the other departments, and hence leave no law to be enforced."

CASE SIGNIFICANCE
This 1916 case in effect placed an offender on a type of system of probation but without existing state law establishing such a system. Judge Killits asserted the court's right to impose a permanent suspension, and thereby refused to impose the sentence fixed by law for four reasons: (1) inherent judicial power; (2) a right established by common law; (3) prevailing federal and state court decisions; and (4) prevailing practice. The Supreme Court found none of these arguments to be

viable. Common law grants the right to suspend a sentence only temporarily in order to obtain a pardon or to prevent some other violation of the law or miscarriage of justice. The Court found, in a review of state cases, that most state cases found the power to permanently suspend a sentence did not exist. The cases relied upon to show that the power did exist were either weakly reasoned or the power to suspend the sentence was sanctioned implicitly by state law. There was only one applicable federal case, and that particular case decision did not find that the power existed. As far as the reason of prevailing practice, the Court acknowledged that the practice did exist. In Massachusetts, for example, the practice of "laying the case on file" had existed for the past sixty years. However, the Court emphasized that this practice was "by no means universal," and "[t]he fact that it is said in argument that many persons, exceeding two thousand, are now at large who otherwise would be imprisoned as the result of the exertion of the power in the past, and that misery and anguish and miscarriage of justice may come to many innocent persons by now declaring the practice illegal, presents a grave situation."

MEMPA v. RHAY
389 U.S. 128 (1967)

FACTS

Two cases were combined in this case. In the first case, 17-year old Mempa received two years probation in Washington State after pleading guilty, "with the advice of court-appointed counsel," to "joyriding." Under state law, the sentence was deferred. When Mempa was involved in a burglary about four months later, the prosecutor moved to have his probation revoked. Mempa "was not represented by counsel, was not asked about his previous court-appointed counsel, or if he wanted counsel" at his revocation hearing. A probation officer gave testimony regarding Mempa's involvement in the burglary and also testified to Mempa's denial of that involvement, although Mempa did not deny his involvement at the revocation hearing. The court revoked Mempa's probation, imposing the maximum ten year sentence with a recommendation to the parole board that Mempa serve one year. Mempa filed a petition for a writ of habeas corpus in the Washington State Supreme Court, alleging that he was denied his right to counsel at the probation revocation hearing. This petition was denied.

The second case, *Walkling v. Washington State Board of Prison Terms and Paroles,* involved similar issues. Walkling pled guilty, on advice of his private attorney, to second degree burglary and received three years probation with sentence deferment. He was arrested over one year later and charged with committing forgery and grand larceny while on probation. His probation revocation hearing was continued for one week to allow him to retain an attorney, but Walkling appeared at the hearing without counsel. He told the court that he did have an attorney, and the court waited for fifteen minutes for the attorney to appear. The court then "proceeded with the hearing in the absence of counsel and without offering to appoint counsel." Walkling's probation was revoked based upon hearsay testimony by a probation officer that Walkling had committed the crimes, and the second degree burglary charge's deferred sentence of fifteen years maximum was imposed. Walkling petitioned for a writ of habeas corpus with the Washington State Supreme Court one year later, alleging the denial of the right to counsel at the combined hearings for probation revocation and sentencing. The petition was denied based on the state court's previous ruling in Mempa's case, which had been heard a short time before. The Supreme Court granted certiorari and the two cases were joined for argument.

ISSUE

Does a defendant have a right to counsel at the imposition of a sentence that was deferred subject to probation?

HOLDING

Yes. The Sixth Amendment, as applied through the due process clause of the Fourteenth Amendment, requires that counsel be afforded to a felony defendant in a posttrial proceeding for revocation of his probation and imposition of deferred sentencing.

RATIONALE

In a decision written by Justice Marshall, the Court reasoned that sentencing hearings are critical stages requiring assistance of counsel "to ensure that the conviction and sentence are not based on misinformation or a misreading of court records." The State's argument was that felony probationers were sentenced at the time they were given probation, so imposing the sentence after a revocation was only "a mere formality." Judges were restricted by state law

MEMPA v. RHAY *(cont.)*

from exercising any discretion in the sentence and were required to impose the maximum sentence, with actual time served to be determined by the parole board. The Court noted though that judges and prosecutors are required to give information to the board about the offender and the criminal acts, so counsel for defendants would have the opportunity to assist in that "marshaling of facts." Further, the right to appeal would be protected by the assistance of counsel, especially in cases such as these two that involved guilty pleas to the initial offenses. At the probation revocation stage, it was possible to withdraw those guilty pleas, and counsel was necessary to make defendants aware of that right.

CASE EXCERPT

"[I]n a case where an accused agreed to plead guilty, although he had a valid defense, because he was offered probation, absence of counsel at the imposition of the deferred sentence might well result in loss of the right to appeal."

CASE SIGNIFICANCE

Prior to 1963, the prevailing decision in *Betts v. Brady*, 316 U.S. 455 (1942) was that the right to counsel depended on various "special circumstances." In 1963, however, *Betts* was overruled by *Gideon v. Wainwright*, 372 U.S. 335, with the Court holding that "the Sixth Amendment as applied through the Due Process Clause of the Fourteenth Amendment was applicable to the States and, accordingly, that there was an absolute right to appointment of counsel in felony cases." Cases prior to *Gideon* established the right to counsel for an indigent "at every stage of a criminal proceeding where substantial rights of a criminal accused may be affected." In the two consolidated cases at hand, both Mempa and Walkling had already been sentenced before they were placed on probation. Thus, the state maintained that the imposition of their sentences at the probation revocation hearings were only mere formalities. While Justice Marshall acknowledged that the Board of Prison Terms and Paroles would actually determine the length of incarceration, both the sentencing judge and prosecutor are required to submit recommendations and information relating to the crime and character of the offender. Counsel would thus be of help to the defendant in presenting any mitigating circumstances or other evidence in the defendant's favor. Washington law also provided

that a case in which the defendant pleads guilty and is given probation can not be appealed unless probation is revoked and the sentence is imposed. Washington law also gave a judge the discretion to allow a guilty plea to be withdrawn at any time prior to the imposition of sentence, if it would serve the ends of justice. Counsel thus is necessary to make defendants aware of this opportunity at a probation revocation, especially since in the cases at hand, the sentences being imposed are actually based on the "alleged commission of offenses for which the accused is never tried." It is important to note that the Court did not rule in this case that individuals have the right to counsel at a probation revocation hearing; it is only when deferred sentencing is being imposed at a probation revocation hearing that the right to counsel exists.

GAGNON v. SCARPELLI
411 U.S. 778 (1973)

FACTS

Gerald Scarpelli, a felony probationer from Wisconsin, was arrested after committing a burglary the day after he was accepted for probation supervision in Illinois. He admitted involvement in the crime, but later claimed that the admission was made under duress, and was false. Scarpelli's probation was revoked by the Wisconsin Department without a hearing and without counsel representation. He was incarcerated at the Wisconsin State Reformatory to begin serving the original 15-year sentence.

ISSUE

Is a previously sentenced probationer entitled to a hearing when his probation is revoked? If so, is he entitled to be represented by appointed counsel at such a hearing?

HOLDING

"1. Due process mandates preliminary and final revocation hearings in the case of a probationer under the same conditions as are specified in *Morrissey v. Brewer*, 408 U.S. 471, in the case of a parolee. 2. The body conducting the hearings should decide in each individual case whether due process requires that an indigent probationer or parolee be represented by counsel. Though the State is not constitutionally obliged to provide counsel in all cases, it should do so where the indigent probationer or parolee may have difficulty in presenting his version of disputed facts without the examination or cross-examination of witnesses or the presentation of complicated documentary evidence. Presumptively, counsel should be provided where, after being informed of his right, the probationer or parolee requests counsel, based on a timely and colorable claim that he has not committed the alleged violation or, if the violation is a matter of public record or uncontested, there are substantial reasons in justification or mitigation that make revocation inappropriate. 3. In every case where a request for counsel is refused, the grounds for refusal should be stated succinctly in the record."

RATIONALE

The Court reasoned that probation revocation was the same as a revocation of parole for purposes of due process protections. While neither revocation is a stage of a criminal prosecution, they both entail a grievous loss of liberty. Thus, as the Court held in *Morrissey*, individuals are entitled to limited due process protections of a preliminary and final revocation hearing. The question of whether or not indigent probationers and parolees are entitled to appointed counsel is a more difficult question. The Court concluded that the right to counsel for an indigent probationer or parolee should be decided on a case by case basis. While counsel would probably not be required in most revocation proceedings, "it may be said that counsel should be provided in cases where, after being informed of his right to request counsel, the probationer or parolee makes such a request, based on a timely and colorable claim (i) that he has not committed the alleged violation of the conditions upon which he is at liberty; or (ii) that, even if the violation is a matter of public record or is uncontested, there are substantial reasons which justified or mitigated the violation and make revocation inappropriate, and that the reasons are complex or otherwise difficult to develop or present. In passing on a request for the appointment of counsel, the responsible agency also should consider, especially in doubtful cases, whether the probationer appears to be capable of speaking effectively for himself. In every case in which a request for counsel at a preliminary or final hearing is refused, the grounds for refusal should be stated succinctly in the record."

CASE EXCERPT

"Introduction of counsel into a revocation proceeding will alter significantly the nature of the proceeding. If counsel is provided for the probationer or parolee, the State in turn will normally provide its own counsel; lawyers, by training and disposition, are advocates and bound by professional duty to present all available evidence and arguments in support of their clients' positions and to contest with vigor all adverse evidence and views. The role of the hearing body itself, aptly described in *Morrissey* as being 'predictive and discretionary' as well as factfinding, may become more akin to that of a judge at a trial, and less attuned to the rehabilitative needs of the individual probationer or parolee. In the greater self-consciousness of its quasi-judicial role, the hearing body may be less tolerant of marginal deviant behavior and feel more pressure to reincarcerate than to continue nonpunitive rehabilitation."

CASE SIGNIFICANCE

This case, coming before the Court a year after the landmark *Morrissey* decision, gave the Court the opportunity to extend the limited *Morrissey* due process protections to probation revocation proceedings. Despite minimal differences between parole and probation, revocation of either status entails a significant loss of liberty. Justice Powell noted that "[i]t is clear at least after *Morrissey v. Brewer*, 408 U.S. 471 (1972), that a probationer can no longer be denied due process, in reliance on the dictum...that probation is an 'act of grace.'" Still unsettled was the question regarding the need for counsel at probation and parole revocations, specifically the right to appointed counsel for indigent probationers or parolees. In 1967, the Court held in *Mempa v. Rhay*, 389 U.S. 128 (1967), that a probationer is entitled to be represented by appointed counsel at a combined revocation and sentencing hearing. In *Mempa*, sentencing was deferred when the offender was placed on probation and was being imposed at the revocation hearing. The Court had reasoned that "counsel is required 'at every stage of a criminal proceeding where substantial rights of a criminal accused may be affected.'" Mempa, however, was found to not apply to the instant case because Scarpelli had been sentenced at his trial. The Court was reluctant in this case to decide that indigent probationers and parolees are entitled to appointed counsel at revocation proceedings primarily because this right would change the nature of the nonadversarial proceeding into an adversarial process. In the case at hand, the Court stated that Scarpelli's admission to the burglary was the kind of situation where counsel would not need to be provided. However, given that he later said he did not commit

GAGNON v. SCARPELLI *(cont.)*

the burglary and that his admission was made under duress, the decision by the Wisconsin department not to provide him with counsel should be reexamined.

CABELL v. CHAVEZ-SALIDO
454 U.S. 432 (1982)

FACTS

California Government Code requires "public officers or employees declared by law to be peace officers" to be United States citizens. Since California probation officers are considered to be "peace officers," they must be American citizens. A class action suit was filed by a group of lawfully admitted permanent resident aliens who had unsuccessfully applied for positions as deputy probation officers in Los Angeles County. They claimed violation of the equal protection clause of the Fourteenth Amendment and sought declaratory, injunctive, and other relief.

ISSUE

Is statutory citizenship an unconstitutional requirement for probation officers and deputy probation officers?

HOLDING

No. Statutory citizenship is not an unconstitutional requirement.

RATIONALE

Because probation officers partake of the government's power to exercise force over an individual, it is important that they have citizenship status. Although the range of individuals over whom such officers exercise supervisory authority is limited, the officers' power with respect to those individuals is broad.

CASE EXCERPT

"A citizenship requirement is an appropriate limitation on those who exercise and, therefore, symbolize this power of the political community over those who fall within its jurisdiction."

CASE SIGNIFICANCE

In this case, the lower court had agreed with the permanent resident aliens that the statutory citizenship requirement imposed upon probation officers in California was a violation of the equal protection clause. In 1978, the Supreme Court vacated and remanded that judgment for further consideration. The Supreme Court had upheld both a New York statute that required state troopers to be citizens and a statute that allowed a state to deny employment to elementary and secondary school teachers who are aliens eligible for United States citizenship but who fail to seek naturalization. The lower district court reconsidered the case at hand but reached the same conclusion as before that the California statute violated the equal protection clause. Upon subsequent appeal in the case at hand, the Supreme Court reversed the lower court's judgment. Writing for the majority, Justice White stated: "One need not take an overly idealistic view of the educational functions of the probation officer ... to recognize that the probation officer acts as an extension of the judiciary's authority to set the conditions under which particular individuals will lead their lives and of the executive's authority to coerce obedience to those conditions. From the perspective of the probationer, his probation officer may personify the State's sovereign powers; from the perspective of the larger community, the probation officer may symbolize the political community's control over, and thus responsibility for, those who have been found to have violated the norms of social order. From both of these perspectives, a citizenship requirement may seem an appropriate limitation on those who would exercise and, therefore, symbolize this power of the political community over those who fall within its jurisdiction." While state laws that discriminate against legal aliens are usually subject to strict scrutiny, the highest standard of review, the lower standard of rational basis review is appropriate for state laws that ban aliens from certain positions with "political functions," and "[i]n those areas the State's exclusion of aliens need not 'clear the high hurdle of `strict scrutiny,' because [that] would 'obliterate all the distinctions between citizens and aliens, and thus depreciate the historic value of citizenship,'" Foley v. Connelie, 435 U.S. 291 (1978) at 295.

BEARDEN v. GEORGIA
461 U.S. 660 (1983)

FACTS

In 1980, Bearden pleaded guilty in a Georgia trial court to burglary and theft by receiving stolen property, but the court, pursuant to the Georgia First Offender's Act, sentenced him to probation on the condition that he pay a $500 fine and $250 in restitution, with $100 payable that day, $100 the next day, and the $550 balance within four months. Bearden borrowed money and paid the first $200, but about a month later he was laid off from his job, and, despite repeated efforts, was unable to find other work. Shortly before the $550 balance became due, he notified the probation office that his payment was going to be late. The state then filed a petition to revoke Bearden's probation because he had not paid the balance, and the trial court, after a hearing, revoked probation, entered a conviction, and sentenced him to prison. The record of the hearing disclosed that Bearden had been unable to find employment and was indigent. Bearden subsequently filed suit, alleging equal protection violations under the Fourteenth Amendment due to imprisoning him for inability to pay his fine and make restitution.

ISSUE

Yes. Does the Fourteenth Amendment prohibit a state from revoking an indigent defendant's probation for failure to pay a fine and restitution?

HOLDING

The Fourteenth Amendment prohibits a state from revoking an indigent defendant's probation for failure to pay a fine and restitution without determining that he or she had not made sufficient bona fide efforts to pay or that adequate alternative forms of punishment did not exist.

RATIONALE

In this decision, the Court noted its tradition of being "sensitive to the treatment of indigents in our criminal justice system," and quoted an observation from Justice Black in 1956 that "[t]here can be no equal justice where the kind of trial a man gets depends on the amount of money he has" (in *Griffin v. Illinois*, 351 U.S. 12, 19 (1956). The Court noted that the most relevant case to Beardon was its holding in *Williams v. Illinois*, 399 U.S. 235 (1970). In *Williams*, the Court ruled that convicted indigent defendants cannot be imprisoned beyond the statutory maximum solely because they are too poor to pay the fine. This decision was extended in *Tate v. Short*, 401 U.S. 395 (1971), where the Court held "that a State cannot convert a fine imposed under a fine-only statute into a jail term solely because the defendant is indigent and cannot immediately pay the fine in full." In the case at hand, "[t]he question presented here is whether a sentencing court can revoke a defendant's probation for failure to pay the imposed fine and restitution, absent evidence and findings that

the defendant was somehow responsible for the failure or that alternative forms of punishment were inadequate.... There is no doubt that the State has treated the petitioner differently from a person who did not fail to pay the imposed fine and therefore did not violate probation. To determine whether this differential treatment violates the Equal Protection Clause, one must determine whether, and under what circumstances, a defendant's indigent status may be considered in the decision whether to revoke probation.... [T]he issue cannot be resolved by resort to easy slogans or pigeonhole analysis, but rather requires a careful inquiry into such factors as 'the nature of the individual interest affected, the extent to which it is affected, the rationality of the connection between legislative means and purpose, [and] the existence of alternative means for effectuating the purpose.' *Williams v. Illinois*, supra, at 260 (Harlan, J., concurring).... We hold, therefore, that in revocation proceedings for failure to pay a fine or restitution, a sentencing court must inquire into the reasons for the failure to pay. If the probationer willfully refused to pay or failed to make sufficient bona fide efforts legally to acquire the resources to pay, the court may revoke probation and sentence the defendant to imprisonment within the authorized range of its sentencing authority. If the probationer could not pay despite sufficient bona fide efforts to acquire the resources to do so, the court must consider alternative measures of punishment other than imprisonment."

CASE EXCERPT

"Only if alternative measures are not adequate to meet the State's interests in punishment and deterrence may the court imprison a probationer who has made sufficient bona fide efforts to pay. To do otherwise would deprive the probationer of his conditional freedom simply because, through no fault of his own, he cannot pay the fine. Such a deprivation would be contrary to the fundamental fairness required by the Fourteenth Amendment."

CASE SIGNIFICANCE

This case recognizes "substantive limits on the automatic revocation of probation where an indigent defendant is unable to pay a fine or restitution" (*Black v. Romano*, 471 U.S. 606 (1985) at 611). Indigent persons on probation can not have probation revoked solely because, through no fault of their own, they fail to pay fines or make restitution. Such a situation is very different, however, from a situation where the probationer "willfully" refuses to pay fines or restitution when he

BEARDEN v. GEORGIA *(cont.)*

has the means to do so, then "the State is perfectly justified in using imprisonment as a sanction to enforce collection." Likewise, the state is also justified in revoking probation and imprisoning the probationer if he or she does not make genuine efforts to find a job or does not try to borrow money to pay fines or make restitution. The state argued that imprisonment was necessary in this case for three reasons: to further its interest in ensuring that restitution be paid to crime victims, to remove the probationer from the temptation of committing future crimes, and to punish the probationer and deter others from committing crimes. Justice O'Connor countered that the first reason would not make restitution suddenly appear in a situation where the offender has already done all he could to find a job or borrow money. In fact, the threat of imprisonment could have the effect of inducing him to raise money illegally. The second reason would mean that the state is incarcerating the probationer because of his poverty. In a footnote, the Court noted that "indigency is itself no threat to the safety or welfare of society." With regard to the third reason, Justice O'Connor acknowledged the state's interest in punishment and deterrence, but observed that there were alternatives to incarceration, such as extending the time to pay fines and restitution, ordering community service, or reducing the fine. This case is not without controversy. While the judgment of the Court was unanimous, three Justices joined Justice White in a separate opinion. These four Justices concurred in the judgment because the court had imposed a lengthy prison term on Bearden after revoking his probation and apparently did not make a good-faith effort to impose a sentence that would be "roughly equivalent to the fine and restitution that the defendant failed to pay." Prior to Bearden, the Court had addressed the treatment of indigents in several cases, ruling that a state practice of granting appellate review only to persons able to afford a trial transcript was unconstitutional, and that indigents are entitled to counsel on first direct appeal and free transcripts of preliminary hearings for use at trial. Further, and most relevant to Bearden, were previous holdings that states can not impose fines or restitutions and then convert those sentences to prison terms because the person is indigent and lacks resources to pay those fines or restitution. Limitations placed on the rights of indigents include the decision that indigents do not have a constitutional right to appointed counsel for a discretionary appeal. Also, federal statutes which allow an indigent defendant to be provided with a free trial transcript only if the court certifies that the challenge to his conviction is not frivolous and the transcript is necessary to prepare his petition have been upheld by the Court.

MINNESOTA v. MURPHY
465 U.S. 420 (1984)

FACTS

In 1980, Murphy was prosecuted for criminal sexual conduct in a Minnesota court and pleaded guilty to a lesser charge of false imprisonment. He was given a suspended prison sentence and placed on probation, the terms of which included participating in a treatment program for sexual offenders, reporting to his probation officer periodically, and being truthful with the officer "in all matters." In September 1981, Murphy's probation officer received information from a treatment counselor that Murphy had admitted committing a rape and murder in 1974. During a meeting with his probation officer, Murphy, upon questioning, admitted to this rape and murder. He was subsequently indicted for first-degree murder and tried to suppress the confession he made to the probation officer on the ground that it was obtained in violation of the Fifth and Fourteenth Amendments. The Minnesota trial court admitted the confession, finding that Murphy was not in custody at the time he spoke to his probation officer and what he told her was neither compelled nor involuntary, despite the absence of Miranda warnings. The Minnesota Supreme Court reversed the trial court's decision, holding that even though Murphy was not in custody in the usual sense, he should have been given Miranda warnings because of the nature of the meeting with the probation officer, the fact that he was under court order to respond truthfully, and because the probation officer already had reason to believe that his answers to her questioning would be incriminating.

ISSUE

Is a statement made to a probation officer by a probationer admissible in subsequent criminal proceedings if given without the Miranda warnings?

HOLDING

Yes. The Fifth and Fourteenth Amendments do not prohibit the introduction into evidence of a probationer's admissions to a probation officer in a subsequent criminal prosecution.

RATIONALE

In a decision written by Justice White, the Court reversed the Minnesota Supreme Court and ruled that the statements that Murphy gave to his probation officer were not compelled. It was up to Murphy to decline to answer any of the officer's questions, asserting his Fifth Amendment right. Further, he was not "in custody" when the officer questioned him, which would have been required in order to trigger *Miranda* warnings. Murphy maintained that he had been compelled to meet with his probation officer and answer all question truthfully or face revocation, but the Court ruled that "the general obligation to appear and answer questions truthfully did not in itself convert Murphy's otherwise voluntary statements into compelled ones." The Court compared Murphy's position to "the ordinary witness at a trial or before a grand jury who is subpoenaed, sworn to tell the truth, and obligated to answer on the pain of contempt, unless he invokes the privilege and shows that he faces a realistic threat of self-incrimination."

CASE EXCERPT

"Since Murphy was not physically restrained and could have left the office, any compulsion he might have felt from the possibility that terminating the meeting would have led to revocation of probation was not comparable to the pressure on a suspect who is painfully aware that he literally cannot escape a persistent custodial interrogator."

CASE SIGNIFICANCE

Prior to this decision, both state and federal courts were in conflict over the issue of whether or not incriminating statements made by probationers without *Miranda* warnings to officers could be used in subsequent criminal proceedings. This case thus clarifies Fifth Amendment protections in the context of probationer-probation officer relations. The Court emphasized that Murphy had not been under arrest when he met with his probation officer and that he had been free to leave at the end of the meeting. If the officer had questioned him while he was held in police custody, or if the police were questioning him in a "custodial setting," then *Miranda* protections would have applied. Further, the Court stated that, "since Murphy revealed incriminating information instead of timely asserting his Fifth Amendment privilege, his disclosures were

not compelled incriminations." Whether or not a probationer is in custody depends on the issue at hand. As the Court noted, probationers are subject to various restrictions and are to be regarded as "'in custody' for purposes of habeas corpus." However, "custody for *Miranda* purposes has been more narrowly circumscribed." Thus, because Murphy was not under arrest and his freedom of movement had not been restrained, he was clearly "not 'in custody' for purposes of receiving *Miranda* protection."

BLACK v. ROMANO

471 U.S. 606 (1985)

FACTS

In 1976, Romano pled guilty in a Missouri state court to two controlled substance offenses, was given suspended prison sentences, and was put on probation. Two months after being given probation, he was arrested for leaving the scene of an automobile accident and subsequently charged with striking and seriously injuring a pedestrian with an automobile in addition to leaving the scene. After a probation revocation hearing, the judge who had sentenced Romano on the controlled substances charges found that Romano had violated his probation conditions by committing a felony. Romano's probation was revoked, and the judge ordered that the previously imposed sentences be executed. After unsuccessfully seeking postconviction relief in state court, Romano filed a habeas corpus petition in Federal District Court, alleging that the state judge had violated due process requirements by revoking probation without considering alternatives to incarceration. The District Court agreed, holding that "under the circumstances alternatives to incarceration should have been considered, on the record, and if [the trial judge] decided still to send Romano to jail, he should have given the reasons why the alternatives were inappropriate." The Court of Appeals affirmed the district court's decision.

ISSUE

Does the due process clause of the Fourteenth Amendment require a sentencing court to consider alternatives to imprisonment before revoking probation?

HOLDING

No. The due process clause of the Fourteenth Amendment does not require a sentencing court to indicate

BLACK v. ROMANO *(cont.)*

that it has considered alternatives to incarceration before revoking probation.

RATIONALE

The Court reasoned that probation revocation is a subjective determination and there are no limitations on substantive grounds for doing so. A reviewing court should not second-guess the sentencing court's decision, and requiring a court to detail the reasons for revoking probation would be unduly burdensome. Romano was represented by counsel at his probation revocation proceeding , and the court concluded there was sufficient evidence to find he violated his conditions of probation.

CASE EXCERPT

"We believe that a general requirement that the fact-finder elaborate upon the reasons for a course not taken would unduly burden the revocation proceeding without significantly advancing the interests of the probationer."

CASE SIGNIFICANCE

The procedures to be followed in probation and parole revocation hearings established by *Morrissey v. Brewer* in 1972 and *Gagnon v. Scarpelli* in 1973 do not include requiring a consideration of alternatives to incarceration. In *Black v. Romano*, the Court noted its disagreement with the two lower courts' reading of Morrissey and Gagnon requiring "a sentencing court to state explicitly why it has rejected alternatives to incarceration." Admittedly, the Court's 1983 decision in *Bearden v. Georgia* "recognized that in certain circumstances, fundamental fairness requires consideration of alternatives to incarceration prior to the revocation of probation"; however, those circumstances involved an indigent probationer who could not pay a fine or make restitution through no fault of his own. In this situation, Romano committed a felony by leaving the scene of an accident after running over a pedestrian, an action that caused the court to no longer view him as a good candidate for rehabilitation.

GRIFFIN v. WISCONSIN
483 U.S. 868 (1987)

FACTS

In 1980, Griffin, a probationer, had his apartment searched without a warrant by probation officers, who were acting on information from a police detective. Officers found a handgun that later served as the basis of Griffin's conviction of a state-law weapons offense. Wisconsin law permits any probation officer to search a probationer's home without a warrant as long as his supervisor approves and as long as there are reasonable grounds to believe the presence of contraband. In determining whether reasonable grounds exist an officer must consider a variety of factors, including information provided by an informant, the reliability and specificity of that information, the informant's reliability, the officer's experience with the probationer, and the need to verify compliance with the rules of probation and with the law. Another regulation forbids a probationer to possess a firearm without a probation officer's advance approval. At trial for felonious possession of a firearm by a convicted felon, Griffin sought to suppress the evidence seized by the probation officers during the search of his apartment. The state trial court denied his motion, concluding that no warrant was necessary and that the search was reasonable. Griffin was convicted, and both the Wisconsin Court of Appeals and the Wisconsin Supreme Court affirmed his conviction.

ISSUE

Does a search without a warrant violate a probationer's Fourth Amendment rights when search is made by a probation officer and is based on reasonable grounds?

HOLDING

No. The search of Griffin's residence did not violate Fourth Amendment rights and was reasonable within the meaning of the Fourth Amendment because it was conducted pursuant to a valid regulation governing probationers.

RATIONALE

The Court, in an opinion written by Justice Scalia, reasoned that a warrantless search on "reasonable grounds," a lesser requirement than probable cause, was valid under the "special needs of law enforcement" exception to the warrant requirement. This exception applies to situations where requiring a warrant and probable cause would interfere too greatly with the government's objective of protecting the public and supervising the parolee. Justice Scalia stated, "It is reasonable to dispense with the warrant requirement here, since such a requirement would interfere to an appreciable degree with the probation system by setting up a magistrate, rather than the probation officer, as the determiner of how closely the probationer must be supervised, by making it more difficult for probation officials to respond quickly to evidence of misconduct, and by reducing the deterrent effect that the possibility of expeditious searches would otherwise create."

CASE EXCERPT

"Unlike the police officer who conducts the ordinary search, the probation officer is required to have the probationer's welfare particularly in mind. A probable cause requirement would unduly disrupt the probation system by reducing the deterrent effect of the supervisory arrangement and by lessening the range of information the probation officer could consider in deciding whether to search. The probation agency must be able to act based upon a lesser degree of certainty in order to intervene before the probationer damages himself or society, and must be able to proceed on the basis of its entire experience with the probationer and to assess probabilities in the light of its knowledge of his life, character, and circumstances. Thus, it is reasonable to permit information provided by a police officer, whether or not on the basis of firsthand knowledge, to support a probationary search."

CASE SIGNIFICANCE

This case illustrates how courts attempt in their decisions to balance the degree of intrusion into a person's right to privacy with the government's burden to protect society. The decision in *Griffin* establishes a "special needs" exception to Fourth Amendment requirements that searches be based on probable cause and with a warrant. Justice Scalia observed that "[a] probationer's home, like anyone else's, is protected by the Fourth Amendment's requirement that searches be 'reasonable.'" Most searches must be accompanied by warrants and are thus subject to the higher standard of probable cause. However, warrantless searches are permitted when "special needs, beyond the normal need for law enforcement, make the warrant and probable-cause requirement impracticable." Accordingly, the operation of a probation system presents such special needs. It is important to note that the Court in this case upheld Wisconsin's law which allowed warrantless searches based on reasonable suspicion. Any reading that all searches of probationers must be based on a showing of "reasonable suspicion," regardless of the terms of probation goes beyond the reach of *Griffin*.

FORRESTER v. WHITE
484 U.S. 219 (1988)

FACTS

White, an Illinois state court judge, had authority under state law to appoint and discharge probation officers at his discretion. White hired Cynthia Forrester as an adult and juvenile probation officer in 1977 and later promoted her. In 1980, White demoted and then discharged Forrester. She filed a damages action in Federal District Court, alleging that she was demoted and discharged on account of her sex in violation of the equal protection clause of the Fourteenth Amendment. The jury found in her favor, and White moved for a new trial. The District Court granted this motion, holding that the jury verdict was against the weight of the evidence. White then moved for summary judgment on the ground that he was entitled to "judicial immunity" from a civil damages suit. This motion, too, was granted. Forrester appealed, and a divided panel of the Court of Appeals for the Seventh Circuit affirmed the grant of summary judgment.

ISSUE

Does a state court judge have absolute immunity from damages for his decision to dismiss a subordinate court employee?

HOLDING

No. A state court judge does not have absolute immunity from a damages suit under 42 U.S.C. 1983 for his decisions to demote and dismiss a court employee.

RATIONALE

In a unanimous decision written by Justice O'Connor, the Court reasoned that the decision to demote and discharge petitioner were administrative in nature. Only decisions involving judicial acts are entitled to absolute immunity.

CASE EXCERPT

"Such decisions are indistinguishable from those of an executive branch official responsible for making similar personnel decisions, which, no matter how crucial to the efficient operation of public institutions, are not entitled to absolute immunity from liability in damages under §1983."

CASE SIGNIFICANCE

According to the Court, judicial immunity has a long history, originating in medieval times as a means of

FORRESTER v. WHITE *(cont.)*

"discouraging collateral attacks and thereby helping to establish appellate procedures as the standard system for correcting judicial error." Judicial immunity also serves to protect a judge's independence. In its decision, the Court stated that "[b]ecause the threat of personal liability for damages can inhibit government officials in the proper performance of their duties, various forms of official immunity from suit have been created. Aware, however, that the threat of such liability may also have the salutary effect of encouraging officials to perform their duties in a lawful and appropriate manner, this Court has been cautious in recognizing absolute immunity claims other than those decided by constitutional or statutory enactment. Accordingly, the Court has applied a 'functional' approach under which the nature of the functions entrusted to particular officials is examined in order to evaluate the effect that exposure to particular forms of liability would likely have on the appropriate exercise of those functions." Accordingly, judicial functions which fall under administrative, executive, or legislative headings, such as administrative personnel decisions, would not qualify for absolute immunity. The Court of Appeals for the Seventh Circuit had reasoned that the threat of lawsuits by disgruntled ex-employees could interfere with judicial decision making. The Supreme Court acknowledged this possibility but observed that this threat is no different from that faced by other public officials who have to hire and fire employees and is not a great enough threat to justify absolute immunity. On the other hand, employment decisions by judges may be protected by qualified immunity, although the Court did not reach this decision.

ALDEN v. MAINE
527 U.S. 706 (1999)

FACTS
In 1992, a group of probation officers sued their employer, the State of Maine, alleging that the state had violated the overtime provisions of the 1938 Fair Labor Standards Act (FLSA). While this suit was pending, the Supreme Court decided in *Seminole Tribe v. Florida*, 517 U.S. 44 (1996), that states are immune from private suits in federal court and that Congress lacks the authority to abrogate that immunity. Applying the decision in *Seminole Tribe*, the federal district court dismissed the probation officers' suit, and the Court

of Appeals affirmed the decision. Alden and the other probation officers then sued Maine again for violating the Fair Labor Standards Act, this time in state court. The state trial court and the state supreme court both held that Maine had sovereign immunity and could not be sued by private parties in their own court.

ISSUE
May Congress use its powers under Article I of the Constitution to abolish a state's sovereign immunity from private suits in its own courts?

HOLDING
No. The powers delegated to Congress under Article I of the United States Constitution do not include the power to subject nonconsenting states to private suits for damages in state courts.

RATIONALE
Writing for the Court, Justice Kennedy stated that "[f]ederalism requires that Congress accord States the respect and dignity due them as residuary sovereigns and joint participants in the Nation's governance." The Court clearly stated that nothing in the Constitution allows Congress to repeal a state's immunity from "private suits in their own courts." The Court reasoned that if the federal government could force on states such suits seeking monetary relief, then this would put a strain on the "financial integrity" of states as well as a cost to state sovereignty. Further, given the fact that the federal government cannot repeal a state's immunity from suit in federal court, if Congress could repeal state immunity in a state court, then the federal government would have "greater power in state courts than in federal courts." Maine's consent to be sued in certain instances while claiming immunity from suit in other instances, as in the case at hand, was nothing more than implementing the "privilege of sovereignty."

CASE EXCERPT
"A review of the essential principles of federalism and the state courts' special role in the constitutional design leads to the conclusion that a congressional power to subject nonconsenting States to private suits in their own courts is inconsistent with the Constitution's structure."

CASE SIGNIFICANCE
This case concerns the scope of a state's immunity from suit. At issue was the allegation that Maine had

not followed the Fair Labor Standards Act in paying overtime to probation officers. Maine did not claim that the officers were not covered by the FLSA, only that Maine could not be sued in state court. As the Court noted, "[t]he Constitution, by delegating to Congress the power to establish the supreme law of the land when acting within its enumerated powers, does not foreclose a State from asserting immunity to claims arising under federal law merely because that law derives not from the State itself but from the national power. A contrary view could not be reconciled with *Hans* v. *Louisiana, supra,* which sustained Louisiana's immunity in a private suit arising under the Constitution itself; with *Employees of Dept. of Public Health and Welfare of Mo.* v. *Department of Public Health and Welfare of Mo.* , 411 U.S. 279, 283 (1973), which recognized that the FLSA was binding upon Missouri but nevertheless upheld the State's immunity to a private suit to recover under that Act; or with numerous other decisions to the same effect. We reject any contention that substantive federal law by its own force necessarily overrides the sovereign immunity of the States. When a State asserts its immunity to suit, the question is not the primacy of federal law but the implementation of the law in a manner consistent with the constitutional sovereignty of the States." The Court cited various decisions from early cases making clear that states are immune from suit in their own courts: "We have often described the States' immunity in sweeping terms, without reference to whether the suit was prosecuted in state or federal court. See, *e. g.* , *Briscoe* v. *Bank of Kentucky,* 11 Pet. 257, 321–322 (1837) ('No sovereign state is liable to be sued without her consent'); *Board of Liquidation* v. *McComb,* 92 U.S. 531, 541 (1876) ('A State, without its consent, cannot be sued by an individual'); *In re Ayers,* 123 U.S. 443 , 506 (1887) (same); *Great Northern Life Ins. Co.* v. *Read,* 322 U.S. 47, 51 (1944) ('The inherent nature of sovereignty prevents actions against a state by its own citizens without its consent').... *Beers* v. *Arkansas,* 20 How. 527, 529 (1858) ('It is an established principle of jurisprudence in all civilized nations that the sovereign cannot be sued in its own courts, or in any other, without its consent and permission'); *Railroad Co.* v. *Tennessee,* 101 U.S. 337, 339 (1880) ('The principle is elementary that a State cannot be sued in its own courts without its consent. This is a privilege of sovereignty') ...." The Court made clear in this decision, however, that the principle of sovereign immunity does not give states the right to ignore the Constitution or valid federal law. Likewise, states are subject to judicial review of compliance with the Constitution and federal law. Sovereign immunity applies to suits brought against nonconsenting states. Many states have passed laws consenting to various suits. The principle of sovereign immunity does not extend to suits brought "against a municipal corporation or other governmental entity which is not an arm of the State." Also, state officers are not protected against certain suits seeking injunctive or declatory relief. Money damages against a state officer may be sought when the relief sought is from the individual officer and not the state and in the officer's capacity for unconstitutional or wrongful conduct fairly attributable to the officer himself. The state of Maine had a "good-faith" disagreement about the requirements of the FLSA. Since the suit was brought, Maine amended its practices and pays overtime to probation officers. As the dissent observed, however, "[w]hy the State of Maine has not rendered this case unnecessary by paying damages to petitioners under the FLSA of its own free will remains unclear ... had it done so, the case before us would be moot."

DISCUSSION QUESTIONS

1. After reviewing carefully both *Mempa v. Rhay* and *Gagnon v. Scarpelli*, discuss when a probationer is entitled to legal representation at a probation revocation hearing.

2. Do you agree with the Court's line of reasoning regarding legal representation at probation revocations? Why or why not?

3. Four Justices dissented in *Cabell v. Chavez-Salido* (1982), describing the exclusion of legal aliens from deputy probation officer positions as stemming from "parochialism and hostility toward foreigners who have come to this country lawfully." Review the majority opinion as presented in this chapter and formulate an argument answering the dissent's charge of parochialism.

4. Discuss possible alternative measures that might be available to courts when faced with indigent probationers unable to pay their fines or make restitution.

5. In your opinion, what do the cases of *Minnesota v. Murphy* (1984) and *Griffin v. Wisconsin* (1987) say about the role of a probation officer? What dilemmas are faced by probation officers in carrying

out their duties to aid in the rehabilitation of their clients?

6. The decision in *Griffin v. Wisconsin* was a 5–4 decision. One of the dissenting opinions acknowledged that probation officers may need to conduct searches of probationers' homes in order to ensure compliance with the conditions of probation, and "reasonable suspicion," rather than the higher probable cause standard, allows an officer to intercede at an earlier stage of suspicion, thus protecting the public and aiding rehabilitation. However, the dissent felt that warrants should still be required in these cases. Would you agree? Why or why not?

7. Discuss the Court's reasoning in *Aldine v. Maine* that states who do not consent can cannot be subject to private suits for damages in their own courts. What is the rationale behind sovereign immunity?

8. Why are judges not protected by absolute immunity when they make administrative decisions? What was the administrative decision the state court judge made in *Forrester v. White*?

9. Discuss the problems faced by indigent defendants in the criminal justice system. Why is the decision in *Bearden v. Georgia* important?

10. What about a probation officer's relationship with a probationer removes the requirement for *Miranda* warnings?

GLOSSARY

Aggravating factors Circumstances in a particular case that support imposing a more severe punishment on a convicted offender. Many states have statutes that list the aggravating factors that jurors can consider in making the death or life decision in a capital case.

Capital Offense Any offense punishable by death.

Collateral attack An indirect challenge to a criminal conviction or proceeding.

Discretion A legally sanctioned exercise of judgment by a governmental agent.

Double jeopardy Subjecting a criminal defendant to more than one prosecution for the same criminal offense. Protection against double jeopardy is provided in the Fifth Amendment to the US Constitution.

Due process clause A clause found in both the Fifth and Fourteenth Amendments to the US Constitution prohibiting the federal government and the states from depriving citizens of life, liberty, or property without due process of law.

Equal protection clause A clause found in the Fourteenth Amendment to the US Constitution stating that no state shall deny any person within its jurisdiction the equal protection of the law.

Ex post facto clause A clause found in Article I, section 9 of the US Constitution protecting against the government retroactively applying criminal statutes.

Forfeiture Statutes that provide for handing over to the government any interest in, claim to, or property or contractual right in property constituting or derived from a violation of the law.

Good time Reduction of the time actually served in prison as a reward for not violating prison rules.

Habeas corpus Latin phrase that means "you have the body." It is a writ filed as a civil proceeding asking an official who has custody of an individual whether that individual is legally incarcerated or detained.

Harmless error An error made by a trial court judge that is not considered sufficiently damaging to a defendant's case to result in a reversal of the judgment.

Indigent A person who cannot afford to hire an attorney.

Mitigating factors Circumstances in a particular case that support imposing a less severe punishment on a convicted offender. Some states have statutes that list the mitigating factors that jurors can consider in making the death or life decision in a capital case.

Money damages Money that compensates a plaintiff for the actual injury they suffered.

Punitive damages Money damages that are awarded to a plaintiff who has been injured intentionally or maliciously. Punitive damages are meant to punish the defendant.

Remand   A decision by an appeals court to send a case back to the court from which it came for further action.

Reverse   A decision of an appellate court that disagrees with the result reached by lower court.

Reversed and remanded   A decision by an appellate court that a guilty verdict reached by a lower court be set aside and the case retried.

Tort   A private or civil wrong in which a defendant caused harm to a plaintiff or to the plaintiff's property (but not a wrong arising out of a contract).

Writ of certiorari   A writ issued by an appellate court asking a lower court to forward to it its records of the proceedings in a particular case.

INDEX